Modern China and International Economic Law

This book series offers an essential forum for Chinese economic law scholars, as well as international scholars interested in China's practice in the context of international economic law. It is thus the aim of this book series to publish essential monographs/compilations in the field of international economic law that focus on China, or on uniquely Chinese characteristics. This book series above all focuses on research that closely relates current practices with past history, and future policies with current circumstances, pursuing a philosophy of understanding legal practices by combining the past and present. Accordingly, top scholars in China and beyond its borders will be invited to contribute to this project from their respective areas of focus, which can cover broad topics related to international law in the current context of China's peaceful rise, such as China's economic policy with various countries, its participation in the WTO legal system and bilateral investment treaty practices, etc.; as well as more specific topics such as China's domestic legislation regarding foreign business, its unique "one country, two systems" policy and its implications on external economic interactions between different "systems" within China.

Yanming Huang

Commentaries on Commercial Arbitration in Modern China

By A Chinese Practitioner

中国国际经济法学会
Chinese Society of International Economic Law, CSIEL

Springer

Yanming Huang
Shenzhen, Guangdong, China

ISSN 2364-8317 ISSN 2364-8325 (electronic)
Modern China and International Economic Law
ISBN 978-981-95-0167-0 ISBN 978-981-95-0168-7 (eBook)
https://doi.org/10.1007/978-981-95-0168-7

This Springer imprint is published by the registered company Springer Nature Singapore Pte Ltd.
The registered company address is: 152 Beach Road, #21-01/04 Gateway East, Singapore 189721, Singapore

Preface

Before the promulgation of the Arbitration Law of the People's Republic of China in 1994, there was only one commercial arbitration institute in China: The Foreign Trade Arbitration Commission under the China Council for the Promotion of International Trade (CCPIT). This institute was later renamed the China International Economic and Trade Arbitration Commission (CIETAC).

As China implementing its reform and open-door policies, Shenzhen, being the first special economic zone, Shenzhen Arbitration Office of the CCPIT's arbitration commission in 1984 formally established with the approval of the State Council. This office was later successively named CIETAC Shenzhen and CIETAC South China. Since 2012, it has been known as the Shenzhen Court of International Arbitration (SCIA).

The commentaries collected in this book were primarily published in Mealey's International Arbitration Report from 1998 to 2013. Therefore, the arbitration institutes referred are mainly CIETAC and CIETAC Shenzhen. Generally speaking, in terms of the cases discussed, they were mostly under the jurisdiction of SCIA's predecessor. After 2013, SCIA has undergone significant development, having experienced a fundamental transformation in management concepts and approaches. The types and case load it has accepted and handled, the regions and industries involved, and its overall influence have grown beyond what outsiders could have imagined.

From 1984 to 1992, the executive team of the Shenzhen Arbitration Office and CIETAC Shenzhen primarily consisted of Mr. Dong/Yougan, Mr. Zhou/Huandong, and Mr. Zhengdong Luo. They were pioneers in foreign-related commercial arbitration in Shenzhen. Since 1992, for a period, the executive team of CIETAC Shenzhen mainly consisted of Prof. Xiao/Zhiming and Dr. Guo/Xiaowen. The institute in that period made constant progress, such as the progress in the stylization and regularization of the management and operation.

As a staff member of the institute, I, the author of this book, had numerous opportunities to receive lawyers, barristers, law professors, other professionals of various jurisdictions engaging in discussions with them. For a long period, my daily work was to receive parties to the cases under the jurisdiction of SCIA.

As an arbitrator at this institute and other arbitration bodies, I had many chances to deal with commercial cases alongside experienced and knowledgeable co-arbitrators. Further, I gained channels to get English arbitration literature. This enabled me to access first-hand information of the commercial arbitration of some developed coun-ties and on a variety of cases. Consequently, I wrote commentaries on various aspects of commercial arbitration, addressing foreign colleagues' critiques of China's only commercial arbitration institute at the time from an insider's perspective. I also discussed the ethics of Chinese arbitrators, the combination of arbitration and mediation in China, and other relevant topics. Commentaries in English before 1995 were published in the Journal of International Arbitration, while those after 1998, focusing on Chinese commercial arbitration, appeared in Mealey's International Arbitration Report.

The commentaries in this book, mainly published in the latter journal, cover topics such as the drafting of arbitration clauses and agreements, jurisdictional decisions, due process and manifest disregard of the law, arbitrators' decision-making processes and the essential abilities and skills required, the determination of applicable law, and the application of CISG and law merchant, and so on.

Thanks to the opportunities afforded by the arbitration institute where I served, therefor I was able to write and publish some. These writings, to some extent, might record and reflect the development of the arbitration institute in that historical period and in Shenzhen, a dynamic city.

Shenzhen, China Yanming Huang

Acknowledgments During the process of compiling this book, my nephew, **Zefeng Ye**, converted my original PDF manuscripts into Word documents, while my daughter-in-law, **Xiuyao Tang**, assisted in organizing the **preface, chapter outlines, and footnotes** for each section. Without their dedicated efforts, this book would have been difficult to complete.

Thanks are due to Mr. Lee Kui Lam, solicitor, consultant, notary public, and China Appointed Attesting Officer, with Hastings & Co, Hong Kong, for his pieces of advice relating to some legal terms kindly given in the course of my writing.

Thanks are due to Prof. An CHEN, without his encouragement and guidance, there would be no chance for me to have this book compiled.

Competing Interests The author has no competing interests to declare that are relevant to the content of this manuscript.

Contents

Part I
Decision-Making Powers over Jurisdiction of Arbitration

Outlines

Commentary 1: On Decision-Making Powers over Jurisdiction of Arbitration at CIETAC

CIETAC's first arbitration rules were adopted in 1956 and were referred to as "Provisional Arbitration Rules." Surprisingly, these "provisional" rules remained in effect for over 32 years until they were replaced by the 1988 rules, which took effect in early 1989. This prolonged use of the provisional rules indirectly reflects the lack of dynamism in China's economic and trade environment prior to the reform and opening-up period.

With the onset of economic reforms, foreign capital began pouring in, leading to rapid growth in foreign investment and international trade. Between 1988 and 1998, CIETAC revised its rules three times within a decade, incorporating international arbitration norms and practices. The evolution of commercial arbitration in China serves as an indicator of the country's increasing openness and economic vitality.

A key issue in commercial arbitration is the determination of jurisdiction: should it be controlled by the arbitration institution itself, or should it be delegated to the arbitral tribunal for each specific case? The author explores and analyzes different perspectives from both domestic and international arbitration practices. Based on the operational realities of CIETAC (Shenzhen) and case-specific arbitration proceedings, the commentary argues—through case-based legal analysis—that jurisdictional decisions should primarily rest with the arbitral tribunals handling individual disputes.

The author also highlights the advantages of institutional arbitration. One of its advantages is that when a case is initiated, but the tribunal has not yet been formed, procedural delays can occur. A permanent arbitration institution can mitigate such issues, ensuring the arbitration process moves forward without unnecessary obstruction or delay.

Unlike a mere observer, the author writes from the perspective of an insider—having served as a "witness", participant, manager to a case or secretary to a tribunal, or a member of a tribunal. Using a first-person narrative, the author provides detailed rather than generalized or selective accounts, aiming to offer an objective view that enables fellow arbitrators, corporate counsels and all the readers who come into contact with this book to form their own judgments, rather than simply proving a predetermined argument.

Commentary 2: An Arbitrator Looks Back—Did CIETAC Have Jurisdiction over Foshan Jiadian Lighting Co., Ltd vs. Prestige Lighting Co., Ltd?

In this case, the author served as a member of a three-person arbitral tribunal. The British respondent failed to appear after receiving the arbitration notice and ultimately lost the case by default. In this commentary, the author provides an in-depth analysis of the evidence involved and directly addresses the respondent's objections in absentia. The author demonstrates the tribunal's jurisdiction over the case and the legal reasoning behind the respondent's defeat.

Ordinarily, in ad hoc arbitration or arbitration administered by certain international institutes, a losing party that failed to appear would not necessarily receive a detailed, post-award explanation of the tribunal's jurisdiction. However, in this particular instance, the author believes that the openness of China's arbitration system is evident. The arbitration institute he once worked for was willing to engage with parties—even those who defaulted—to provide explanations and clarifications.

This openness allows the losing foreign party to recognize that its default appearance was not the true cause of its loss; rather, the loss was due to its contractual breaches. Furthermore, as discussed in Part III of this book, theory and practice suggest that respondents should participate in arbitration proceedings, as non-participation constitutes both a procedural and substantive breach of contract. And there might be heavy risks and costs.

Following the issuance of the arbitral award, the author closely followed the enforcement of the decision abroad and actively responded to criticisms questioning CIETAC's jurisdiction. This engagement was not a legal duty of an arbitrator and a tribunal and a permanent arbitration institute but a reflection of the institute's commitment to service. More importantly, it was an academic effort of the author of this book to dissect and analyze the case, contributing to a broader understanding of arbitration practice.

On Decision-Making Powers over Jurisdiction of Arbitrations at CIETAC

1 Introduction

The history of the China International Economic and Trade Arbitration Commission (CIETAC) reveals that there are five sets of arbitration rules promulgated since 1956.

The First Rules were promulgated on 31 March 1956 (hereinafter referred to as the 1956 Rules). The Second Rules were promulgated on 12 September 1988,effective on 1 January 1989 (here- in after referred to as the 1988 Rules).On 17 March 1994, at the First Session of the Standing Committee of the Second Congress of the China Council for the Promotion of International Trade (CCPIT)which is also known as the China Chamber of International Commerce (CCOIC), the Third (revised) Rules were formally adopted with effect from 1 June 1994(hereinafter as the 1994 Rules).The 1994 Rules were revised and adopted subsequently on 4 September 1995 by COIC. The Fourth Rules were implemented on 1 October 1995 (hereinafter referred to as the 1995 Rules).The 1998 Rules have been effective as from 10 May 1998 (hereinafter referred to as the 1998 Rules) and have superseded all the previous rules mentioned.

The Arbitration Law of the People's Republic of China (hereinafter referred to as the Arbitration Law) was adopted at the Ninth Meeting of the Standing Committee of the National People's Congress and promulgated by Order No.31 of the President of the PRC on 31 August 1994 and effective of 1 September 1995.Logistically, the 1995 Rules should have been revised to comply with the stipulation of the Arbitration Law and should have come into effect simultaneously with the former.

There is no stipulation in the 1956 Rules about objection to the validity of an arbitration agreement and/or jurisdiction of CIETAC.

This commentary was published in Mealeys International Arbitration Report, Vol.13, # 7, July 1998, pp 18–37.

The author is grateful to Dr. Thomas Chiu and Prof. Sam Blay with the Faculty of Law, University of Technology, Sydney for their valuable pieces of advice.

Y. Huang, *Commentaries on Commercial Arbitration in Modern China*, Modern China and International Economic Law, https://doi.org/10.1007/978-981-95-0168-7_1

Unlike the 1956 Rules, the 1988 Rules and Rules promulgated thereafter have stipulation to address these issues. Paragraph 3 of Article 2 of the 1988 Rules read:

> "The Arbitration Commission has power to decide on the validity of arbitration agreements and the jurisdiction over arbitration cases."

The 1994 Rules were the result of experience gained after the implementation of the 1988 Rules.

Here are some of the examples:

> "Article 4.The Arbitration Commission has the power to decide on the existence and validity of an arbitration agreement and the jurisdiction over an arbitration case."

> "Article 5.An arbitration clause contained in a contract shall be regarded as existing independently and separately from the other clauses of the contract, and an arbitration agreement attached to a contract shall be treated as a part of the contract existing independently and separately from the other parts of the contract. The validity of an arbitration clause or an arbitration agreement shall not be affect by the modification, recession, termination, invalidity or revocation of the contract."

> "Article 6.Any objections to an arbitration agreement and/or jurisdiction over an arbitration case may not be raised after the Respondent has presented his first substantive defense in writing. Any objections to jurisdiction over a counterclaim may not be raised after the Claimant has submitted his first substantive defense in writing in respect of the counterclaim."

It is worth noting that under the 1994 Rules, Article 5 is of vital importance. It demonstrates for the first time that China's commercial arbitration body follows the principle of the severability of the arbitration clause in accordance with the practice in the West. Later that is provided in the Arbitration Law.! However, there is no provision concerning the power of the arbitrator to determine his own jurisdiction in all the Rules and the Arbitration Law. Our counterparts in the international commercial arbitration circle treated it as a drawback of Chinese arbitration. endnote 2

The 1995 Rules on the role of an arbitration clause in a contract clause (Article 5) and objections to an arbitration agreement (Article 6)are exactly the same as those in the 1994 Rules.

The first paragraph of Article 20 of the Arbitration Law provides a similar to Article 6 of 1994; it reads:

> "If a party challenges the validity of the arbitration agreement, he may request the arbitration commission to make a decision or apply to the People's Court for a ruling. If one party requests the arbitration commission to make a decision and the other party applies to the People's Court for a ruling, the People's Court shall give a ruling."

As it is provided in the Arbitration Law that a people's court has the last say in deciding the validity of an arbitration agreement, there is some amendment in Article 4 of the 1995 Rules which reads:

"The Arbitration Commission has the power to decide on the existence and validity of an arbitration agreement and the jurisdiction over an arbitration case. If a party challenges the validity of the arbitration agreement, and when one party requests the Arbitration Commission to make a decision and the other party applies to the People's Court for a ruling, the People's Court shall give a ruling."

There is no amendment in Articles 4, 5 and 6 of the 1998 Rules.

I wrote an article on the 1994 Rules.3 Since then, there have been some developments in this area in the last three years. I would like to address these developments as well as my observations in this article through studying some cases.

II. ***Case 1. Jurisdiction Within the Power of an Arbitration Tribunal.***

There is a case of dispute arising from a joint venture contract. The claimant (coded as A1) is a company located in Jiangmen City, Guangdong Province. The first respondent (coded as B) is a Hong Kong company. The second respondent (coded as A2) is a company in Xinhui City, Guangdong Province. On 20 April 1988, A1 as Party A concluded a Joint Venture Contract (J-V Contract) and articles of association with B to set up a Joint Venture to produce emulsion gloves. On 10 June 1988, A1 and A2 entered into an Agreement. Article 1 of the Agreement provides that both parties should observe the J-V Contract and articles of association signed by and between A1 and B. The main stipulations of the Agreement are as follows:

A1 and A2 jointly invest in the Joint Venture. The profits, losses and risks should be borne by them in proportion of their respective contribution to the registered capital. Al is in charge of getting a loan of US$322,500 from a bank, Al and A2 equally share it and have it contributed to the Joint Venture and respectively accounts for 32.25% of the total registered capital and investment of the Joint Venture. A sum of RMB 1,200,000 (Chinese currency) is needed for the infrastructure of water, electricity and gas for the Joint Venture, A2 is in charge of getting a loan of that sum. The loan and interest is included as production cost of the Joint Venture and is discharged by it. A2 leases out a factory building of 1800 square meters to the Joint Venture for 10 years, the rent is borne by the latter.A1 and A2 respectively appoints two person to be on the Board of Directors of the Joint Venture. The chairman is appointed by A1 and A2 appoints a vice-chairman. A2 recommends two candidates respectively as manager and deputy manager. The duration of the Agreement is 10 years. Any unsettled disputes arising from the execution of the Agreement shall be submitted to an arbitral institute.

On 9 October 1990, a meeting of the Board of Directors of the Joint Venture was held. The Minutes of this meeting (in brief) read:

1. The total amount of investment of the Joint Venture is US$400,000, each party has paid its own shares. Al's accounts for 37.5%, A2's 37.5%, B's 25%.
2. The equipment was imported without installation as the price of latex gloves in the international market is kept on falling. The decision are as follows:July 1998
    (a) The equipment is kept and sealed in the rented factory building. The expense is shared by three parties according to the ratio of their respective investment;
    (b) Three parties jointly look for a chance to sell the equipment or try to produce other products;
    (c) Before the selling of the equipment, three parties should in line with the principle on mutual benefits and good-cooperation jointly share the risks, the

total price and other expense in accordance with the ratio of their respective investment.

There was a form attached to the Minutes. It recorded some figure about the investment and expenses until the date of the meeting.

Afterward disputes arose. A1 filed an application for arbitration with CIETAC, Shenzhen, in accordance with the arbitration clause contained in the J-V Contract and Article 1 of the Agreement CIETAC, Shenzhen, accepted the application on 26 June 1994.

Upon receiving a notice of arbitration from CIETAC, Shenzhen, A2 submitted a demurrer on 19 July 1994 with the following arguments:

1. There is no agreement made by and between Al and A2 about submitting any disputes to CIETAC.
2. The J-V Contract was signed by the claimant as Party A independently in its own name with B. That is proved by some approvals from some governmental departments concerned. Those approval documents also fully prove that the contradictor A2 is not a side to the J-V Contract and so it is no subject to the arbitration case.
3. There is no clause in the J-V Contract stipulating that the internal disputes of one side should be referred to CIETAC. However there is a provision in the J-V Contract which provides that disputes should be referred to CIETAC.
4. Al in the application for arbitration declares that its claims are based upon the arbitration clause in the J-V contract and Article 1 of the Agreement between Al and A2. But the meaning of that Article 1 is that A1 and A2 combine to form an independent party, namely the Chinese Party (Party A) should observe the J-V Contract and the articles of association.
5. Al on 20 March 1994 started legal proceedings against A2 at a people's court. Its claim, facts, reasons and evidence in the lawsuit are exactly the same as in its application for arbitration. A2 on 30 March 1994, handed over its defense. In accordance with the aforesaid viewpoints and facts A2 holds that CIETAC, Shenzhen, should overrule Al's unreasonable claim.

B appointed an arbitrator on 18 July 1994. According to CIETAC Rules, B and A2 should jointly appoint one arbitrator from the Panel of CIETAC Arbitrators. B did consult A2 accordingly, but A2 made no response.

A1 sent a letter on 13 August 1994 to CIETAC, Shenzhen, to rebut the issues mentioned in the demurrer as follows:

1. A1, A2 and B in reality formed a joint venture relationship after the signing of the Agreement. Three parties reached an agreement concerning the disposal of the deficit contained in the Minutes. It is no doubt that A2 is a party to the Joint Venture. Al is in a position to initiate the proceedings for liquidation.
2. A2 is not in a position to raise any objection over the arbitration case of CIETAC.
3. In March 1994, Al took a debt recovery action against A2 at a people's court. The lawsuit was based on the Agreement between A1 and A2.However the application for arbitration was based on the J-V Contract between Al and B and the actually

formed joint venture relationship among B, A1 and A2. The reasons and facts of the arbitration case are recorded in the Minutes. The lawsuit and the arbitration case are completely different.

4. For the purpose of thoroughly settling the disputes about Joint Venture after the termination of the J-V Contract, A1 intended to resort to arbitration, and it revoked the court action on 25 April 1994. The people's court issued on 20 July 1994 a ruling, allowing Al's withdrawing and the ruling has come into force. In the course of Al′s resorting to the law, A1 and A2 once tried to settle the disputes through conciliation but without result. So Al has to submit tie application for arbitration. Now there is no grounds anymore for A2 not to join the arbitration.
5. What A2 did was to delay the arbitration process and shirk responsibility. A1 strongly requests that CIETAC, Shenzhen, should urge A2 and B lo:

   (a) appoint an arbitrator jointly, confirm the one appointed by B, or,
   (b) authorize the Chairman of CIETAC, Shenzhen, to appoint one in accordance with the 1994 Rules.

A1 stressed that any of the above would achieve fairness and save time for every party.

I submit that the aforesaid Minutes have at least demonstrated that B had no objection to the Agreement and agreed that A2 was a party to the Joint Venture. According to Chinese Law the contracts of a joint venture are subject to examination and approval, and the assignment of the rights and obligations of an approved contract shall be subject to approval too.

A2 was originally a third party to the Joint Venture. Its joining in the Joint Venture means a substantial amendment to the J-V Contract. According to the facts of this case, Al assigned part of its contractual rights and obligations to A2. This assignment should have been referred to the approval authorities for examination.

CIETAC's acceptance of a case is based on the prima facie evidence provided by a claimant. A conclusion is subject to the decision of a tribunal after some hearing. That is to say the question should be decided by the tribunal to be in line with the applicable and substantive law. You could not confirm that the assignment was not referred to the approval authorities before some hearing.

After the receipt of the letter from B, CIETAC, Shenzhen, communicated a notice of composition of the tribunal and the date of hearing to the three parties. The notice simply mentions A2's ideas expressed in its demurrer without any comments and informs the parties of the name of the arbitrator appointed by B.

Al's attorney on the phone urged us to make a decision to press A2 to participate in the arbitration. We were not in a position to force anybody to execute his rights or obligations. We did not think what A2 said in its demurrer was a procedural matter; instead, it was a vital issue which should be ruled by the tribunal.

But that attorney who might not have much knowledge and experience in dealing with external-related commercial arbitration case. He protested to the Chairman of CIETAC, Shenzhen, without following the Rules of CIETAC rigorously. He also insisted that according to Article 4 of the 1994 Rtles, that question should be first decided.

In September 1994, that attorney wrote to the Chairman of CIETAC, Shenzhen, accusing that the composition of the arbitration tribunal did not conform to the 1994 Rules. He quoted Article 27 of the 1994 Rules in his letter and said that the two respondents were unable to jointly appoint an arbitrator within the time limit, so the appointment should be done by the Chairman; otherwise, it would jeopardize the validation of the award-to-be. He demanded that CIETAC should first make a decision on the jurisdiction over the case.

Here arises a question: When there are two respondents in an arbitration case, one of the respondents refuses to arbitrate, does it implicate that the two respondents fail to agree on the choice of an arbitrator?

If the answer is affirmative as suggestion held by Al's lawyer, there arises another question. If a respondent gives up his rights or believes that he is not a party to the case, he refuses to do anything as required by the arbitration, does it imply that the co-respondent is forced to give up his rights or automatically lose his right to appoint an arbitrator?

I don't think the answer to these two questions is affirmative. On the contrary, I believe when there are two respondents in an arbitration case and if one of them refuses to arbitrate or gives up his right, the other has the right to make his choice by appointing or entrusting the Chairman of CIETAC to appoint one arbitrator.

CIETAC was forced to satisfy AI's demand. A decision on the jurisdiction over the case was issued on 6 September 1994. It stipulates:

> "After examining the Claimant AI's application for arbitration and related documentary evidence, A2's demurrer and relevant evidence, we have found no documents which show the consent the Board of Directors of the Joint Venture concerning A2's joining in and the approval of the local government. CIETAC holds A2 is not a subject to the J-V contract; the approval document presented by the Al and approval certificate turned in by A2 all show that A2 is not a party to the above mentioned contract, the disputes arising from the Agreement between Al and A2 are the disputes of one side to the J-V contract, they are not within the scope of the arbitration clause of the J-V Contract. So those disputes between A1 and A2 are not within the jurisdiction of CIETAC.
>
> "CIETAC decides and informs: A2 does not have to participate in the arbitration; it is lawful and valid of the appointment of the arbitrator by the Respondent B; the hearing is held according to the original schedule, the Claimant A1 and the Respondent B are required to send their legal representatives or agents to appear at the hearing on time."

The decision was drafted by me. But it does not represent any views of mine. Since then, I have held that the question of jurisdiction of vesting of decision-making powers over many critical matters in CIETAC rather than an arbitral tribunal is not in line with international trends and norms.

III. Case2: Pleas To Jurisdiction That Should Be Ruled On By A Tribunal In Its Final Award.

On 11 June 1985, a Hong Kong company (coded as P) and a factory in Guangdong Province (coded as D) signed a joint venture contract to set up a company to make hardware. When disputes arose from the contract and could not be resolved by the board of directors, on 19 August 1994, P filed an application for arbitration to CIETAC, Shenzhen, in accordance with an arbitral clause in the contract. P's claims are as follows:

1. To distribute fixed assets, residual products, tools and residual materials of the joint venture according to the appropriate law.
2. To decide that the sum of HK$1,066,500 paid to some of those Hong Kong expatriates employed by the joint venture and that P should be indemnified by the joint venture.
3. The arbitration fees are borne by D.

D submitted a defense and plea concerning CIETAC's jurisdiction. It deals with four questions

1. To reply to the first claim of P;
2. To analyze the responsibility for the losses suffered by the joint venture;
3. P does not make any plea on the sum of HK$1,066,500. Thus this sum is not within the jurisdiction;
4. The responsibility on whose paying the arbitration fee.

D appointed an arbitrator before submitting his defense. A tribunal was formed and it first reviewed the defense and the plea.

In the plea, D dealt with the second claim of P.D argued that P's claim was not within the jurisdiction of CIETAC. Hereunder are his reasons:

1. The claim is related to the credit and financial liability between P and the joint venture. There are two issues of that relationship, namely the subject of the disputes and the debt itself. D is neither one of them. Consequently, D has no direct relation with the second claim of P. And, P is not in a position to have a claim against D. As the joint venture was dissolved and liquidation was executed by the liquidation group. P may have a claim to the liquidation group.
2. This claim is based on no arbitration clause. P's application for arbitration is based on the arbitral clause set forth in the joint venture contract. But that clause only stipulates that any disputes arising from or in connection with the interpretation or execution of the joint venture contract as well as the articles of association of the joint venture. P's second claim is obviously neither within he area for arbitration nor within the sphere of the arbitral clause. D therefore argues that this issue should be decided before hearing.

Usually D might raise the plea and state the reasons. His plea and reasons would form the basis for examination and/or rulings in the tribunal's award. The tribunal originally intended to proceed in accordance with the arbitration rule. It did not do so because of D's argument.

The tribunal had to make its decision to consider the jurisdiction over P's second claim in accordance with the meaning of Article 4 of the 1994 Rules.

The tribunal found in the name of CIETAC stated that it had the power to arbitrate this case by reference to those provisions of the joint venture contract signed by the parties, namely:

> "...any disputes arising from the interpretation or execution of the joint venture contract should be referred to arbitration. dissolution and liquidation of the joint venture forms the provision of Article 6 in the joint venture contract. And P's second claim is concerning liquidation under Article 6.The tribunal found it no problem to construe P's second claim as within the meaning of Article 6, not to mention that the joint venture had been dissolved and liquidation is under execution. Moreover, both parties' representatives have formed a liquidation group."

The tribunal went on to decide on the size of debt incurred by the joint venture:

> "This debt has a direct impact on the distribution of the set of the joint venture. The tribunal holds that D should acknowledge the amount of this debt, so that the liquidation group would be able to reach a decision. Consequently the dispute about P's role as a creditor to the joint venture is another issue of this case."

This premature decision (i.e., without a full and complete hearing) of CIETAC might be correct. However, we have to re-assess the attitude of the attorney of D. The attorney filed his statement together with documentary evidence before the hearing of the tribunal. In the statement, he indicated that his client would respect the decision of CIETAC with a condition. That condition was in relation to the debt owed by the joint venture to P. It was because his client did not believe the joint venture owed P any money. Usually, it is the tribunal who decides this jurisdictional problem/issue after some examination at some hearing.

The tribunal should first ascertain whether that P had paid the employees of the joint venture from Hong Kong, and whether it was authorized by the joint venture. If so, how much? This reflects a major defect in Article 4 of both the 1994 and 1995 Rules. These articles (with the identical wordings from each other) have vested CIETAC with the sole and exclusive authority in deciding jurisdiction over an arbitration case even before an arbitration tribunal commences first hearing.

In the part of Facts of the Award rendered by the tribunal, it deals with the problem of the second claim of P, quoting both parties' statements and counterattacks. The tribunal deals with the problem of the second claim of P in relation to the facts of the Award. The tribunal also takes notice of both parties' statements of claims and counter-claims. In the second claim, P mentions the debt owed by the joint venture to him. D argues that the joint venture had paid the Hong Kong employees 80%of their wages, the balance is approximately HKS15, 781, 92. The tribunal holds that if the joint venture owes its employees, the employees would have a claim against the joint venture. If the joint venture did ask P to pay some sum of wages to the employees, P would have a claim against the joint venture. However, P does not produce any evidence to support his claim and the claim is untenable.

IV Case 3: The Powers of CIETAC And/Or Its Branches to Decide an Objection Against CIETAC's Jurisdiction.

There is a case of disputes arising from a contract about a restaurant that is sub-contracted to a third party. In June 1988, Ms. Zhu (a Hong Kong resident) and Mr.Chen (coded as C) entered into a contract with a Shenzhen Corp (coded as R). According to this contract, R has the right to sub-contract the restaurant to C. At the time the business floor space of the restaurant was only a bit more than 100 square meters.

In May 1990, C renewed the contract with R to continue running the restaurant. This contract expired on 1 July 1994. C argued that R had orally promised them to renew the contract for another term. C claimed that they invested RMB5, 6000,000 for extending the floor space and re-decorating the restaurant. The floor space has since extended from 100 square meters in 1988 to about 800 square meters in 1994. C paid a certain sum of contract fees monthly for this restaurant to R. There is an arbitration clause in the contract.

In January 1994, C, for the purpose of recovering all the investment, wrote to R, expressing the hope of extending the time limit. R orally agreed and in June of the same year they gave C a blank contract form to fill in, saying that they would sign it.

R did not sign the contract. Disputes arose. On 5 July 1994, C brought a suit against R at the People's Court of Luohu District, Shenzhen City and applied for property preservative measures. The Court sealed up the restaurant.

On 26 July 1994, C requested a dismissal of the case, stating that they preferred an alternative resolution. R did not submit their defense.

Two days later, C's request was satisfied by the court through rendering a ruling.

On 5 August 1994, C in accordance with the arbitration clause of the contract submitted their application for arbitration to CIETAC, Shenzhen, claiming the repayment of their investment of RMB5,600,000 yuan in the restaurant and the interests of it. CIETAC, Shenzhen, took cognizance of the case and issued a notice of arbitration. Having received the notice, a representative of R made a few phone calls to CIETAC, Shenzhen, claiming the dispute was not within CIETAC's jurisdiction. Upon the request of CIETAC, Shenzhen, R submitted their demurrer on 26 September 1994. It states:

1. Arbitration must be based on the voluntary of both parties. There is indeed an arbitration clause in the contract. But C brought an action against our company to the People's Court of Luohu Distract. That shows they do not want to settle the disputes through the means of arbitration. So both parties have no more willingness of arbitration at all.
2. The Court's acceptance of the case shows that the arbitration jurisdiction has been excluded. Normally, the Court should have not received the case because in the contract there is an explicit arbitration clause. However the Court had the imprudence to receive the case and sealed up the restaurant of our company. That has excluded the possibility of arbitration.
3. When the two parties are dissent from each other, namely one wants to have it settled at a people's court and the other wants to adopt the means of arbitration, a people's court enjoys priority.

In response to the demurrer, CIETAC, Shenzhen, replied in writing as follows:

> "It has been established that there is an arbitration clause in the contract between C and your company. That shows that both of you have been voluntary to agree on arbitration. According to Article 257 of the Civil Procedure Law of PRC, if there is an arbitration clause in a contract

> between two parties, when disputes arise from or in connection with it, disputes should be referred to arbitration but not to a court. C did once lodge an action against your company with the People's Court of Luohuo District, Shenzhen City. Nevertheless, your company did not respond with any defense. That shows that your company is unwilling to accept the jurisdiction of a court, and you have not given up the arbitration agreement. Subsequently, C requested the dismissal of the case from the Court, and the Court issued a ruling to dismiss the case. That shows that the arbitration clause of the aforesaid contract is still valid. There is no such thing of exceeding arbitration jurisdiction. Any party of the contract is authorized to file an application for arbitration."
>
> "The dispute of the contract is external-related. CIETAC is an institute specially in handling disputes arising from external-related contracts. Since there is an arbitration clause in your contract, CIETAC has the power to take cognizance of the case. Therefore your company should present your defense in accordance with the Arbitration Rules, exercising your power authorized by the Arbitration Rules."

Every now and then CIETAC would come across this kind of event. The whole arbitration process runs into some obstacles at the very beginning. It is not uncommon to find that a respondent may refuse to comply with the arbitration agreement; deny there is a valid arbitration agreement or raise an objection to the jurisdiction of CIETAC. Hence CIETAC, being a permanent arbitration institute, should enforce the arbitration process without interference or interruption. It is CIETAC's obligation to promptly guide the parties concerned to a correct track. This work should not be delayed until the formation of a tribunal. In China, it is an aid needed usually at the first stage of arbitration proceedings. What CIETAC has done in this respect has been realistically significant in the past years.

According to our experience, almost every single commercial contract between a foreign party and a Chinese party would contain an arbitration clause with wordings similar to the following prevailing clause:

> "Any disputes arising from or in connection with this contract shall be settled through amicable negotiations. In case no settlement can be reached, the case shall be submitted to CIETAC for arbitration in accordance with its Arbitration Rules. The arbitral award shall be accepted as final and binding upon both parties. The fees for arbitration shall be borne by the losing party unless otherwise awarded."

Technically, in these commercial contracts, we can say that the arbitration clause stipulated therein would convey the same meaning as the above-mentioned prevailing clause.

To avoid confusion and further disputes, CIETAC suggests the following wordings as a model for an arbitration clause in a commercial contract:

> "Any dispute arising from or in connection with this contract shall be submitted to CIETAC for arbitration which shall be conducted by CIETAC or its Shenzhen sub-commission or its Shanghai sub- commission at the option of the Claimant in accordance with its existing rules of arbitration. The arbitral award is final and binding upon both parties."

People can see that the prevailing clause and the model clause do not mention the nomination or appointment of one or more arbitrators. This is different from those recommended by other arbitration institutes, such as the clause for ICC arbitration, which reads:

> "All disputes arising in connection with the present contract shall be finally settled under the Rules of Conciliation and Arbitration of the International Chamber of Commerce by one or more arbitrators appointed in accordance with the said Rules."

In China, a claimant submitted its application for arbitration to CIETAC. CIETAC then takes cognizance of the case in accordance with the arbitration clause set forth in the contract signed by and between the claimant and its respondent and upon the application for arbitration by the claimant. By virtue of its Arbitration Rules, the case is referred to a tribunal that will be formed for this purpose.

Before forming the tribunal, the respondent does nothing but first make an objection to the jurisdiction of CIETAC upon receiving an arbitration notification. In the above case, what the respondent objects to was the jurisdiction of CIETAC but not a tribunal-to-be. CIETAC should promptly clear up the misunderstanding of the respondent, preventing any potential antagonism between the claimant and the respondent, or between the respondent and the parties and CIETAC from happening or deteriorating at this stage of the proceedings.

Though in reality, a case will be heard and settled by a tribunal. An award will be made and signed out by the members of a tribunal. Thereafter, the award document will be stamped by CIETAC before it is handed down to both parties. It is up to this stage that the award could be called a CIETAC award. When a CIETAC award is applied for enforcement at either a domestic or foreign court, the award may be recognized and enforced or refused or set aside or suspended by that jurisdictional authority. This jurisdictional measure would only refer to the CIETAC award but not the arbitrators who handled the case. As a permanent arbitration institute, it is reasonable and logical for CIETAC to be vested with some authority at some stage of a process to execute its jurisdiction. This can be regarded as the difference between an institutional arbitration and an ad hoc arbitration. To do so, it will enhance the work of CIETAC. Furthermore, the CIETAC Award is a "Trade Mark." It has been created by the staff and arbitrators of CIETAC. It is used by all the arbitrators on its panel when they are appointed to handle cases under the jurisdiction of CIETAC. One of the rights and obligations of the executives of CIETAC is to safeguard its reputation and credit. At least the secretariat of CIETAC should see to it that there are fewer slips or errors in its daily operation and the work of all the tribunals and furnish service such as clearing off some obstacles for the tribunals. That is why there is a screening group within the secretary to review draft awards, for the purpose to remind arbitrators of any issue related to the form of the awards on condition that the arbitrators' independence of decision is not affected. That is one of the reasons CIETAC has to select and appoint qualified arbitrators by maintaining a panel. But I have to add a few words here. It is only provided in the 1995 and 1998 Rules that the CIETAC could remind the arbitration tribunal of any issue related to the form of the award. 'Anyhow the practice in CIETAC in this regard is as that in the International Court of Arbitration of the International Chamber of Commerce. Namely CIETAC, without affecting the arbitral tribunal's liberty of decision, may also draw its attention to points of substance.8 So this related provision should also be contained in Article 56 of the 1998 Rules.

In reality, in most disputes, when a tribunal is formed, members(three of them)of a tribunal may live in different places or countries. A thorough discussion among them is not an easy job. Usually, they meet a day or two before a hearing at the headquarters of CIETAC in Beijing or at CIETAC's two branches respectively in Shenzhen and Shanghai. Though some of the arbitrators on the CIETAC's Panel might have easy access to a fax set or now a computer with E-Mail, a final version of a decision relating to procedure problems could be sent by these means. The professional secretaries of CIETAC are able to have it done more effectively than the arbitrators. During the five working days in every week, there are always staff at the end of the telephones, fax sets or computers at CIETAC. Efficiency is the life of every business.

2 Some False Concepts of some Respondents Should be Cleared As Quickly as Possible by CIETAC

A prompt and brief reply might clear the false concepts of some respondents and guide them onto the right track.

A Chinese company (Buyers) and an Australian company (Sellers)entered into a sales contract concerning the sale of wool grease. The arbitration clause of the contract reads:

> "All disputes in connection with this Contract or the execution thereof shall be settled friendly through negotiation. In case no settlement can be reached, the case may then be submitted for arbitration to the Arbitration Committee of China Council for the Promotion of International Trade. The decision of the Arbitration Committee shall be final and binding upon both parties; arbitration fee shall be borne by the losing party or the Arbitration may be settled in the third country mutually agreed upon by both parties."

When disputes arose and could not be settled by the parties themselves, the Buyers submitted an application for arbitration to CIETAC, Shenzhen. The Summary Procedure applied to the case as the amount of the claim totaled not more than RMB 500,000 yuan.

After receiving a notice of arbitration, the Sellers (respondent) made a reply which reached CIETAC, Shenzhen, three days before the hearing, saying:

> "May we emphasize that we are unable to attend personally in the Arbitration to be held on 18 September(1995).Especially we do not understand the Chinese Language in hearing but we would like to settle this matter in Australia. If the Buyers submit their claim to Arbitration Commission of Australia with English as communication."

In the award rendered by me as a sole arbitrator dealt with the quoted question as follows:

> "It is explicitly provided that the disputes should be submitted for arbitration to CIETAC. Without furthermore negotiation, neither party could amend the provision. Though it is provided that 'the Arbitration may be settled in the third country mutually agreed upon by both parties, 'the two parties have not negotiated over the issue of a third country. There is

> not a third country agreed upon by the two parties to substitute China. Both parties have not agreed on the arbitration under the jurisdiction of the Arbitration Com-mission of Australia. Both parties have not agreed on the language for arbitration, according to the provision of CIETAC Rules, the Chinese Language is the official language of its arbitration."

If the respondent's reply had reached me some days earlier, what I said in the award would have been written in a letter in the name of CIETAC to the respondent for the purpose of clearing their false concepts.

On 1 June 1995, a Chinese company (the Buyers) and a Thai company (the Sellers) signed a purchase contract with a total value of US$1,757,500.Under which the Sellers should supply three brands of Thai fragrant or white rice of 500MT for the Buyers at the unit price respectively of US$420/MT, US$330/MT, US$355/MT CNF Shenzhen, China.

The arbitration clause of the contract reads:

> "All disputes arising out of the contract or concerning the contract shall be submitted to the China International Economic and Trade Arbitration Commission for arbitration in accordance with its Arbitration Rules. The arbitration shall take place in Shenzhen, China.
>
> The arbitral award is final and binding upon both parties." The law application clause provides that:
>
> "It will be governed by the Law of the People's Republic of China under the circumstance that the contract is signed or the goods while the disputes arising are in the People's Republic of China or the defendant is a Chinese legal person. Otherwise it is governed by the United Nations Convention on Contract for the International Sale of Goods."

The price terms clause goes:

> "The terms in the contract are based on INCOTERMS 1990 of the International Chamber of Commerce."

The version clause is as follows:

> "This contract is made out in both Chinese and English of which versions are equally effective. Conflicts between these two languages arising there from, if any, shall be subject to Chinese version."

On 16 August 1995, the Buyers as claimant in accordance with the arbitration clause in the contract submitted an application for arbitration to CIETAC, Shenzhen.

After receiving an arbitration notice, the Sellers as respondent made a reply, raising an objection to the jurisdiction of CIETAC, Shenzhen, over the case and presenting their first substantive defense. The main points about the objection are summed up as follows:

> The contract was not signed at Shenzhen, China (though it is recorded in the contract that the signature place is Shenzhen, China, in fact it was concluded by facsimile).When the disputes arose, the goods were not in China. Furthermore we respondent are no Chinese legal person, so, we hold the disputes of the contract should not submitted to CIETAC, Shenzhen.

To the objection, I drafted a letter, which was rendered in the name of CIETAC, Shenzhen, to the respondent. The main points are as follows:

The arbitration clause set forth in the contract not only explicitly expresses both parties' will of arbitration but also choose an arbitration body, i.e. CIETAC. This choice can't be changed unless otherwise agreed upon by both parties through further negotiation.

CIETAC is an international arbitration institute. It resolves commercial disputes between foreign legal persons and Chinese legal

persons, between foreign legal persons and/or natural persons. The facts that the signature place and subject matter are not in China won't result in the invalidation of the arbitration clause of the contract.

Law application and jurisdiction of an arbitration institute are different issues. Article 5 of the Foreign Economic and Trade Law of PRC specifies "The parties to a contract may choose the proper law applicable to the settlement of contract disputes. In the absence of such a choice by the parties, the law of the country that has the closest connection with the country shall apply." The tribunal-to-be would settle the issue of proper law in light with international practices and the above-mentioned conflict rule. Furthermore it is provided in the law application clause that "it is governed by the Unites Nations Convention on Contract for the International Sale of Goods." We believe this choice would be fully respected by the tribunal.

3 The Viewpoints in the Chinese Legal and Arbitration Circles

I purpose to briefly introduce some of the viewpoints and opinions in the Chinese legal and arbitration circles about the decision-making powers over jurisdiction in arbitration. I should say what I have known is limited.

A. Being aware of the trend and general practice of the world commercial arbitration but expresses no one's own opinions.

Dr. Guac Fei said:

"In the world, while determining the validity of an arbitration agreement or an arbitration clause, rendering a decision or an interlocutory award of jurisdiction, the power is first entrusted to arbitrators or arbitration tribunals. As the validity of an arbitration agreement directly affect the jurisdiction of a case, hence an arbitration tribunal's power to decide its own jurisdiction and the validity of an arbitration agreement is usually provided in law."

Dr. Guao said in the same article:

"The validity of an arbitration agreement and the jurisdiction of an arbitration case is seldom decided by an arbitration institute Nevertheless, the China International Economic and Trade Arbitration Commission and the China Maritime Arbitration adopt this approach."10

Dr. Guac did not analyze the advantages and shortcomings of each way, and expressed no of her own opinions in this regard.

B. Holding the doctrine of competence–competence in esteem.

Mr. Tao Chunming and Mr. Wang Shenchang mentioned the doctrine of severability and the doctrine of competence-competence in one of their books, holding that both the doctrines are closely related and the doctrine of competence-competence is reasonable both in theory and practice. According to that doctrine, when parties to a case are divergent in views on the validity of their arbitration agreement and the jurisdiction of the case, the dispute should not be referred to a court but to a tribunal or arbitrators. That would avoid delay of the formation of the tribunal and the arbitration procedure.

The two compilers said that the doctrine of competence-competence had been widely confirmed and applied in conventions, treaties, and precedents. They hold Article 2 of the Arbitration Rules of CIETAC also embodies the doctrine. As the book was published in 1992, so it must refer to Article 2(3) of the 1988 Rules, which reads:

> "The Arbitration Commission has power to decide on the validity of arbitration agreements and the jurisdiction over arbitration cases."

I do not think the Article 2 of the 1988 Rules and the Article 4 of the 1995 Rules embody the doctrine of competence-competence, as the power is not vested in tribunals or arbitrators. Namely, the tribunals and arbitrators, according to the stipulation in CIETAC Rules, have no power to determine their jurisdiction.

About the Article 20 of the Arbitration Law Professor Wu Huanning held:

> "That stipulation goes against the original intention of the parties at the time they signed the arbitration agreement. As the arbitration agreement expresses their intention to refer their dispute to arbitration, the dispute over the validity of the arbitration agreement itself should also be referred to the arbitration body for a final settlement."

What Prof. Wu said is quite correct. However, he did not mention the power of a tribunal or an arbitrator in this regard.

Two scholars held that an arbitration agreement is the base upon which an arbitration institute takes cognizance of a case. The system of the arbitration agreement is the cornerstone of the commercial arbitration system.

The two scholars touched the issue about the power to decide the existence and validity of arbitration agreements. They were of the view that the power should be entrusted to arbitration tribunals or arbitrators. They positively commented on the doctrine of competence-competence, saying the application of that doctrine would avoid first having a judicial procedure for settling the issue of the validity of an arbitration agreement, and then referring the case to arbitration for settling the substantive issues. Time would be saved.16 I am all for these two viewpoints.

C. Explicitness and validity of an arbitration agreement are of two conceptions.

Three arbitrators of CIETAC held that an explicit arbitration agreement is different from a valid arbitration agreement. They are two conceptions. The two important conditions for a valid arbitration agreement are: the parties' real intention to apply for arbitration; the matters for arbitration being within the sphere provided by law. But an explicit arbitration agreement should contain many factors, such as the arbitration matters or sphere, the name of arbitration body, the application of a set of arbitration rules, venue of arbitration, the validity of the award, namely the finality of the award and the exclusion of appeal to a court, etc.

The three arbitrators said that a court should help the parties to a case to perfect their defective arbitration clause, so that their arbitration intention would be realized and an arbitration body would be able to smoothly finish arbitration procedures, safeguarding the social economic order.

I quite agree with the views expressed above by the three arbitrators. But I am sorry that they did not talk about the question concerning the power of an arbitrator to determine his jurisdiction.

D. A dispute over the validity of an arbitration agreement should be decided by an arbitration institute, but a court has the last say.

Two teachers of law said that a dispute over the validity of an arbitration agreement should first be decided by an arbitration institute. If any party to the case is of objection against the decision, the objection should be referred to a court. The ruling made by the court is final.9.

Mr. Dai Yue said that an arbitration tribunal should have power to determine its own jurisdiction, as that is the need and a prerequisite for the tribunal to execute its function. 20 But Mr. Dai did not think that the decision made by a tribunal over the jurisdiction is final. Instead, he held that a people's court has the final say.

I do not agree with the above-mentioned views.

E. A people's court is more authoritative than an arbitration body, the issue of validity of an arbitration agreement should be decided by a people's court.

> "According to the stipulation of the Arbitration Law, if a party challenges the validity of the arbitration agreement, he may request the arbitration commission to make a decision. If at the same time the other party applies to a people's court for a ruling, the people's court shall give a ruling(Article 20 of the Arbitration Law).A people's court is a state judicial organ, it is more authoritative than an arbitration institute."

The viewpoint shows that some professionals just ignored the trend in the commercial arbitration circle of the whole world.

4 Conclusion

In dealing with the issue of the arbitrator's right to rule on his own jurisdiction, we should take full notice that in the practice of CIETAC parties concerned usually first challenge the jurisdiction of CIETAC, a permanent arbitral body, so there are grounds for CIETAC to be vested with some powers to make decisions over the matter of challenging its jurisdiction. I am aware that:

> "If there is one thing over which modern writers on arbitration seem to agree, it is that arbitrators must be allowed to rule on their jurisdiction. Lalive recently suggested that this might now be regarded as a 'principle d'orde public transnational'. Earlier, in similar vein, Mezer had remarked that modern arbitration could hardly prosper without such a concept. Other authors seem to be no less enthusiastic.

> "This support for the arbitrator's right to rule on his own competence is reflected in a number of international conventions, national laws and arbitration rules. The European Convention 1961 [Art.V(3)], the Washington Convention 1965 [Art.41(1)] and the UNCITRAL Model Law [Art.16(1)] all expressly permit the arbitrator to rule on challenges to his own authority. This is also the case as regards to the Belgian Code judiciaire [Art.1697(1)], the Swiss Concordat and Loi federale sur le droit international prive("LDIP")[Concordat suisse sur l'arbitrage ("IAC")Art 8(1);LDIP,Art.186(1)],the Dutch [Burgerlijke Rechtsvordering,Art.1052(1 and West German Codes of Civil Procedure [Zivilprozessordnung("ZPO")Art.1037]and the ICC [Rules of the ICC Court of Arbitration,Art.8(3)]and UNCITRAL Arbitration Rules [Art.21(1].The English and Swedish courts have also taken the same view."

We should recognize that many businessmen the world over are not familiar with arbitration. If a permanent arbitration institute is obligated to give them some advice or has the power to rule on objections to its jurisdiction, that at lease would be helpful to create an harmonious atmosphere for arbitration.

Having consulted UNCITRL Arbitration Rules, and on the basis of our experience reflected in the examples which I have presented above, I have worked out an article to substitute Article 4 of the 1998 Rules in regard to the pleas as to the jurisdiction of CIETAC and an arbitral tribunal as follows:

> "CIETAC before the formation of the arbitration tribunal has the power to rule on objections that it has no jurisdiction, including any objections with respect to the existence or validity of the arbitration clause or of the separate arbitration agreement. In general, CIETAC should rule on a plea concerning its jurisdiction as a preliminary question. However it may authorize the arbitration tribunal formed later on to deal with it.
>
> "The arbitration tribunal has the power to rule on objections that it has no jurisdiction, including any objections with respect to the existence or validity of the arbitration clause or of the separate arbitration agreement. In general, the arbitration tribunal should rule on a plea concerning its jurisdiction as a preliminary question. However, the arbitration tribunal may proceed with the arbitration and rule on such a plea in its final award."

Accordingly, the principles embodied above should also be contained in the articles concerned in the Arbitration Law.

Notes

1. Article 3 of the Law of the People's Republic of China on Chinese-Foreign Equity Joint Venture.
2. M. J.Moser,China's New International Arbitration Rules,11,J.Int.Arb.3,September 1994,p.5–24.
3. Huang Yanming,Some Remarks About the 1994 Rules of CIETAC and "China's New International Arbitration Rules," 11, J.Int.Arb.4,December,1994,pp.105–116.
4. Article 3 of the Law of the People's Republic of China on Chinese-Foreign Equity Joint Venture.
5. Article 27 of the Law of the People's Republic of China on Economic Contracts Involving Foreign Interest.
6. See Article 56 of the 1995 Rules and the same article of the 1998 Rules.

7. Id.
8. See Article 27 of ICC Rules (1998).
9. Dr.Guao Fei,On Arbitration Agreements,Arbitration &Law Report, CIETAC, Issue 2, 1996, p. 11.
10. Id.
11. Tao Chunming and Wang Shenchang, China International Economic and Trade Arbitration—the Procedure Theory and Practice, Publishing House of the People's China, October 1992, pp.108–113.
12. Id. p.112.
13. Id. p.113.
14. Prof. Wu Huanning,Comments on the Arbitration Law,Arbitration &Law Report, CIETAC, Issue 3, 1995, p.11.
15. Prof.Li Shuangyuang, Huang Yie, Issues Concerning Arbitration Agreement, a paper presented at the Conference of Arbitration Law held on 24–25 March 1995,Beijing,jointly sponsored by the Working Commission of the Standing Committee of the National People's Congress, the Legislation Burau of the State Council,the China Council for the Promotion of International Trade.pl.
16. Id.p.14.
17. Chen Dejun, Wen Shenchang and Kang Ming,International Usage and Foreign-Related Arbitration Practice, China Youth Publishing House, August 1993, pp. 181–196.
18. Id. p. 189.
19. Pro:.Zhang Zhongbai and Liou Weiguo, Aspects Relating to the Validity of Arbitration Agreements, Private International Law and International Commercial Arbitration with Prof.Huang Jin as chief editor, Publishing House of Wuhan University,March, 1994, pp. 181–187.
20. Dai Yue, On the Theory of Autonomy of Arbitration Clause, Private International Law and International Commercial Arbitration, Publishing House of Wuhan University, March, pp.214–215.
21. Id. p. 218.
22. Tan Bing(Chief Editor),Research on the Chinese Arbitration System, Law Publishing House, Octo-ber 1995, p. 198.
23. Adam Samuel, Jurisdictiona:A Study of Belgian, Dutch, English, French, Swedish, Swiss, U.S.and West German Law, Schulthess Polygraphis cher Verlag Zurich 1989, pp.178–179.

An Arbitrator Looks Back: Did CIETAC Have Jurisdiction over Foshan Jiadian Liqhtinq Co., Ltd. vs Prestiqe Liqhtinq Co., Ltd.?

1 Introduction

There are many scholars in the field of commercial arbitration with a deep understanding in both theory and practice. I, the author of this article, though working in this field for quite a long time, incline to regard myself as an artisan only. I suppose I have gained some experience in the practice including lessons drawn from mistakes made by my colleagues and myself as well. So I am fond of collecting feedback after an award is issued especially when the award is the focus of enforcement proceedings. I try to contact the parties and lawyers concerned and request their feedback. When feedback especially including written materials obtained, I would always like to review the issues contained in them.

There is an old Chinese saying which states past experience, if not forgotten, is a guide for the future. I believe mistakes are the cost on the road forward. To share experiences and lessons is worthwhile. Here are some of the lessons I have learned.

In this article I will explain how an arbitrator considers the case before him.

Next, I will review some of the issues revealed in the enforcement proceedings of a CIETAC award brought in Britain. I served on the Tribunal at the China International Economic and Trade Arbitration Commission, Shenzhen (CIETAC, Shenzhen) in the arbitration between Foshan Jiadian Lighting Co., Ltd. (hereinafter referred to as Claimant, or Applicant in the proceedings in UK and Jiadian) and the Respondent Prestige Lighting Co., Ltd.. (hereinafter referred to as Respondent or Prestige).

This commentary was published in Mealey's International Arbitration Report, Vol.16, #9, September 2001, pp. 52–75.

Thanks are due to Mr.Huang/ Zhongquan of Foshan Jiandian Lighting Co., for the materials provided to me which enable me to have a picutre of the overall proceedings in the UK. Thanks also to Dr. John Mo, associate professor with the Law School, City University of Hong Kong for some reference material, and Dr. Xenos M. Yuen with the Law Offices of Yuen & Associates, PLLC for his advice.

Y. Huang, *Commentaries on Commercial Arbitration in Modern China*, Modern China and International Economic Law, https://doi.org/10.1007/978-981-95-0168-7_2

2 The Proceedings of Arbitration at CIETAC, Shenzhen, and the Main Contents of the Award

A. About the Procedure of the Arbitration

CIETAC, Shenzhen, in accordance with the arbitration clauses contained in the two sales contracts between the Claimant Foshan Jiadian Lighting Co., Ltd. and the Respondent Prestige Lighting Co., Ltd. and upon a written Application for Arbitration submitted by the Claimant, on 16 July 1999 took cognizance of this case (Case No. SHEN G99048). The two arbitration clauses contained in the two contracts are identical:

> Any disputes and controversies arising between the parties from the execution of, or in connection with, this contract should be settled through friendly negotiation. In case no settlement can be reached, the case shall then be submitted to China International Economic and Trade Arbitration Commission Shenzhen Commission for settlement by arbitration in accordance with the Commission's Arbitration Rules in effect at the time of applying for arbitration. The award rendered by the Commission shall be final and binding upon both parties.

The Secretariat of CIETAC, Shenzhen, sent the Respondent by EMS a Notice of Arbitration, a copy of the Application for Arbitration by the Claimant and the appendices thereto, a copy of the Arbitration Rules with Arbitration Fee Schedule, a copy of the Panel of Arbitrators of CIETAC. The Respondent made no direct response thereto but a law firm without formal authority in the name of the Respondent wrote to CIETAC, Shenzhen.

The revised Arbitration Rules of CIETAC (hereinafter referred to as the "Arbitration Rules"), which came into force on 10 May 1998, apply to the procedure of this case.

An Arbitration Tribunal (hereinafter referred to as the "Tribunal") was formed on 2 August 1999, consisting of the presiding arbitrator Mr. Qiu appointed by the Chairman of CIETAC pursuant to Article 24(2) of the Arbitration Rules, myself Mr. Huang (the author of this article) appointed by the Chairman of CIETAC authorized by the Claimant, Mr. Wu appointed by the Chairman of CIETAC pursuant to Article 26 of the Arbitration Rules. The Notice of Formation of the Tribunal was sent by registered mail that day to the two parties, respectively.

In consultation with the Secretariat of CIETAC, Shenzhen, the Tribunal decided to hold an oral hearing on 3 November 1999. The notice of hearing was sent by registered mail on 17 September 1999 to the parties, respectively.

On the date of the oral hearing, Mr. Huang Z.Q., the representative of the Claimant, was present. The Respondent failed to send any representative. The Tribunal had to proceed with the hearing and make an award by default pursuant to Article 42 of the Arbitration Rules.

After the hearing the Claimant produced supplementary submission. The Secretariat of CIETAC, Shenzhen, sent the supplementary submission to the Respondent by registered mail, but received no reply.

The Tribunal made an award([99]Shen Guo Zhon Jue Zhi No.96 Award—attachment) in absentia under the relevant provisions of the Arbitration Rules.

B. **Facts of the Case Confirmed And Recorded in the Award**

On 13 November 1998, the Claimant (as Seller) and the Purchaser) by means of fax concluded the sales contract Proforma Invoice P/I No. ELP981113 consisting of two pages, of which the transaction value is up to USD22170.00. The goods are energy-saving lamps of eight descriptions. The terms and conditions, which are more connected to this case, are as follows:

Brand: CLASSIC.

Dispatch Time: 17 November 1998 Delivery Terms:By Air.

Freight Clause: Freight Collect.

Payment Terms: T/T prior to the shipment Remarks:

1. No order will be accepted without a valid purchase order.
2. Prices supplied are not subject to change.
3. (Omitted)
4. This P/I stands valid after being signed by both Seller and Purchaser.
5. The facsimile copy of this P/I is also valid. Payments information:
   *Beneficiary: Jiadian Lighting Co., Ltd. *Bank: Bank of China, Foshan Branch.

General Terms and Conditions are on page 2.

The Claimant states that after the receipt of the facsimile transfer document of payment from the Respondent on 16 November 1999, it dispatched the goods by air as per the request of the Respondent.

By request of the order of the Respondent, on 25 November 1998, both parties made another sales contract Proforma Invoice P/I No. ELP981125 consisting of two pages with the Claimant as the Seller, of which the transaction value is up to USD16034.00. The goods are the energy-saving lamps of four descriptions. All the terms and conditions except for the Dispatch Time stipulated as arranged and Remarks and Payments Information are exactly the same as under the aforesaid sales contract.

In the Application for Arbitration the Claimant alleges:

> That on the very day when the second sales contract was concluded, the Respondent sent by fax the transfer document of payment to the Claimant requesting the latter to dispatch the goods as soon as possible. The Seller noticed that the payment under the proceeding contract had not been paid into its account, and accordingly, ceased the delivery of the order.

As a matter of fact, to this day, the above-mentioned two payments have not yet been received. Therefore, the Claimant demands the following:

1. On account of the Respondent's breach of contract and fraudulently obtaining goods from the Claimant through the use of fake transfer document of payment, the Claimant requests that the Respondent pay the sum of USD 22170.00 under P/I No. ELP981113, and interest (6% per diem rate) of the arrears amounting to USD

25273.80 in all 190 days, namely from 20 November 1998 to 30 May 1999 and (10%) contractual fine amounting to USD2217.00, total amount is USD49660.80.

2. Because of the default of the Respondent and its attempt of obtaining the Claimant's goods by means of fake transfer document of payment, the Claimant has suffered great losses in the overstocking of the products and in the circulation of fund, though it still retains the goods. Therefore, the Respondent shall pay the Claimant the sum of USD16034.00 under the sales contract P/I No.ELP981125 for the finished products.

CIETAC, Shenzhen, on 22 August 1999 received a letter dated 19 August 1999 from J.E. Rothery &Co. Solicitors (hereinafter referred to as the Letter of Rothery), a British law firm. The first paragraph reveals that the Respondent of this case has consulted the law firm. The second and third paragraphs of the letter are as follows:

> "Our instructions are that it was an expressed part of the agreement between our clients and Jiadian Lighting Co Ltd. that any disputes between the two Companies would be resolved in accordance with UK Law and in the UK Courts. Indeed, we enclose a copy of a letter signed on behalf of Jiadian Lighting dated 15th August 1997 to this effect.
>
> "The dispute between the parties in this matter arises from the supply of 15 volt transformers by Jiadian Lighting Co to our clients. The transformers should have conformed to European Standards and CE compliant. The transformers were not. Our clients have been prosecuted for the supply of defective transformers and have incurred total costs and compensation claims exceeding mp150,000."

Attached to this letter there was a copy of a letter dated 15 August 1997 (hereinafter referred to as the Letter of 15 August 1997) from the Respondent to Mr. Huang of the Claimant, as follows:

> "I am writing to ask you to reply to my letter dated 19th May, 1997.If you agree to the final paragraph of the letter which said:
>
> "The parties will take measures to settle disputes which may arise in connection with this contract(emphasis added)in a friendly and amicable way. In case the parties will not come to an agreement, the discrepancies will be settled in a UK Court of Law. At all times our dealings will be governed by UK law(emphasis added)".
>
> "Please sign below at the side of my signature."

The three Chinese characters "Huang Z.Q." were signed on the letter.

After receiving the copies of the Letter of Rothery and a copy of the Letter of 15 August 1997 transferred by the Secretariat of CIETAC, Shenzhen, Mr. Huang Z.Q. of the Claimant wrote a letter dated 9 September 1999 to the Secretariat of CIETAC, Shenzhen. A copy of the latter was transferred from Mr. Huang Z.Q. to the Respondent.

The second paragraph of the letter from Mr. Huang Z.Q. reads:

> "The letter dated August 15, 1997 provided by the Appellee (i.e. Respondent)is fake document because we have not received the said letter before, and what is more, the signature of the Chinese name was not my own handwriting signature."

The Respondent made no response to this letter.

After the oral hearing, the Claimant produced an additional submission. The main part of it is as follows:

> "Due to the order from Prestige Lighting Co., ltd. Under P/1 No.ELP981125 is OEM order, which were produced according to buyer's brand name and specifications. The color temperature of the lamps is warm white with base B22 to meet the standard of the British electrical appliance. However, general speaking, in Chinese domestic market, the Chinese people like to purchase the lamps in cool white color with base E27, under above circumstances, we have to replace base B22 with E27,and change the color gift box for each lamp, and clean buyer's brand name for each lamp which were printed on the lamp housing, and re-print our own brand name on them again. For so many modifications on the lamps, we have to sell them at lower prices."
>
> "In brief, on the one hand, it gives rise to the loss for us to complete the above jobs, on the other hand, reducing prices also causes loss for us, so the total loss is at least 50%."

In this additional submission the Claimant amends its second claim as USD8017.00

C. The Views of the Tribunal in the Award

The facts confirmed and views expressed by the Tribunal are as follows:

1. The Claimant and the Respondent respectively as Seller and Purchaser signed Proforma Invoice P/I No. ELP98113 on 13 November 1998. It consisted of two pages. The lamps (subject matter of the contract) were warm white with base B22 to meet the standard of the British electrical appliance, and in all of eight descriptions. The Claimant on 16 November 1998 performed the contract by dispatching the goods by air as per the request of the Respondent. The Respondent received and accepted the goods. On 16 November 1998 the Respondent faxed the Claimant a transfer document of payment but in fact the document was a remittance application filled in by the Respondent and not a telegraphic transfer prior to dispatch as required in the contract and the sum of USD22170.00 was not paid to the Claimant after the goods were received.
2. The Claimant and the Respondent, respectively as Seller and Purchaser, signed Proforma Invoice P/I No. ELP981125 on 25 November 1998. It consisted of two pages. The lamps (subject matter of this contract) were warm white, the same as that of the former sales contract, and in all of four descriptions. The Claimant had the goods produced. The Respondent once more asked the Claimant to dispatch the goods by faxing the Claimant a remittance application. Such remittance application was not an effective means of payment, and in fact the Respondent had not paid for the goods under the former contract. As the Claimant discovered that the Respondent had not paid for the amount due under the former contract, it suspended the performance of its obligation by ceasing delivery of the goods. Obviously, the Respondent did not perform its obligation under the latter contract by T/T prior to the shipment. The Respondent was in breach of contract. As the goods of the contract were produced in the light of the descriptions of the Respondent, if the Claimant wants to have this batch of goods modified to be sold in China by removing the Respondent's trademarks, reprint trademarks

and change the color to white that would cause it much trouble and cost. The Claimant claims that it would at least suffer a loss of USD8017.00. The Tribunal sustains the Claimant in its claim on 50% of the price of the goods.

3. Both of the aforesaid sales contracts consist of two pages. That is clearly recorded in the first page. The two-second pages are exactly the same titled as General Terms and Conditions. The arbitrators have quoted Article 7 Arbitration (Clause)at the beginning of this Award and make more quotations from it.

   "1 Validity.

   "1.1 This Proforma Invoice/Sale Contract, including terms and conditions stated herein, constitutes the entire agreement between buyer and seller unless otherwise is agreed upon in writing. Terms and conditions in this P/I or S/C shall take precedence over any conflicting terms and conditions printed on Buyer's purchase or-der and /or related documents."6. Claims.

   "In case of quality discrepancy, claim should be filed by the Buyer within 30 days after the arrival of the goods at port of destination; while for quantity discrepancy, claim should be filed by the buyer within 15 days after the arrival of the goods at port of destination. It is understood that the Seller shall not be liable for any discrepancy of the goods shipped due to causes for which the insurance company, shipping company, other transportation organization or post office are liable. If no claims are filed within term of validity, Buyer shall be deemed to have waived its rights to assert any claim."

The Tribunal ascertains that the Respondent did not sign on the second page of both contracts. But it did receive the pages. The "Header (telefax transmission details at the top)" on the second page of the two contracts explicitly reveals that the Respondent faxed the second pages back to the Claimant after receiving them. That shows that the Respondent did not raise any objection to the terms and conditions on the second pages. As part of the contracts, the terms and conditions on the second pages are binding upon both parties.

4. The Respondent has produced no evidence to show that within time limit it had the goods inspected, had an inspection certificate sent to the Claimant, and made claims against the Claimant.
5. After examining the attachment to the Letter of Rothery, the arbitrators find out that the signature was obviously not Mr. Huang's handwriting.
6. It is not provided in Proforma Invoice P/I No.ELP981113 damages of breach. Therefore the Claimant's claim that the Respondent pay damages of USD2217.00 is not allowed.
7. Based on the above-confirmed facts and the viewpoints, the Tribunal allows the two claims of the Claimant except for the 10% contractual fine amounting to USD2217.00 in the first claim.

And the arbitration fee shall be borne by the Respondent.

D. Decisions of the Tribunal in the Award.

1. The Respondent shall pay the Claimant the arrears under Proforma Invoice P/I No.ELP981113 plus the interest loss totaling USD47443.80.
2. The Respondent shall compensate the Claimant in the sum of USD8017.00 for loss incurred in performing the obligation under Proforma Invoice P/I No.ELP981125.
3. The arbitration fee to be paid to CIETAC, Shenzhen, is fixed at USD3833.00, which shall be borne by the Respondent. The sum has been deposited with CIETAC, Shenzhen, in advance by the Claimant. Accordingly, the Respondent shall reimburse that sum to the Claimant.
4. The Respondent shall make payment of the amounts referred to in 1, 2 and 3 above within 30 days from the date this Award is rendered, beyond which an interest at a rate of 10% per annum shall be added.

3 Some Issues the Tribunal Took Seriously And That of the Author

A. About the Second Pages of the Two Sales Contracts

The Claimant claimed that there was an effective arbitration clause in each disputed contract CIETAC, Shenzhen, took cognizance of the case according to the prima facie evidence provided by the Claimant.

When the case was in the Tribunal's hand the Respondent did not submit a formal written defense. Instead its agents sent the Letter of Rothery to CIETAC, Shenzhen, with an attachment (the Letter of 15 August 1997). The solicitors claimed that in the attachment the parties had agreed to have their discrepancies settled in UK Court of law and the dealings would be governed by UK law. By the agreement in the Letter of 15 August 1997, the agents of the Respondent denied the jurisdiction of CIETAC and the Tribunal.

The Tribunal should first find out the authenticity of the attachment. The arbitrators did ascertain that the signature of the three Chinese characters was not the handwriting of Mr.Huang Z.Q, the representative of the Claimant.

Then the Tribunal had to inquire into the matter whether the two-second pages previously prepared by the Seller containing General Terms and Conditions had been faxed to the Purchaser as the Purchaser only signed page one of the two contracts. The arbitrators found out after examining the documents submitted by the Claimant that the Respondent had received the two-second pages and then faxed them back to the Claimant. The headers (the telefax transmission details at the top) on the second pages of the two contracts revealed that fact. At the top of the second page of the first contract, it was clearly recorded as header as follows:

13-11-9810:59 FROM:PRESTIGE LIGHTING CO 0113–273-5038 TO:00867573320531 PAGE:02.

At the top of the second page of the second contract, the details of the telefax transmission were identical to the aforesaid other than the time and date:25-11-9818:41.

The Respondent was not in a position to deny that. It was recorded in the first page of the contracts that each contract consisted of two pages. We the arbitrators came to the conclusion that under the General Terms and Conditions there was an arbitration clause in each contract that was binding upon both parties.

The agents of the Applicant (Claimant in the arbitration) in the enforcement proceedings of the CIETAC Award in the UK, upon my inquiry, said:

> "As regards the Tribunal's decision in relation to page 2 of both of the sales contracts, we considered that there appeared sufficient evidence that this had been received by Prestige and was incorporated into the contract. In fact this did not appear to be an issue, save for the fact that Prestige claimed the arbitration clause(only) was not binding on the grounds that they alleged a separate arbitration clause had been agreed (in the Letter of 15 August 1997)."1.

As we arbitrators voted down the authenticity of the signature of Mr. Huang Z.Q. in the copy of the Letter of 15 August 1997 to the Letter of Rothery, then according to the doctrine of competence-competence, we held the case was under the jurisdiction of the Tribunal at CIETAC.

B. **Whether the Respondent in Material Breach of Contract**

The Respondent, as purchaser of the disputed contracts, owned the right to receive the goods and did receive and accept the goods stipulated in the first contract. The Respondent did enjoy the right upon the first contract. The Claimant, as seller, did perform its obligation stipulated in the first contract but without obtaining the corresponding right stipulated in the first contract. In the first contract, the Respondent was in material breach. In the second contract, the Respondent was also in breach, and the Claimant was in a position to suspend the performance of its obligation. The two transfer documents of payment faxed to the Claimant by the Respondent in fact were remittance applications only. Should we have the word "defraud" used by the Claimant in its Application For Arbitration repeated and stressed? Could we say that it was wrong for the Claimant to have used the word?

C. **Application of Law**

In my draft award there was an item dealing with this issue:

> "There is no law application clause in the two contracts. We the three arbitrators hold that law Merchant is applied to the instant case, namely that we would abide by the fair and reasonable principle."

This idea was not accepted by my co-arbitrators. Without mentioning law application, there would be no problem. If you owe someone a debt, you have to pay. It is an unalterable principle valid everywhere.

D. Language of the Arbitration And Especially of the Award

It is provided in the Arbitration Rules applied to the procedure of this case that the Chinese language is the official language of CIETAC, and if the parties have agreed otherwise, their agreement shall prevail.2 This provision is not bad, though it is not up to the requirement of the parties yet and should be more flexible in view of the position of CIETAC as an international arbitration institute and as autonomy and flexibility are the inherent features of arbitration.3 The main problem is how it should be interpreted. Does it mean no matter what the language of a contract with an arbitration clause is—in Chinese or in English only, or the contract is bilingual (in both Chinese and English) but there is no mention of the language of arbitration—when there is an arbitration under the jurisdiction of CIETAC, the language of arbitration must be Chinese only in each case? It seems to me in practice the staff at CIETAC have this interpretation of the provision, and it does prevail within it.

The contracts of this case and all the communications between the parties were in English. The Claimant submitted its Application for Arbitration in both Chinese and English. Arbitration notice and some other documents issued to the parties by CIETAC, Shenzhen and its Secretariat were in both Chinese and English. That was good. The hearing was conducted in Chinese with only the Claimant appearing. But when I, one member of the three-arbitrator engaged in drafting the Award, I first wrote it in English. My co-arbitrators and colleagues at CIETAC, Shenzhen, did not accept that, pointing out that according to the Arbitration Rules the Award should be in Chinese. I was in the minority and gave up and wrote in Chinese instead with the quotations of original language. Only one of my colleagues suggested that I have the quotations turned into Chinese. But this opinion was not accepted.

I am quoting some provisions concerning the language of arbitration from the arbitration rules of some other arbitration institutes:

> "In the absence of an agreement by the parties, the Arbitral Tribunal shall determine the language or languages of the arbitration, due regard being given to all relevant circumstances, including the language of the contract."

> "If the parties have not agreed otherwise, the language(s)of the arbitration shall be that of the documents containing the arbitration agreement, subject to the power of the tribunal to determine otherwise based upon the contentions of the parties and the circumstances of the arbitration."5.

I do think the above-quoted provisions relating to the language of arbitration are good ones. If we respected the parties' autonomy, we would have written the Award in English. My English is not good enough, but my two co-arbitrators are good at English. One of them is a retired professor of the University of International Business and Economy in Beijing. The other one is a professor of the University of Foreign Studies in Guangzhou. With them joining hand, the Award could have been written in good English, I believe.

4 Furthermore Comments on Letters from Rothery.

The Letter of Rothery reached CIETAC, Shenzhen, on 17 August 2000. The letter is of four paragraphs and the second and third paragraphs have been quoted in the proceeding part of this article, and the first and fourth paragraphs are as follows:

> "We have been consulted by Prestige Lighting Company Limited...in connection with an Application to your Commission by the above Company for arbitration in a dispute. We have received certain documents relating to this matter and would ask you to note that our clients do not accept that arbitration in China is appropriate in the circumstances (emphasis added)."

> "Our clients' position is that if Jiaadian Lighting feel that they have any claim against our clients, that claim should be pursued in the UK Courts. Our clients point out however that any such claim will be strenuously defended and our clients will pursue a counterclaim for the balance of the compensation costs which they have incurred in this matter."

This letter revealed that the Respondent had received the Notice of Arbitration.

We, the Tribunal, did mention and comment on the Letter of 15 August 1997 in the Award. On 19 November 1999, the Rothery for the second time wrote CIETAC, Shenzhen, as follows:

> "We note that we have not received any response from you to our letter of the 19th August.

> "Our clients have received a copy of a letter sent to you by Jiadian Lighting Co. Ltd. in which it is clear that further correspondence and proceedings are continuing in this matter(emphasis added). "Our clients' position is that they are still sustaining losses and claims arising out of the supply of the original low voltage trans-formers. Our clients' agreement with Jiadian expressly provided for all disputes to be dealt with under the UK Law and in the circumstances, if Jiandian wish to pursue a claim against our clients the matter should be pursued by court action in England and our clients do not accept that the Arbitration Commission has jurisdiction to deal with this matter."

The emphasized part of the two letters showed that the Respondent had received all the arbitration documents from CIETAC, Shenzhen, including all the ones from the Claimant and transferred by CIETAC, Shenzhen. But we were not in a position to directly communicate with the Rothery as they had not produced any power of attorney rendered by their clients the Prestige. I was sorry that the Rothery had never realized that they should have sent to us with their first letter a document issued by the Respondent and at least signed by the representative who signed the contracts if they did not have it notarized.

5. What CIETAC, Shenzhen, Required of the Applicant's Solicitors in Britain

A. **Providing the Solicitors with Relevant Documents Demonstrating the Principle of Due Process Was Abided By**

I had kept an eye on the course of the enforcement action in Britain, asking the representative Mr. Huang Z.Q. of the Claimant in the arbitration to keep me informed.

Mr. Huang on 31 March 2000 wrote the secretary of the Secretariat of CIETAC, Shenzhen, who was assisting the Tribunal in handling the procedure affairs (hereinafter referred to as the secretary), conveying his British solicitor's request as follows:

> "It is not clear from the documents provided to us whether Prestige Lighting was notified of the arbitration proceedings. The English Court may refuse to recognize the award if it transpires that Prestige Lighting was not given proper notice of the appointment of the arbitrator or of the arbitration proceedings or was otherwise unable to present its case. Please therefore could you provide copies of any relevant documents demonstrating that adequate notice of the arbitration proceedings was given to Prestige Lighting."6.

Therefore, the copies of the sender's copies of the mailing bills (receipts) kept on file with CIETAC, Shenzhen, showing that the Respondent had been timely informed, were given to the Applicant and its solicitors in the UK. That showed the Respondent's procedural rights had been fully respected, namely the principle of due process had been abided by, though the Respondent had given up its rights, failing to submit its defense and failing to appear at the hearing, etc.

B. **Authentication And Certification of Arbitration Award**

The solicitors with Denton Wilde Sapte (hereinafter referred to as DWS) engaged by the Applicant learned I was a CIETAC staff member, and wrote me on 5 September 2000 asking me to sign on behalf of the Tribunal the revised Authentication and Certificate of Arbitration Award. The Certificate is as follows:

> IN THE MATTER OF THE ARBITRATION ACT 1996.
>
> AND IN THE MATTER OF AN ARBITRATION.
>
> BETWEEN:
>
> JIADIAN LIGHTING COMPANY LIMITED Applicant.
>
> -and-.
>
> PRESTIGE LIGHTING COMPANY LIMITED Respondent.
>
> AUTHENTICATION AND CERTIFICATION OF ARBITRATION AWARD.
>
> I, HUANG YANGMING, of the China International Economic and Trade Arbitration Commission ("CIETAC"), "Shenzhen Commission, 19/F Block B, Zhongyin Building, 5015 Caitian Road Futian District, Shenzhenc 518,026 China, Arbitrator. I was appointed an Arbitrator by the president of the above CIETAC, Shenzhen, Commission Arbitration by authority of the Applicant under Article 26 of the Arbitration Rules. I confirm that I acted in this Arbitration along with Mr. Qiu N.Z., President, and M.Wu X.G.I certify that the documents attached hereto are an accurate copy of the Award returned against the Respondent in the above matter on 6 December 1999 which was handed down at the end of the Arbitration hearing and the Arbitration Agreement clause on which the Award was issued. I also confirm that the signatures on the Award are mine and those of my fellow Arbitrators.

The next day I made a response, writing to the solicitor:

> "Upon request, I am willing to issue a Certificate of the Award. I've got enlightenment from the British practice of enforcing an award in light with the New York Convention. As an arbitrator I've got some awards enforced abroad such as in America but never come across such problem. Nevertheless, I am always to do my bit for anyone if I can. I wish that I could get feedback when the matter is settled.

"I would like to draw your attention to the amendment to the Certificate made by me. Is it ok?"

The Certification rendered by is as follows:

IN THE MATTER OF THE ARBITRATION LAW OF P.R.CHINA and.

IN THE MATTER OF AN ARBITRATION Between.

Jiadian Lighting Company Limited Claimant.

And

Prestige Lighting Company Limited Respondent.

AUTHENTICATION AND CERTIFICATION OF ARBITRATION AWARD.

I, HUANG YANMING, of the China International Economic and Trade Arbitration Commission("CIETAC")located on 6/F, Golden Land Building,32 Liangmaqiao Road, Beijing 100,016, China, Arbitrator. The Claimant of the instant case submitted its application for arbitration to the China International Economic and Trade Arbitration Commission, Shenzhen Commission ("CIETAC, Shenzhen), 19/ F Block B, Zhongying Building, 5015 Caitian Road, Shenzhen, 518,026 China. I was appointed as Arbitrator by the Chairman of CIETAC under Article 26 of the Arbitration Rules. I confirm that I acted in this Arbitration along with Mr. Qiu N.Z., the Presiding Arbitrator, and Mr. Wu X.G..I certify that the documents attached hereto are an accurate copy of the Award returned against the Respondent in the above matter on 6 December 1999 which was handed down at the end of an oral hearing and the Arbitration Clause on which the Award was issued. I also confirm that the signatures on the Award are mine and those of my fellow Arbitrators.

The aforesaid Certificate was presented by the solicitors with DWS on 20 October 2000 when they filed a Witness Statement signed by one of the solicitors John Manners Miles to an honorable justice in the High Court of Justice Queen's Bench Division Commerce Court on behalf of the Applicant to seek to enforce the Award in accordance with the provisions of the New York Convention.7.

In this regard we could see that an institute arbitration has a strong advantage over an ad hoc arbitration. A permanent arbitration institute has kept its files. When a case is closed, parties concerned could still seek assistance from the institute or even the members of a tribunal. As to an ad hoc arbitration, after the award is issued, how could parties concerned find easy access to the arbitrators and the files?

C. The Enlightenment I Have Received

In the course of writing this article I have consulted some professionals and really obtained some knowledge. I asked an attorney in America for advice on some issues relating to the enforcement of a foreign arbitration award.

"Did the court require that the award should have been notarized by a notary in China when you were engaged in dealing with the case of Cause No.H-96-3188? 8 And did the court require that a Certificate of the Award should have been signed and issued by a member of the Tribunal?"

I've got this advice.

"According to the Federal Rule of Evidence 902[3] foreign documents: requires: 1. the execution or attestation, and accompanied by a final certification as to the genuineness of the signature and official position a. of the execution or attesting person or b. of any foreign official whose certificate of genuineness of signature and official position relates to the execution or attestation or is in a chain of certificates of genuineness of signature and official position relating to the execution or attestation. A final certification may be made by a secretary of embassy, consul general, vice consul,...assigned or accredited to the United States.

"So, to prove a., we need CIETAC personal who has authority to issue a certified copy on CIETAC behalf to make a certification or attestation, then he needs to go to the U.S. consulate office and certify that before a U.S. consul, vice consul, secretary of embassy to certify his authority and signature to be in compliance to the FRE 902[3] so the document can be admitted in the evidence. Or else, the document will be excluded as hearsay rule."9.

Similar provisions could be found in Sect. 102 of the Arbitration Act 1996 of UK. The aforesaid Certificate of Award prepared by DWS is used in the UK, and the certificate issued by me could be used in any country or region. Mentioning the CIETAC award enforced in America reminds me of the fact that one of my colleagues did go to the American Consulate General to certify the award before a US consul.

But a question remains unsettled as for me. I have to issue a second document to certify a first document rendered by my co-arbitrators and me.

Time is money and efficiency is the life of any undertaking. I believe the easiest approach is to have an award of a permanent arbitration institute such as CIETAC, the American Arbitration Association, the ICC International Court of Arbitration, London Court of International Arbitration, etc., certified by writing to the institute's secretariat. An official reply from the institute should be regarded as a certification. It would take less time and expense and would benefit the parties concerned. A permanent arbitration institute should regard that as its duty.

5 Studies of Feedback Issues of Applying Enforcement of the Award

A. Brief Introduction to the Course of Proceedings in UK

The solicitors of the Applicant had a Claim Form No. (or Folio No.) 2000F 1188 issued in the Commercial Registry, Room E200 Royal Courts of Justice, Strand, London WC2A 2LL [DX 44450 Strand] on 20 October 2000, and on the same day the Witness Statement of John Manners Miles with DWS was produced.

The Honorable Mr. Justice David Steel rendered an Order on 25 October 2000. A Witness Statement of Christopher Brown was issued on 11 December 2000.

A hearing was scheduled to take place on 21 May 2001, at which the court was to hear an application by Prestige and determine whether or not the underlying arbitration agreement was valid, in view of Prestige's purported Letter of August 15. A solicitor with DWS tells me:

> "If it was valid, Jiadian could then have proceeded to enforce the Award. We were optimistic the court would dismiss Prestige's application but could not be certain bearing in mind the issue with the arbitration agreement, the interest claim and the large counterclaim(emphasis added)."10.

It is said that it was probably partly due to the imminence of that hearing which prompted Prestige to make offers of settlement at that time. A final offer was accepted by Jiadian on 18 May. It was unnecessary for the hearing to go ahead, and the draft consent order with the settlement terms was lodged with a clerk of the Right Honorable Mr. Justice Colman of the Commercial Court, and the judge on 8 June 2001 rendered a Consent Order. Prestige will pay Jiadian the aggregate sum US$30,000 by 30 August 2001, and then it will be a full and final settlement of the claims under the Award.

B. Main Contents And Some Views in Witness Statement of John Manners Miles

Mr. Miles with DWS on 20 October 2000 on behalf of the Applicant submitted the Claim Form 2000F 1188 in the High Court of Justice Queen's Bench Division Commercial Court but it was sealed by the Court on 31 October 2000.

It turned out Mr. Miles' Witness Statement was submitted on the same day. It contains an introduction to the solicitor, his status and authority; tells of the legislation base of the Statement; the solicitor exhibits together with the Statement a Notarized and certified copy of the Award and the official translation of the Award, copies of disputed contracts which contain inter alia the arbitration clause between the parties; briefs some information about the parties; mentions the important matters about the arbitration proceedings such as the acceptance of the arbitration, the delivery of Notice of Application, Arbitration Rules with fee schedule and the Panel of Arbitrators, the Formation of the Tribunal and the sending of the notice by registered mail to the parties; stresses that the Respondent clearly received all the documents, etc. In all, the solicitor's Statement sought to illustrate that the principle of due process in the arbitration has been abided by and the Award was based on confirmed facts and thus was final and binding upon both parties.

Mr. Miles is also informed by My Huang Z.Q. and believes that the Applicant is entitled to enforce the Award in China and that no enforcement proceedings have been stayed or taken or are pending against the Respondent in China. Therefore, the solicitor asks the honorable court's permission to enforce the Award in the same manner as a judgment or order of the honorable court and requests that the Respondent be ordered to pay the cost of the Application.

That is my understanding of the Statement. Furthermore I would like to quote form the Statement some passages relating to the Letter of 15 August 1997:

> "9.In the letter (of) Rothery also asked the Tribunal 'to note that our client do not accept that arbitration in China is appropriate in the circumstances.' Attached to their letter was a copy of a letter dated 15 August 1997, supposedly sent from the Respondent to the Applicant's General Manager, Mr.Huang ZQ, asking to change the Arbitration Clause in the Applicant's Purchase Invoice General Terms and Conditions, to UK Law. The 3 characters Huang Z. Q, had purportedly been counter-signed on the letter, on behalf of the Applicant.

"10.The Applicant strongly refutes that there was any such agreement and on receiving from CIETAC, a copy of Rothery's letter and its attachment, the Applicant's Mr. Huang Z.Q. wrote to CIETAC stating 'the Letter dated 15 August 1997 provided [by the Respondent] is [a]fake document because we have not received it before and the signature of the Chinese name was not my own handwriting signature.'"11.

"11.It is also, in my view, compelling that the Respondent did not amend, annotate or communicate any such purported changes to the Purchase Invoices and the General Terms and Conditions, which they obviously received later, in November 1997."

For the interest of their principal, the attorneys must safeguard the legal effect of the Award. And according to the analysis, conclusion, and decision in the Award and the evidence provided by the Applicant, they at the initial stage could not find opposite or negative grounds to have the Award set aside or suspended or annulled.

In the later part of this article I will look further into the matter of the Letter of 15 August 1997.

C. **The Order of the Honorable Mr. Justice David Steel**

Justice David Steel on 25 October 2000 rendered his order as follows:

UPON THE EX PARTE APPLICATION by the Solicitors for the Applicant AND UPON reading the Witness Statement of John Manners Miles dated 20 October 2000, filed on behalf of the Applicant herein.

IT IS ORDERED THAT:

The Applicant does have permission to enforce the Arbitral Award made by the China International Economic Trade Arbitration Commission dated 6 December 1999, against the Respondent in the same manner and effect as Judgment or Order of this honorable Court; and.

The Respondent pay the Applicant's costs of this application, to be assessed if not agreed.

At the date of the issuing the Order, the Respondent had not yet made response to the Claim Form No.2000F 1188 and the Witness Statement of Mr.Miles. According to the Notes for the Respondent of the Claim Form a time limit of 14 days is fixed for the Respondent.12.

Being a commercial arbitrator, I am grateful to those justices and judges and respect them who are always ready to abide by the provisions of the New York Convention.

Still I want to know more.

D. **The Main Contents And Some Views in the Witness Statement of Christopher Brown**

Mr. Brown was the managing director of the respondent.

In response to the Witness Statement of Mr. Miles, Mr. Brown on behalf of the Respondent on 11 December 2000 made the Statement. After revealing his status and authority he first inquires about the reason why the Order of Mr. Justice Steel on 25 October 2000 was made as it is stipulated in the Notes accompanying the Claim

Form (pp.4–5) that the Respondent has 14 days in which to respond by returning the acknowledgment of service form, and that the Award may not be enforced until after the expiration of such period, or if the Respondent applies within that period to set the Order aside, until after the application is finally disposed of. Therefore he asks the Court to treat his Statement as an application to set aside the Order of Mr. Justice Steel if that is necessary and appropriate; and otherwise to treat it as evidence in opposition to the Applicant's claim for such an order. He confirms that the respondent's solicitors duly returned the Acknowledgment of Service, indicating an intention to contest the application and the claim for costs, on 10 November 2000,within the 14-day time limit.13.

Fairly speaking what Mr. Brown says in this regard is reasonable or with legal grounds and I believe it should have been sustained. It must be drafted by solicitors of the Respondent.

Mr. Brown then talks about the jurisdiction of CIETAC in the following paragraphs:

5. "The Respondent wishes to contest this application (or alternatively, seeks to have the ex parte order set aside)upon the ground that there was no arbitration agreement between the parties and that accordingly CIETAC has no locus standi or jurisdiction to make any award against the Respondent(emphasis added)."14
6. "The Applicant is aware that the existence of the alleged arbitration agreement is disputed by the Applicant [It must be a clerical error. It should be Respondent—the author], and indeed this is dealt with in Paragraphs 9&10 of Mr. Miles Witness Statement. The substance of this dispute over jurisdiction is also referred to in the alleged arbitral award of CIETAC, at page 23.15

7. "Briefly, it is the Respondent's case that the contracts which were the subject matter of the alleged arbitration award were not governed by the arbitration provision contained in Clause 7 of the Applicant's General Terms and Conditions, having been superseded or replaced by a different provision relation to the resolution of disputes between the parties which had been expressly agreed between the Respondent and the Applicant, acting by its representative Mr. Huang Z.Q (emphasis added).
8. "The dispute between the parties turns upon whether Clause 7 of the Applicant's General" Terms and Conditions governs the contracts which are subject of the alleged arbitration, or whether that arbitration clause was replaced by an express agreement between the parties, as contained in the Letter of 15 August 1997 (Exhibit"CB4"). It is the Respondent's case that this express agreement was made between the parties, and that accordingly the effect thereof was that in relation to all contracts between the parties entered into after August 1999 Clause 7 of the Applicant's General Terms and Conditions did not apply (emphasis added)...
9. "(omitted)."
10. "10. I believe that the Letter of 15 August 1997 was sent to the Applicant by fax only. This would be the normal method of communication with the Applicant

in China, due to the unpredictable nature of the postal system and the time taken for ordinary mail to be delivered.

11. "It is the Applicant's case, as indeed was apparently stated to CIETAC, that the Letter of August 15 was duly countersigned by Mr. Huang Z.Q., to indicate the Applicant's agreement to the alteration in the future dispute procedure, and was then faxed back to the Respondent. I have been able to trace the original of the return(countersigned)fax, a copy of which appears as Exhibit 'CB4'.It can be seen from the fax imprint at the head that it is recorded as having originated from fax number 867573320531, which is the Applicant's fax number to which the original version was sent for signature (as appears on the Pro Former Invoices). It is shown as having been received back on 19 August 1997 at 4:37 pm (emphasis added)."
12. "I am aware from the contents of the alleged arbitral award, and Paragraphs 10 and 11 of Mr. Miles 'Statement, that the Applicant contends that the signature, in Chinese characters, which appears on the returned fax (of the Letter) of 15 August 1997 immediately above the typed name 'Huang Z.Q.' is a fake and is not the genuine Chinese signature of Mr. Huang Z.Q. Although not stated specifically, it is a clear implication from this that the Applicant accuses the Respondent, or rather someone on its behalf, of forging Mr. Huang Z.Q's signature upon this document. I strongly reject such an allegation, and the insinuation that the Respondent and its employees are prepared to perpetrate a criminal offence in order to gain a jurisdictional advantage in this dispute (emphasis added)."

After pursuing the Statement of the Mr. Brown, I scrutinize its Exhibit CB4. I do find from the copy of the Letter of August 15 as Exhibit CB4 the two lines as the fax imprint at the head as follows:

07-12-0012:32 FROM:PRESTIGE LIGHTING 01132795038 TO:01924387112 PAGE:02.
FROM:JIADIAN LIGHTING CO.,LTD.
PHONE NO.867573320331 Aug.19199704:37 PM P01.

Now it turns out what the Respondent says about the genuineness of the letter in his Statement is true and Mr. Brown's indignation expressed in the Statement is understandable as he thinks he is correct and was wronged. But the deep reason is not dug out yet and it seems to me that neither the parties in the British proceedings has found it. Furthermore they have overlooked a key issue.

I examined my file and the file of the case kept in the CIETAC archives.16 I found the imprint at the head of the duplicate provided by the Rothery together with their first letter dated 19 August 1999 to CIETAC, Shenzhen. The solicitors didn't mention the fax imprint and there is no sign showing that it originated from the Applicant. There is only some imprint at the head on the right side of the duplicate as follows:

IO.01274851230 PAGE:02.

I guess "IO" should have been "TO." And now I am in a position to infer from the fact that the Respondent had made a big mistake (I am not sure whether I could say people of the Respondent had made a foolish mistake or say they had made a blunder) when Mr. Brown or his colleagues duplicated the Letter of 15 August 1997 and gave it to Rothery. It was not duplicated from the very back-faxed page from the Applicant but from the page originated from the Respondent to the Applicant. Mr. Brown or his aids who had drafted the Letter of 15 August 1997 and knew the purpose of it and had pursued it, but they had not seen that the duplicate was made from that copy back-faxed by the Applicant after it was signed by someone over there. Mr. Brown or his aids should have shown the solicitors with the Rothery the original copy from the Applicant telling them the key to prove that the parties had reached a new agreement which finally substituted the arbitration agreement contained in Clause 7 of the General Terms and Conditions of the two contracts. The solicitors with the Rothery should have first shown the arbitrators that they were the Respondent's attorneys. They should have shown there existed a second expressed part of the agreement between the parties that any dispute between the two companies would be resolved in accordance with UK Law and in the UK Courts. In a word, the solicitors should not have only repeated what words were in the Letter of 15 August 1997, they should have tried to convince the CIETAC Tribunal of the second agreement that amended and substituted the former arbitration clause.

We, the arbitrators, did find out that the three Chinese characters Huang Z.Q. signed by someone were quite similar to the signature of Huang Z.Q. Someone with the Applicant must have imitated the signature of Mr. Huang when he was not available, though it was not signed by Mr. Huang himself, we could tell. If we had found the fax imprint showing that it really originated from the Applicant, we would have dealt with that point in the Award. The Claimant could not deny it had concluded an agreement with the Respondent by signing in the Letter of 15 August 1997.

Should we have given up the jurisdiction? If there were really a new agreement between the parties and it really replaced the old ones in the disputed contract, no doubt, we should have given it up without any hesitation.

Take it easy. I have to talk more about the matters contained in the Letter of 15 August 1997.

First of all, I would like to draw your attention to the date of the Letter of 15 August 1997 and the date of the two contracts of the instant case. The first one is dated 13 November 1998 and the second one dated 25 November 1998. The views of the parties are not divergent on this question. When the "expressed agreement between the parties contained in the Letter of 15 August 1997" 17 concluded, the disputed contracts of the instant case might not have been on the minds of the parties' representatives.

Which is new and which is old? It is a simple question.

The second matter in the Letter of 15 August 1997 is that it is provided "The parties will take measures to settle dispute which may arise in connection with this contract (emphasis added)... In case the parties will not come to an agreement, the discrepancies will be settled in a UK court." Does "this contract" mean any contract of the disputed contracts of the instant case? Does not "this contract" mean a particular contract at that time? It is very interesting.

Mr. Brown says:

> "It is the Respondent's case that this express agreement was made between the parties, and that accordingly the effect thereof was that in relation to all contracts between the parties entered into after August 1997 Clause 7of the Applicant's General Terms and Conditions did not apply, and there was thus no arbitration agreement between the parties in relation to the contracts which are the subject of the current dispute and which form the basis of the alleged arbitral award."18.

The agreement in the Letter of 15 August 1997 was prior to the arbitration agreement in Clause 7 of the General Terms and Conditions of the two contracts. Parties could have amended all the contracts. People know that a new contract supersedes or replaces an old contract but not the opposite. Could not the agreement between the parties reached on 16 and 25 November 1998 replace the one concluded on 15 August 1997?

The third matter in the Letter of 15 August 1997 is expressed in the following wording: "At all times our dealings will be governed by UK Law." It relates to the application of law but not the jurisdiction of an institute in handling disputes.

Now let me return to the other side of the issue relating to the Letter of 15 August 1977. Even if that is so, i.e., if the argument of the Respondent holds water, the agreement in the letter should have superseded or replaced the arbitration agreement in Clause 7 of the General Terms and Conditions of the two contracts. What would be the situation? The Award would be set aside or refused to be enforced? Should we the arbitrators be held fully responsible for the result? This question is of practical and theoretical significance.

People know that the arbitrators deal with the case based on the evidence provided by the parties. As the negligence of the Respondent and its attorneys (though not formerly authorized), which resulted in the Tribunal's failing to find out the parties did have a second agreement (in fact it should be regarded as the first agreement and later replaced by the new ones in the disputed contracts of the instant case). Then the Award could not be enforced or "[i]t would appear that the enforcement of the Award could be vulnerable to a similar allegation in the future which it seems the English court would be bound to investigate."19.

I believe that up to now Mr. Brown, his colleagues, and the solicitors with the Rothery have not realized that key yet.

E. **The Quality of the Goods**

To challenge the jurisdiction of CIETAC, Mr. Brown says the Respondent also has a counterclaim (for over To100000)[20] against the Applicant arising out of the supply of faulty goods that did not meet required specifications. Mr. Brown argues that the size of this counterclaim significantly exceeds the amount claimed by the Applicant and the amount allegedly awarded by CIETAC.

> "In the circumstance I respectfully submit that the Respondent has a good set-off in respect of the amount of the Award even if it is otherwise found to be binding upon the Respondent."21.

If the solicitors of the Applicant find out the reason when comparing the copies of the August 15 letter submitted by the Respondent respectively in the course of arbitration and in the proceedings of applying for the enforcement of the Award, what would be the situation? The Award would be set aside or not enforced? This question is of practical and theoretic significance.

According to Clause 6 of the General Terms and Conditions of the contract, the Respondent should have the goods inspected after receiving goods under the first contract, and if there was any problem, it should have the claim filed within 30 days. The Applicant dispatched the goods on 20 November 1998 by air. Roughly speaking, the Respondent should have had the goods inspected and any claim filed around 30 December 1998.

Together with his statement, Mr. Brown submitted exhibits CB6, CB7, and CB8 for the purpose of proving that the goods supplied by the applicant were faulty and did not meet the required specifications.

CB6 was a Product Report issued by a manager of Micron Laboratory Food Technology Consultants dated 21March 1997. The date of it shows it has nothing to do with the disputed contracts of the instant case.

CB7 is a Report of Examination issued by AMTAC Laboratories Division dated 11 December 1996. Again, the date itself shows it has no connection with the disputed contracts of the instant case. There are about nine pages in all with the aforesaid Reports of Examination, judging them from the dates recorded on each one, I could hardly find the relationships among them and with the instant case. They were all issued before the conclusion of the two disputed contracts.

CB8, it is a reminder letter (non-payment of fines etc.) by Bury Magistrates' Court (1732) on 8 October 1998 to the respondent, reminding the latter of an overdue payment of the court order and urging it to pay. It is unnecessary to repeat the meaning of the date of the document.

If there is no mistake in my understanding of the aforesaid Exhibits, I believe no matter which court hands the case, there would be no difference."4.The Respondent has produced no evidence to show that within time limit it had the goods inspected and had an inspection certificate sent to the Claimant and had claims against the Claimant." 22 That conclusion in the Award is correct.

F. **The Interest**

Mr. Brown, on behalf of the Respondent, "[d]isputes the amount of interest which has been added to the Applicant's claim by CIETAC." 23 He puts an emphasis on that point, saying, "It should also be noted that in the Application for Arbitration at pages 1&2 the Applicant seeks interest at 6%for a period of 190 days—which is inconsistent with an award of 25,273.80." 24 Let me make a quotation from the Application for Arbitration.

> "Jiadian (the Claimant)demands that Prestige pay the outstanding P/L ELP981113 amounting to USD22170.00,6% interest per diem rate (emphasis added)of the arrears amounting to USD 25273.80 (dated from 20 November1998 to 30 May 1999 in all 190 days)and 10%contractual fine amounting to USD2217.00,namely,total amount is USD 49660.80."

I wonder whether my understanding of the"6% interest per diem rate" was not correct. To make sure I consult a dictionary.

"per diem: adv. by the day; for each day(computed the total of man-hours saved per diem—C.D Lewis)."25.

The solicitors with DWS wrote the Applicant, inquiring "[h]ow this interest figure was calculated, including the rate and period of interest, and on what basis the interest was claimed, i.e. is it a contractual or statutory entitlement?"26.

The solicitors with DWS realized the interest rate was too high. So they consulted Chinese lawyers and obtained a legal opinion of 30 March 2001 from Siway & Seaway Law Office (hereinafter referred to as Siway). The main text of the legal opinion is as follows:

"As regards the interest, amounting to US$25273, as set out in CIETAC Shenzhen's decision, based on the application for a rate of 0.6 per day for 190 days, we don't think that such high rate was reasonable and also fail to find out any relative proofs supporting this high rate provided by Claimant. For this purpose, we consulted with ['with' should be omitted—the author of this article guesses] Bank of China Shanghai Branch (unifying rate in the whole China) for the current interest rate and the one in November 1998. The oral reply said that the interest rate of US Dollar loan on liquid assets was 7.625% per year in November 1998 and the current one was 7.3125%.

"Besides, we look through the 'Reply to the Calculation Based on Which Standard on the Breach of Contract Damages for the Undue Payment' issued by the Supreme People's Court on May 16, 1999. Additionally, the Supreme People's Court made a revised Reply on January 29,1999 [hereinafter referred to as fashi [1999] No.8 Document—the author of this article][27]. Both Replies regulate that the calculation standard of breach of contract damages shall refer to the regulations on the interest rate of deposit and loan issued by the People's Bank of China (the Central Bank of China), which states that the breach of contract damages shall be calculated by 0.05% to 0.04% per day.

"Moreover, we looked through the regulation of reduction of interest issued by the People's Bank of China on 10 June 1999, which provides that since 10 June 1999 the interest rate of the undue loan per day shall be lowered from 0.03% (i.e., annual interest rate is 10.8%) to 0.021% (i.e., annual interest rate is 7.56%).

"In conclusion, the reasonable, interest rate shall be 0.05%to 0.04% per day. However, the interest rate in this case alleged by the Claimant is 0.6% per day (i.e.,10-time more than 0.05% which is apparently too high)."

What the law firm says in the above-mentioned legal opinion is correct. Lawyers in China are quite familiar with the regulations, as arbitrators are. A solicitor with DWS sent me a copy of the legal opinion with a letter.28 He says in the letter:

"To our knowledge there is also no contractual basis for this high rate of interest which in the circumstances appears to be quite arbitrary (emphasis added).

"This is a cause for concern because it is potentially a ground for resisting the application to enforce the arbitral award on the basis that, under the New York Convention, the arbitral award was not in accordance with the law of the country in which the arbitration took place, i.e. Chinese law."

I was willing to heed his criticism. But I was not in a position to reply on behalf of the Tribunal.

One of my colleagues, the secretary mentioned in the preceding part of this article, replied saying the Respondent did not present at the hearing and did not raise any defense against the rate of interest proposed by the Claimant. Therefore, the Tribunal rendered the default Award against the Respondent.29.

The solicitors were not satisfied with the reply, they said they needed to show from where the "authority" to award a rate of 0.6% per day was deserved.30 They tell us:

> "In England, in the absence of a contractual right to interest, a statutory rate of 8% can be claimed, subject to the Court's discretion to award the full amount.
>
> "However, there does not appear to be anything in the Jiadian contract or the arbitration rules and Siway say there is nothing under China law which allows the rate awarded. It is simply customary or is there some other valid grounds for entitlement?"31.

I have been enlightened from the letter, and no doubt what the lawyer says is not wrong. The secretary at CIETAC, Shenzhen, was required to reply:

> "...as I personally know, there is not any law in China, which sets a statutory rate as in England for the time being. It customarily leaves the issue for the tribunal to exercise their discretion in the absence of a contractual right and/or any statutory rules."32.

Usually, we, arbitrators, would follow the stipulations contained in the documents issued by the Supreme People's Court, the documents mentioned in the aforesaid legal opinion. But I could not say my colleague's reply to the solicitors was wrong. It is not against any principle of law.

Because fashi [1999] No.8 stipulates that in dealing with the issue of damages resulting from the breach of contract a (people's) court "kevi canzhao [may refer to the calculation standard of breach of contract damages" formulated by the People's Bank of China. The meaning of "keyi canzhao" is "may refer to," the standard of the People's Bank of China can be followed and meanwhile a judge or arbitrator can or is in a position to make appropriate adaptation in light of specific conditions.

The interest rate is an issue I do not think could be treated independently because it could cause the Award to be set aside or not enforced.

Could any UK court judge find that the arbitrators of CIETAC are in manifest disregard of law?

> "'[m]anifest disregard' of law...would require an American court to consider whether foreign arbitrators had disregarded foreign law. It is one thing to ask an American judge to hold American Arbitrators guilty of manifest disregard of American law. It is quite another to ask an American judge to determine whether foreign arbitrators manifestly disregarded the internal, substantive law of a foreign nation by which the parties agreed in their contract to be bound. That seems to [be]...a slippery slope upon which American judges should not embark, in clear derogation of the public policy underlying the Convention."33 Won't this principle apply in England?

I, now, could guess the representative of the Claimant made a mistake in writing 0.06% per diem rate as 0.6%.

As for me, I confess that I should at least have suggested that the rate be reduced according to the standard formulated by the People's Bank of China and confirmed in the fashi [1999] No. 8 Document. I should not conceal my faults and gloss over my wrongs. I did overlook it. If the Respondent had argued about it, there would have been no such problem. But as we judged on the evidence submitted by the parties that we had jurisdiction and the Respondent gave up its rights in the arbitration proceedings. I suppose the enforcement of the decision of interest is not a very serious problem as it is a small sum calculating from 20 November 1998 to 30 May 1999, when the Claimant drafted and intended to submit its application for arbitration, in all 190 days.

In our practice, a claimant could claim an interest calculated to the date when a respondent pays. In the instant case, in fact it was accepted by CIETAC, Shenzhen, on 16 July 1999 and the Award was rendered on 6 December 1999. From 30 May to 6 December 1999, there are about 186 days; the interest is calculated without including this period of 186 days. In this regard, the claimant is not "insatiably greedy."

I am not very sure whether the claimant could have argued this way and these factors would have been considered by a UK judge.

I am confused with the alleged counterclaim Mr. Brown files in his Statement. He says the counterclaim falls into two parts: the first relating to the disputed contracts of the instant case and the second relating to the earlier supply of low-voltage transformers.34 I have mentioned that from the Exhibits CB6, 7 and 8 and all the documents consisting of the Exhibits submitted by Mr. Brown with his Statement I could not find any relation with the deals between the Applicant and the Respondent. The name of the Applicant is not mentioned in all the Exhibits. Being a private judge I could hardly believe that the counterclaim would be sustained. To my mind what the Respondent said about its counterclaim was only swashbuckling.

Being merchants in the field of international trade, Mr. Brown and his colleagues should have known how to execute their rights within time limit. They received the goods and accepted them but without performing their obligation to pay. No matter which court has the jurisdiction over the case, the Respondent would always be regarded as in material breach of contract.

It is said that arbitrators have been permitted to award punitive damages and such decisions have been affirmed, such as in the Supreme Court of New York[3]5, and that has been the trend of most court decisions since Mastrobuono was decided.36 It is reported that in securities arbitration, several New York appellate decisions have made inroads into the enforceability and scope of mandatory arbitration agreements in the securities industry.37.

> "At a time the industry is struggling to revamp the entire arbitration system, the Appellate Division, First Department, has held that arbitrators may award punitive damages, reversing the 1976 case of Garrity v.Lyle Stuart,Inc.,40 N.Y.2d 354,386 N.Y.S.2d 831 (1976). In Mulder v. Donaldson, Lufkin & Jenrette, No.59192 N, 1996 N.Y. App.Div.LEXIS 9920 (Oct.81996), the appellate court ruled that, unless parties specifically agree to exclude them, punitive damages are available in arbitration in New York."38.

I have no idea if the decision on interest is regarded as punitive damages and whether it could be affirmed by a UK court.

6 Conclusion

CIETAC, Shenzhen, its Secretariat and the Tribunal of the instant case abided by the principle of due process. The Tribunal came to the decision that it had jurisdiction over the case after carefully examining the scope of the Letter of 15 August 1997 provided by the Respondent through its attorney, though the latter had no former power of attorney.

In fact, the Letter of 15 August 1997 was prior to the arbitration agreements in Clause 7 of the General Terms and Conditions of the contracts. It is the arbitration agreements in the contracts that supersede or replace the agreement in the Letter of 15 August 1997 but not the opposite. After re-examining the Letter of 15 August 1997 and other documents of the case, I confirm that we had jurisdiction over the case.

Even if that was so, i.e. the argument of the Respondent should have been tenable, because of that lost opportunity. I don't think it would have got another opportunity in the proceedings of applying for the enforcement of the Award, otherwise it would be unfair to the Claimant and the Tribunal and the latter's institute. They had done nothing wrong in the arbitration with respect to this question and it was the responsibility of the Respondent. Would the work of the arbitrators be null and void because of the Respondent's fault? Would the Claimant have to go through another proceeding for the purpose of enjoying its rights because of the fault?

To my great relief, I have got to know about it through reading feedback documents.

I think the attorneys and their principals should have worked more closely together. They should have paid better attention to the details of the case such as the duplicates of original documents.

The arbitrators should be more careful in calculating. For instance, they should ask themselves whether the interest rate awarded is too high or whether they should award punitive damages. In the instant case, the rate of interest was too high, the sum was small because it was in respect to a short period. So the problem is not so serious as having been regarded.

Notes

1. Michael Pridge with Denton Wilde Sapte:The letter of 12 July 2001 to Mr.Yanming Huang.
2. Article 75 of the 1998 Arbitration Rules of CIETAC.
3. John Mo,Probing the Uniformity of the Arbitration System in the PRC, J.Int.Arb.Vol.17, No. 3, June 2000, p14.
4. Article 16 of the ICC rules of Arbitration.
5. Article 14 of International arbitration Rules of the American Arbitration association.
6. Huang Zhongquan,Letter of 31 April 2000 to Mr.Mingquan Qian.
7. In the High Court of Tustice Queen's Bench Division Commercial Court,liaidan Lighting Company Limited v.Prestige Lighting Companv Limited, Claim No.2000 F 1188.Hereinafter referred to as Case No.2000 F1188.

8. In the United States District Court Southern District of Texas Houston Division. Shenzhen Food- stuff-Drinks Industrial Import and Export Companv v.Louisiana-Pacific Corporation,Cause No.H- 96-3188
9. Xenos M.Yuen,attorney with Law Offices of Yuen &Association,PLLC.Letter of 14 August 2001 to Mr.Yanming Huang.
10. Michael Pridge,Letter of 21 August 2001 to Mr.Yanming Huang.
11. The quotation is exact as the original other than some abbreviations.
12. See Notes for the Respondent of the Claim (Case) No. 2000 F1188, p. 5.
13. Witness Statement of Christopher Brown,Paragraphs 2, 3, 4 and 5, pp. 2–4, Case No.2000 F1188.
14. Witness Statement of Christopher Brown,Paragraph 5,p.4,Case No.2000 F 1188.
15. See the English version produced by the 1st Applied Translation in London.
16. See Files of CIETAC, Shenzhen No.1135–1, p. 77.
17. See Paragraph 8 of the Witness Statement of Christopher Brown,p5,Case No.2000 F 1188.
18. Id.
19. Michael Pidge with DWS,Letter of 12 July to Mr.Yanming Huang.
20. Id.
21. See Paragraph 16 of the Witness Statement of Christopher Brown, p. 9, Case No.2000 F1188.
22. See [99]Shen Guo Zhon Jue Zhi No.96 Award.
23. See Paragraph 24 of the Witness Statement of Christopher Brown,p12,Case No.2000 F 1188.
24. Id.
25. Philip Babcock Grove Ph.d(ed.)Webster's third New International Dictionary, G.&C. Merriam Company Publishers Springfield, Massachusetts, U.S.A. p. 1676.
26. Michael Pridge, Letter of 23 November 2000 to Connie GF with the Claimant and CC to Mr. Yanming Huang.
27. Fashi means judicial interpretation and the document was numbered fashi [1991] No. 8.
28. Michael Pridge, Letter of 3 April 2001 to Mr. Yanming Huang.
29. Mingqiang Qian, Letter faxed on 5 April to Mr.Michael Pidge with DWS.
30. Michael Pridge, Letter of 5 April 2001 to Mr. Mingqiang Qian.
31. Id.
32. Mingquang Qian,Second letter faxed on 6 April 20001 to Michael Pridge.
33. Brandes, 635 F, Supp, at 167.
34. See Paragraph of the Witness statement of Christopher Brown,p.9,Case No.2000 F1188.
35. Id.
36. See Mastrobuono v Shearson Lehman Hutton,512 US 52,and see, e.g., Smith Barnev v Schell,53 Fed 807 [7th Cir 19951; Kellev v Michaels,59 F3d 1050 [10th Cir 1995]; Davis v Prudential Sec.,59 F3d 1186 [11th Cir 1995];Shearson Lehman Bros.Neurosurgical Asocs.,896 F Supp 844 [SD Ind 1995], etc.
37. Recent New York Court Decisions Benefit Plaintiffs,World Arbitration And Mediation Report, Vol.7, No.9;September 1996,pp.216–217
38. Id

Part II
Issues Relating to Due Process

Outlines

This chapter contains a single commentary in which the author, serving as an arbitrator, reflects on the legal and procedural issues that arose during the enforcement of an arbitral award in the United States. Given the complexity and significance of the case, it warrants an independent chapter within this book.

Throughout the author's career as an arbitrator, involvement in international commercial arbitration cases has been relatively limited. Among the arbitral awards enforced in the United States, this case remains the only one for which the author received direct feedback. The case and its enforcement raised critical issues beyond **due process**, including **manifest disregard of the law**, the applicability of the **United Nations Convention on Contracts for the International Sale of Goods (CISG)**, and the interpretation of the **Convention on the Recognition and Enforcement of Foreign Arbitral Awards (New York Convention)**.

The author reflects on personal shortcomings as an arbitral tribunal member. For instance, in the English translation of the arbitral award, the phrase:

"In the course of the hearing, the Arbitration Tribunal heeded the oral statements and arguments of both parties and did investigations."

This wording inadvertently provided grounds for the losing party to misinterpret the actions and professional conduct of the majority arbitrators. It was only after consulting a senior lawyer in Hong Kong while drafting this commentary that the author learned that the more appropriate English phrasing should have been:

"The Tribunal inquires into the matter at the hearing."

Under the applicable arbitration rules, the official working language of the proceedings was Chinese. However, the respondent, a U.S. company, had appointed a British arbitrator who was employed in Hong Kong at the time. It appeared that this arbitrator lacked proficiency in Chinese. The author retrospectively examines the communication gaps within the tribunal, particularly between the two Chinese arbitrators and the foreign arbitrator.

This commentary highlights the various objections raised by the U.S. company during the enforcement proceedings, as well as the judicial reasoning of **United States District Judge Vanessa D. Gilmore** in addressing the issues at hand. The judge's assessment, including her discussion of the respondent's allegations against the majority arbitrators—both Chinese—was objective and precise. The author regards her ruling as a textbook example of judicial reasoning in international arbitration.

The two Chinese arbitrators constituted the majority of the tribunal. So far as the author knows that a formal dissenting opinion by the minority arbitrator dealing cases under the jurisdiction of CIETAC had never been issued, nor was there a perceived need to elaborate further on the matter. Instead, it was agreed that all case materials would be forwarded to both parties. The judicial analysis cited under **Section IV-C** of this commentary provides a clear and accurate summary of the issues involved, demonstrating Judge Gilmore's expertise in international trade law.

This case serves as an important reference for understanding the challenges of enforcing foreign arbitral awards, the potential pitfalls in drafting arbitral decisions, and the necessity of precise legal language in cross-border arbitration.

Reflections on Some Issues of Due Process

1 Introduction

The China International Economic and Trade Arbitration, Shenchen Commission (CIETAC, Shenzhen) on August 5, 1994, took cognizance of a case arising from a contract of international sale of goods (Case File: [1994] Shen Guo Zhong Shou Zi No. 78). The Claimant was a Chinese company (hereinafter referred to as "SZF") with its principle office in Shenzhen. The Respondent was an American corporation (Herein after referred to as "LPC") organized under the laws of Delaware, with its principle office in Oregon, United States of America. LPC was principally in the pulp, lumber and building products business, and was one of the largest and respected companies in the industry. The Arbitration Rules of CIETAC which came into force on June 1, 1994, (hereinafter referred to as the 1994 Rules) were applied to the procedure of this case.

CIETAC, Shenzhen, on September 9, 1994, formed an arbitration tribunal, which was composed of Mr. X as the presiding arbitrator, Mr. Huang and Mr. K. as arbitrators to hear the case.

An arbitration award numbered as (95) Shen Guo Zhong Jie Zi No. 91 was issued by the majority of the arbitrators of the Tribunal on August 22, 1995. The Tribunal partially satisfied the Claimant 's claims, awarding within 50 days from the date the Award was rendered the Respondent should indemnify the Claimant the profit loss, the other losses and the attorneys fees in dealing with the case.

The Respondent did not automatically implement the Award. The Claimant (is called Plaintiff in the action at law) on September 25, 1996, petitioned the United

☆ This commentary was published in Mealey's International Arbitation Report, Vol, 14, # 8, August 1999, pp.26–56.

The author is grateful to Mr. Xenos M. Yuen with the Law Offices of Yuen and Associates, PllC located in Houstan, for the Files of Cause No. H -96–3188 provided.

Y. Huang, *Commentaries on Commercial Arbitration in Modern China*, Modern China and International Economic Law, https://doi.org/10.1007/978-981-95-0168-7_3

States District Court For the Southern District of Texas Houston Division for confirmation of the arbitral Award under the Convention on the Recognition and Enforcement of Foreign Arbitration Awards (hereinafter referred to as the Convention), implemented by 9 U.S.C. § 201-208(1997). SZF required that the Court order LPC (is called Defendant in the action at law) to pay the awarded damages, bearing the applicable interest.[1]

The parties exchange several documents, such as the requests for admissions, interrogatories, request for production, answers or objections to each other 's request or interrogatories, motion for summary judgement, and reply or response to each other 's summary judgement.

On August 29, 1997, LPC filed a motion for summary judgement, arguing that the Court should vacate the arbitration Award because the arbitration process violated LPC 's due process rights. LPC also contends that the panel 's decision was procured by fraud, in manifest disregard of the law, and beyond the scope for the arbitrators' authority.

On August 29, 1997, SZF also filed a motion for summary judgment, contending that it is entitled to judgment as a matter of law. It is undisputed that CIETAC rendered an award of US$363,908.88 in favor of SZF. Since LPC has failed to pay the damage award. SZF argues it is entitled to the payment with interest pursuant to the panel's decision. After several confrontations, the two parties through their attorneys reached an agreement disposing of all the outstanding issues in the case and request the Court enter the following agreement.

Both parties agree that the [95] Shen Guo Zhong Jie Zi No.91 Arbitration Award rendered by an arbitration tribunal of the CIETAC on August 22, 1995, shall be recognized and enforced. The Plaintiff SZF expressly waives the accrued interest portion of the Award provided the principal amount of US$370,887.92 is paid on or before March 24, 1998. The Defendant LPC shall pay the plaintiff the sum of US$370.887.92 on or before March 24, 1998.

Based on the foregoing agreement, an Agreed Order was signed by the honorable Vanessa D. Gilmore, the United States District Judge on February 23, 1998.

The Law Offices of Yuen and Associates, Pllc located in Houston were engaged by the Plaintiff SZF to take over the case from some predecessor on February 3, 1997. Two lawyers Mr. Xenos M. Yuen and Mr. Stephan Honore of the law firm attended a conference on the enforcement of CIETAC's arbitral awards in America held in Shenzhen on August 14, 1998. They delivered speeches at the conference. Mr. Yuen made presentation of the instant case.

I have talked with Mr. Yuen about the case for several times, as he visits China now and then. He has raised quite a few questions about the conduct of arbitration s at CIETAC as well as the instant case and gave me some advice, stressing the key factor, which would ensure that a foreign arbitral award is to be successfully enforced in America.

Upon request of me, Mr. Yuen gives me a copy of the court proceeding. When I first glance over the documents contained in the bound volume, the Original Answer of LPC issued by its attorney attracts my attention and I've got to know that the Defendant condemns, saying that the Award was procured by corruption, fraud or undue means. That attorney strongly attacks the two arbitrators signing the Award. It is the first time for me in my career as a professional to have had experience of being attacked on that so solemn occasion. I have got some lawyer friends of America. But to tell the truth, my knowledge about them is mainly gained through watching TV series, such as "L-A Law," "The Practice". The resourceful heroes and heroines of those TV series, bravely fighting for justice and legal sanctity, have made lasting impressions on me. Now that event, taking me to a court of America once more in other way, impresses me more directly and deeply. It seems that I am a character of a TV program, sitting over there but without any lines.

I pour over the documents of the case proceedings of the Cause No. H-96-3188, and review the Case File No. 490-1 of CIETAC, Shenzhen, which [94] Shen Guo Zhong Shou Zi No. 78 Case and (95) Shen Guo Zhong Jie Zi No. 91 Award and all the documents of the instant case were in. To my great relief, the Award on the whole is correct. Meanwhile, I examine myself, looking back on the course of the arbitration, finding out some slips of the Tribunal or myself that could have been avoided. It was these slips that gave someone a handle against the winner, jeopardizing the enforcement of the Award. After reflections on some issues concerning due process I feel I have better understanding of those questions.

For the purpose of giving a general view of the arbitration case, so that readers could have a general idea of it and then they could comment on the opinions and decisions as well as the work of the Tribunal, I would like to outline the Award as follows and have the whole Award as an appendix to this article (Text of Award and Dissenting Award in Section A. Mealey 's Document #05-990830-101).

2 The Excerpts of [95] Shen Guo Zhong Jie Zi no. 91 Arbitration Award

A. *Procedural Matters*

CIETAC, Shenzhen, on August 5, 1994, took cognizance of the case. The 1994 Rules are applied to the procedure of this case. CIETAC, Shenzhen on September 9, 1994, formed an arbitration tribunal, which is composed of Mr. Xiao as the presiding arbitrator, Mr. Huang and Mr. K. as arbitrators to hear the case.

The Tribunal heard the case in Shenzhen on December 10, 1995. The Claimant and the Respondent both attended the hearing. Mr. P., a staff member of the American Plywood Association ("APA") was present as a witness. In the course of the hearing the Tribunal heeded the oral statements and arguments of both parties and did investigations. After the hearing, both parties handed in their additional statements and evidence.

This Award is decided by the majority of the arbitrators and rendered on August 22, 1995.

B. ***Facts***

On September 9, 1993, the Claimant (buyer) and the Respondent (seller) signed the Contract No. 93A8811 (hereinafter referred to as the Contract); the subject matter is American Southern Yellow Pine Plywood of US$1,077,534.50. The terms and conditions that are closely related to the dispute are as follows:

Grade: BCX O&ES;

Price: US$610.00/PER MSF, C&F Shanghai, PRC;

Packing: 46 PIECES/UNIT (1,200 UNITS); Shipping Mark: 94130/SHANGHAI;

Terms of Payment: The buyer shall open an irrevocable at sight L/C to the seller with the Bank of China, Shenzhen, (hereinafter referred to as BOC, Shenzhen) with notification of opening through the First Chicago International (hereinafter referred to as First Chicago). The credit shall be payable against the presentation of the draft drawn on the opening bank together with the documents specified. The L/C to be subject to the Uniform Customs and Practice for Documentary Credits (1983 Revision), International Chamber of Commerce Publication No. 400 (hereinafter referred to as UCP400).

Documents: Commercial invoice indicating the Contract No., L/C No., commodity, quantity, unit price and total amount; full set of clean on-board ocean bills of lading; packing list/weight memo indicating quantity, gross and net weight of each package; certificate of quality issued by APA indicating the Contract No., L/C No. and certificate of origin.

Arbitration: All disputes may then be submitted to CIETAC for arbitration.

On September 25, 1993, the Claimant opened a letter of credit in favor of the Respondent with a sum of US$606,096.00. During the performance of the Contract, an agreement was reached by and between the two parties to deliver the goods in two shipments instead of one on November 10, 1993, the Respondent made the first shipment and then on November 17, sent all the documents respectively to BOC, Shenzhen and First Chicago. On December 2, BOC, Shenzhen refused to accept the documents, alleging that there were seven discrepancies between the documents and the L/C. On December 22, the Claimant declared the Contract avoided. Afterward, the parties consulted with each other but failed to reach any agreement. The Claimant on August 4, 1994, applied to CIETAC, Shenzhen for arbitration, claiming for damages of US$1,082,086.60, which included profit loss US$731,869.99, its end user 's loss US$270,216.68 and attorneys fees US$80,000.00.

The main issues of the parties are as follows:

1. Whether the Respondent was aware of the end user of the subject matter upon conclusion of the Contract;
2. Reasons for the delivery of the goods in two shipments;
3. The discrepancies of the documents;
4. About the Certificate of Quality;
5. Quality of the goods and remedy measures.

C. *The Tribunal's Opinions and Decisions*

1. *The Applicable Law*

Both parties hold that CISG[2] is applicable to the Contract, the reasons they express are correct. This common wish should be fully respected.

2. *Whether the Respondent Knew that There Was an End User of the Subject Matter upon Conclusion of the Contract*

Facts demonstrate that upon conclusion of the Contract, the Respondent should have known about the end user of the subject matter. As a big company engaged in timber, construction materials and other products for years, the Respondent should certainly make sure of the requirements of the customer and process the goods according to such requirements. The Respondent alleges that the Claimant bought the goods for itself even at the time of delivery. This is, however, not true.

3. *Delivery of Goods in Two Shipments*

In the course of performing the Contract, both parties changed one shipment into two should be regarded as a new agreement.

4. *The Certificate of Quantity Issued by APA and the Quality of the Goods*

In the light of Article 38 of CISG, unless there is a special provision between both parties, the buyer's right to have the goods inspected at the destination is not excluded.

Regarding to this case, the documents were refused by the issuing bank as result of discrepancies; it is meaningless for both parties to argue whether the Certificate of Quality is effective or whether there is any defect in the quality of the goods.

5. *The Discrepancies in the Documents and the Claims*

There are seven discrepancies in the documents. Grade of Goods in the Invoice, Bill of Lading, Packing List/Weight Memo differs from that in the L/C. It was written as BOX O AND ES instead of BCX O & ES which technically indicates water proof and oil-sealing for engineering use in concrete templates. The product is highly customized. Since the Respondent misprinted BCX as BOX in the above-mentioned document, it is reasonable for the Claimant to doubt that the shipped goods were not up to the originally required grade. This discrepancy is essential.

In the Packing List/Weight Memo, there are two contract numbers: 94130 and 93A8811; in the Certificate of Quality, the contract number is 94130. They differ from the number in the other documents. The name of goods in the Certificate of Origin is Southern Pine Plywood, different from those appeared in Shipment Advice, Invoice, Bill of Lading and Packing List/Weight Memo. It is stipulated in Article 15 of UCP400 that documents which appear on their face to be inconsistent with one another will be considered as not appearing on their face to be in accordance with the terms and conditions of the L/C.

The Certificate of Quality does not carry the name of goods. According to Article 23 of UCP400, the data content in the document makes it possible to relate the goods and/or services referred to therein to those referred to. Furthermore, as in the Certificate of Quality the name of the goods isn't indicated and the contract is No. 94130, there is sufficient reason for the Claimant to doubt whether the goods are the subject matter of the Contract.

In the Packing List/Weight Memo two kinds of units are listed with only one weight. Moreover, two different contract numbers appear in the same document.

The above-mentioned documents are of material ones. In accordance with the principle established in UCP400 that documents should appear on their face to be in accordance with the terms and conditions of a credit, the issuing bank is in a position to refuse to pay for the documents. The content of the documents presented by the Respondent are not in line with the terms and conditions in the L/C which means that the Respondent failed to deliver the goods in line with the L/C under the Contract. The Respondent is in fundamental breach of the Contract.

The Tribunal partially satisfies the claim for damages of profit loss of the Claimant, 10% of the price for the first shipment, i.e.. US$60,609.60. The Tribunal awards the Respondent to pay the damages of the Claimant for what it needs to compensate its end user, US$270,216.68 and compensate the Claimant part of its attorneys fees in dealing with the case, US$33,082.60.

3 The Full Text of the Opinion of Dissenting Arbitrator

It is with regret that I cannot agree with the Award of the majority. I propose to state my reasons very briefly.

I am satisfied that there was at least one discrepancy in the letter of credit, which justified the bank in rejecting the document. That point was the BCX/ BOX point. I am not impressed with the other alleged discrepancies relied upon.

I am also satisfied that the Respondent knew the Claimant intended to sell these goods to an end user.

No evidence produced, whether oral or written, has satisfied me that the goods delivered were other than up to standard. The live evidence given by a representative of the APA was compelling and there was no satisfactory evidence to gainsay it. I also accept the Respondent's oral and written evidence as to quality and reject any contrary assertions.

I am satisfied that in this case the Claimant acted opportunistically when the documents were rejected. They tried to get the price reduced substantially.

In my view, the Claimant did not mitigate its loss. If it indeed had a genuine sub-purchaser it should have waived the discrepancies, delivered the goods according to the sub-contract and taken its profit on the sub-contract. Instead the Claimant attempted to negotiate a price reduction.

The Loss of Profit claim, as my co-arbitrators have noted, is extravagant and unreasonable. It is significant to note that on 13 December 1993 (document A14) the

Claimant was seeking compensation of US$45,000. I have never been satisfied as to why when this arbitration commenced the Claimant was seeking roughly ten times that amount and later it sought, without any satisfactory explanation, to double even that exaggerated claim on the first day of the hearing. They gave no explanation as to why the increased claim. I was not aware that my co-arbitrators formally gave leave.

I also have the gravest doubts about the very existence of the sub-contract relied upon by the Claimant. I am not satisfied on the evidence that any genuine sub-contract had been entered into by the Claimant. The exorbitant claim for loss of profit is, in my judgment, some evidence that this sub-sale was not a genuine transaction. It also appears to me that the Claimant manufactured some documents, which it put before us in support of its claim. On the day of the hearing, the Claimant submitted a batch of exhibits. Six of these are said to be communications from the Claimant to the Respondent. The Respondent denies receiving them. Document A.18 is alleged to be a document sent by the Claimant to First Chicago. First Chicago denies receiving the document. When one examines these documents, one's suspicion is excited. The real document A.15 had in fact been in the Chinese language and sent to Excelsior (the Broker) without the references to documents A.13 and A.14. However, later the Claimant submitted one document A.15 which did refer to documents A.13 and A.14, the documents allegedly sent to the Respondent but not received by them. One has to ask why there was fabrication of evidence and one answer is that it was done in some way to cover up a non-existent sub-sale.

I do not feel that the Claimant has discharged the burden of proving that it entered into the sub-contract alleged.

If I were wrong about that, then I would conclude that the Claimant is only entitled to damages under Article 76 of the CISG namely the difference between the contract price and the current price at the time of the breach of contract. The Claimant failed to produce any evidence on this topic. Further, under Article 74 the Claimant will be entitled to its reasonable loss of profit on the sub-contract. No law requires the Tribunal to compensate extravagant and unusual bargains. As the Claimant has failed to satisfy me that a sub-sale was entered into I would not have awarded them 20% of the value of such alleged contract.

I would have dismissed this claim in its entirety.

As to costs I am surprised that my colleagues think it right to award the Claimant by way of costs a sum equivalent to 10% of the total award. I am not aware of any evidence being presented to the Tribunal on the issue of the Claimant 's expenses and to award them without any verification the maximum permitted by Article 59 is in my opinion quite unacceptable. The Respondent has had no opportunity of commenting on this issue.

As I would have found for the Respondent I would have awarded them not more 10% of the claim as their expenses after having called for verification of such expense and after having given the Claimant an opportunity to comment—a privilege denied to the Respondent by my co-arbitrators.

4 Issues Arising in the Course of Applying for the Enforcement in America and the Arguments and Viewpoints of the Parties and the Judge

A. *Questions Raised by the Parties*

1. *The Formation of the Tribunal*

The Plaintiff SZF appointed Mr. Huang as arbitrator. The Defendant LPC appointed Mr. K as Arbitrator. CIETAC appointed Mr. Xiao as the presiding arbitrator. Both parties confirmed that. But it remains a problem, as there was some discrepancy between the account and the fact. I'll make further reference to this later.

2. *At What Time or on What Occasion Plaintiff Amended Its Claims and the Defendant Submitted Its Statement of Defense and Exhibits*

In the action at law, the Defendant requests the Plaintiff to admit that it amended and nearly doubled its claim for lost profits allegedly caused by LPC on the first day of the arbitration hearing and that SZF never introduced any evidence during the arbitration hearing to support this amendment. The last-minute amendment was permitted by the majority of the Tribunal.

That amendment to the Plaintiff's claim at the hearing exceeded the authority of the Tribunal. LPC was seriously prejudiced by the amendment as it got no notice or meaningful opportunity to respond.

The Defendant admits that it submitted documentary materials to the Tribunal before and at the time of the hearing and the Tribunal accepted them. Both parties were permitted to and did submit additional documents to the Tribunal following the hearing.

3. *An Unauthorized Third Party Present at the Hearing*

The Defendant alleges that an unauthorized third party was also present at the hearing in violation of the confidentiality requirements governing the arbitration. During the introductions of the hearing, SZF misrepresented to the Tribunal the identity of this individual. LPC learned of this after the hearing and lodged its protest immediately.

4. *The Claim of Attorneys Fees*

With reference to the Award giving the Claimant attorneys fees in the amount of US$33,082.60, the Defendant affirms that there was absolutely no evidence in support of this claim. LPC was neither presented with evidence of the expenses reasonably incurred by the SZF nor was given an opportunity to comment on any such evidence. The Defendant treats the award of that sum of attorneys' fees as fundamentally unfair practices, as SZF introduced no evidence to the Tribunal. LPC labels the Tribunal a "kangaroo court."

5. ***The Tribunal Undertaking Investigations and Collecting Evidence on Its Own Initiative***

The Defendant condemns that the Tribunal conducted its own discovery, gathered its own "evidence" regarding the plywood transaction and evaluated this "evidence" without any notice to LPC. LPC was informed for the first time of this "evidence" when it was provided with the majority award; months after the arbitration was complete. As a result, LPC was not given an opportunity to comment on any of this "evidence" during the arbitration, though the arbitration rules entitled LPC to do so.

6. ***The Tribunal Exceeding Its Authority by Concluding that an Inspection at the Destination Being Warranted to See the Condition and the Quality of the Goods***

The Defendant censures the Tribunal for its view on the right enjoyed by the buyer to have an inspection at the destination, saying the majority exceeded their authority by concluding that an inspection in China was warranted to see whether any damage had occurred during shipment. The point was not raised by the Claimant at the hearing and there was no evidence presented of any possible damage during shipment. Furthermore, the parties had previously rejected all proposed inspections in China, so such an inspection was beyond their agreement.

LPC says it was always willing to have the goods inspected for defects. Although the Tribunal could have conducted such an inspection, it refused to do so. Also, the ultimate buyer denied all access to the plywood. Nevertheless, the Tribunal somehow concluded without any credible evidence that the plywood was defective.

7. ***The Constitution of the Award***

The Defendant admits only that the Award was signed by two members of the Tribunal and that these two members constituted a majority. However LPC denies that the opinion of the majority constitutes the Award. Rather, the Award also contains a written dissent by a third member of the Tribunal.

The Defendant requests the Plaintiff to admit that the minority wrote a Dissenting Opinion in the arbitration and that each and every sentence and/or paragraph referring, in whole or in part to the "Claimant is accurate, true, and correct."

The Plaintiff objects to the relevancy of the Dissenting Opinion of Mr. K appointed by LPC. With respect to this action for enforcement of the Award, what he said in his opinion is irrelevant since it is the Tribunal's majority decision, and not a dissent that is enforceable.

SZF holds that the Dissenting Opinion is neither a part of the Award nor part of the evidence upon which the Award was rendered. The minority merely expresses some personal opinion after the Tribunal judgement was rendered.

8 ***The Award Being Procured by Undue Process and Undue Means***

The Defendant asserts that the Award and the procedures attendant to it lack due process, impose improper and unauthorized arbitral procedures beyond the scope of the arbitration agreement entered into by the parties, and are a violation of public policy under Article V of the New York Convention. Further, the Award was procured by collusion, corruption, fraud or undue means, in violation of Section 10 of the Federal Arbitration Act, 9 U.S.C. § 10, and the two arbitrators signing the Award acted in manifest disregard of the applicable, controlling law. The Award was also fundamentally flawed because the SZF committed fraud on the Tribunal by inducing it to render a fraudulent and fundamentally unfair award.

9. *Allegation of False Documents Manufactured by SZF*

LPC says that at the hearing SZF introduced a series of documents purporting to be faxes from it to LPC and to First Chicago. LPC had never seen these documents before the hearing and it strenuously objected to these documents on the basis that they appeared to be false, fraudulent documents prepared solely for the hearing. SZF introduce d no evidence to show that the faxes had been sent by it and/or received by LPC. These documents were critical to support SZF's claim for losses related to its alleged resale of the plywood.

The Dissenting Opinion characterized these documents as "manufactured." The majority opinion fails to discuss these documents. Under Article 54 of the 1994 Rules, the Tribunal was required to give the parties a "reasoned award." Nevertheless, although the Award never justified the use of these documents, the documents necessarily had a substantial impact on the principal award rendered against LPC, US$270,216.88 for losses related to the alleged resale. The Award was obtained through fraud on the Tribunal and is invalid.

B. *Some Viewpoints and Comments on Some Issues Expressed by the Judge of the United States District Court for the Southern District of Texas, Houston Division*

The United States District Judge Vanessa D. Gilmore on December 12, 1997, issued an Order. He makes reference to the case, saying that on September 25, 1996, SZF petitioned this Court for confirmation of the arbitral Award under the Convention, implemented by 9 U.S.C. § 201–208 (1997). SZF requests that this Court order LPC to pay the awarded damages, bearing the applicable interest.

On August 29, 1997, LPC filed a motion for summary judgment, arguing that this Court should vacate the arbitral Award because the arbitration process violated LPC 's rights. LPC also contends that the Tribunal's[3] decision was procured by fraud, in manifest disregard of the law, and beyond the scope of the arbitrators' authority.

On the same day, SZF also filed a motion for summary judgment, contending that it is entitled to judgment as a matter of law. It is undisputed that CIETAC rendered an award of US$363,980.88 in favor of SZF. Since LPC has failed to pay the damage award, SZF argues that it is entitled to payment with interest pursuant to the Tribunal 's decision. SZF also asserts that LPC fails to present any credible and relevant evidence warranting the refusal of recognition or enforcement of the Award. Conversely, LPC maintains that this Court must vacate the Award because no evidence was introduced at the hearing to support the arbitrators' decision. Furthermore, LPC argues that the fraud committed by SZF on the Tribunal requires this Court to refuse to enforce the Award (Order—I).

The judge states his views about the case, saying that summary judgment is appropriate if no genuine issue of material fact exists and the moving party is entitled to judgment as a matter of law. Fed. R Civ. P. 56. A fact is " material" if its resolution in favor of one party might affect the outcome of the suit under governing law. Anderson v. Liberty lobby, Inc., 106 S. Ct. 2505, 2510 (1986). An issue is "genuine" if the evidence is sufficient for a reasonable jury to return a verdict for the non-moving party. Anderson. 106 S. Ct. At 2510 (ORDER—II).

The only issue before this Court is whether it must confirm the arbitration Award rendered by CIETAC.

The United States district courts have original jurisdiction over an action or proceeding falling under the Convention 9 U.S.C. § 203 (1997). There are three requirements for a district court to exercise jurisdiction under the Convention: "the award (1) must arise out of a legal relationship (2) which is commercial in nature and (3) which is not entirely domestic in scope." Cargill Int 'l S.A. v. M/T Pavel Dybenko, 991 F.2d 1012, 1017 (2d Cir. 1993).

"Judicial review of an arbitration award is extraordinarily narrow[.]." Forsythe Int'l, S.A. v. Gibbs Oil Co. Of Texas, 915 F.2d 1017, 1020 (5th Cir. 1990). As the party opposing confirmation, LPC "bears the burden of proof of establishing an Article V reason prohibiting confirmation" (ORDER—III).

LPC argues that the Tribunal did not provide an opportunity to respond either to the award of attorneys fees or to the evidence that the Tribunal gathered and evaluated on its own.

"Due process is flexible and calls for such procedural protections as the particular situation demands. "The fundamental requirement of due process is the opportunity to be hear d at a meaningful time and in a meaningful manner."

With respect to evidence matters, "arbitrators are not bound by the rules of evidence." An arbitrator is not bound to hear all of the evidence tendered by the parties.... [H]e [simply] must give each of the parties to the dispute an adequate opportunity to present its evidence and argument." Essentially, "an arbitrator must provide a fundamentally fair hearing.... A fundamentally fair hearing is one that 'meets the minimal requirements of fairness—adequate notice, a hearing on the evidence, and an impartial decision by the arbitrator.'"

Regarding the decision of attorney 's fee, the judge quotes the last paragraph of the Tribunal's Opinion of the Award and the last paragraph of the Dissenting Opinion. Concerning the evidence of that claim, Mr. M., a representative of LPC presenting at the hearing, argues that LPC was not "presented with evidence of the legal expenses incurred by SZF nor given an opportunity to comment on any such evidence or on the propriety, if any, of an award to SZF of attorney 's fees."

SZF contends that "[c]ertainly the Tribunal had evidence, as did [LPC]... that attorneys were working on the case and that their efforts were substantial, since these attorneys appeared before the Tribunal." Furthermore, SZF continues, it requested attorney 's fees in its claim for damages. Based on the evidence submitted, the Court finds that a genuine issue exists as to whether the Tribunal 's award of attorneys fees, purportedly in the absence of any evidence, violated LPC 's due process rights. Therefore, summary judgment in favor of LPC based on this defense would be improper.

LPC also argues that the Tribunal collected and evaluated its own evidence without giving LPC an opportunity to respond to the propriety of this evidence. In support of this assertion, Mr. M 's affidavit states that during the arbitration hearing he discovered that the Tribunal had collected its own evidence regarding the parties' plywood transaction and that LPC was not given an opportunity to comment on any of this evidence.

Conversely, Mr. Hu, SZF 's attorney at the arbitration hearing, contends that LPC 's accusation of an independent investigation by the Tribunal is groundless because under China law the Tribunal "has the power of independent investigation outside the evidence pro- vided by the parties involved." Mr. Hu argues that he was never informed that the Tribunal had collected its own evidence in this case and questions whether an in dependent investigation ever occurred.

Based on the record, the Court finds that LPC fails to present sufficient evidence warranting a grant of summary judgment as to this defense. Although Mr. M. claims to know about the Tribunal's independent investigation, he does not explain how he learned of this information. Unlike Mr. M.'s affidavit, in its motion for summary judgment, LPC argues that it found out about the evidence allegedly collected from the independent investigation when it received the Tribunal's written decision. However, given the conflicting account by LPC on this issue and Hu's response, the Court finds that a fact issue exists as to whether CIETAC deprived LPC of a fundamentally fair hearing by collecting evidence on its own initiative without providing LPC an opportunity to be heard on the propriety of this evidence.[4] Summary judgment is, therefore, improper (ORDER—IV).

LPC argues that the acts of fraud committed by SZF on the Tribunal require this Court to vacate the Award as against the public policy of the United States. In particular, LPC claims that at the arbitration hearing SZF introduced at least eight to ten fraudulent documents purporting to be faxes sent between LPC to SZF. The documents were admitted into evidence and considered by the Tribunal. LPC maintains that these fraudulent documents "were the primary 'evidence' underlying the award" of US$270,216.88 to SZF for loss profits.

Given LPC's admission that it both discovered the allegedly fraudulent faxes during the arbitration hearing and "strenuously objected" to their authenticity, the Court finds that, as a matter of law, the Award was not procured through fraud. SZF 's motion for summary judgment is granted as to this defense (ORDER—V).

LPC contends that this Court must vacate the Award because the Tribunal issued an award in manifest disregard of the law. According to LPC, the Tribunal's decisions to award lost profits and attorney's fees without any supporting evidence, to allow SZF to dramatically increase its damage request during the hearing, and to conduct an in dependent investigation without notice to LPC were in manifest disregard of the law. LPC also claims that the Tribunal acted in manifest disregard of the law by ignoring LPC 's defense of mitigation.

"Manifest disregard of the law" requires an error by the arbitrators that was obvious and capable of being readily and instantly perceived by the average person qualified to serve as an arbitrator. Moreover, the term 'disregard ' implies that the arbitrator appreciates the existence of a clearly governing legal principle but decides to ignore or pay no attention to it. Judicial inquiry under the 'manifest disregard' standard is therefore extremely limited. The governing law alleged to have been ignored by the arbitrators must be well defined, explicit, and clearly applicable. " Merrill Lynch, Pierce, Fenner & Smith, Inc. v. Bobker, 808 F.2d 930, 933-34 (2d Cir. 1986). Consequently, "[m]anifest disregard of the law may be found... if the arbitrator 'understood and correctly stated the law but proceeded to ignore it.'" Siegel v. Titan Indus. Corp., 779 F.2d 891, 893 (2d Cir 185).

As mentioned, the Court must confirm the Award unless LPC establishes one of the defenses provided in Article V of the Convention. The ground advanced by LPC—that the arbitrators issued an award in manifest disregard of the law—is not explicitly provided as a defense in Article V. Therefore, LPC cannot rely on the plain meaning of Article V to invoke this defense.

Furthermore, LPC does not provide nor has the Court found any authority for LPC's proposition that "manifest disregard of the law" is available as an independent defense to the enforcement of a foreign arbitration award.

The Court refrains from applying the defense of "manifest disregard of the law" to the Award rendered by CIETAC for policy reasons. One court has stated that, within the context of foreign arbitration, the defense of

> "manifest disregard" of law... would require an American court to consider whether foreign arbitrators had disregarded foreign law. It is one thing to ask an American judge to hold American arbitrators guilty of manifest disregard of American law. It is quite another to ask an American judge to determine whether foreign arbitrators manifestly disregarded the internal, substantive law of a foreign nation by which the parties agreed in their contract to be bound. That seems to [be]... a slippery slope upon which American judges should not embark, in clear derogation of the public policy underlying the Convention.

Brandeis, 656 F. Supp. at 167.

In the instant case, the parties agreed to arbitrate all disputes before CIETAC. Therefore, the arbitration rules of CIETAC apply to all of LPC 's arguments concerning the various procedural errors committed by the Tribunal. (The Award, Instrument No. 19, at 2, 13-16.)

LPC also argues that the Tribunal ignored its defense of mitigation. The parties' Contract is governed by the CISG (Id. at 18-19). Unlike LPC's contention, the Tribunal, in its written decision, clearly recognizes SZF's obligation to "take reasonable ways to purchase a substitute for the end user as to reduce the loss" (Id. at 24). However, the Tribunal concluded that such a "replacement could not be possible to make up for the loss suffered by the end user" (Id. at 25). The "manifest disregard" defense "means more than error or misunderstanding with respect to the law" (Brobker, 808 F.2d at 933).

Accordingly, the Court finds that there is no authority for recognizing "manifest disregard of the law" as an independent ground for vacating a foreign arbitration award under the Convention. See, e.g., Brandeis, 656 F. Supp. at 167 (holding that the "manifest disregard " defense is not available to a party opposing enforcement of the award within the context of the Convention). Therefore, as a matter of law, the Court grants SZF's motion for summary judgment as to LPC's defense of "manifest disregard of the law" (ORDER—VI).

LPC maintains that the arbitrators exceeded their authority by awarding US$363,908.88 in damages to SZF. In particular, LPC contests the Award for lost profits and for attorneys' fees. According to LPC, SZF failed to submit any evidence supporting an award for lost profits or attorneys fees. LPC also argues that it got no meaningful opportunity to respond to SZF's eleventh-hour amendment to its claims. In support of vacating the Award for this reason, LPC relied on Article V(1)(c) of the Convention which provides that a court may refuse to recognize and enforce an arbitration award where it "contains decisions on matters beyond the scope of the submission to arbitration[.]" 9 U.S.C. § 201 (1997). The Court finds that LPC 's reliance on Article V(1)(c) for authority is misplaced.

As mentioned, the Court must confirm the Award unless LPC establishes one of the defenses provided in Article V of the Convention. Unlike Article V of the Convention which governs the Court 's refusal to enforce a foreign arbitral award, Chapter 1 of the existing FAA specially authorizes a court to vacate an award "where the arbitrators exceeded their powers." 9 U.S.C. § 10(d) (1997). This language is not included in Article V of the Convention. Consequently, the Court concludes that LPC cannot simply rely on this broad language in order to advance an additional defense to confirmation of the foreign arbitral Award.

Furthermore, LPC's arguments are not properly addressed under Article V(1)(c) of the Convention. LPC does not contend that the Tribunal decided matters beyond the scope of submission to arbitration. Rather, it argues that the arbitrators exceeded their authority by rendering a damage award despite the lack of supporting evidence on the issue of damages. Accordingly, the Court finds that as a matter of law this defense—that the arbitrators exceeded their authority given the lack of evidentiary support for the damage award rendered by the Tribunal—is not available under the Convention to prevent the confirmation of the foreign arbitral Award issued by CIETAC. SZF 's motion is, therefore, granted as to this defense (ORDER—VII).

Accordingly, this Court denies Defendant LPC 's Motion for Summary Judgment. This Court grants Plaintiff SZF 's motion as to Defendant 's claims that the Award was procured by fraud, issued in "manifest disregard of the law," and beyond the arbitrators' authority and denies Plaintiff's motion with respect to Defendant 's due process defense (ORDER—VIII).

C. *Summary of Plaintiff's Comments upon the Dissenting Opinion*

The attorney for the Plaintiff in his Supplemental Response to Defendant 's Motion for Summary Judgement analyses and comments on the Opinion of the Dissenting Arbitrator [hereafter "Dissent"]. The excerpts are as follows:

First of all, Mr. K. concurs with the majority that the Bank of China was justified in rejecting the documents tendered pursuant to the letter of credit and thus withholding payment for the plywood. He cities one major discrepancy as supporting this result, and then says that he is "unimpressed with the other alleged discrepancies relied upon," hardly a ringing endorsement of LPC 's allegations of fraud (Paragraph 2 of Dissent).

He then concurs with the majority "that the Respondent knew the Claimant intended to sell these goods to an end user" (Paragraph 3 of Dissent). These two conclusions concurring with the majority are enough on which to base a predicate for the finding of fundamental breach and assessment of damages.

Mr. K. states, "No evidence produces, whether oral or written, has satisfied me that the goods delivered were other than up to standard" (Paragraph 4 of Dissent). However, this misses the point that this was a documentary transaction, dealing in documents, and a letter of credit. In this kind of transaction, one looks only at whether the documents submitted pursuant to the letter of credit are defective, not at the underlying merchandise covered by the documents. Therefore, it is irrelevant whether the plywood itself was actually up to standard or not. The importer/buyer is entitled to rely on the documents in determining whether to reject the shipment.

Here, the nature of the defective documents entitled SZF to conclude that the shipment did not meet the terms of the letter of credit and to decide to declare a fundamental breach, and refuse to pay or take delivery.

Despite the fundamental breach, in an effort to mitigate damages, SZF accompanied its end user to Shanghai Port (at considerable distance from their base of operations) in the hopes that they could examine the actual shipment (which they had not yet seen) and arrange for a cash sale. Mr. K. concludes that in doing this, "the Claimant acted opportunistically" and "tried to get the price reduced substantially," and failed to mitigate its losses (Paragraph 5, 6 of Dissent).

The majority arrived at a different conclusion, finding that "the Claimant did want to receive the goods and therefore persuaded the end user to go to Shanghai to check the goods for purpose of mitigating the loss" (Award, p. 25). The Tribunal goes on to find that "Claimant even tried to obtain the Respondent 's authorization to receive the documents for the inspection of the goods. But the Respondent didn't agree." Id. Again, the dissent and the majority are merely in disagreement over the key facts which underlie the basis for the Award.

The Dissent then concurs with the majority in the view that the loss-of-profits claim is "extravagant and unreasonable" (Paragraph 7 of Dissent). The Award reduces SZF's claim for loss of profits from 121% of the price of the shipment to only 10%, i.e., US$60,609.60. Award, bottom of p.23–top of p.24. Thus, even if it were error (which is not conceded) to allow SZF to increase its claim drastically on the eve of the oral hearing, the error is cured by the end result since the Tribunal lowered the amount to what would be commercially reasonable lost profits under the circumstances.

Mr. K. expresses his "gravest doubts" that SZF had entered into any sub-contract, discussing some of the documents, which he apparently believes to have been "manufactured" or "fabricated" (Paragraphs 8, 9, 10 of Dissent). Though we cannot be sure, since LPC has not identified or produced the "fraudulent" documents, these are apparently some of the documents strenuously objected to by LPC during and following the hearing. "As the Claimant has failed to satisfy me that a sub-sale was entered into I would not have awarded them 20% of the value of such alleged contract." The majority concluded differently in the Award, pp. 24–25. They determined that "the total price of the Contract between the Claimant and its end user equals to US$1,351,083.43... " Award, p. 23. Since the Contract provided that SZF would be liable for 20% of the amount of the Contract if they failed to deliver, this was determined by the arbitrators to constitute "other losses" actually suffered by SZF. Twenty per cent of US$1,351,083.43 is US$270,216.68, the amount awarded as "other losses." The fact that the dissenter disagreed is not evidenced of any fraud.

Mr. K. says he would have dismissed this claim in its entirety (Paragraph 11). This is not consistent with his earlier statement agreeing with the majority that the bank was justified in not paying under the letter of credit. Since LPC did not cooperate when SZF asked to inspect the goods to see if they were acceptable to the end user, there was no way to avoid the damages that ensued. Surely it was proper for the Tribunal to order compensation for those damages.

With respect to attorney fees, even though Mr. K. acknowledges Article 59 of the 1994 Rules permits payment of 10% of the Award, he is critical of the majority 's decision to award the maximum. Again, there merely is a disagreement among the arbitrators about how to assess the attorney fees.

It is true that the majority does not directly address the question of the challenged documents. It may well be because the issue of the documents did not loom as large as a problem as LPC now would make it out. On the other hand, maybe the Tribunal took LPC 's protestations into account when they decided to drastically cut the amount awarded for loss of profits. If so, then the accusations of fraud have been factored into the arbitral decision.

Summarizing, an analysis of the Dissent just highlights the fact that the arbitrators both agreed at times and disagreed at other times on the various aspects of the case. As pointed out, the Dissent is at times even inconsistent (emphasis added). On the one hand the dissenter agrees that LPC knew that SZF intended to resell the goods to an end user, but later suggests he be not convinced that there was a sub-sale. It is to be noted that Mr. K. states that the evidence does not satisfy him that a sub-sale was entered into. He does not say that no evidence was introduced on that subject. It is at least reasonable for the majority to have concluded differently; finding that there was a sub-sale.

5 Retrospection and Reflections on Some Issues of the Arbitration Proceedings

A. *The Formation of the Tribunal*

The author of this article drafted the Award, both Chinese and English versions. To be exact and from the viewpoint of law, the final Award was translated by the author of this article. But the preface was drafted by the secretary of the Tribunal (hereinafter "the secretary"). It accounts for the acceptance of the case, the appointment of the arbitrators and the formation of the Tribunal, the receiving of documents submitted by the parties, the date for hearing, the service of all the arbitration documents, etc. The preface does not accurately account for how the Tribunal was formed. I was to blame for overlooking the errors.

Perhaps it should be added here that, before the oral hearing, the two arbitrators of Chinese nationality who signed the Award had never met with the representatives and attorneys of both parties.

Looking up the files of this case, one could find out that a brief and explicit statement of appointing an arbitrator is contained in the Application for Arbitration by SZF: It is hereby to authorize the chairman of CIETAC, Shenzhen, to appoint an arbitrator. The secretary general of the secretariat of CIETAC, Shenzhen, on behalf of the chairman wrote down his opinion appointing Mr. Huang as arbitrator for SZF in the column provided on the form, the Examining and Approving of the Acceptance of an Arbitration Case for this case.[5] The notices of arbitration in Chinese respectively issued to LPC and SZF on August 5, 1994, all recorded that Mr. Huang was appointed by the chairman of CIETAC, Shenchen, as arbitrator upon authorization by SZF.[6] But when the notices were turned into English and the notice of composition of the Tribunal was drafted, through an unfortunate oversight of the secretary, the wording goes that "The Applicant has appointed Mr. Huang as the arbitrator for this case."[7] That mistake was also overlooked by someone who was in charge of checking, signing and issuing documents.[8] Arbitrator, Mr. K. was appointed by LPC and the presiding arbitrator Mr. X. was appointed by the chairman of CIETAC, Shenzhen.[9]

B. ***The Claimant's Amendments to Its Claims; Respondent Submitted Documentary Materials to the Tribunal at the Time of the Hearing***

In SZF's Application for Arbitration, the Claimant claims for damages of US$538,056.08 and requests the Respondent to bear the arbitration fees. On December 7, 1994, three days before the oral hearing, the Claimant revised its claims, claiming for damages of US$1,082,086.60, which includes profit loss of US$731,869.99, attorneys' fees of US$80,000, and its end user's loss of US$270,216.68. SZF re-submitted Statement of Defense and submitted additional documentary materials on the day of the hearing.

The Claimant had a right to amend its claims. Was it too late to amend the claim? Would the amendment affect the arbitration proceedings? Might the Tribunal refuse such amendment?[10] No hearing had ever been held yet. It seemed not to be too late. But regarding the oral hearing at hand it was indeed too late. It did cause the secretary great difficulty to have the amendment and its appendixes served to the Respondent and the arbitrators before the hearing. The secretary did criticize the attorney of the Claimant, pointing out that it would bring real and potential trouble to the secretariat of CIETAC, Shenzhen[11] and the Tribunal. Should the secretariat and the secretary have refused to accept the amendment and its appendixes? One should not neglect that the parties to a case do not send their documentary materials directly to the arbitrators of a tribunal at CIETAC. But on December 7, 1994, the same day of receiving the Claimant's revision, the secretary succeeded in having it faxed to Mr. K and one of the attorneys of the Respondent, who was staying in Hong Kong at that time.[12] I could not remember whether on the day of hearing, Mr. K expressed his opinion on refusing the amendment. "The mere fact that SZF may have claimed what may have been regarded as excessive damage estimates does not mean that the Tribunal accepted these claims."[13] Isn't it an objective comment? Any reasonable man won't deny it.

The Respondent did submit its Statement of Defense and appendixes within the time limit on September 24, 1994. There were about 64 pages in all including the Chinese version of the Statement of the Defense. On the day of the hearing, LPC re-submitted its Statement of Defense without any amendment and various appendixes without any Chinese version. There were about 315 pages in all. It was 4.9 times of the pages of 64 submitted previously. Was it too late? Would it affect the arbitration proceedings? Were the secretariat and the Tribunal in a position to refuse the documentary materials at the oral hearing? It was only at the beginning of the first hearing. It seemed not to be too late. But the arbitrators, who were holding the hearing, were unable to go over the documentary materials of 315 pages, making preparations beforehand and amending their outline for inquiring of the parties about the matter, it was indeed too late. That must remain fresh in the memory of the arbitrators of the Tribunal and the agents of both parties and the secretary, I guess. For the representatives and the attorney of the Claimant, could they make any comments on and respond to the documentary materials of 315 pages at the hearing without going over them beforehand? Did they have so good a command of English which enabled them to comprehend all the main points in the materials by glancing over them while paying attention to the statement of LPC and the inquiries by the Tribunal about the matter? Let us not forget among the materials, about 251 were just received by SZF and by the Tribunal.

Did the Tribunal have any better alternative? I could not figure out. To the best of my memory, I did not air any opinion and the presiding arbitrator did not ask my opinion on that matter. I could not remember whether Mr. K expressed his idea to refuse or accept the documentary materials submitted by LPC.

Facing the great trouble caused by the parties to the Tribunal and to them each other, did the Tribunal get room for maneuver? The parties put pressure on the Tribunal. Did they make any self-examination? The representatives and the attorneys of the Respondent (except for one lawyer engaged from Shanghai, China) were from afar which cost LPC a great sum of money. If the Tribunal could overcome the difficulties and ascertain the facts that would enable it to decide the case by only a hearing, why shouldn't it have a try? The arbitrators should have had a tacit understanding on this matter. But what a pity that it turned out that we didn't!

In retrospection, I suppose the Tribunal should have first revealed the issues that the Claimant had amended its claim three days before the hearing and now the Respondent submitted its great quantity of documentary materials at the hearing. The Tribunal should have suggested or even decided the hearing be delayed to the next day, so that the parties and the arbitrators would have time to go through the materials. Perhaps the Tribunal should have convened a pre-hearing conference. One of our colleagues of America says, "A preliminary conference with the parties and the arbitrator is a very useful means of ensuring that a large commercial arbitration proceeds quickly and well. There is no problem getting a conference held. Arbitrators will almost certainly call a preliminary conference in a large case if asked, and the AAA rules require that it be held at the request of any party or at the discretion of the arbitrator or the AAA."[14] No party to the case asked to call such a conference. And under the 1994 Rules parties and arbitrators were not free or encouraged to adopt such a means. Since 1988 CIETAC has amended its rules four times, respectively 1988, 1994 1995 and 1998. But there have been no stipulations about pre-hearing conference in its rules.

May I point out that the Chinese language is the official language of the CIETAC.[15] The parties to the case didn't agree otherwise in their contract. If they had done so, their agreement should have prevailed. According to the 1994 Rules, the secretariat of the CIETAC may, if it deems it necessary, request the parties to hand in corresponding translation copies in Chinese language of the various documents and evidential materials submitted by the parties.[16] In light of this provision the Tribunal and SZF have the rights to require LPC to submit Chinese version of some documents such as LPC 's memorandum of law and some affidavits and exhibits. I would like to mention that when the Claimant submitted its revision, English translation of it was provided by its attorney Mr. Hu. Furthermore, CIETAC, Shenzhen engaged an interpreter for the parties at the hearing. The expense was RMB 3,000 shared by the parties. SZF bore two-thirds and LPC one-third.[17] Don 't neglect that it was the representatives and attorneys (except for a Chinese lawyer) of LPC that needed an interpreter more.

Now you could make your judgment whether the Tribunal had the parties in mind and tried to provide them with convenience and whether the parties were treated with equality. In fact the Respondent enjoyed more " privileges." But it turns out that the Respondent did not appreciate our "kindness." And it is natural that a losing party would not be ready to accept any negative result. With the help of lawyers, the business executives of the Respondent should have roughly predicated that result and then after receiving the Award they would treat it somewhat objectively and calmly. I do not think it was too harsh.

During the enforcement proceedings LPC holds that the amendment to the SZF 's claims at the hearing exceeded the authority of the Tribunal. LPC was seriously prejudiced by this last-minute amendment, since the amendment doubled the amount of SZF 's claims without any notice to LPC or meaningful opportunity to respond. The Tribunal was in favor of one party in this regard. In the action at law SZF only raises the question that the Tribunal accepted the documentary material submitted by LPC at the time of the hearing. But SZF does not mention the quantity of pages of the documentary evidence submitted by LPC at the time of the hearing, placing emphasis upon that it was of about 315 pages, and it was 4.9 times of the number of that submitted before the hearing. Why?

In dealing with the above-discussed matter, the members of the Tribunal did not have proper communication and coordination. I, being one member of them, won't shirk responsibility. Was it because we were unable to bridge over the gap of two languages and two cultures? But people all know that in the international commercial arbitration circle arbitrators have many common speeches. Nevertheless, I have to acknowledge that cooperation among the three arbitrators was not a successful one, up to our expectation. In spite of this, I would like to point out that that was a rare event in CIETAC. Furthermore, we could have had it done properly.

C. *Accusation Against the Tribunal of Collecting and Evaluating Its Own Evidence*

Mr. M, one of the agents of LPC at the arbitration, in his affidavit submitted to the United States District Judge states that during the arbitration hearing he discovered that the Tribunal had collected its own evidence regarding the parties' plywood transaction and LPC was not given an opportunity to comment on any of this evidence. LPC argues that it found out about the evidence allegedly collected from the independent investigation when it received the Award. "For example, the majority 's Award clearly provides that "[i]n the course of (the) hearing, the Arbitration Tribunal heeded the oral statements and arguments of both parties and did investigations."'[18] (Emphasis added)

Could the majority of the Tribunal go so far to pull the wool over the minority's eyes and privately undertake investigations outside and collect evidence on their own initiative? What a strange story from over the seas, namely a tall story! Anyone of our profession would judge that in arbitrating the instant case, the Tribunal did not need collect any evidence of its own.

Furthermore, I would like to quote a few lines to show the cooperation among the arbitrators of Chinese nationality and other nationalities. One of our colleagues who is an American says:

> I have had the pleasure of serving on the panel of CIETAC arbitrators since 1989, when CIETAC first appointed foreign parties to its panel, and I am pleased to report that my experiences as a foreign arbitrator have reinforced my respect for CIETAC. As a foreign arbitrator, I have been included fully in all aspect of each matter to which I was appointed, including all internal discussions involving other members of the appointed tribunal. While all of my experiences have been as the sole foreign arbitrator on the tribunal, I have at all time felt that my views were weighed equally with those of other arbitrators, and all procedural and substantive is- sues I have raised were handled diligently and conscientiously by the other arbitrators, with the full support of the secretariat where so required. I expect this will come as very good news for any foreign company which is concerned about issues of impartiality or which may wonder about the significance of the list of international arbitrators.[19]

Criticisms, suggestions to CIETAC, to its staff members and its arbitrators should be highly appreciated. I do not think that the foregoing accusation against the Tribunal was aimed at smearing the reputation of the Tribunal and CIETAC. We have enjoyed encouragement and proper appraisal from our colleagues the world over. For instance, one of our colleagues in London comments on CIETAC, saying "[i]f the place of arbitration is China then it is suggested that the choice should be the China International Economic and Trade Arbitration Commission: CIETAC enjoys a high international reputation."[20] And he also says, "Internationally, CIETAC is highly regarded. It is probably now the world 's busiest international commercial arbitral institution."[21]

Nevertheless, what is the reason for that accusation? I could not work out up to now how Mr. M during the hearing discovered that the Tribunal had collected its own evidence regarding the parties' plywood transaction. How and what could he read in the eyes and on the face of the arbitrators? As for the same accusation of LPC, I guess the trouble or misunderstanding was caused by the translation of a Chinese word "diaochao." It is used three times in the Award in Chinese original. I have thought "investigation" is the equivalent of it. The preface of the Award deals with the procedural matters, accounting that the Arbitration Tribunal heard the case in Shenzhen on December 10, 1994. "In the course of (the) hearing, the Arbitration Tribunal heeded the oral statements and arguments of both parties and did investigations." (Emphasis added)

One might not misunderstand the meaning of the word or phrase from the context. The Tribunal raises questions for the purpose to find out the how s and whys of the dispute. The parties are required to make responses. That is the course of doing investigations at the oral hearing. It does not mean that the Tribunal undertook investigations outside and collected evidence on its own initiative.

The second "diaochao" is used in the first sentence of the first paragraph of the Tribunal 's Opinion of the Award in Chinese original. In translation, I did not use its "exact equivalent." Instead, I had the meaning contained in the sentence "after carefully examining the written statements and evidential documents produced by both parties and listening to their oral statements and arguments, the Tribunal expresses its opinions.... "

The third is in the second item on the Tribunal's Opinions. I turned "tingshen diaochao" of Chinese into English as "[t]he investigation at (the) hearing."

An English version of a legal provision of a Chinese law with the word of "diaochao" is as follows:

> Court investigation shall be conducted in the following order:"

(1) statements by the parties;
(2) informing the witnesses of their rights and obligations, giving testimony by the witnesses and reading of the written statements of absent witnesses;
(3) presentation of documentary evidence, material evidence and audio-visual material;
(4) reading of expert conclusions; and
(5) reading of records of inspection.[22]

I am not sure whether the translation is accurate. I just want to say that it seems to me that "investigation" could also be done within the court. English is not my mother tongue. I have to consult an American dictionary.

"Investigate. To follow up step by step by patient inquiry or observation. To trace or track; to search into; to examine and inquire into with care and accuracy; to find out by careful inquisition; examination; the taking of evidence; a legal inquiry."[23]

If I do not wrongly understand, "investigation" could be conducted within a court. Still I regard my translation of "diaocha" as a lesson. There must be quite a few idiomatic ways to express the idea. If I had turned it this way "In the course of the oral hearing, the Tribunal conducts its own inquiries to verify evidence submitted by the parties," it would have been better. Or I'll follow a piece of advice of Mr. Kui-lem Lee, a solicitor of Hong Kong to express the idea in another way. "The

Tribunal inquires into the matter at the hearing." I suspect that must be a legal term and there would be no misunderstanding.

D. *The Majority of the Tribunal Exceeding Their Authority by Concluding that an Inspection in China Was Warranted to See the Quality of the Goods*

The documents are not in accordance with the terms and conditions of the credit and that results in the fundamental breach of the Contract by the LPC and unlimited damages it should bear. That is the key of the instant case and all the other factors are subordinate. SZF stresses the point by making a quotation "In credit operation all par- ties concerned deal in documents, and not in goods, services and/or other performances to which the documents may relate."[24] It sticks to this point from beginning to end, including in the action at law in America. The majority of the Tribunal could not negate the viewpoint of the Claimant. I believe the differences among the arbitrators should have been ironed out or at least could have been greatly narrowed.

The parties argue about the validity of the Certificate of Quality, the quality of the goods and the adoption of remedy measures for mitigating losses.[25] They must hold that their views were related to the dispute. The viewpoints should be mentioned in the Award. The Tribunal should make some comment on them. It discusses the questions, saying, "Though the inspection clause provides that the goods are inspected by APA, it doesn't provide that the inspection of APA is final. In light of Article 38 of CISG, unless there is a special provision between both parties, the buyer's right to have the goods inspected at the destination is not excluded."[26]

Concerning the argument about the quality of the goods, the Tribunal's viewpoint is "In this regard it is meaningless for both parties to argue whether the Certificate of Quality is effective or whether there is any defect in the quality of the goods."[27] The Tribunal only touches on the questions without concluding whether the goods are up to the standard.

E. *About the 'Fraudulent Faxes Fabricated by SZF'*

LPC holds that there was a lack of due process in the process in the arbitration. For instance, at the hearing SZF introduced a series of documents purporting to be faxes sent between LPC and to SZF. LPC had never seen these documents before the hearing and LPC strenuously objected to these documents on the basis that they appeared to be false, fraudulent documents prepared solely for the hearing. The majority opinion fails to discuss these documents. Under Article 54 of the 1994 Rules, the Tribunal was required to give the parties a "reasoned award."

Judge Gilmore concludes correctly in her Order, saying the Award was not procured through fraud. I would like to reiterate that the key to the case is a discrepancy in the documents. There are seven discrepancies. Five of them are of substantial nature.

In LPC's Objections and Answers to SZF's First Set of Interrogatories, LPC says "The Dissenting Opinion characterized the new documents offered by SZF at the hearing as 'manufactured.' The majority's opinion fails to discuss these documents. Under Article 54 of the 1994 Rules, the Tribunal was required to give the parties a 'reasoned award.' Nevertheless although the Award never justifies the use of these documents, the documents necessarily had a substantial impact on the principal Award rendered against LPC, US$270,216.88 for losses related to the alleged resale."[28]

I should frankly admit that as a party had held that some contentions or documents were related to the case, the Tribunal should have made response in the Award, no matter how brief it would be.

F. ***The Drafting of the Award***

After the hearing and receiving the additional documents of both parties, the author of this article, following the advice of the presiding arbitrator, commenced to draft the Award. For Mr. K.'s sake, I first draft it in English. Respecting our co-arbitrator, I first only drafted the factual part of the Award, the statement of the facts and the parties' contentions. While transferring the additional documents of the parties, the secretary informed Mr. K. of the matter on February 27, 1995.[29] On March 31, 1995, the secretary sent the draft factual part of the Award to Mr. K.,[30] asking him to draft the Tribunal's opinion and decision. On April 19 of the same year, the secretary faxed Mr. K., reminding him that according to the Article 52 of the 1994 Rules the Award should be issued before or on June 22, 1995, hoping that he could have his opinion expressed by the end of the coming May.[31] On the May 17 Mr. K. posted to the secretary a corrected copy of the factual part of the Award together with his observations on the merits of the dispute.[32] Contrary to expectation, between the majority and the minority there were differences in principle. The majority had to put forward their own observations.

As the divergence appeared, the Tribunal had to request CIETAC to postpone the time limit to August 22, 1995, and promptly informed the parties of that.[33]

When Mr. K. received the draft substantive conclusions of the majority in English, he on August 17, 1995, by fax wrote to the presiding arbitrator, saying that he was "[u]nable to agree with the decision of the majority in this case and I enclose a brief dissenting opinion which I would be grateful if you would append to the majority award."[34] The majority and the minority failed to come to a consensus. According to the provisions in the 1994 Rules, the Award was decided by the majority and it was written in Chinese.[35] An English translation was provided to the parties and Mr. K.

After rendering the Award, the presiding arbitrator on August 25, 1995, wrote Mr. K., saying, "In our practice, the opinions of dissenting arbitrators are docked into the file other than the awards. So, your written opinion is kept in the case file in accordance with Article 55 of the 1994 Rules."[36] Mr. K. wrote to the presiding arbitrator, strongly requiring that we have his opinion sent to the parties, otherwise he would send it to the parties by himself.

"Where a case is heard by an arbitration tribunal of three arbitrators, the arbitration award shall be decided by the majority of the arbitrators and the minority opinion can be written in the record and docketed into the file...."[37] This provision has been in the Rules of CIETAC since 1956.[38] Many of my colleagues don 't think that is a good provision. In our mind it is out of date. We hold that the minority opinion could and should be recorded in the award so that the parties could have easy access to the different views of different arbitrators. Quite a few of us have had such experience as a minority in a three-member tribunal. Once I was the minority in a Tribunal. I argued with my co-arbitrators and sent my dissent opinions in writing several times to the secretary of the Tribunal and she would pass them to the other two arbitrators in Beijing. I did not sign the award. Having received the award, the attorneys of the respondent that had appointed me came to my office two times, urging me to reveal my opinions about the issues. The first time they came in January 1997. The attorneys (now worked for the defendant in an action at law) came again in April 1998 when I returned from abroad after an absence of more than a year. But I had to decline to answer.

Being one arbitrator on a CIETAC Panel and a member of a particular tribunal, you have to follow the Rules, but you have the right or duty to level constructive criticisms at the Rules and advance suggestions. We did send Mr. K.'s opinion to the parties, braving potential criticisms or misunderstandings with calm and confidence. It was mainly because of the words in the last paragraph of the Dissenting Opinion. I am going to say a few more words about that later. I don't think it was fair to SZF. It is provided in the 1994 Rules that "Once the parties agrees to submit their dispute to the Arbitration Commission for arbitration, it shall be deemed that they have agreed to con—duct the arbitration under these Rules."[39] Did the Tribunal comply with the 1994 Rules particularly Article 7 and Article 55 in this regard?

G. *About the Accusations of the Accepted False Documents, Lack of Due Process, Manifest Disregard of the Law, an Unauthorized Third Party Presenting at the Hearing and the Claimant's Attorneys Fees*

Dealing with allegations of the Tribunal's acceptance of some false documents manufactured by SZF, and the Award violating due process and being in manifest disregard of the law, the exposition of Judge Gilmore is so brilliant. I should say no more.

Let me try from another angle to view the aforesaid issues and the matter of an unauthorized third party presenting at the hearing and the affair of the Claimant's attorneys fees. If the Tribunal had handled more thoroughly and properly, having the handling process recorded in writing, in tape and in the Award, I suppose the natural justice would have been better reflected.

Now summing up our experience, a document titled Procedural Matters Needing Attention was promulgated within CIETAC last year. It is provided that when commencing a hearing, a presiding arbitrator or a sole arbitrator should first explain how the tribunal is formed and ask whether any party has a challenge to any arbitrator. The presiding arbitrator or sole arbitrator should check the identities and authorities of the agents and ask whether a party has doubt about that of anybody in the hearing room. A tribunal should make sure whether any party has objections to the effect of the arbitration agreement between the parties and the arbitration rules under which the arbitration is conducted. During the hearing, a tribunal should ensure that the parties are treated equally and that each party has the right to be heard and is given a fair opportunity to present its case. A tribunal is to see to it that evidence is examined at the hearing or parties give up their right to examine. The stipulation in the Arbitration Law of PRC must be followed that the parties shall have the right to carry on debate. At the end of the debate, the presiding arbitrator or the sole arbitrator shall solicit final opinions from the parties,[40] even if the tribunal cannot decide yet whether there will be a further hearing.

The aforesaid requirements or measures have been the standards of CIETAC.[41] In my practice, as there is no period of time fixed for submitting documents or further written statements, at the end of the first hearing, I always consult with both parties and then decide or rather we agree upon a deadline by which the parties shall present any additional statements. Then the right to due process of parties would be better safeguarded. If the Tribunal had handled the case that way, most or even all the allegations against the Tribunal in enforcing the Award would have been obviously groundless.

I have found an inspiration from a brilliant exposition by one of our colleagues. "The beauty about procedure is that no harm is done until an award is rendered that is affected by a procedural mistake. If you make a mistake, that is not the end. You are not on a tightrope. If a party thinks that you went wrong, it will often tell you spontaneously. You should even encourage the parties to tell you if they believe you committed a procedural mistake, say, at the end of each hearing day (emphasis added). Procedural mistakes can almost always be rectified on the spot. You can re-establish the balance between the parties. You can reopen reasonable opportunity for a party to present its case."[42]

I still remember vividly. At the hearing the parties were angry with each other because the revision of the claims of Claimant was done only a few days before and the large quantity of documents presented by the Respondent on the spot. If it could be regarded as a procedural mistake, the Tribunal missed the chance to have it rectified on the spot. Or it may say that particular mistake could not be rectified this way. The Tribunal should have made appropriate adaptation in the light of specific conditions. We should have delayed the hearing to the next day or had the hearing lasted to or resumed on the next day, so that the parties would get time to study each other's revised claims and added documents. One more way, the Tribunal should have held one more hearing which would provide it with a chance to re-establish balance between the parties and to solicit the final statements from the parties or re-open reasonable opportunity for a party to present its case.

Some more words about the issue about the SZF attorneys ' fees. LPC complains that it was denied due process (1) because of the award of attorney 's fees and (2) because the Tribunal allegedly gathered "evidence" not disclosed to LPC until it received the majority 's opinion.[43] SZF 's attorneys in the action at law retort as follows:

> Article 59 (of 1994 Rules) provides that the tribunal may award attorney fees up to 10% of the total amount awarded to the winning party. The Tribunal awarded 10%. The concept of contingency fees based on a percentage of the dam - ages is not unheard of. Certainly the Tribunal had evidence, as did LPC, that attorneys were working on the case and that their efforts were substantial, since these attorneys appeared before the Tribunal (emphasis added — he author of this article). SZF included a request for attorneys ' fees in its claim for

damages. In the prayer of its statement of defense submitted to the Tribunal on September 24, 1994, LPC sought 'that the Claimant 's claims be dismissed, and all costs and expenses of this proceeding including attorneys ' fees... ' Award, at 10 (emphasis added). LPC knew that attorneys fees had been requested and had an opportunity to address this is- sue further during the arbitration process if it had chosen to do so.[44]

The aforesaid quotation is very plain; namely the argument is in simple language. On cursory examination, one may judge that SZF 's attorneys in the action at law were reasoning fallaciously. As a matter of fact, their argument is reasonable. Let us review Article 59, it goes:

The arbitration tribunal has the power to determine to rule in the arbitral award that the losing party shall pay the winning party as compensation a portion of the expenses rea- son ably incurred by the winning party in dealing with the case. The amount of such compensation shall not in any case exceed 10% of the total amount awarded to the winning party.[45]

I consulted some secretaries at CIETAC, Shenzhen, whom I always regarded as arbitration experts. Some of them hold that the original intention or meaning of Article 59 is to empower a tribunal to use its discretion. No doubt an arbitration or a lawsuit cost a winning party some money. Arbitrators or parties concerned should not misunderstand. In this regard, documentary evidence is less important.

H. *Some More Words About the Work and Cooperation of the Co-Arbitrators and the Rules of CIETAC*

Everyone in the circle of international commercial arbitration knows very well, that "All arbitrators should devote such time and attention as the parties may reasonably require, having regard to the circumstances of the case, and shall do their best to conduct the arbitration."[46]

The three arbitrators respectively resided in Hong Kong and Shenzhen, which are neighboring cities with only a small boundary river in between. It had been very convenient for the residents of Hong Kong to come to Shenzhen. But a Shenzhen resident must get a special permission after going through some formalities and only after that could he go to Hong Kong with a pass. Before the hearing, the arbitrator residing in Hong Kong should have come a bit early to have a meeting with his co-arbitrators. After the hearing there should have been a discussion or more among the three arbitrators. If we had done so, some problems might have been avoided or settled. Divergences might have been narrowed or even eliminated. English was the mother tongue of one of the three; there would have been a good English version of the Award.

My co-arbitrators were veteran ones, I felt highly honored to work with them. Being a member of the Tribunal, I might have suggested or urged some discussion among the three arbitrators after the hearing in Shenzhen.

No matter how convenient or effective the electronic communication means are, such as telephone, fax, even hot line and e-mail, they could not substitute the meeting of people. The effect of two meetings of two arbitrators of a tribunal is not equal to that of one plenary session of the tribunal.

Moreover, my co-arbitrator. K. says in the last paragraph of his Dissent Opinion, that his co-arbitrators did not give the Respondent an opportunity to comment on the issue of Claimant's expenses. Did Mr. K. mention that problem to his co-arbitrators during the hearing and talk about this problem with his co-arbitrators in the hour's break for lunch? Did he point out that mistake to the presiding arbitrator after the hearing and suggest that the Tribunal should hold a hearing more for the purpose of rectifying the procedural mistake, re-establishing the balance between the parties and re-opening reasonable opportunity for LPC to present its case? Did the Tribunal lose an opportunity to rectify the mistake due to the turning down of his suggestion by his co-arbitrators? I had no idea but felt disappointed about that.

I have gained some enlightenment from the practice and experience of our colleagues of another permanent arbitral institute. Last December, CIETAC, Shenzhen, received a letter from the chairman of an international arbitration under the auspices of the International Chamber of Commerce (ICC) in Paris. He says in the letter that the other arbitrators in the arbitration are a professor of China University of Politics and Law in Beijing and a lawyer of a law firm in Washington D.C. One of the parties in the arbitration is a Chinese company domiciled in Shenzhen whilst the other is a US corporation. The tribunal schedules a site visit at the Chinese party 's production facility in Shenzhen. In connection with the site visit, the tribunal also schedules a hearing where some of the witnesses in the arbitration will be heard by the tribunal. The chairman inquires whether it would be possible for the tribunal to conduct the witness hearings in the facilities at CIETAC, Shenzhen. He says that the site visit and witness hearings are scheduled in the week January 11-16, 1999. He estimates that possible hearings could commence on January 12 and possibly last until January 16. The three arbitrators and their administrative secretary arrived in Shenzhen on January 10.

I had met the chairman seven years before in Guangzhou and made acquaintance of the Chinese professor in December 1997 in the University of Canberra. When I got to know that they were in a hotel, I initially called them up, saying hello to them. At that time they were engaged in further studying of the case. They told me that the tribunal had drawn up a document as terms of reference and established a provisional procedural timetable before the first hearing held in Stockholm, after the hearings in Shenzhen they would finally decide the date and place of the third hearing. The hearing actually lasted three days (January 12 through January 14, 1999).

One can see that the parties were from different countries, the three arbitrators were of different cultural backgrounds and from different countries, which are far away from one another; the time and energy that the three arbitrators devoted to the case were sufficient. It seems to me that the co-arbitrators had good cooperation. In fact, commercial arbitrators of different nationalities have a tradition of good coordination in dealing with international disputes.

It should be provided in the CIETAC Rules that an arbitrator "[m]ay conduct a preparatory conference with the parties for the purpose of organizing, scheduling and agreeing to procedures to expedite the subsequent proceedings."[47] To be more explicit, a tribunal should be delegated more power and shoulder more responsibility. It is revealed that recently the secretariat of CIETAC has a practice where the secretariat would draw up a document defining the main points for the hearing (tingshen yaodian) signed by the parties. It is in nature a list of issues to be determined. The signing of the document would serve as a confirmation of the jurisdiction of CIETAC and the formation of the tribunal. The document would be an effective measure to speed up the subsequent proceedings.[48] It must be similar to the practice of drawing up a document defining its terms of references and a document of a provisional timetable by a tribunal and signed by the parties and the tribunal provided in the ICC Rules of Arbitration (1998).[49] I have no idea why that has not been provided for in the 1998 Rules of CIETAC. An amendment to the CIETAC Rules should have been done on the basis of absorbing more opinions and wisdom of our colleagues.

6 Conclusion

After going through [95] Shen Guo Zhong Jie Zi No. 91 Award, most our colleagues, I believe, would see eye to eye with the majority of the Tribunal. But it is not a perfect one. The preface of the Award does not accurately reflect what the process was. Some argument should have been mentioned. We had other shortcomings while dealing with the arbitration. The lessons that should be gained from this case are as follows:

A. ***The Communication Among the Co-Arbitrators***

Before a hearing, more time, at least half a day should be arranged for a meeting of the arbitrators to draw up a provisional timetable. During a hearing, when there is some unexpected event, a recess should be arranged for discussion to reach an consensus. After a hearing, co-arbitrators should exchange ideas about the case. The drafting of an award should be based upon a thorough discussion or some debate. The discussion usually should be done at some plenary session of the tribunal.

B. ***Procedural Matters***

When commencing the first hearing, a tribunal should as mentioned above first tell the parties how it is formed and ask whether any party has any challenge to any arbitrator. The status and authority of the representatives or agents should be checked and the tribunal should inquire whether any doubt exists. The tribunal should make sure that evidence is examined. Before closing of the hearing, the tribunal shall solicit final opinions from the parties; namely the parties make their last statements.

C. ***Hearing***

In dealing with an international case of large size and complexity, a tribunal holding a preparatory conference with the parties is a good way. Drawing up terms of reference and procedural timetable with the parties is proper. As there is somewhat good preparation beforehand, the tribunal should direct the parties to focus the presentations on the terms of reference. More days or more hearings should be planned.

D. *The Constitution of a Tribunal*

For an international commerce arbitration, when the parties fail to jointly appoint the third arbitrator, namely the presiding arbitrator, they should jointly or respectively specify the conditions of a prospective arbitrator such as the nationality or his/her specialty. Under similar circumstances, the Chairman of CIETAC should consider the nationality and had better appoint an arbitrator whose nationality is different from the parties and his/her two co-arbitrators.

E. *The Independent Status of an Arbitrator and His/Her Team Spirit*

Being a member of a tribunal, you are of independent status, subjected to no co-arbitrator. You, however, should attach importance to teamwork among your co-arbitrators. If you find out any procedural mistake committed by your co-arbitrators, or any problem of the tribunal in handling the case, you are obligated to point it out timely and join hands with your co-arbitrators to have it rectified.

Notes

1. In the United States District Court Southern District of Texas Houston Division, Shenzhen Foodstuff-Drinks Industrial Import and Export Company v. Louisiana–Pacific Corporation, Cause No. H-96-3188, unpublished, herein after referred to as Cause No. H-96-3188.
2. United Nations Convention on Contracts for the International Sale of Goods.
3. In the Order of Cause No. H-96-3188, the honorable judge uses "panel" that is equal to "tribunal," I suppose. For the sake of consistence and easy understanding, I use "Tribunal" instead of "panel" in this article.
4. An arbitration under the jurisdiction of CIETAC is handled independently and impartially by a particular tribunal. If there is any problem or error concerning process or any category, it is the tribunal, the author of this article believes, that should bear the responsibility but not the institution CIETAC.
5. See CIETAC, Shenzhen Files No. 490–1, p. 035.
6. Id., pp. 036–039.
7. Id., pp. 040–043 and pp. 074—077.
8. For the documents issuing procedures of CIETAC, Shenzhen, please consult the Stylization and Regularization of the Management and Operation of the Chinese Arbitration Institute by Huang Yan ming, the author of this article, Huang is his family name, 11, J. Int. Arb. 2, June, 1994, pp. 77–98.
9. Id. pp. 042–043 and p.075, and see Article 24 of the 1994 Rules.
10. See Article 19 of the 1994 Rules.
11. About the function and duty of the secretariat, please see Article 11 of the 1994 Rules.
12. See CIETAC, Shenzhen Files No.490–1, pp85-86.
13. See Plaintiff's Supplemental Response to Defendant's Motion for Summary Judgment, Cause No. H-96-3188.

14. David M. Heilbron, the Arbitration Clause, the Preliminary Conference, and the Big Case, Arbitration Journal, American Arbitration Association, June 1990, Vol. 45, No. 2. pp. 38–44. And See Commercial Arbitration Rules (CAR) of the AAA (as Amended and in Effect January 1,1990) § 10.
15. See Article 75 Of the 1994 Rules.
16. Id.
17. See CIETAC, Shenzhen Files No. 490–1, p. 087 and p. 093.
18. Files of Cause No. H-96-3188.
19. Sally A. Harpole, A Perspective on CIETAC Arbitration, China International Commercial Arbitration Yearbook (1993–1994), p. 158.
20. Anthony Connerty, Trade with China: How and Where Disputes Can Be Resolved, Arbitration, the Journal of the Chartered Institute of Arbitrators, Vol. 64, No. 2, pp. 129–136, May, 1998.
21. Id.
22. Article 124 of the Civil Procedure Law of the People's Republic of China, Handbook of Foreign Economic Law Publishing House of Law, China, p. 124.
23. The Black's Law Dictionary, Fifth Edition, p. 740.
24. Article 4, UCP.
25. See [95]Shen Guo Zhong Jie Zi No.91 Award, at pp. 13–14.
26. Id. at p. 20.
27. Id. at pp. 20–21.
28. See Files of Cause No. H-96-3188.
29. See Files of CIETAC, Shenzhen No. 490-I, p. 094.
30. Id., p. 095.
31. Id., p. 096.
32. Id., p. 101.
33. See Files of CIETAC, Shenzhen No. 490–1, pp. 104–107 and Article 53 of the 1994 Rules.
34. See Files of CIETAC, Shenzhen No. 490–1, pp. 030–033.
35. See Article 55 and 75 of the 1994 Rules.
36. See Files of CIETAC, Shenzhen No. 490–1, p. 034.
37. Article 55 of the 1994 Rules. And that provision almost remains unchanged in the Article 54, Section 1 of the 1998 Rules, which are effective as from May 10, 1998.
38. See Article 29 of the 1956 Rules, Article 33 of the 1988 Rules and Article 54 of the 1995 Rules of CIETAC.
39. Article 9 of the 1994 Rules.
40. Article 47 of the Arbitration Law of P.R.C.
41. Procedural Matters Needing Attention of CIETAC.
42. Dr. Pierre A. Karrer, Don't be Afraid — A Pep Talk, Arbitration, the Journal of the Chartered Institute of Arbitrators, Vol. 65, No.1, February 1999, pp. 24–25.
43. See LPC's Motion for Summary Judgement, at pp. 18–19, Files of Cause No. H-90-3188.
44. See Plaintiff' s Supplemental Response to Defendant's Motion For Summary Judgment, at p. 11, Files of Cause No. H-90-3188.
45. This article is not amended in the 1995 Rules and 1998 Rules.
46. Article 7 of the Ethics for International Arbitrators, International Bar Association.
47. Article 16–2 of the International Arbitration Rules of the American Arbitration Association (1997).
48. See Bulletin of the Arbitration Research Institute, China Chamber of International Commerce, Vol. 6, No.1, March 11, 1999, p. 5.
49. See Article 18 of ICC Rules of Arbitration (1998).

Part III
Legal Issues Relating to Absence and Potential Risks and Costs

Outlines

Through the analysis of specific cases, the author touches on some respects of some **permanent arbitration institutions** The primary objective is to **urge parties to take arbitration agreements seriously**, cautioning against **casually denying their validity or refusing to participate in arbitration proceedings**—actions that could result in loss **of rights and severe financial consequences**.

This commentary emphasizes that, in the **international arbitration community**, an arbitration agreement—whether incorporated within the main contract or separately signed—is fundamentally treated as a **contract** in itself. Parties are expected to **honor their commitments**. When a case falls under the jurisdiction of a permanent arbitration institution, once the arbitration proceedings commence and the **notice of arbitration** is serviced or received, the respondent should not reject the appointment of an arbitrator, refuse to submit a defense, or decline to appear at the hearing. Participation is both a **contractual right and an obligation**. A **defaulting party who loses the case is not only in breach of the main contract but also in violation of the arbitration agreement**, constituting a **double breach**—breaching both the main contract and the arbitration agreement itself.

Irrational Approaches to Arbitration: A Cautionary Case Study

This chapter also references a case from the early 1990s that drew significant attention from the Chinese arbitration community:

Revpower Ltd. v. The Shanghai Far-East Aero-Technology Import and Export Corporation, an international commercial dispute of relatively modest monetary value that was arbitrated abroad.

In a striking **miscalculation**, the Chinese respondent initially appointed a **foreign arbitrator**, resulting in a three-member arbitral tribunal composed **entirely of foreign arbitrators**. The fact should be stressed that the proper law of the case under discussion was Chinese law. The respondent then **refused to participate in the proceedings** and, in an astonishing move, attempted to submit the dispute to an **Intermediate People's Court in Shanghai**.

Upon reviewing the arbitral award, the author discovered a **highly concerning issue**: there were **nine different versions of the timeline of dispute initiation**. Despite this inconsistency, the arbitral award ordered the respondent to pay **twenty times** the amount originally stipulated in the disputed contract. As a consequence, the respondent was **forced into bankruptcy**.

This case serves as a **stark reminder** that when drafting contracts and arbitration clauses, parties should **not rely solely on the reputation of an arbitration institute** as the deciding factor. Similarly, once arbitration has commenced, the **reputation of the candidate of an arbitrator alone should not dictate a party's approach to the proceedings**.

Cases such as this remain vivid examples of **the risks of disregarding arbitration obligations**. Although they may belong to the past, the **lessons they embody must be revisited and remembered** by future parties to arbitration.

Legal Issues on Absence of a Party at the Hearing

1 Introduction

In the past decodes, while being a secretary or a case manager of some permanent arbitration institutions, I assisted many arbitral tribunals to deal with procedural affairs relating to cases conducted by the tribunals. Also as a member in three-arbitrator tribunals or a sole arbitrator of single-arbitrator tribunals, I sat to hear various foreign-related and domestic cases. In some of these cases and despite the fact that the notice of arbitration with the hearing date(s) and all the arbitral documents had been duly served and every stage of the arbitral proceedings had been notified by the secretariat of a permanent arbitration institution or the secretaries appointed by the secretariat to tribunals, the respondents failed or refused to attend the hearing and/or did not submit to the tribunals written representations and evidence so as to defend their cases against the claimants. Some respondents would keep silent form the commencement to the end of the arbitral proceedings.

Since a defaulting party makes no response at all and before a tribunal is formed, the secretariat of the permanent arbitration institutions (mainly means CIETAC and SCIA) and the secretary appointed for the tribunal-to-be are under heavier psychological pressure as he/she would always worry that various arbitration notices and documents might not have been properly serviced or might be deemed as not properly serviced in the future, and therefore he/she would be forced to be more prudential with the affairs relating to service of all the notices and documents, ensuring that the principle of due process is fulfilled. And after the tribunal is formed, the tribunal would share the worries and anxieties with the permanent arbitration institution, the

☆This commentary was published in Meraley's International Arbitration Report, Vol. 28, # 12 December 2013, pp.19–49.

The author is grateful to Dr. T. C. Foo of Liu, Choi and Chen (Solicitors and Notaries), solicitor and notary public and China-appointed attesting officer located in Hong Kong for his valuable advice, without his guidance, this article would not be in this form.

Y. Huang, *Commentaries on Commercial Arbitration in Modern China*, Modern China and International Economic Law, https://doi.org/10.1007/978-981-95-0168-7_4

secretary, and the case manager mentioned above. They would worry that without any response from a defaulting respondent would leave room or (potential) possibilities for the losing respondent and for a people's court on the pretext that there have been some defects in the proceedings, therefore refusing to enforce or setting aside the final award. For the purpose of proper service, generally, the arbitration correspondence would be sent to the respondent or one of the respondents more than one time and would at last to the addressee's last known place of business, registration, domicile, and habitual residence or mailing address after reasonably and repeatedly inquiring. In a word, it is troublesome.

If you are an outsider, or even if you are a legal professional and you are familiar with commercial arbitration in other legal jurisdictions, you would hardly have the similar feeling.

In my practice, I have seldom come across that the default by a party mainly by the respondent or one of the respondents would paralyze the progress of the arbitral proceedings, but objectively speaking, in most of such cases and such proceedings, the default of a party would slow or even greatly delay the progress of the proceedings.

In my professional career, I know that I am of very limited knowledge and scanty information, I have never run across any comments on the legal issue relating to the omission of a defaulting party by any arbitrator or any tribunals in his or their awards rendered in the respondent's absence.[1] Most colleagues believe that the respondent's failing to appear at an oral hearing or refusing to participate in any arbitration proceedings is of waiving its right only. He is under no legal duty to take part in arbitration proceedings. Or the parties to the arbitration would hold that the participation is not mandatory.

I myself up to June 2013 in the capacity of an arbitrator in my arbitral awards had never made any comments on the negative act of a party absent from arbitral proceedings.

In an award, should an arbitrator or a tribunal make any comments on the act or omission of a defaulting party? Is a respondent's failing or refusing to appear at an oral hearing or even the whole arbitration proceedings of a case neither a legal issue nor related to the moral dimension of contract in our contemporary society? Should the act or omission of a defaulting respondent be deemed not within the claims of a claimant or not within the scope of the disputes between or among the parties, therefore which should not be commented on, criticized, condemned, or even touched? Is an arbitrator or a tribunal given power or authority to comment on any respect of the absence of a party, or is that or not at the discretion of an arbitrator or a tribunal?

Some of my respected colleagues who are senior and experienced solicitors or other legal professionals from common law countries or regions, might have no such feeling or experience as I, an arbitrator located in a developing country, have got, and they might not be able to share or understand. They might not agree with my viewpoints above and below and those points of views of some colleagues within the commercial arbitration circle form whom I have been making quotations below, for the purpose of trying to support and strengthen my arguments. Most of the legal professionals from developed common law jurisdictions believe and hold that being a judge or an arbitrator, when facing the situation that a respondent is absent from some hearing, just following the provisions of the applying procedure law and arbitration rules, there would be no trouble at all. Further, some of them are of the view that an arbitration clause contained in a contract amounting to no contract.

The different views of those legal professionals from common law jurisdiction of developed countries and regions have enlightened me and have caused me to examine the absent events of respondents in the arbitral proceedings from some other angels. I would try to examine the absence of a respondent from the perspective of a Chinese arbitrator and the perspective other than an arbitrator.

I grew in China. Being a commercial arbitrator, I have been in quite different social-cultural, political, and legal environment from those, for example, solicitors or arbitrators located in developed common law countries or regions.

Simply put, in the mainland of China, though people and legal professionals might expect that a bright prospect is in store for us, judicial independence is somewhat distant ahead. China is on her way to the rule of law.

Chinese citizens, when they come across or suffer unjust treatment or decisions or hear about and talk about the similar phenomena or events they would frequently joke and complain that the Chinese character "guan" (official) consists of "two mouths",[2] vividly describing and reflecting the structure of the lower part of the character and simultaneously vesting the structure of the character with some satirical function. That implies that officials have the last say in deciding some matters under the jurisdiction of them or even beyond their authority or duties and some of them would sometimes not abide by any procedure rules, instead they are used to abusing power on some pretext or even at liberty not deal with matters in line with existing rules. I was delighted with what President Xi Jinping of China said on January 22, 2013, to put power into the cage. I suppose that is to say to strengthen the balance and check and supervise the operation of power.

We arbitrators would be always on our guard against leaving any room or any grounds or any opportunity that an award would be set aside or annulled or refused to enforce by a people's court. Further a people's court in China is entitled to notify a tribunal for a new award within a certain limit of time.[3] There is some cases below that the tribunals were required to have a re- arbitration.

And I myself as a presiding arbitrator with my co-arbitrators some years ago handled a foreign-related case under the jurisdiction of Huizhou Arbitration Commission. The award of majority opinion in favor of the claimant, a Hong Kong natural person, was directly set aside or annulled by the Huizhou Municipality Intermediate People' Court. The judges might have overlooked that the case was foreign-related and according to a judicial interpretation document issued by the Supreme People's Court of PRC ("Supreme Court"),[4] only the Supreme Court has the last say in denying the validity of an award of a foreign-related case. What a pity! The lawyer of the claimant was unable to make a defense on the provisions of the judicial document above. I am to have an article specially based on this case.

Now before dealing with the aspects on the subject of this article, I am to give some examples of final awards of CIETAC, showing the twisted fate of some awards beyond your imagination.

2 Part One: The Long And Twist Course of the Winning Parties' Application for Enforcement of Some Awards of CIETAC

I. Case One: A (A Company Located In Shenzhen), B (A Trust Investment Corporation Located In Yinchuan Of Linxia Hui Autonomous Region) And C (An Electronic Company Located In Shenzhen) V. Matsue (Matsue Limited Located In Hong Kong)

For saving space, I would give no details of the case but outline some events and their respective times relating to the case and the award and drop down some comments.

In April, 2001, Shenzhen Overseas Chinese News had the event relating to the case as the headlines; the coverage revealed that when the enforcement of the final award was suddenly suspended, the national and some local federations of the returned overseas Chinese and their legal advisory committees strongly expressed their different opinions and closely followed the development of the case. Readers would have access to the case.[5] A long commentary titled Irrational Challenges to the Finality of an Arbitral Award—Analyzing Some Issues Arising from the Course of Enforcing (96) Maozhong Caizi No. 0271 Award ("Irrational Challenges") based on the case by me was published in 2002.[6] And I got some materials more in 2011.

1. Some Material Times and Events Relating to the Case

In June 17, 1989, a foreign-related joint venture of three parties producing mini-soft disks was established in Shenzhen, Guangdong Province.

On December 9, 1989, A, B, C and Matsue joined the joint venture to substitute the original equity partners. The members of the Matsue were returned overseas Chinese from Indonesia in 1970s and ever since have resided in Hong Kong.

On October 5, 1992, upon the request, department concerned under the Shenzhen Municipality Government allowed Matsue to withdraw from the joint venture and it would be substituted by a company from the United States. But it was not the intention of Matsue and it was not aware of the matter as the fact was not previously revealed to it. It was ridiculous.

In September 1994, A, B and C, as the claimants, according to the arbitration clause contained in the joint venture contract referred the disputes to CIETAC with Matsue as the respondent, claiming that Matsue was in breach of the joint venture contract and requiring the tribunal-to-be to award that Matsue should pay the claimants the liquidated damages USD69,000.00. Matsue filed a counter-claim requesting to terminate the joint venture contract and refund its investment USD2, 000,000.00.

On September 6, 1994, CIETAC accepted the case (numbered V94574) referred by the three mainland partners.

On July 30, 1996, the award as (96) No.0271 ("Award 0271") was issued in favor of Matsue, and the main decision was that the three claimants should refund Matsue the sum of USD1,600,000.00, the sum of price paid by Matsue for the joint-venture to import equipments, plus the interest on the principal.

From July 1997 to December 2000, the losing parties the three claimants tried all means to deny the validity of the Award 0271, challenging the finality of it.

In October 2000, after the denying the challenges by the three losing parties, the Shenzhen Court adopted some acts to seal up and freeze over 10 million corporate shares of the A, B and C.

In November 2000, the enforcement carried out by the Shenzhen Court was suspended.

2. **The Challenges to the Validity of Award 0271 And the Damage to the Justice And to the Private Right of the Winning Party by the Abuse of Public Power**

A. **The First Challenge**

On July 29, 1997, after receipt of an application for cancellation (annulment) of the Award from the three claimants, the Second Intermediate People's Court of Beijing ("Beijing Court") informed CIETAC, holding that according to the provisions of Art 70 of the Arbitration Law of the PRC that the award involved one of the circumstances prescribed in Paragraph 1, Art 260 of the Civil Procedure Law of PRC, the tribunal should re-arbitrate the case. I take it as the first challenge to the finality of the award.

On June 30, 1998, the three-member tribunal, after an oral hearing on December 30, 1997, rendered an award again (without re-numbered), holding that the further submissions by the three claimants would not effect the Award 0271 at all. The arbitrators affirmed the original Award 0271.

B. **The Second Challenge**

Upon receiving the Award issued through re-arbitration proceedings affirming the original Award 0271, Matsue applied Shenzhen Court for enforcing the Award 0271 (including the Award affirmed it). The Shenzhen Court had the jurisdiction because two of the losing parties to the case had assets in Shenzhen.

On October 16, 1998, A and C submitted an application to the Shenzhen Court for not enforcing the Award. They mainly relied on the grounds:

(1) There was no arbitration clause in the contract (the contract according to which Matsue paid the price of USD1,6000,00.00 to buy the equipments for the joint-venture, that contract should not be regarded as an attachment to the joint venture contract);
(2) The procedure was not in line with the Arbitration Rules of 1994 of CIETAC, Art 18 which provided that any counterclaim should be filed within 60 days from the date of receipt of the Notice of Arbitration. Matsue did not file its counterclaim within the time-limit;
(3) The tribunal was beyond its authority, dealing with matters of infringement or tort acts that were out of the scope of the arbitration agreement or the limits of authority of an arbitration institution, and;
(4) The Award rendered after the re-arbitration procedure had not been served to the claimants.

On December 30, 1998, the collegial bench of the Shenzhen Court, after an oral hearing on November 11, rendered a **final ruling**, rejecting the application of the applicants. The legal fee was RMB50.00, borne by the applicants. Fifty RMB yuan, a challenging chance would only cast the losing parties. It is unbelievable!

C. The Third Challenge

Before the ruling above was rendered, B as the applicant filed an application on the same grounds to the Shenzhen Court for not enforcing the said Award. The collegiate bench consisted of the same judges rendered a **final ruling**, rejecting the application of B. The legal fee was RMB50.00, borne by B. Again Fifty RMB yuan would have enabled one of the losing parties to have a chance to make a challenge. Believe it or not!

D. The Forth Challenge

After the receipt of the said two **final rulings** by the parties, A, Band C applied the Beijing Court for setting aside the Award, because CIETAC resided in Beijing, therefore the Beijing Court had the jurisdiction.

On February 4, 2000, the Beijing Court in its **final ruling** rejected the application of the applicants mainly on the grounds that the said Award was not about a domestic case, but the reasons given by the applicants were applied to a domestic one but not a foreign-related case (from the viewpoint of private international law). Further the collegial bench revealed that the applicants did not based on the grounds that the Award involved was one of the circumstances prescribed in Paragraph 1, Art 260 of the Civil Procedure Law of P RC. The legal fee of RMB30,000.00 was borne by the losing applicants. That sum was 60 times of that the losing parties had to spend and bear in the proceedings before the Shenzhen Court.

Actually there were some challenges more to the finality of the Award 0271. From June to September 2000, the losing parties referred the case to the Yinchuan Intermediate People's Court of Linxia Hui Autonomous Region. Thus the Higher People's Court of the Region was also involved.

E. An Interior Letter Form the Supreme Adjudicatory Agency to the Shenzhen Court

In October 2000, after denying the challenges by the three losing parties, the Shenzhen Court adopted some acts to seal up and freeze over 10 million corporate shares of the A, B and C.

In November 2000, the enforcement carried out by the Shenzhen Court was suspended because it received an "Interior Letter (Restricted Document)" from an office of the Supreme Court, instructing the Shenzhen Court not to enforce the Award 0271 anymore.

The final Award 0271, being confirmed by an award of the re-arbitration proceeding and its validity also being confirmed by three final rulings of two competent courts, was, for a period, destroyed by the Interior Letter issued without any proper procedure or due process of law and not in line with the existing legal system.

For writing this commentary, I review and re-consult the materials, in particular those provided to me by Matsue in 2011. The chairperson of the board of Matsue ("Chairperson") asked quite a few celebrated political figures of Hong Kong and some agencies of the Government of the Hong Kong Special Administrative Regions for help, who did forward her petitions to the chairman of the Standing Committee of the National Congress, the premier of the State Council at that time, to the Supreme People's Court and the Supreme People's Procuratorate and the National Office For Petition (handling letters submitted by and complaints from petitioners), etc., for their respective attention.

I would like to mention some feedback information to the petitions above. On December 14, 2000 and on December 30, 2002, the Liaison Office of the National Deputies of the Supreme Court ("Liaison Office") respectively gave reply to two deputies (Mr./Ms Zhu Tianhua and Mr. Cheng Yiu Tong) to the National People's Congress of the PRC, saying that after examination of the Award, its Trial and Judicial Committee held that there was some procedure errors with the Award 0271, therefore the Award should not be enforced. The Supreme Court had instructed the Higher People's Court of Guangdong Province to see to it that the Shenzhen Court should not enforce the Award (supervise that the Shenzhen Court should not continue the enforcement of the Award). The two replies were respectively numbered as [2000] No. 294 and [2002] No. 431. A staff member of the office of the woman deputy (Madam Fan Hsu Lai Tai) located in Hong Kong to the National People's Congress in a replay dated on January 18, 2003, to the Chairperson quoting the contents of the document [2002] No 431 of the Liaison Office above.

I would like to further mention that the Legal Advisory Committee of China Federation of the Returned Overseas Chinese located in Beijing on January 12, March 9 and March 12, April 16, 2001, in a row submitted letters (or titled as Report or Opinion) to the then president or the chief justice of the Supreme Court, airing their different opinions toward the decision by the Supreme Court revealed by the reply [2000] No. 294 from the Liaison Office to the National deputy Zhu Tianhua. The legal experts in their letters analyzed the reasons that the Award 0271 should be respected and enforced and the Interior Letter being not in line with existing rules or it was not made through due process. No doubt, the chief justice got those letters but I have got no access to his response.

Citizens expect and they have the rights to require that statesmen, high-ranking officials, public servants and judges should respected law as supreme principle. Civil and commercial disputes, if the parties fail to have them settled which should then be referred to mediators, judges or arbitrators. Once there is a final judgment or an award and the parties concerned do not automatically execute the decisions; upon the request of the winning party, it is the duties of a competent court to enforce the judgment or the award. All the other agencies, authorities or outsiders should not lay a finger on, in respecting the rule of law.

In the course of writing this commentary, I produced those replies above to my colleague Dr. Foo, as a senior solicitor in Hong Kong, out of professional sensitivity; he immediately raised a question, why those letters were not attached to any final ruling to the non-enforcement of the Award 0271 from a competent court?

F. Matsue Never Give up and They Were Enjoyed Warm Supports

After the Award was declared (not publicly) no longer in force, Matsue was unable to continue its business in Hong Kong and its Chairperson had never given up her effort by writing various letters to some Hong Kong deputies to the National People's Congress, some Hong Kong Members of the Chinese Political Consultative Conference, to the Constitutional Affairs Bureau of the Government Secretariat, Hong Kong, the Office of the Chief Executive of the Hong Kong Administrative Region of the PRC, the Office of the Government of the Hong Kong Special Administrative Region in Beijing, etc., revealing all the suffering Matsue had suffered because of the Interior Letter.

For a long period the Chairperson was a petitioner. She was supported by some lawyers in the mainland, the legal council of the National Federation of the Returned Overseas Chinese and many law experts in the mainland. I would like to particularly mention that a popular figure the Honorable Mr. Tsui Sze-Man, GBM (Xu Simin, the Great Bauhinia Medial Winner) of the Hong Kong Special Administrative Region of the People's Republic of China not only forwarded some petitions written by the Chairperson and her lawyer in mainland to the then premier but also personally in May, November 2001 and in March 2002 wrote letters to the then premier, condemning the wrong act reflected by the issuing of the Interior Letter. On the Interior Letter, Mr. Tsui also had written letters to some VIPs of China, holding that it was against the principle of due process. Mr. Tsui passed away in September 2007, at the age of ninety-three.

Prof. Wang Youjin, a famous political and law commentator of Hong Kong, in May 2001 had a series of commentaries on this case carried in Hong Kong Economic Journal.

In the spring of 2011, I got to know from the Matsue's former lawyer that a judge with the Shenzhen Court, who was not a member of the collegial bench of issuing the final rulings above, after receiving a petitioning letter from the Chairperson, he re-examined the files of the case and came to realize that the Interior Letter was groundless and should be withdrawn. It was said that judge called on some official or some senior judge with some department of the Supreme Court and the communications between the two judges, the Shenzhen Court submitted a report on the case and the Award 0271 and the Interior Letter. Upon receiving the report, the Supreme Court officially withdrew the Interior Letter. The lawyer suggested that I should pay a visit to the judge with the Shenzhen Court, as I had published the Irrational Challenges.

Prof Wang Youjin and I had a meeting in Hong Kong with the Chairperson and her sisters in the spring of 2011 after I got the information that the Interior Letter had been withdrawn and the enforcement procedure of Award 0271 had been restored. Prof. Wang passed away in winter 2011, at the age of eighty-four.

If a Chinese arbitral award would face so many obstacles and so many uncertain factors, wouldn't that do the reputation of the rule of law of China a lot of harms? If the enforcement of a Chinese arbitral award would cost a winning party over 12 years, how would you take "Time is money and efficiency is the life of every business" as a motor in China? If now and then arbitrators would receive feed-back information that their awards are in fact of no final effect at all, would they have full of confidence of their course? And would any businessmen believe in arbitration in China? Is it a rare negative example?

G. **Some Thoughts on Matsue Case**

(1) **How Many Chances Do the Three Losing Parties Should Have to Challenge the Finality of the Award 0271?**

According to the provisions of Arts 58 and 63 of the Arbitration Law of PRC and the provisions concerned of the Civil Procedure Law of PRC, a losing party has some chance to apply to the intermediate people's court at the place where the arbitration institution resides or at the place of the access of the losing party for non-enforcement or cancellation of (set aside) a final award. According to the general principle of resjudicate, once a final ruling is rendered, one of the three losing parties or the three losing parties of the said case would be jointly and severally bound by it, any one of the three or all the three would have no more chance. So it would be irregular and illegal to have three final rulings regarding to the challenges to the Award 0271. And it would be more ridiculous that despite of the final Award together with the award confirming it through re-arbitration proceedings and the three final rulings, the nal Award 0271 would be ruined by the Interior Letter.

(2) **The Interior Letter Being in Conflict with the Principle of Due Process**

Art 198 of the Civil Procedure Law of PRC (1991): "If the president of a people's court at any level finds definite error in a legally effective judgment or written order of his court and deems it necessary to have the case retried, he shall refer it to the judicial committee (trial or judgment committee) for discussion and decision."

"If the Supreme People's Court finds definite error in a legally effective judgment or written order of a local people's court at any level, or if a people's court at a higher lever finds some definite error in a legal effective judgment or written order of a people's court at a lower level, it shall respectively have the power to bring the case up for trial by itself or direct the people's court at a lower level to conduct are trial."

There is no provision or procedure provided in the Arbitration Law of PRC similar to the procedure for trial supervision in the Civil Procedure Law of PRC. And Art 198 does not apply to any arbitration proceedings in China.

Matsue had no idea of the procedure leading to the Interior Letter. And before the issue of it, Master should have received any copy of the application to the Supreme Court by the three losing parties to set aside or refuse to enforce the Award 0271. However Matsue had not been provided with any chance to present their case.

(3) The Cost of the Realization of Justice and Maintaining Social Economic Order

How much time, energy and money Matsue and its Chairperson had spent? If the time Matsue had spent on the arbitration proceedings is included, the case was accepted on September 6, 1994, from that date to 2011, Matsue spent 17 years on the case. How many authorities, agencies, officers, political and popular figures, lawyers and law professors have been involved?[7] I would only mention some of those attending the conference specially organized by the legal Adversary Committee of the National Federation of the Returned Overseas Chinese according to the news carried in the Shenzhen Overseas Chinese News (2001-04-12–2001-04-18), they were Mr. Liang Qinhan, Mr. Xie Chonqin, Mr. Yang Yiping and law professors: Yang Jiansun, Liu Jiaxin, Jian Wei and Yin Songnian.

If the time, energy and money of Matsue and other agencies and people involved had been spent on creating property or any jobs, how great it would be?

(4) "Fairness And Justice More Glorious Than the Sun"

A sum of two million of US dollars (or USD1.6 mil- lion) might not be a big sum to a nation, but was really a big sum to a family or a company in operation. And we should also take account of the time when Matsue had owned this sum. It was in 1990s.

Without judicial independence and without the system of check and balance, there would be abuse of power. Once there is any abuse of power, legal principle will be put on the shelf. The national leaders, such as the premier, should not be troubled with such a matter, such as the enforcement of an arbitral award.

On November 11, 2013, I got a message sent by mobile phone from Matsue's former lawyer Mr. Yang Yiping, revealing that in 2012, the Award 0271 was at last successfully enforced. He said that the good judge Mr. Yang Kecheng with the Shenzhen Court should be never forgotten.

Many Chinese never forget that in the press session on March 14, 2010, the then Premier Wan Jiabao said in response to the last question "I think fairness and justice are more glorious than the sun." That line turned out to be the most quoted one in domestic media and it became an immediate catch phrase in China. His words warmed the hearts of the people.

(5) Ensuring Independent and Impartial Exercising Adjudicative and Procuratorial Powers According to Law

In the communiqu´e of the 3rd Plenary Session Of 18th CPC Central Committee, one of the main points strengthened is the rule of law, inter alia, ensuring that the adjudicative and procuratorial powers would be exercised independently and impartially. We have reasons to believe that administrative intervention to judiciary would be greatly restrained.

II. Case Two: Walmart Dalian V. Dalian Wanguo

1. Overview of the Case Relating to the Enforcement Proceedings of CIETAC Award [2005]0168

Walmart Dalian as tenant and Dalian Wanguo Shopping Square Corporation Limited (I am not very sure whether it is the official translation of its name, hereinafter referred to as "Dalian Wanguo") as landlord entered into a tenancy agreement for letting its commercial premises, the annual rent was over RMB10 million. According some message in the People's Daily, November 4, 2011, Since June 2002 Walmart Dalian had never paid any sum of rent and the aggregated outstanding sum up to November 2011 was over RMB100 million.[8]

2003 Walmart Dalian filed the case to CIETAC against Dalian Wanguo on grounds that the landlord had been in breach of the tenancy agreement, claiming to annul the agreement.

On April 28, 2005, the final award [2005] Zhongguo Maozhong Jincaizi No. 0168 ("Award 0168") was rendered. Among the decisions, the tribunal awarded that Walmart Dalian should pay Dailian Wanguo the rent due and owing. Dailian Wanguo, on September 25, 2006, applied to the Dalian Municipality International People's Court ("Dalian Court") for enforcement of the award.

Walmart Dalian, according to the reports above, applied for arbitration for the second time. The tribunal with CIETAC rendered an award affirming the Award 0168 in favor of Dalian Wanguo. I have no idea how it could be re-instituted. For saving space, and further, the ordinary journalists or reports are not legal professionals and usually are hardly able to report or describe a case or relevant proceedings with proper terminologies. I have consulted some staff members with CIETAC, but they have to abide by the principle of maintaining the confidence of the case unless the parties have revealed it fully to the public. Therefore I prefer not to inquire into the details of the case and am not in a position to comment on the merits of the case. The following pieces of information mainly based on the coverage of China's official CCTV and I have added some sub-headings.

2. The Enforcement Proceedings Have Been Followed and Covered by CCTV

Walmart Dalian, through retaining the services of a Chinese law firm, thereby has rendered the Dalian Court to terminate without reason or justification the enforcement proceedings in connection with the Award 0168 against Walmart Dalian ("enforcement proceedings").

This incident has been covered by China's official CCTV twice in the past 2 years. CCTV's recent coverage on May 15, 2013, shows the facts of the malpractice. The CCTV program, which is in Chinese, may be viewed at: http://video.sina.com.cn/p/news/v/2013-05-15/205562431383.html. In the following I would summarize the main points of the translated version of the transcript of the program.

3. **Walmat Dalian Refusing to Pay Rents and the Dalian Court Declared that They Are Determined to Enforce the Award**

Two years ago in our "Focus Talk" program, we covered a story entitled "How Come It's Walmart Again?" in which it was reported that Walmart Dalian had been in default in paying rents to its landlord Dalian Wanguo for the past 12 years.

It was reported that Dalian Wanguo claimed the outstanding rents by lodging an application for arbitration to CIETAC (actually Walmart Dalian was the claimant—the author), which conclusively decided that the disputing parties should continue to honor the tenancy agreement, meaning that Dalian Wanguo should continue to let the premises to Walmart Dalian and the latter should pay its rents, accrued and accruing, in full to Dalian Wanguo under the agreement. However, Walmart Dalian refused to comply with the arbitration award. CCTV's reporter spoke to Mr. Liu K, then director of the Enforcement Bureau of the Dalian Court, who said, "*In order to uphold Chinese law and to protect the legitimate rights of the applicant, we shall in accordance with the law resolutely enforce the arbitration award against the obligor no matter who he is and no matter what difficulties we may face.*" It looked as if the Dalian Court was demonstrating a strong stance and was prepared to enforce the award against Walmart Dalian.

Two years have since lapsed. What has happened to the enforcement case now?

4. **The Enforcement Proceedings Have Been Terminated Under a Resolution of the Dalian Court And an Alleged Directing Note From the Supreme Court**

Recently CCTV's reporter approached the Dalian Court again and discovered that the original director of the Enforcement Bureau has been transferred to some other post. His successor Mr. Liu CC met with the reporter. He said that the enforcement proceedings of the case had been terminated under a resolution of the Trial and Judgment Committee of the Dalian Court.

This surprising outcome stunned the reporter, because terminating the proceedings means closing the case for good. Mr. Liu CC said that the reason for termination was the enforcement had faced extreme difficulties. The reporter still remembered that during the last reporting, the Dalian Court showed to the reporter a copy of the notes of a court enquiry, which recorded two panel judges Mr. Yu Zhou and Mr. Lin Chi at the hearing said: "*The case is about an enforcement of a commercial lease which relates to the performance of acts only, and therefore there can be seen no external obstacle to prevent the parties from performing such acts under the agreement.*"

Why were their statements contradictory to that of Mr. Liu CC, the current director of the Enforcement Bureau? The reporter asked for meeting with the previous panel judges for clarification, but was told they were either no longer in that court or currently not available for interview.

On reading relevant official documents, the reporter discovered that to terminate any enforcement proceedings, certain conditions must first be satisfied. Art 14 of a document effective since 2007 entitled "*Certain Rules on the Transparency in Conducting Enforcement Proceedings Issued by the Supreme People's Court of China*" stipulates: "*A court should first call for a public hearing before exercising its power to terminate any enforcement proceedings instituted in connection with an enforceable legal document*"."

Had the Dalian Court held such a public hearing before it decided to terminate the enforcement proceedings against Walmart Dalian?

The attorney for Dalian Wanguo Mr. Duan HX said that Dalian Wanguo had never been served any notice of public hearing in connection with the proceedings, and they absolutely had no idea how the decision of the Dalian Court came about.

What was the legal basis for the Dalian Court to reach such a decision without going through the required statutory procedures then?

According to Mr. Liu, the said director of the Enforcement Bureau, the Trial and Judgment Committee of the Supreme Court of China, after considering the case, issued a **directing note instructing the Dalian Court to terminate the enforcement proceedings**. The Supreme Court note stated: "*For an enforcement proceeding that aims to enforce the performance of an unfulfilled contract, if the parties involved have widely different views on their respective rights and obligations in the course of performing the contract, causing the enforcement unrealizable, then the enforcement proceeding of the case shall be terminated, and the parties may resort to litigation to resolve their dispute.*"

5. "An Arbitration Award is Final" Provided in the Arbitration Law of PRC

Madam Gao F, member of the Experts Consultative Committee of CIETAC, told the reporter: "*Under Art"9 of the Arbitration Law of the People's Republic of China, an arbitration proceeding once completed, its award is final and conclusive and binding on the parties. So upon the completion of the arbitration proceedings and the grant of the arbitration award, neither of the parties would be able to institute another set of arbitration proceedings or file a claim to a court for litigation in respect of the same issue. That is to say, since the Dalian Court has terminated the enforcement proceedings filed on the basis of the arbitration award, there is no other legal venue at all for Dalian Wanguo to litigate against Walmart Dalian.*"

6. The Reporter Allowed no Access to the Alleged Directing Note

The reporter requested for inspection of the Supreme Court's note, but Mr. Liu the director of the Enforcement Bureau said that it was not convenient for him to produce the document. But he further said: "*Even if there were no such a Supreme Court's note, the Dalian Court still has legal grounds to terminate the proceedings, which are provided for, among others, in Article 235 of the Civil Procedural Law of the People's Republic of China*".

The reporter searched for this Article 235. It provides, "*In any of the following events, the court shall decide to terminate the enforcement proceedings*":

"*(6) where the court sees fit to terminate it.*"

Then, what is meant by "*where the court sees fit*"?

According to Mr. Liu, it is entirely in the court's discretion. The legal expert whom the reporter consulted, however, said: "*This stipulation is not applicable to the case concerned. Only when the court concludes that the arbitration award is against public policy can it resort to this stipulation to terminate the enforcement proceedings. Otherwise, there is absolutely no possibility for the proceedings to be terminated.*"

7. **A Forged "Written Request" to Withdraw the Application for Enforcement by Dalian Wanguo?**

The reporter discovered in the course of his investigation that this was not the first time for the Dalian Court to decide for termination of the enforcement proceedings. There was another such decision in 2006, as shown in the case files. Such termination was stated to be as a result of the applicant withdrawing the application for enforcement. A memo attached to the Dalian Court's decision to terminate the enforcement proceedings indicated that a Ms. Zhou YL, purportedly an employee of Dalian Wanguo, told the Dalian Court that the applicant requested to withdraw the application for enforcement and agreed to terminate the proceedings. She signed her name on the memo to confirm the statement.

Whereas, Dalian Wanguo said that they had been awaiting the result of the enforcement from the Dalian Court since 2006, but nothing turned out. They checked with the Dalian Court again in 2011 when they discovered in the case files the "Written Request" to withdraw the application for enforcement, which they had never filed with the court. Ms. Zhou YL indeed was an employee of Dalian Wanguo responsible for contacting the Dalian Court for the proceedings, but she had never signed such a document.

Realizing that the signature was forged, Dalian Wanguo immediately reported the case to the police. The Dalian Court called for experts to verify the signature of Zhou YL and concluded that it was forged, but no forensic expert report was issued.

Who forged the signature of Zhou YL? With the puzzle in mind, the reporter requested to interview the trial judge Mr. Wang GY but the Dalian Court refused to provide the reporter with information for communicating with the Judge Wang.

Who did it then? Why did the Dalian Court rely on a forged document to arrive at the decision for termination of the enforcement proceedings? The incident was not pursued by the Dalian Court because the Court considered it unnecessary. Instead, the Dalian Court took initiative to claim that the 2006 decision for termination of enforcement proceedings was obsolete (?), and allowed the proceedings to be continued.

……

The reporter retrieved and viewed the video recording of the hearing. He noticed that the attorney representing Walmart addressed herself to the (Dalian) Court as Xu XD, an attorney with KW law firm. And at last the reported revealed that she was the daughter of the president of the Dalian Court.

III. Some Thoughts on the Issues Relating to the Two Cases Above

1. How Long is the Journey to Have a Promise Made by CIETAC Realized by a People's Court?

Without the support of the courts, an arbitral award might be a useless scrap of paper. If the enforcement proceedings of an award would come across so many obstacles that could hardly be predicated, people would lose trust in the arbitration and in the arbitral institutes in China. Do you have any confidence that the Award 0168 would be finally enforced and it wouldn't take a long period more?

2. Is There Any Back-Door Practice in the Enforcement Proceedings?

As I have no access to first-hand materials of the Award 0168 and its enforcement proceedings, I don't touch on the merits of the case. But I could guess someone had something done through back door to the Darlian Court. Don't you think that we could take that the "Directing Note" relating to the Award 0168 was another "Interior Letter" to the Award 0271? The coverage done by the reporter of the CCTV has provided enough information and room for you to infer and imagine.

3. Would an Arbitrator Feel Disappointed with Such Events?

If as an arbitrator your painstaking efforts reflected in the course of hearing and drafting an award, it gets no active result, you wouldn't feel that your work is no value as it should be or as you expect or predict? If such event takes place frequently, you would gradually lose confidence. An act in line with law is much louder than any number of empty slogans and declarations.

4. Both Sides of the Enforcement of the Two Awards Above

Following my friend Mr. Marcus S. Jacobs QC of Australia and funded by him, I attended the 57th Congress of the International Association of Lawyers (from November 1–3, 2013, in the Macau Special Administrative Region of PRC), on the topic of International Commercial Arbitration. A woman lawyer (as I was some minutes late at the seminar, I did not know which country she came from) had got sufficient materials or cases about the enforcement of awards in mainland China. Her outlines were on the screen, revealing that the shortest period and the longest period for the enforcement, saying for the latter, an atypical case cost the winner over 4000 days. I had got no chance to exchange ideas with her. But it seems to me that the period of enforcement of Matsue is longer than that she was aware of. If we take into account that Award 0271 was issued on July 30, 1996, then from 1996 to 2012, roughly, the application for enforcement cost Matsue 16 years.

The two typical cases mentioned above do reflect some reality in mainland China. Nevertheless, I don't think they represent the mainstream of commercial arbitration in China. CIEAC and many arbitration institutes, such as Beijing Arbitration Commission, SCIA, and some local arbitration institutions, are developing. If we look at the dark side of the matter, some agencies and some ones in high positions for a certain period did not respect the rule of law, you would feel disappointed. If you look at the bright side, so many social associations, legal professionals and law professors, popular figures, and such judges as Mr. Yang with the Shenzhen Court showed great concern for the case, for fairness and justice, you should lose no hope in arbitration in mainland China. Further, CCTV (its "Focus Talk Program") and People' Daly have been engaging in the tasks of exposure of illegal acts.

3 Part Two: An Arbitration Clause Should Be Regarded as a Contract

Now I should return to the main subject of this commentary, touching on some legal issues pertaining to the absence of a party at the hearing.

In July and August 2013 respectively, as a president arbitrator of a three-member tribunal and as a sole arbitrator of a single-arbitrator tribunal, I dealt with (including joining hands with my co-arbitrators) two cases under the jurisdiction of CIETAC. In the two awards drafted by me, I have made observations on the omission of the defaulting parties.

In the first case my co-arbitrators did not quite agree with my comments on the act or omission of the defaulting respondent. But in both awards, the scrutiny professionals within CIETAC had no objection to my comments in this regard.

I would below review some concepts of the nature of an arbitration agreement and its binding force. What I am to quote and my discussion might not be divided into proper classification and in logical order.

IV. **Legal Nature of an Arbitration Agreement or an Arbitration Clause**

1. **An Arbitration Agreement Being of a Contract Nature**

For the sake of argument and supporting my view point, I would like to make some quotations from some dictionaries, monograph and comments popular within the legal and commercial arbitration circle:

"***(a)greement; contract***. *The former may refer either to an informal arrangement with no consideration (e.g., a 'gentlemen's agreement') or to a formal legal arrangement supported by consideration. Contract is used only in this second sense. The distinction applies also with the verbs* **agree** and **contract**. The intended sense of **agree(ment)** is usually clear from the context."[9]

"***(a)greement***: *a manifestation of assent by two or more people to a course of action. An agreement is normally enforceable only if it meets the requirements of a contract, in which case the terms 'agreement' and 'contract' are interchangeable.*"[10]

Based on the aforesaid definitions, it is understandable that in the context of commercial arbitration and in this article, the terms "agreement" and "contract" are interchangeable or they are synonyms; and an arbitration clause is synonymous with an arbitration agreement or an arbitration clause and an arbitration agreement are of the same function.

Please see the following quotations:

"*Since commercial arbitration is* ***a creature of contract*** (emphasis added), *generally only parties to an arbitration agreement are bound to participate. National Broadcasting Co. Inc. v. Hear Stearns & Co., Inc., 165 F34 184 (CA2 1999).*"[11]

Though an arbitration agreement is with no consideration or it is not supported by consideration, without arbitration agreement there would be no arbitration. Arbitration agreement is of a contract nature.

I would like to recall a principle reflected in UNIDROIT Principles of International Commercial Contracts 2010. "*Article 1.3 (Binding character of contract) A contract validly entered into is binding upon the parties...*".

The Comment attached to this Article 13:

"*1. The principle pacta sunt servanda*". That is another basic principle of contract law.[12]

About this principle, I would like to consult some book more:

"*The Latin maximpacta sunt servanda (agreements must be kept) comes from Canon law. It reflects* the **longstanding moral dimension of contract in our law** (emphasis added)—*that there is an* ***ethical*** *as well as legal* ***obligation*** *to* ***keep one's contractual promises****. Contracts should be honored not only because reliability is necessary to foster economic interaction, as discussed in section 1.4.3, but simply because it is morally wrong to break them.*"[13]

Without contract there would be no arbitration. No matter whether an arbitration agreement is reached by the parties concerned before or after some disputes arose. Once there is a contract containing an arbitration clause or an independent and separate arbitration agreement relating to the underlying contract, on the one hand the contracting parties enjoy a contractual right to refer any disputes arising from the underlying contract to arbitration and on the other hand the contracting parties shall be obliged to participate in commenced arbitral proceedings.

"*Arbitration agreements are* ***a matter of contract law*** (emphasis added) *and a court interpreting such agreements should consider the parties' intent. Med Centre Case, Inc. v. Smith, 727 So 2d 9 (Ala 1998).*"

"*Parties may contract to make the decision of an arbitrator or other third party a condition precedent to a right of action on the contract. State ex rel. United Asphalt Suppliers, Inc. v. Standers, 204 W Va 23, 511 SE2d, 134 (1988).*"[14]

When interpreting an arbitration agreement, a court or a judge should keep in mind that it is a matter of contract law and so does a private judge, an arbitrator.

2. An Arbitration Clause Being an Exclusively Contractual Right

I have further consulted some other American arbitration expert with profound knowledge in this regard. Please see the following viewpoint and its corresponding discussion:

"*Generally,* ***an arbitration clause is a contractual right*** (emphasis added) *which cannot be invoked by a nonparty to the arbitration agreement are bound to arbitrate [Dayh- off Inc. v. H. J. Heinz Co., 86 F3d 1287 (CA3 1996); Gingiss International v. Bormet, 585 F3d 328 (CA7 1995); United States v. Harkings Builders, Inc., 45 F3d 830 (CA4 1995) (judgment creditor/garnishor); American Ins. Co., NAP v. Cazort,*

316 Ark 314, 871 SW2d 575 (1994); Curtis G. Testerman Co. v. Buck, 340 Md 569 A3d 649 (195).]"[15]

Could anyone enjoy some contractual rights but he should shoulder no correspondent legal duties? The viewpoint above is that only parties to an arbitration clause or agreement are of possession of the arbitration right. But it seems to me that the principle of right equal with obligation is effective herewith and *an arbitration clause is also a contractual obligation and so is an arbitration agreement.*

Immediate following the words of the quotation above, the American colleague continues to say that:

"*The rule that an arbitration clause is a contractual right which cannot be invoked by someone who did not sign the contract in which it appeared reflects the principle, basic to contract law,* ***that only parties who have manifested an intent to be bound to the arbitration clause should be obligated to do so*** (emphasis added) *[Thomson-CSF, S. A. v. American Arbitration Ass'n, 64, F3d773(CA2 1995);Bullis v. Bear, Stearns & Co., Inc, 553, NW2d 599 (Iowa 1996)].*"[16]

The parties to an arbitration clause or agreement enjoy an exclusive contractual right and they are bound by a corresponding contractual obligation.

3. A Contract Containing an Arbitration Clause Traded as Two Contracts

Article 5-4 of the CIETAC Arbitration Rules (2012):

"*An arbitration clause contained in a contract shall be treated as a clause independent and separate from all other clauses of the contract, and an arbitration agreement attached to a contract shall also be treated as independent and separate from all other clauses of the contract. The validity of an arbitration clause or an arbitration agreement shall not be affected by any modification, cancellation, termination, transfer, expiry, invalidity, ineffectiveness, rescission, or nonexistence of the contract.*"

The core of the provisions of that paragraph of that Article is that an arbitration clause contained in a contract is deemed to be "separable" or "severable". Similar provisions of slight different wordings could be found in arbitration rules of many arbitral institutions all over the world.

For the purpose of writing this article, I review the following viewpoint:

"*When the parties to an agreement containing an arbitration clause enter into that agreement,* ***they conclude not one but two agreements*** (emphasis added), *the arbitral twin of which survives any birth defect or acquired disability of the principal agreement.*"[17]

So concise and precise of the viewpoint, it is in line with the principles of contract law, including the doctrine of autonomy, the principles of fairness and of good faith. So in my opinion, if an award is rendered, for example in the respondent's absence, in favor of the claimant, that would show that the defaulting respondent is not only in breach of the underlying contract but also in breach of the arbitration clause incorporated in the underlying contract or a separate arbitration agreement relating to the underlying contract, the respondent is in breach of two contracts, of double-default.

4. Parties to an Arbitration Agreement Having Outstanding Promises to Each Other

I am of the view that an arbitration agreement is a contract. What category of an arbitration agreement as a contract is?

I am of the opinion that the execution of an arbitration agreement showing that both parties agree to have any of their future or existing disputes referred to arbitration. That is their common wish or common promise.

Professional legal dictionaries have definitions on contracts of various categories. I would prefer to choose concise definitions or explanations from a book of contracts:

"*Because, at the point of contract formation, both parties have outstanding promises to be performed in the future, the contract is said to be* ***bilateral***." [18]

"*Because, at the point of contract formation, only one of the parties has a promise outstanding, the contract is said to be* ***unilateral***." [19]

I think that at the point of formation of an arbitration agreement, the parties have outstanding promises to be performed in the future. If there are any disputes out of or in connection with their main contract and could not be settled through amicable negotiation, a party as the claimant shall refer the disputes to arbitration, and the other as respondent shall follow suit and take part in the arbitral proceedings. That is to say, not only the potential claimant having an outstanding promise shall refer the dispute to arbitration, the other party as the potential respondent would have no outstanding promise. On the contrary that the other party as the potential respondent shall abide by the arbitration agreement and keep the outstanding promise contained therein and he is obliged to take part in the arbitration proceedings.

Arbitration proceedings are provided in a contract, once it commences, the participation of a contracting party is of obligation nature. A contractual right could be wavered but a contractual obligation must be abided by. That is to say once the arbitration proceedings commence, contracting parties to the arbitration clause or agreement shall be under obligation to follow the applicable arbitration rules and the requirements provided in the notices from a permanent arbitral institute or the tribunal of the case to appear or present his case. No matter which party (Party A or Party B, the Seller or the Buyer, the Assigner or the Assignee, the Landlord or the Tenant, etc.) to an underlying contract and its separate arbitration agreement first refer the dispute concerned to arbitration. That principle is applied to ad hoc arbitration.

A colleague in plain English begins his lecture, saying that:

"*Arbitration proceedings are frequently commenced by the issue of a Notice of Arbitration or a Request for Arbitration by which the claimant calls on the other party, the respondent,* ***to take part in the contractual process for the appointment of the arbitral tribunal***. (emphasis added)." [20]

Any arbitral proceedings, though, are commenced by the issue of a notice of arbitration based on the request for arbitration submitted by a claimant, but actually he is following the previous arbitration clause contained in the contract with the respondent, or is abiding by the previous arbitration agreement with the respondent.

And the respondent is required or obliged to take part in the proceedings specifically provided in their mutual agreement.

1. The Principles Operate in Any Arbitral Proceedings in the Absence of a Party

The principles contained in UNCITRAL Model Law on International Commercial Arbitration prevail in the practices of many arbitral institutions the world over. Let's review the Model Law and some of its articles.

"Article 25 Default of a party"

Unless otherwise agreed by the parties, if without showing sufficient cause,

"(a) the claimant fails to communicate his statement of claim in accordance with article 23 (1), the arbitral tribunal shall terminate the proceedings;

"(b) the respondent fails to communicate his statement of defense in accordance with article 23(1), the arbitral tribunal shall continue the proceedings ***without treating such failure in itself as admission of the claimant's allegations*** (emphasis added);

"(c) any party fails to appear at a hearing or to produce documentary evidence, the arbitral tribunal may continue the proceedings and ***make the award on the evidence before it*** (emphasis added)."

Explanatory Note by the UNCITRAL secretariat on the 9185 Model Law on International Arbitration as amended in 2006.

"(c) Default of a party"

"37. The arbitral proceedings may be continued in the absence of a party, provided that due notice has been given. This applies, in particular, to the failure of the respondent to communicate its statement of defense (article 25(b)). The arbitral tribunal may also continue the proceedings where a party fails to appear at a hearing or to produce documentary evidence without showing sufficient cause for the failure (article 25 (c)). However, if the claimant fails to submit its statement of claim, the arbitral tribunal is obliged to terminate the proceedings (article 25(c)).

"38. Provisions that empower the arbitral tribunal to carry out its task even if one of the parties does not participate are considered of practical importance. As experience shows, it is not uncommon for one of the parties to have little interest in cooperating or expediting matters. Such provisions therefore provide international commercial arbitration its necessary effectiveness, within the limits of fundamental requirements of procedural justice."

The principles contained or reflected in the provisions of Art 25 of the Model Law have been abided by the arbitrators with CIETAC and SCIA. Although similar provisions of CIETAC Arbitration Rules in this regard might not be so expressed or specified as it should have been or should be. Let's refer to similar Articles of CIETAC Arbitration Rules.

Art 42 of the CIETAC Rules of 1994?

"Should one of the parties fail to appear at the hearing, the arbitration tribunal may proceed with the hearing and ***make an award by default*** (emphasis added)."

Art 42 of the CIETAC Rules of 1995 and 1998 is exactly worded as its former one in the CIETAC Rules of 1994.

The principles, in particular the ones contained in Art 25 (b) and (c) of the UNCITRAL Model Law, are not reflected. That is to say that the tribunal shall not treat the failure of the respondent as the admission of the claimant's allegations and making the award on the evidence before it.

Then the previous set of rules was substituted by the CIETAC Rules of 2005. Art 34 Default:

"*1. If the Claimant fails to appear at an oral hearing without showing sufficient cause for such failure, or withdraws from an ongoing oral hearing without the permission of the arbitral tribunal, the Claimant may be deemed to have withdrawn its Request for Arbitration. In such a case, if the Respondent has filed a counterclaim, the arbitral tribunal shall proceed with the hearing of the counterclaim and* ***make a default award*** (emphasis added)."

"2. *If the Respondent fails to appear at an oral hearing without showing sufficient cause for such failure, or withdraws from anon-going oral hearing without permission of the arbitral tribunal, the arbitral tribunal may proceed with the arbitration and* ***make a default award*** (emphasis added). *In such a case, if the Respondent has filed a counterclaim, the Respondent may be deemed to have withdrawn its counterclaim.*"

The provisions in the CIETAC Rules of 2005 were much better than the similar provisions of their previous versions. Nevertheless the English expression of "***making a default award***" might not have reflect edits original meaning and might lead some misunderstanding and further that "*without treating such failure in itself as an admission of the claimant's allegations*" and "*the arbitral tribunal (may) make an award on the evidence before it*" remained short in CIETAC Rules.

Now the said article is renumbered as Art 37 Default incorporated in CIETAC Rules of2012, as effective as of May 1, 2012, the wording remains unchanged or exactly the same as that quoted above.

Up to now, after revising and adopting many sets of arbitration rules (save the first set of Provisional Rules of 1956, there are Rules of 1988, 1994, 1995, 1998, 2005 and 2012), the actual practice of CIETAC without treating such failure (of the respondent) in itself as admission of the claimant's allegations and making the award on the evidence before it incorporated or specified in its arbitral rules. Those in charge at CIETAC and its experts should have known what the provisions of Art 30 of the UNCITRAL Arbitration Rules (as revised in 2010) are and should think over the reason for the provisions including its wording.

And about the wrong introduction of the expression "*making a default award*," I once said "*What a pity, a mistake, in my humble opinion, would remain uncorrected for some decades.*"[21] Because making a (the) default award is not in line with the actualities and practices of the arbitrators with CIETAC. And it is not in conformity with the guiding principle of not treating the failure in itself of the respondent as an admission of the claimant's allegations and making the award on the evidence before the tribunal.[22]

VI. The Practices at CIETAC When a Party Fails to Appear at a Hearing

In this commentary, I would mainly deal with the default of a respondent. Default in this article mainly means that a respondent refuses to make any response to the notice of arbitration properly serviced, does not appear at any hearing, or keeps silent all over the arbitral proceedings. In this article examples are selected mainly from the awards carried in the **Selected Works of China International Economic and Trade Arbitration Commission Awards (1989–1995) Updated to 1997, Authorized English Version**. I would first of all give an example of failure of a claimant with proper reasons.

1. **Case One Award 32**[23]

The Claimant's Failure Of Appearing At A Hearing Is Not Without Sufficient Cause And That Was Accepted By The Arbitral Tribunal.

A. **Outline**

The claimant a Bangladesh buyer and the respondent a Chinese seller **on April 20,1986** signed a contract for the sale of 100 tons of Sulphur black BR 200%, at a price of USD1,350 per ton, C & F Chittagong, payment by letter of credit, shipment between June and September, 1986.

On November 25, 1986, the goods of 60 tons arrived at Chittagong Port. The buyer resold some to its domestic clients. Upon receiving complaints from its clients, the buyer **on December 29, 1986**, telexed the seller to challenge the quality of goods. The buyer **on January 19, 1987**, got two inspection reports from a local inspection agency which respectively revealed that the goods were not in crystal form but "partly luped/ crystal form and/or powder", and "in powder/party crystal form". The conclusion was that the goods were not in conformity with the stipulations in the contract. Based on the inspection reports, the buyer claimed for indemnity.

The seller denied the claim and refused to indemnify. Therefore **on September 5, 1988**, the buyer referred the dispute to CIETAC, asking for USD57,000.00 from the respondent to compensate for the loss arising from the part of the goods not being in crystal form. The amount requested increased to USD60,915.30 **on June 14, 1989**.

The arbitral tribunal held an oral hearing in Beijing **on May 29, 1989**. The claimant, due to financial problems, failed to appear but had informed the tribunal of its problems and asked the tribunal to examine the case according to the written statement of claim and other documents. ***The tribunal expressed its understanding of the claimant's request***. After the hearing, the claimant submitted supplementary statements and documents.

The respondent attended the hearing, presenting its case and making response to the inquiries of the tribunal. The tribunal found out that the part of the goods arrived at the destination on **November 25, 1986**, and in accordance to the contract the claimant should have claimed for compensation on or before **December 25, 1986**, the commodity inspections certificates were not issued until **January 19, 1987**. Therefore **on May 15, 1990**, the tribunal dismissed the claimants' claim. That had nothing to do with the default of the claimant, or we should say that the claimant's failure of appearing at the hearing was not without proper cause.

B. **Commentary**

The award was not a defaulting one. Talking about a deal of international trade, the defaulting claimant might have neglected that a time limit was of essence. For such a claim in small sum and of not a complicated case, I do believe the parties to the deal should have sought for some consensus on the appointment of a sole arbitrator to hear their case alone[24] and requested that the tribunal should examine the case and make an award on the basis of documents submitted by the parties and *vice verse*, the tribunal with the parties consent could examine the case on the case of document only.[25] That would save the parties much trouble, time and money.

2. **Case Two Award 38**[26]

The Defaulting Respondent Did Put Many Obstacles To Prevent And Slow The Arbitral Proceedings From Moving On. Indeed The Respondent Tried Many Means.

A. **Outline**

On November 16, 1981, a Chinese seller and a Thailand buyer concluded a sales contract, providing that the seller should supply 1,610 diesel-engine water-pumps and spare parts for USD779, 424.36 including 6% interest, CIF Bangkok, D/A 360 days payment; 150 water-pumps should be delivered in December 1981, 628 ones in February 1982, 102 in March 1982, and 730 ones in April 1982. After the conclusion of the contract, the seller delivered all the goods under the contract. The buyer accepted the goods but left USD165,493.39, the value for 299 water-pumps, unpaid. The parties had some negotiations but failed to reach a settlement.

On April 17, 1987, the seller as claimant according to the arbitration clause in the contract referred the case to CIEAC Shenzhen.[27] The buyer as respondent, on July 17, 1987, wrote to CIETAC Shenzhen, saying that the contract clearly provided that arbitration should be conducted in Beijing. Respecting the parties' wish, CIETAC Shenzhen transferred the case to the headquarters of CIETAC in Beijing.

On February 22, 1988, ten months lapsed, CIETAC accepted the case and informed the respondent to appoint an arbitrator and submit its statement of defense. The respondent failed to do so. According to the CIETAC Rules of 1956, the Chairman appointed an arbitrator for the respondent.

On August 11, 1988, almost six months lapsed, the three-member arbitral tribunal held an oral hearing in Beijing. The respondent received the notice but failed to appear.

On January 17, 1989, the tribunal authorized an arbitrator on the panel of CIETAC to take relevant materials to the respondent in Thailand.

On November 3, 1989, CIETAC gave the respondent one more chance by telex urging it to submit a statement of defense by November 20, 1989, saying that "*You could also require the arbitral tribunal to hear the case (once more). Otherwise the tribunal will make an award.*"

On November 24, 1989, the respondent made response, repeating what it had said to CIETAC Shenzhen that CIETAC had no jurisdiction over the case.

On December 20, 1989, over one year was gone after the oral hearing was held, CIETAC replied to the said response, giving it one month of grace period for submitting its statement of defense. But the respondent made no more response.

On July 14, 1990, the tribunal, based on the materials before it, held "*[t]hat the respondent had been given enough opportunity to defend the case, but had failed to present its statement of defense and other documents. Therefore, the arbitration tribunal decided to award the case in accordance with the current materials.*".

The tribunal confirmed the facts that after delivering the 1610 water pumps under the contract and having an outstanding sum for 299 water-pumps, the claimant dispatched some representative to the respondent's place of business to investigate. The parties reached an agreement that the respondent would pay the out- standing sum. But respondent failed to perform the agreement. The tribunal held that the agreement was supplementary to the contract, being merely concerned with the payment of the debt and did not replace the original. Therefore, the tribunal rendered an award in favor of the claimant, all the claims succeeded.

B. **Commentary**

Though there were great obstacles put and great troubles caused by the defaulting respondent, CIETAC and the arbitral tribunal tried their best to ensure the principle of nature justice was fully satisfied. The award rendered at the end of the defaulting proceedings and the award was not a default one but based on the evidence submitted by the claimant to the tribunal.

3. **Case Three Award 57**[28]

The Respondent Acknowledged Receipt Of The Notice Of Arbitration And The Attached Request For Arbitration By The Claimant With Supporting Evidence But Thė Respondent Failed To Submit Any Statement Of Defense. Nevertheless Only Part Of The Claims Of The Claimant Succeeded.

A. **Outline**

On April 27, 1985, a Chinese buyer (an import corporation) upon the authorization of its client entered into a contract for purchasing an S-model body CT scanner system with an American seller. The price of the scanner was USD5,100,000.00. An attachment to the contract provided the sale price included service of the scanner and warranty in respect of the parts for one year after the scanner arrived. Moreover, erection of the scanner should be finished by the seller within 2 or 3 weeks after receiving the goods by the buyer.

In September of 1985, the seller delivered the goods and the buyer paid the price. But the seller failed to erect and adjust the scanner in the specified time limit. At the buyer's repeated request, **on August 5, 1985**, the parties signed an agreement concerning the erection and test running of the scanner with the main points: The seller shall be in charge of arranging for engineers to erect and adjust the scanner at the client's premises of the buyer free of charge **by August 25, 1985**. If the engineers fail to come in time, the seller will automatically return all the payment to the buyer. On receipt of the refunded sum, the buyer shall return the scanner to the seller. The expenses incurred therefore shall be borne by the seller; after installing and completing a test run of the scanner, the seller shall at its own expense dispatch a resident engineer to China to maintain the scanner so as to ensure that the scanner works properly for the warranted one-year, etc.

Until October 5, 1986, the seller dispatched engineers to install and adjust the scanner. Since some parts were burnt down, the installation was unsuccessful and the engineers returned to the United States. Thereafter the respondent dispatched no engineers more and refused to reply to the buyer. The client of the buyer could not have the scanner erected and was unable to properly operate it.

The buyer as claimant in accordance with the arbitration clause referred the dispute to CIETAC, "*[r]equesting that the respondent indemnify the loss(es) of USD157, 594.00 (emphasis added) suffered by it because of the respondent's failure to (properly) perform the contract, and that the respondent* **bear all expenses relating to arbitration** (emphasis added)."

The award neither gives the date of submission by the claimant nor reveals that when and how the three- member tribunal was formed.

On June 3, 1987, the notice of arbitration with the request for arbitration and its supporting evidence was sent to the seller respondent, and on August 26, 1987, the addressee acknowledged receipt of the documents. "Thereafter the arbitration tribunal repeatedly asked the respondent to submit its statement of defense, but the respondent failed to do so and presented no request. The arbitration tribunal carefully examined the documents only in accordance with the provisions of the Arbitration Rules."[29] But the respondent did not submit any statement of defense and kept silence.

On February 1, 1988, as the respondent did not reply to the CIETAC, to avoid further loss, the tribunal rendered an intermediate award, allowing the claimant to engage domestic technicians with local spare parts to install the scanner; permitting the claimant to take the necessary measures to install and adjust the scanner under the contract.

On July 27, 1990, the claimant, in its letter to the tribunal, said that "*[t]he installation and test run had identified difficulties as the machine* (the scanner) *had been damaged by internal electrical fault when the respondent's engineers were erecting the machine. The installation incurred the following expenses*:

"*1. RMB435,000.00 for installation, test run and maintenance (of the scanner)*;

"2. *RMB66, 972,60. for spare parts and repair (of the scanner)*

"*3. RMB4,980 for labor*;

"*4. RMB19, 268.17 for business trip.*"

The total of the above was RMB526, 220.77.

On November 5, 1990, over three years was gone since the respondent confirmed its receipt of the notice of arbitration, the tribunal rendered its final award based on the documents submitted by the claimant. The tribunal awarded that the respondent shall pay USD88,179.09 indemnity to the claimant without interest; the claimant's other claims shall be rejected and; the arbitration fee shall be borne by the respondent.

B. **Commentary**

According to the direct quotation above, there was no oral hearing. The award itself does not make full details of the delaying of the arbitral proceedings, though readers could connect to some extent the delay with the omission of the respondent, for not a complicate case of the said one, over three years is a rather long period.

The aggregated sum of the claims of the claimant were eUSD157, 594.00 and RMB562, 220.77. The sum awarded by the tribunal was USD88,179.09. As I could not recall the rate between the USD and RMB in 1987 or 1990, roughly speaking, only 30-40 percent of the sum claimed by the claimant was awarded. We know that arbitration fee was calculated and collected according to the claimed sum and the burden of the arbitration fee is closely dependent on the liability for breach. It is not proper to require that the sum claimed should be exactly equal to that of the sum the tribunal would award. But roughly speaking, in my humble opinion, between the two sums there should not be too great a difference. So therefore, if I had been in the shoes of the tribunal, I would have decided that the claimant should bear part of the arbitration fee. But I am not very sure whether the tribunal had weighed the moral imperative of the arbitration agreement. Even if the arbitrators had got the ***pacta sunt servanda*** in mind, they should have had some reasons discussed under the Opinion of the Arbitral Tribunal of their final award.

4. **Case Four Award 64**[30]

Though The Respondent Was In Default Of The Oral Hearing And Made No Statement Of Defense, The Fact Is That The Absence Of The Respondent Was Far From Automatically Validated The Arguments And Claims Of The Claimant. Or That Omission Of The Respondent Had Little Connection With The Consequence Of The Arbitration.

A. **Outline**

On April 15, 1988, two companies located in China (one as import and export company and another one as processing company[31]) with a company located in America entered into a contract for processing latex gloves with imported materials. The contract provided that over three years, from December 1988 to November 1991, the American company would provide latex from Thailand to the two Chinese companies. The award revealed that the American company, on January 17, 1989, advised the Chinese side that it could not continue carrying out the contract due to the failure in performing another 26 contracts of the same class with Chinese partners. Some dispute arose, and the two sides failed to settle it through the negotiation held on April 28, 1989, in Guangzhou.

On July 31, 1989, the Chinese side as the claimant submitted a request for arbitration to the CIETAC, applying that the American company as respondent to indemnify the following two sums:

"*1. RMB2, 987,682for the loss in production investment*;

"2. *USD823,500 for economic loss.*".

The award revealed that the respondent received the notice of arbitration but failed to appoint an arbitrator; it received the notice of hearing to beheld **on September 15,**

1990, in Beijing, but it neither attend nor submitted a written statement of defense; and it also received the letter about what had the tribunal inquired in the hearing, it made no response by the time limit.

In the award the three-member tribunal made the following decisions:

"*1. The respondent shall indemnify RMB31,500.00 and USD823,500.00 to the claimant*;

"2. *The claimant's other claims shall be rejected*;

"*3. The arbitration fees shall be borne by the respondent.*"

B. **Commentary**

Without sufficient materials available, I am not in a position to comment on any aspects of the case and the award. It is not a default award. The sum awarded was far from fully satisfying that of the first claim, because in respect of the claimed sum of RMB2,987,682 for the loss in production investment, only RMB31,500.00 was awarded. There was a great difference between the two figures. Taking into account the difference between the two figures and that it could be treated as the miscalculation or misjudgment of the claimant, therefore, the claimant should bear a small portion of the arbitration fee, such as 10 percent, as a token of the claimant's misjudgment.

5. **Case Five Award 82**[32]

The Award Was Rendered In Favor Of The Claimant Upon The Completion Of The Defaulting Proceedings; The Arbitration Fee Was Not Fully Born By The Defaulting Party As The Party In Breach, The Winning Claimant Also Bore A Small Potion Of The Arbitration Fee Due To Its Un-proper Claim.

A. **Outline**

On October 25, 1985 a Chinese seller and an American buyer signed a sales confirmation agreement with TV sets/aerials, control clock and lamp of some models and quantity, the price terms were of FOB Shanghai, the total price was USD91,048.20 and the payment was due 60 days after acceptance.

Having accepted the goods under the sales confirmation, the buyer paid only USD15, 000.00 of the USD91,048 due, and later complained of the poor quality of the goods. An agreement was reached which provided that the buyer could return to the seller the defective goods that could not be re-sold and that the buyer should pay for the goods which had been re-sold. The value of the returned goods was USD27,391.55. Furthermore, on three occasions the seller, at the buyers' request, had delivered samples of USD350,65. That sum was not paid. Dispute therefore arose and was unable to resolve by the parties. The seller as claimant referred the case to CIETAC, Shanghai Sub-commission, applying for an award to confirm that:

"*1. The respondent shall be liable to pay the claimant USD48,656.65 as the outstanding balance of the price of the goods; and USD8,991.75 as interest for the period from March 31, 1990 to July 11 at a monthly rate of 0.66%*";

"2. *The respondent be liable to pay USD350.65 for the price of the samples delivered by the claimant on three occasions*";

"3. The respondent shall be liable to indemnify the claimant for the cost of carriage of the returned goods, which was USD2,112.00";

"4. The respondent bears the costs of this arbitration."

The notice of arbitration, the claimant's application for arbitration and all relevant attachments, together with a copy of the CIETAC Rues of 1988 and panel list of arbitrators were served to the respondent. The respondent failed to appoint an arbitrator, submitted no statement of defense, and did not attend the oral hearing on September 15, 1992, in Shanghai and did not explain why.

The arbitral tribunal ascertained the facts and was of the opinion that: the respondent had received all the goods and returned some valued at USD27,391.55, thus it owed the claimant the outstanding balance USD48,656.65, and the respondent should pay the claimant this sum with interest; the claimant had delivered the samples to the respondent on three occasions, for two of which the respondent should pay the price USD250.65, the claimant should not claim for the price of the other samples as they were for inspection by the respondent to see if the goods were up to standard.

In the third decision the tribunal dismissed the claim that the respondent should indemnify the claimant for USD2,112.00 being the cost of carriage of the returned goods. And in the fourth decision, the tribunal awarded that the respondent and the claimant should respectively bear 90% and 10% of the arbitration fee.

B. **Commentary**

Once again, the award rendered in the absence of the defaulting respondent shows that the failure itself was not treated as an admission of the claimant's allegations. The allegations of the claimant were far from fully succeeded.

In all the awards mentioned, except for the Case 1, the tribunal held that the Bangladesh claimant due to financial problems failed to attend the oral hearing faraway in Beijing, all the defaulting respondents did not properly tell the tribunals their reasons or cause of not appearing at an oral hearing or instead submitting their written statements of defense. In the aforesaid cases, the tribunals did not touch on the omission of the respondents at all, not even from the angle of the ethical obligation. I myself in my past professional career had dealt with such matter in the same way.

6. **Case Six—SHEN DM2012008 Case and [2012] Zhongguo Maozhong Shencaizi no.D142 Award**[33]

In Terms Of Area, Shenzhen Is Not A Big City. Within The Same City, The Contact Of The Parties To A Case And Between Them And CIETAC South China, There Should Have Had Little Difficulty To Have All The Arbitration Documents Served. But The Defaulting Respondent Could Have Greatly Slowed The Progress Of The Proceedings.

A. **Outline**

In October 2009, a Shenzhen power company as seller with a Shenzhen property development company as buyer concluded a sales contract with a diesel generator set as the subject matter and the price being RMB580,000.00. The arbitration clause expressly provided that any dispute arising from the contract should be referred to CIETAC South China.

On November 28, 2009, the seller delivered the generator set to the buyer. After inspection and acceptance of the goods, the buyer paid 95% of the price. In January 2011, when the balance became due and payable, the buyer did not pay the balance.

On November 13, 2011, the lawyer of the seller sent a letter to the buyer, urging the addressee to pay the small sum of balance but the buyer refused to make any response.

On January 10, 2012, the seller referred the dispute to CIETAC South China, applying for an award to collecting the balance of the contract price RMB29,900.00; the legal fee of RMB10,000.00 and a sum of liquidated damages RMB31,320.00 (RMB29,000.00 x 360 days), etc.

B. A Prolonged Course of Service

Shenzhen city is only about 2000 km^2 and with excellent communications with all towns or all the communities or even all the corners of the city and with all parts of the country or the world. But the service of some notice of arbitration would have cost the secretary to the tribunal over six months.

On January 17, 2012, the secretary assigned by the secretariat of CIETAC South China to the future tribunal according the address provided by the claimant sent the notice of arbitration to the respondent by EMS, but it failed to reach the respondent.

On February 1, 2012, the secretary for the second time sent the notice to the addressee of the aforesaid address, failed again.

On February 17, 2012, the claimant through its lawyer in his response to the inquiry of the secretariat confirmed the aforesaid address was the respondent's last known place of business, he had checked the information appearing on some website with the market administration bureau of the municipality.

On February 27, 2012, the secretary for the third time sent the notice and all the documents related to the respondent at the aforesaid address. Later it was confirmed that the mail had been serviced.

On March 5, 2012, the lawyer of the respondent came to CIETAC South China, producing some documents showing the respondent's capacity and his authority. The lawyer also produced a copy of an application informing the secretary that he had, on behalf of his principal, filed an application to the Shenzhen Court for an order (ruling) that the arbitration clause was void. In addition, he, on his power of attorney, wrote down a communication address for this case. Thereafter, all the mails sent to that address were successful.

On March 7, 2012, the respondent filed its counter-claim. The claimant was informed of the matter by the secretary. I would like to draw the readers' attention to the fact that two days before that date, the respondent as plaintiff had filed an application to the Shenzhen Court for a ruling that the arbitration clause was void.

On March 30, 2012, the lawyer of the claimant as the defendant submitted to the Shenzhen Court a statement of defense, rejecting the arguments of the respondent as plaintiff.

On May 16, 2012, the lawyer of the claimant submitted a copy of a civil ruling rendered by the Shenzhen Court. That ruling allowing the withdrawal of application for denying the validity of the arbitration clause contained in the sales contract of the said case.

On June 27, 2012, CIETAC South China rendered a jurisdiction decision, confirming its jurisdiction over the case.

On June 29, 2012, the secretariat sent a letter to the parties, informing them of the procedure matters after the rendering of the said Jurisdiction Decision.

On July 23, 2012, I was designated by the Chairman of CIETAC South China as the sole arbitrator to hear the case.

On August 10, 2012, was the date for an oral hearing. On July 23, the date of the formation of the single-arbitrator tribunal, the notice of date for the hearing was by EMS sent to the parties.

On August 9, 2012, the secretary to the tribunal by mobile phone sent a message respectively to the lawyers of the parties, reminding them of the oral hearing. That is not required by the arbitration rules as the duty of the secretary or the arbitrators.

On August 10, 2012, the oral hearing should have commenced at 2:30 pm. The lawyer of the claimant was present but there was no lawyer or agent dispatched by the respondent. I suggested that the lawyer of the claimant wait for the lawyer of the respondent for half an hour. The lawyer present agreed. And I simultaneous asked the secretary to contact the respondent's lawyers. He did dial the two mobile numbers left by the lawyer. But no one answered the phone call.

It was provided in Art 34-2 of the CIETAC Rules of 2005 that "*[i]f the Respondent has filed a counter-claim, the Respondent may be deemed to have withdrawn its counterclaim.*"[34] In accordance with the provision, I proceeded with hearing, inquiring into the matters relating to the claims of the claimant.

At the end of the oral hearing, I suggested to the lawyer of the claimant that if the respondent could show sufficient cause such as there had been *force majeure*, we would arrange for another oral hearing. The lawyer of the claimant agreed.

On August 13, 2012, the secretary by EMS informed the respondent of the main points of the oral hearing, requesting that it should make response within five days. The notice was served.

On August 23 and 29, 2012, the lawyer of the respondent stated that he had not received the notice of oral hearing and without receiving any message mentioning the oral hearing sent by the secretary, requesting another oral hearing.

The tribunal accepted the argument of the lawyer of the claimant that the respondent's failure was short of sufficient cause and that it had taken various measures to delay the proceedings.

On October 20, 2012, the award was rendered in terms of all the claims. In the award, I did not comment on the act and omission of the defaulting respondent and decided to refund part of the arbitration fees for its counterclaim. Actually I had finished the award by that August 25. The secretariat must have been weighing all the aspects of the case and the factors that might influence the finality or the fate of the award, or the ones in charge must have been agonizing over the problem.

C. Commentary

If a defaulting respondent does not keep his contractual promise contained in the arbitration clause, the arbitration proceedings could hardly go forward smoothly. Nevertheless no arbitrator, including me at CIETAC and at SCIA, would have treated an arbitration agreement as a contract and treated the default at a hearing by a party as a breach of contract. And we had never made any comments on the act of omission of a defaulting party.

VII. The Defaulting Respondent Actually not in Breach of the Underlying Contract but in Breach of the Arbitration Clause Only

1. Case Seven—Award [2003] Zhongguo Maozhong Jin (Shen) Caizi No.001X

Actually The Parties Have Got No Dispute At All. The Realization Of The Purpose Of Their Deal Is To The Mutual Benefits. And The Realization Must Go Through Some Formalities With Some Competent Authorities With A Judgment Or An Award Confirming Legality And Validity Of The Deal. So Referring The Deal To An Arbitration Institute Or A Court With Jurisdiction Is The Common Intention Or Wish And That Is Required By Some Policy Covering Such Deals. With- out Such A Judgment Or An Award, Their Common Purpose Could Not Be Finally Realized. Though The Defaulting Respondent Actually Did Not Put Any Obstacles In The Arbitral Proceedings, And Instead To Some Extent, It Did Cooperate With The Claimant. If The Respondent Was Somewhat More Active, The Proceedings Would Have Been More Quick And More Smooth And Saving Time/ Money And Trouble Of The Claimant And Would Have Finally Been Beneficial To Both The Parties As Well.

A. Background

Parties: YY Investment Co., Ltd (located in Guangdong Province, China)V. CT Investment LLC(located in the State of Delaware, USA)

In June 2004, a branch of a state-owned bank of China as assignor and an asset management corporation of China as assignee, both located in Shenzhen, executed a subrogation agreement providing that the assignor would transfer its right to the assignee to collect out- standing loans from 63 debtors (companies). The deal went through formalities required.

In December 2005, CT, the respondent of the instant case as assignee and the asset management corporation of China aforesaid as assignor signed a subrogation agreement, providing that the assignor would transfer its right concerning the 63 debtors mentioned above to the assignee.

During the period from March to June 2006, the parties of the Subrogation Agreement went through the formalities required for an assignee of foreign country. That is to say, the deal with foreign company as a buyer or assignee should be specially approved, confirmed and recorded by some competent authorities under the State Council of China and by announcement in some public media to inform all the debtors.

In March 2012 and in Beijing, YY, the claimant of the instant arbitration case, as **Party B** (**assignee**), and CT, the respondent of the instant arbitration case, **as Party A** (**assignor**), entered into a Subrogation Agreement and then a month later executed a Supplementary Agreement to the former. The two agreements are of Chinese version only, collectively named the Agreement.

All the right and liabilities above first originated from the loans by the bank aforesaid to companies. The series of deals above is of packaged outstanding debts.

The consideration of the assignee, the claimant of the instant case, under the disputed Agreement was RMB5, 200.000.00 and the aggregated sum of the subject matter was over RMB420,000,000.00. By April 17, 2012, the assignee had paid in full the price of the deal to the assignor in two installments. All the debtors concerned and their respective guarantors were aware of the deal under the Agreement.

Article 10 Arbitration Clause: *The Agreement shall be construed according to Chinese law, the rights and obligations thereof shall be determined and confirmed according to Chinese law, however, its conflict law principle is not applicable to the Agreement. As for any dispute out of or related to the Agreement, both parties are supposed to, first of all, seek resolution* via*amicable negotiation. If any dispute could not be settled through negotiation, then the relevant dispute shall be referred to CIETAC for arbitration in compliance with effective arbitration rules when the request of arbitration is submitted. The arbitral tribunal shall be consisted of three arbitrators. Each party shall appoint one arbitrator, while the third one, the presiding arbitrator, shall be jointly designated by both parties. In case that both parties fail to reach agreement over the candidate for the presiding arbitrator within 20 days after receipt of the notice of from CIETAC, then he/she shall be designated by the Chairman of CIETAC. However the presiding arbitrator should not be current of former citizen of China or of the United States. The arbitration award is final and binding on both parties of the Agreement. All the arbitral documents shall be written In English.*

B. The Commencement of the Arbitral Proceedings of This Case

The claimant on March 5, 2013, submitted its Request for Arbitration to the South China Office of CIETAC located in Shenzhen,[35] applying to the tribunal for an award to:

(1) Confirm that the Subrogation Agreement and its Supplementary Agreement are legal and valid.
(2) Confirm that the claimant has since April 2012 obtained the rights to collect outstanding loans form over 60 debtors and enjoyed all the appurtenant rights and interests and documents showing the titles concerned (ownership);
(3) In ten days after the award rendered, the respondent shall transfer the title relating to the outstanding loans of all the debtors to the claimant, going through formalities concerned.

On March 11, 2013, the claimant submitted an application to CIETAC, requesting to have some oral hearings held in Shenzhen and on March 15, to the claimant and the respondent the secretariat of CIETAC by courier delivered an arbitration notice and all the arbitration documents concerned, including the Request for Arbitration and the application by the claimant that the oral hearing should be held in Shenzhen to the respondent. In the above notice, the secretariat of CIETAC inquired the parties what language should be used in the proceedings.

C. The Conduct of the Parties During the Proceedings

Both parties agreed to have an oral hearing held in Shenzhen and only the Chinese language used in the proceedings. In response to the aforesaid notice from CIETAC, on April 10, 2013, the claimant and the respondent respectively in writing officially agreed that the oral hearing should be held in Shenzhen and the language used in the proceedings should be Chinese only. That is the first active act adopted in the arbitration proceedings by the respondent in line with the arbitration clause. Because the Agreement was in Chinese only, the subject matter—the outstanding loans and their debtors were located in China—there would be little possibility to have the award enforced out of China. If all the documents had been bilingual (both in Chinese and English) or as to the provision of the Arbitration Clause that "The arbitration document shall be written in English," that would be a heavy burden to the parties, especially the claimant.

D. The Parties Jointly Appointed the Presiding Arbitrator Located in Shenzhen, But the Respondent Did Not Appoint An Arbitrator

The claimant appointed an arbitrator from the panel of CIETAC and the respondent did not appoint an arbitrator within the time limit provided in the arbitration note and therefore the chairman of CIETAC appointed an arbitrator for the respondent. The two parties jointly appointed me as the presiding arbitrator. That was the second act adopted by the respondent in the proceedings. When I decided to accept the appointment as the presiding arbitrator of the tribunal, I was informed that the working language of the case was Chinese only.

The three-member tribunal was formed on May 6, 2013. The parties agreed on the candidate of the presiding arbitrator located in Shenzhen that would result in paying less arbitration fees by the parties, such as the arbitrator's travel and accommodation expenses incurred in dealing with the case. In the CIETAC Rules of 2012, provisions relating to charging the parties any other extra and reasonable costs covering the matters of this paragraph and the previous one.[36]

E. The Respondent Did not Submit Any Written Statement or Submission and Was Absent from the Oral Hearing

The oral hearing was held on June 7, 2013; the agents (a lawyer and three staff members) of the claimant were present, but no representative of the respondent appeared, though it was said that the respondent had an office or similar authorized agent officially established or residing in Shanghai. The day after the oral hearing, a notice with the summary of the hearing was sent to the respondent, inter alia, inquiring whether the addressee had any opinion or comment about the case and would require a further oral hearing. The respondent did not, within the time limit of June 17, make any response.

Generally speaking the proceedings smoothly went on in spite of the failure of the defaulting respondent. On the one hand it was not properly making response to all the inquiry, notice and requirements; and on the other hand it put no obstacles to slow the proceedings.

F. **The Respondent After the Oral Hearing Submitted Some Document Showing That It Had Obtained Official Permission to the Deal Form Competent Authority Of China**

The second statement of attorney of the claimant (mainly stating and confirming the status and authorities of its three staff members) and some additional documents on June 17 and 19, 2013, reached the case manager of the tribunal. On June 19, the respondent submitted to the case manager of the tribunal a Record Registration Form issued by the State Exchange Bureau (of China) showing that the respondent had properly obtained the permission to buy or dispose of the outstanding loans of the instant case, namely the respondent, as assignee or buyer in the previous deal of the outstanding loans from a Chinese financial assets management corporation as assigner or seller, had gone through procedures and had been approved by some competent authorities ("the Record Registration From"). That was the third act taken in accord with the provisions of the arbitration clause by the respondent in the proceedings.

The documents above were sent to the parties by courier, asking them to make comment within 7 days upon receiving. On June 25, the claimant made response, confirming the authenticity, legitimacy and relativity of evidence, the Record Registration Form.

The final award was rendered by all three arbitrators in favor of the claimant on July 23, 2013. All the claims were accepted by the tribunal and as during the oral hearing, about the allocation of fees, the claimant specially expressed that it would bear all the sum of the case. In the award the tribunal decided in its fourth decisions that the claimant bearing all the arbitration fees including the sum as remunerations to the arbitrators and traveling and accommodation expenses of one of the arbitrators from Beijing to Shenzhen.

G. **Commentary**

Actually there was no dispute between the two parties respectively as assignor and assignee at all. What is required for such deals is that the parties to the Subrogation Agreement finally shall transfer tittles of those outstanding loans from the assignor to the assignee, thus the Subrogation Agreement shall be confirmed by a court or by a tribunal. With a judgment or an award the parties could at last realize their common goal of the Agreement.

This case could be settled more economically and in shorter period. The parties could have agreed on a sole arbitrator instead of the three-member tribunal to handle the case. Further, the respondent could have from its Shanghai office dispatched an authorized representative to negotiate with the representative of the claimant and reach a settlement of agreement during the proceedings or at the oral hearing. Then the parties could have requested the tribunal to render a consent award. That would have save the time, money and trouble of the claimant, the secretariat of CIETAC, the case manager of the tribunal and the tribunal as well.

In this case, as parties might not be so familiar with arbitration, the claimant solely shoulders the great burden, not only paying the arbitration fees, but also preparing copies of submissions in quintuplicate. It was not easy at all. Because the claimant submitted supporting evidence, which, inter alia, consisted of dozens of subrogation agreements concerning the series of deals, notary certificates showing that YY had sent the 63 debtors and their respective guarantors the notices of subrogation and other related documents, roughly 63 judgments or conciliation statements with the aforesaid branch of the bank of the state-owned as the plaintiff and those debtors and their respective guarantors as the defendants regarding their respective outstanding loans and those correspondent warranties, copies of announcements of those previous subrogation agreements published in some dailies of gazette nature and function. In other words, the claimant had to prepare thousands of copies of A4 paper. Actually, almost all the supporting materials and pieces of evidence submitted by the claimant were originally provided by the respondent. When I went to the South China Office of CIETAC to chair the hearing, I had to carry a trolley for holding the files of the case. If it had been a sole-arbitrator tribunal, the number of copies submitted or prepared by the claimant would have been at least reduced by two.

H. Commentary on Some Aspects Pertaining to the Omission of the Respondent During the Proceedings

In the award under the heading The Opinion of the Tribunal, while drafting, I had expounded eight questions, respectively as follows:

(1) The capacity of the parties;
(2) The jurisdiction, the governing law, the nationality of the arbitrators and the working language of the case;
(3) The respondent had, by lawful means, obtained the titles over the outstanding loans owed by the 63 debtors;
(4) The validity of the Subrogation Agreement and its Supplement;
(5) The purpose of the Subrogation Agreement and its Supplement;
(6) The performance of the Subrogation Agreement and its Supplement;
(7) The claimant's allegation that the respondent's refusal to go through the formalities concerning the transfer of the titles and the respondent's failing to appear at the oral hearing; and
(8) About the claims of the claimant.

About Question 1, as a rule an arbitrator or a tribunal had to make clear and confirm the identification, legal status and the capacity of the parties. The claimant was required to produce business certificate as a direct evidence to show its identifications, legal status and capacity. But there were no such certification as first evidence directly produced by the defaulting respondent. I had to confirm its legal status and capacity based on some judgments rendered by Shenzhen Court, such as Judgments (2006) Shenzhon Faminsi Chuzi No. 286 and No. 287 and other documents such as the Record Registration Forms. In those judgments, the judges of the collegial benches ascertained, confirmed and accepted the legal status and capacity in carrying on such deals in China. Nevertheless, YY should have produced its business certificate or legal person ID issued by the competent authority of the State of Delaware, the United States of America.

About Question 7, actually there was no refusal to go through the formalities concerning the transfer of the titles by the respondent. As a case, it seemed to me, that the claimant had to makeup some reasons, otherwise how could a case be referred to a tribunal? There had been some improper acts by the respondent, such as not submitting any statement or submission, not pointing an arbitrator as required by the arbitration agreement and the arbitration notice, absent from the oral hearing. Taking part in the proceedings, appearing at the oral hearing and making response to the tribunal were the respondent's obligations to perform and observe the arbitration rules and procedure, thereby the respondent could be said to some extent in breach of his agreement for arbitration. The respondent's absent from the proceedings, submitting no statement of defense and submitting no identification document was not in line with the spirit of arbitration. Failure to act in any arbitration proceeding would generally slow the progress. Further in this case the parties could have reached a settlement agreement and requested the tribunal to render a consent award that would have been to the benefits of both parties. Referring the case to arbitration was not due to any actual difference between the parties. On the contrary, there were no real disputes between the parties at all, the only reasons were that the parties were required to go through formalities with an award confirming their deals.

My co-arbitrators did not quite agree with my remarks on the omission of the respondent, saying there had never been such comments on it in any CIETAC award, we should focus on the issues of the parties only, as to the attitude of one party, and an arbitrator could orally express his opinion in the course of oral hearing. They also expressed that if I would insist on having the remarks written in the award, they would give up their objection.

I persisted in holding the position towards the omission of the defaulting respondent, holding in this case that the respondent was in breach of his consent for arbitration to some extent, though it was not serious. I would have a try, having my remarks aforesaid carried in the award for the first time. My colleagues of scrutiny of the draft award at CIETAC had no objection.

VIII. The Defaulting Respondent Actually in Breach of the Underlying Contract and the Arbitration Clause as Well

1. Case Eight—Award [2003] Zhongguo Maozhong Jincaizi No.054X

The Respondent Should Have Got No Doubt That It had First Been In Breach Of The Underlying Purchase Contract With An Arbitration Clause Incorporated As It Then Had Accepted The goods Under The Contract Returned Due To Some Reason That Would Be Revealed Below, And Then In Breach Of The Agreement For Compensation. When It Refused To Take Part In The Arbitral Proceedings, It Was Further In Breach Of The Arbitration Clause, A Contract More.

A. The Conclusion of the Contract and Some Related Clauses

Parties: MY Trading Co., Ltd (China) v. Laboratories PNT (France)

On May 20, 2011, MY as buyer and the PNT as seller in Guangzhou, China entered into a Purchase Contract and its Supplemental Agreement, providing that the seller would sell NUTRI YIN and NUTRI YANG respectively 10,000 boxes (200mg/tablet x 60 tablets) and the total amount was EUR58,500.00. The arbitration clause contained in the Contract specifically provided that all disputes thereof shall be submitted to CIETAC and the arbitration shall be conducted in Shenzhen. Clauses closely related to the case quoted as follows:

"10 Payment: 30% (EUR17, 550) at acceptance of order by bank transfer (TT), balance (EUR40, 950.00) to be paid by bank transfer (TT) before delivery." "'Balance (EUR40,950.00) to be paid by bank transfer (TT) before delivery' modified to "balance (EUR40, 950.00) to be paid by bank transfer on delivery(in the Supplemental Agreement)."

"14 Inspection and Claim for Indemnification: The law and regulations of the People's Republic of China prohibits disqualified pharmaceuticals to be imported. It is mutually agreed that for the quality of the contracted goods in this category, the Inspection Certificate issued by the Institute for Drug Control/the China Commodity Inspection Bureau after inspecting the goods within 90 days from the date of completion of discharge of the goods at the port of destination shall be taken as final and binding upon both parties. The Seller shall take back all the disqualified goods and compensate the Buyer for the value of the goods plus all losses and fees sustained due to return of the cargo. Should the quantity/weight be found not in conformity with those stipulated in this Contract upon inspection by the Institute for Drug Control/ the China Commodity Inspection Bureau, the Buyer shall have the right to lodge a claim against the Seller for compensation within 90 days from the date of completion of discharge of the good at the port of destination on the basis of the Inspection Certificate issued by the said Institute/Bureau."

B. The Performance of the Contract and the Agreement for Compensation at no Cost

On June 22, 2011, the buyer by TT paid the deposit of EUR17, 500.00 to the seller.

On July 18, 2011, the cargo delivered by air reached Guangzhou. The buyer went through formalities, handling the import cargo customs clearance procedure, paying customs duties and added values taxes, etc.

On September 23, 2011, the Entry-Exit Inspection and Quarantine of the People's Republic of China issued a sanitary certificate, holding that the labels did not meet the labeling requirements. According to the "General Standards For Health (Function) Food (GB16740- 1997), the Guangzhou Entry-Exit Inspection and Quarantine Bureau rendered a notification that the cargo should be returned to the seller."

In November 2011, the parties signed an agreement titled Agreement for Compensation At No Cost, providing that the buyer returned the goods to the seller and the seller re-deliver such goods of same quantity and specifications with proper labels to the buyer. The seller failed to perform the Agreement of Compensation. Dispute arose.

On February 4, 2013, the buyer referred the case to CIETAC, applying for an award that the seller refund the deposit, various losses sustained, and liquidated damages. A notice of arbitration and other arbitration documents were sent by EMS on April 7, and it was confirmed that the notice had been served.

On May 31, 2013, the sole-arbitrator tribunal was formed because the amount in dispute did not exceed RMB2, 000,000.00.[37] And on the same date the formation of the tribunal and date of oral hearing was sent by EMS to the parties. It was confirmed the notice had been served on June 3, 2013.

The seller respondent failed to submit any statement of defense and on June 25, 2013, failed to appear at the oral hearing and remained silence through the proceedings.

After the oral hearing the secretary by EMC informed the respondent of the hearing and asked whether it would submit any written opinion and need any further oral hearing.

C. The Precondition of the Seller Exporting the Special Goods Under the Contract to China

According to the Food Hygiene Law of the People's Republic of China and the Provisions for Health Food Registration, an exporter must first apply to the China Food and Drug Administration ("CFDA") for a certificate of selling some specified goods. The seller while signing the Contract had two such certificates, their validity periods respectively would be ended on January 23, and March 8 of 2012.

Without any submission from the defaulting respondent, I was unaware of the seller's position on the dispute arising from the Contract and its supplement and the agreement of compensation and the allegations of the claimant.

Based on the evidence of the claimant, I, through the inquiries done at the oral hearing, confirmed that the respondent had been in breach of the Purchase Contract and its supplement, and then in breach of the Agreement for Compensation At No Cost., believing that the respondent without any new valid certificate issued by the CFDA, it would have been unable to perform the contract. The claims of the claimant were sustained.

D. Commentary

Once the seller elected the arbitration proceedings to resolve the contractual dispute, the seller was under legal obligation or at least under an ethical obligation to observe and perform arbitration. If the administration team of the respondent was of the opinion that for a small claim attending an oral hearing in a place far away in China form its place of business in France, they could make response, submitting written materials and suggesting that the case examined solely on the basis of the written materials and evidence submitted by the parties. I did in the award comment on the omission of the respondent, holding that the silence and default of the respondent was in breach of the arbitration clause another contract concluded by the two parties. As the award was in favor of the clamant, that was to say that the single-arbitrator tribunal accepted the claim of the claimant that the respondent, the seller of the disputed contract was in breach. Hence the respondent was in double breach of the underlying contract and the arbitration clause.

4 Conclusion

Commercial arbitration is one of the courses of action open to parties to resolve their contractual disputes. The arbitration clause denotes consent of the parties to go for arbitration and exclude the jurisdiction of any court. Thus, the parties are required to abide by the promise made by them contained in the arbitration clause or arbitration agreement and the arbitration rules and procedure. If a party goes back from his promise and fails to observe and perform the applicable arbitration rules and procedure, the arbitral tribunal shall hear the case or continue the proceeding in his absence and make an award accordingly. The defaulting party bears the natural consequence of his default.

Commercial arbitration is a creature of contract. No contract or no agreement there would be no arbitration at all. An arbitration agreement is of contractual nature and a contract containing an arbitration clause consists of two agreements. Taking parting in or refusing to participate in any arbitration proceedings is not a contractual right only. Parties to an arbitration agreement are under a legal obligation as well as under an ethical obligation to keep their contractual promises. Not the potential or the real claimant enjoys the contractual right or is obliged to refer any dispute to arbitration only. Any potential or the real respondent is abided by the arbitration agreement. Refusing to appear in any arbitration proceedings agreement is not waiving his right only.

The bottom line for a defaulting respondent is that he should be at least under a moral obligation to make response to a notice of arbitration, acknowledging that the documents had been served, submitting some documents showing his identification, telling the tribunal or the other party why he would be absent for many oral hearing. At lease a respondent should not put any obstacle to the arbitral proceedings.

Notes

1. For writing this article I have glanced over the volume of the Selected Awards of the China International Economic and Trade Arbitration—Relating to Finance, Estate Property and Disputes of Other Kinds (1995–2002) and the volume of the Selected Awards of the China International Economic and Trade Arbitration—Relating to Disputes Arising From Sales of Goods (1995–2002), both were com- posed by CIETAC and published by Law Press China. The awards issued in the absence of the respondent or one of the respondents respectively carried in pp.10-23, 23–38, 280–289, 337–342 of the former volume (five in all), and in pp.25–33, 34–7-37, 52–57, 64–75, 227–235, 235–245, 272–277, 277–293, 317–346, 386–391,482–490, 490–497,

520–528, 585–592 of the latter volume (fourteen in all). The arbitrators and tribunals of the case did not touch on the absence of the respondent or one of the respondents from the oral hearing (s) or the proceedings. The books carried no information about their respective date of publishing; the prefaces of the books are exactly the same by CIETAC on August 2002. I have also skimmed through the Selected Works of China International Economic And Trade Arbitration Commission Awards (1989–1995) Updated To 1997, Authorized English Version, Editors-in-Chief Priscilla Leung Mei-fun and Wang Sheng-Chang, Sweet & Maxwell, Asia, 1998. There are 96 awards in all. Awards of the Cases 1, 7, 28, 39, 39, 44, 52, 57, 61, 64, 65, 66, 69, 71, 77, 82 86, 92 and 94 were rendered in the absence of the respondent or one of the respondents.

2. In China, there has been an official standard system; a judge is regarded as an official or equal to an official.
3. Article 61 of the Arbitration Law of the People's Republic of China.
4. The Notice of Supreme People's Court on the Matters Relating to Setting Aside a Foreign-Related Award, April 23, 1998.
5. Please refer the headline of the Shenzhen Overseas Chinese News, April 12–18, 2001.
6. See Yanming Huang, Commentary on the Irrational Challenges to the Finality of an Arbitral Award— Analyzing Some Problems Appearing in the Course of Enforcing (1996) CIETAC Award, Civil And Commercial Law Review, Liang Huixing, Law Professor, as the chief editor, Vol. 24, Golden Bridge Culture Press (Hong Kong) Ltd, September 2002, pp. 254–361.
7. See the message carried in the Shenzhen Overseas Chinese News of Shenzhen 2001-04-12–2001-04-18, it reveals that may law professors or law experts attending the conference on the case specially organized by the Legal Advisory Committee of China Federation of Returned Overseas Chinese.
8. See the overseas edition of the People's Daily of November 4, 2011.
9. See Bryan A. Garner, A Dictionary of Modern Legal Usage, Second Edition, Law Press, China, 2003, p. 40.
10. See James E. Clapp, Random House Webster's Dictionary of the Law, New York, 2000, p. 22.
11. See Domke On Commercial Arbitration (The Law of Practice of Commercial Arbitration), Martin Domke; Revised Edition by Gabriel M. Wilner Professor of Law, The University of Georgia School of Law, 2002 Cumulative Supplement, (Published August 2002), Volume 1, By Nuzhat Hafeez, J. D, Thomson, p. 30.
12. Article 13 and its Comment 1 of the UNIDROIT Principles of International Commercial Contracts 2010.
13. See Brian A. Blum, Contracts (Second Edition), China Fangzheng Press, April 2004, pp. 12–13.
14. See supra Note 11. [Martin Domke, Domke On Commercial Arbitration, Revised Edition by Gabriel M. Wilner, Professor of Law, The University of Georgia School of Law, 2002 Cumulative Supplement (Publish August 2002) Vol. 1 by Nuzhat Hafeez, J.D., Thomson West, p. 30].
15. Id. Chap. 10-p. 1; the author of this article has the original Note 1 carried in Chap. 10-p. 2 copied down and bracketed.
16. Id. The author of this article has the original Note 2 carried in Chap. 10-p. 2 copied down and bracketed.
17. Stephen M. Schwebel, "The Severability of the Arbitration Agreement", International Arbitration: Three Salient Problem (Grotius Publications, Cambridge 1987) pp. 1–60, at p. 5. the author of this article re- quotes it from Philippe Leboulanger, The Arbitration Agreement: Still Autonomous? International Council For Commercial Arbitration, International Arbitration 2006: Back to Basics? (General Editor: Albert Jan Van Den Berg, 2007 Kluwer Law International BV, p. 5).
18. See supra Note 9, p. 77.
19. Id. p. 76.
20. See Anthony Houghton SC, Statement of Case: Claims, Defences and Counterclaims, Asian Dispute Review, April 2013, p. 59.

21. See Yanming Huang, Two Notes On The Application Of The CISG To Cases Under The Jurisdiction Of The CIETAC South China, Mealey's International Arbitration Report, September 2012, Volume 27, Issue # 9, p. 27.
22. Id, pp. 19–29 and please see Yanming Huang, Principles Applying in Default Proceedings and Some Misunderstanding of a Default Award, Journal of Inter- national Economic Law, No.2, Volume 12 (2005), Peking University Press, May 2006, pp. 332–361. The Abstract of this article: When a party to a case neither appears at a hearing not submits its statement of defense, how should the tribunal continue the proceedings?How the principles of Due Process and Natural Justice should be reflected? How should be the award rendered? What are the original meanings of "Proceedings of Quexi Shenli (Defaulting Proceedings) and "Quexi Caijue") to rending the award in the absence of the respondent) in the Chinese legislation? The author shows how tribunals proceed with the arbitral proceedings in the respondent's absence and focuses on those cases under the jurisdiction of CIETAC; reviews the practice and general principles under these circumstance in the international arbitration circle and reveals some misreading to the principles. In the article the author in the article also makes known that in China there have been mistakes in turning the above -mentioned legal terminologies into English.
23. See Selected Works of China International Economic And Trade Arbitration Commission Awards (1989- 1995) Updated To 1997, Authorized English Version, Editors-in-Chief Priscilla Leung Mei-fun and Wang Sheng-Chang, Sweet & Maxwell, Asia, 1998, pp. 178–181.
24. Please refer Article 15 of the CIETAC Rules of 1988.
25. Please refer Article 22 of the CIETAC Rules of 1988.
26. See supra Note 23, pp. 214–219.
27. CIETAC had an office established in February 1984 in Shenzhen for the purpose of providing great convenience to the disputing parties, thus they may have their disputes settled nearby without spending much time and much expenses. The CIETAC Rules of1956 applied to all the cases accepted by CIETAC and its Shenzhen Office. In January 1989, the Shenzhen Office was renamed as CIETAC, Shenzhen Sub- Commission, the abbreviation was CIETAC, Shenzhen. For the purpose of less wordy, the author has the abbreviation used.
28. See supra Note 23, pp. 314–317.
29. The CIETAC Rules of 1956, as its second set of rules adopted on September 2, 1988 and came into force as from the date of January 1, 1989. But this case was accepted in 1987.
30. See supra Note 23, pp. 369–372.
31. At that time, the first stage or initial stage of reform and open to the world, in China only those imported and exported companies of state-owned were authorized to sign contracts with foreign companies.
32. See the supra Note 23, pp. 481–484.
33. This case was under the jurisdiction of former CIE-TAC South China and now name as SCIA. Since the case was accepted in January 2012, therefore its series number reflects the relationship between CIETAC and its former South China Sub-Commission.
34. The independent Arbitration Rules of SCIA came into force as from December 1, 2012.
35. CIETAC before its 2012 Arbitration Rules coming into effect on May 1, 2012, the conflicts between the CIETAC and its former sub-commissions respectively located in Shenzhen and Shanghai arose from the different opinions about the wording or provisions of Article 2–6 of the CIETAC Rules of 2012, and it could not be settled through negotiation and compromise. The contradictions subsequently led to the split- ting of the CIETAC, SCIA and SHICA officially and respectively renamed to substitute the former South China Sub-Commission and Shanghai Sub-Commission. That was the apparent cause for the breaking out of the conflicts.
36. See Article 72 (Arbitration Fees and Costs) of the CIETAC Rules of 2012.
37. Id, Article 54. ■

Price in Denying the Validity of an Arbitration Agreement and Refusing to Participate in Arbitral Proceedings Without Grounds

1 Introduction

In this article, an arbitration clause and an arbitration agreement mean the same thing. The author, in his practice, now and then comes across some party to a case, especially the respondent, who challenges the validity of an arbitration clause by saying that there is no effective arbitration agreement between it and its counterpart. The respondent therefore challenges the jurisdiction of the arbitration institution to which the claimant, according to the arbitration clause, refers its request for arbitration. Some of the respondents' arguments are true. But this article focuses on another side—a respondent acting without grounds in denying the existence or validity of an arbitration clause. The respondent fails to adopt a correct attitude. After the arbitration institution or the appointed tribunal issues a decision on the existence and validity of the arbitration clause and on its jurisdiction over the case, confirmation being made, the respondent still stubbornly adheres to its opinions, without rationally giving up the seesaw battle (tug-of-war) with its counterpart and taking account of the decision of the arbitration institution or the tribunal, without properly exercising its rights to file statements of defense or be present, address the tribunal and make submissions or make convincing argument at oral hearings. Therefore, this usually results in a heavier price. This is a case of that kind.[1]

This commentary was published In Meraley's International Arbitration Report, Vol 21, # 1, January 2006, pp.26–40. The author is grateful to Professor Xiuwen Zhao with the Law School of the People's University,China, Madam Wendy S. W. Wong with S. W. Wang & Associates, Hong Kong and Mr. Qingjun Jin with King & Wood for their assistance such as in providing some materials relating to Revpower case and different cases. The author's sincere thanks must go to Mr. Marcus S. Jabobs, QC, a distinguished arbitrator of Australia, for reading the article, pointing out some mistakes and giving many valuable pieces of advice.

Y. Huang, *Commentaries on Commercial Arbitration in Modern China*, Modern China and International Economic Law, https://doi.org/10.1007/978-981-95-0168-7_5

2 Revpower Ltd. v. the Shanghai Far-East Aero-Technology Import and Export Corporation

(1) **Arbitrators:** There was a tribunal of three arbitrators.[2]

(2) **The Background:** Revpower Limited (Revpower') was solely funded by American Ross Engineering Corporation and incorporated under the law of Hong Kong having its principal place of business in Hong Kong.[3] It entered into a Compensation Trade Agreement (Agreement') with the Shanghai Far-East Aero-Technology Import & Export Corporation (Far-East') on June 5,1988.

Under the Agreement, Far-East was to manufacture industrial batteries for Revpower's specifications with machinery, equipment, raw materials, and engineering expertise supplied by Revpower. The products produced by Far-East were to be sold by Revpower in the United States and elsewhere. Prices of the first three years were provided in Appendix II. Clause 14 was titled Disputes, Claims and Arbitration as following:

(a) All disputes or claims arising out of the Agreement shall be settled by friendly consultation between the parties if possible.

(b) Except for excusable delays and conditions specified under the Force Majeure clauses in Articles 12 and 13 of the Agreement, if one party breaches the Agreement and causes the other party to suffer loss or to be deprived of rights and benefits accorded it under the terms of the Agreement, the injured party has the right to claim compensation from the infringing party for the losses incurred and should set up a claim within 30 days after the predetermined performance date as specified in the Agreement and provide documentary evidence necessary for the claim. Documentary evidence of Revpower shall be issued by the American Arbitration Association. Documentary evidence of Far-East shall be issued by CCPIT(China Council for the Promotion of International Trade). If the party against whom the claim is filed does not accept the claim(after all evidence is issued)the parties shall submit the dispute to arbitration as provided below.

(c) Should either party, after 60 days after the dispute arises, believe that no solution to the dispute can be reached through friendly consultation, such party had the right to initiate and require arbitration in Stockholm, Sweden, in accordance with the Statute(R&P)of the Arbitration Institute of the Stockholm Chamber of Commerce.

(d) Any arbitration award shall be final and binding on both parties. The parties shall make any payments of award or costs within sixty days of such award, and shall otherwise act according to the award.

(e) The arbitration fees and costs shall be borne according to the decision of the arbitrators.

(f) During consultation or arbitration, each party shall continue to perform its obligations under the Agreement.

Disputes arose, with a cover letter dated July 2,1991; Revpower submitted to the Arbitration Institute of the Stockholm Chamber of Commerce('SCC Institute')a document entitled' Request for Arbitration, General Narrative, Selection of Arbitrator and Statement of Claim against Defendant dated June 29, 1991 (Request for Arbitration'). Revpower says that initially the cooperation between the parties appears to have developed according to plan, equipment and machinery supplied by the Claimant was in place at an existing battery factory of the Respondent ('the Battery Factory') and in working order. Various difficulties arose and in November 1989 the Respondent failed to purchase and install necessary equipment which it had undertaken to purchase or construct in China and to reconstruct the buildings within a reasonable time. These failures concerned primarily the equipment necessary for the final stages of the production of batteries called 'formation' and 'charging.' Although the equipment and machinery supplied by the Claimant was in place at an existing Battery Factory of the Respondent and in working order by the end of 1989, enabling a successful—if limited—test production to be carried out, the missing final steps of the production line made production of finished products impossible. The Claimant furthermore submits that after the so-called Tian'anmen Square events in China during June 1989 the Respondent's attitude to the project changed dramatically. From that time the Respondent was no longer able to provide adequate personnel either by way of competence or in numbers to complete the missing part of the production line, finish the building work, absorb training and start production. A total separation was carried out between the Battery Factory and its staff and the very limited facilities and staff that were assigned to the new production line under the name of Qi Bao Factory. In November 1989 the Respondent closed the Qi Bao Factory and representatives of the Claimant were thereafter denied access to it. Simultaneously the Battery Factory demanded substantial increases of the agreed fixed prices in order to make any deliveries in the future. Furthermore, the Respondent failed to arrange for a performance guarantee by the Bank of China which was its duty under the Agreement and which was necessary for financing purposes for the Claimant to obtain. All of the aforesaid circumstances, which in the Claimant's view constituted breaches of contract by the Respondent, led the Claimant to give notice of termination of the Agreement and subsequently to terminate it, effective as of February 1,1990.

During the oral hearing, Revpower adjusted its monetary claim to the amount of US$4,486,086 plus interest and costs.

By letter dated October 5, 1991, Far-East submitted that the SCC Institute did not have jurisdiction over the claims made by the Claimant in its Request for Arbitration.

On April 21, 1993, less than two months before the scheduled June 14 final hearing, Far-East notified the tribunal that it had decided to withdraw from the arbitration proceedings. The panel, having earlier decided that it had jurisdiction over the case, proceeded with the arbitration in Far-East's absence. On July 13,1993,after four days of hearings, a unanimous arbitral panel granted Revpower an award in the amount of approximately US$4,486,086 plus interest from the date the case was submitted in 1991, and attorney's fees.[4] Please compare with Revpower's price of the equipment, raw materials, and expertise of about US$300,000[5] or US$322,086.[6]

Far-East referred the same dispute to the Shanghai Intermediate People's Court[7] ('the SI Court') in March 1993.

3 The Complaint Brought by Far-East at the SI Court

On April, 1993, the SI Court accepted the complaint on the ground that the arbitration clause in the Agreement was ambiguous and incapable of performance because it did not refer to the SCC Institute. Further, the SI Court held that Revpower had breached the clause without taking any step to consult the counterpart.[8] Revpower immediately challenged the SI Court's jurisdiction over the case. On May 18,1995,the SI Court, ruled to reject Far-East's application. Far-East appealed to the Shanghai Higher People's Court. The latter on July 24, 1995, ruled to uphold the former SI Court's ruling.

The author believes if Far-East had been present at the oral hearing, the total amount of the awarded claim would have been and could have been reduced or even be greatly reduced.

4 Nine Versions Relating to the Time and Main Cause of the Disputes

Has the tribunal exactly confirmed the time and the main cause of the disputes? It seems to me that point is still open to question. Let me quote some statements from the Award.

The first: Various difficulties arose, and by the end of 1989 the new factory was still not in operation.[9]

The second: The Claimant furthermore submits that after the so-called Tian'anmen Square events in the *PRC during June 1989 the Respondent's attitude to* the project changed dramatically. From that time the Respondent was no longer able to provide adequate personnel either by way of competence or in numbers to complete the missing part of the production line, to finish the building work, to absorb training and start production. A total separation was carried out between the Battery Factory and its staff and a very limited facility and staff was assigned to the new production line under the name Qi Bao Factory.[10]

The third: In November 1989 the Respondent closed the Qi Bao Factory and representatives of the Claimant were thereafter denied access to it. At about the same time the Battery Factory demanded substantial increases of the agreed fixed prices in order to make any deliveries in the future. Furthermore, the Respondent failed to arrange for a performance guarantee by the Bank of China which was its duty under the Agreement and was necessary for financing purposes for the Claimant to obtain.[11]

The fourth: The main issue to be resolved by the Tribunal is whether or not the Respondent has committed a breach of contract, entitling the Claimant to damages. That issue is mainly related *to the event which took place during the second half* of 1989 and which caused the Claimant to terminate the Agreement.[12]

The fifth: The parties have presented the Tribunal with two different and conflicting versions of the events which led to the result that the new battery factory never reached the production stage and instead was closed in November 1989.[13] In terms of time, that version is identical with the third version.

The sixth: The evidence presented by the Claimant also demonstrates that the failure during the later *autumn of 1989 to start production due to the fact* that machinery, equipment, and facilities were missing, which it was the Respondent's duty to provide, particularly vital equipment that was missing—processing equipment necessary in forming and charging departments.[14]

The seventh: The evidence before the Tribunal also substantiates the submission by the Claimant that the *decision in June 1989 to make a separation between the Battery Factory and the new factory caused consider*able difficulties, such as shortage of staff and lack of management.[15]

Please compare this seventh version with the third and fifth. In the third and fifth versions, the event took place in November 1989, but not in June as in the seventh version.

The eighth: The Tribunal's conclusion is therefore *that the fact the new factory was not in operable condition by the end of 1989 was due to failure by* the Respondent to fulfill its obligation under the Agreement.[16]

The ninth: The Tribunal agrees with the Claimant *that the fact that no production could take place in* the factory by December 1989 was due to such serious failures by the Respondent in meeting its obligations under the Agreement.[17]

The above said versions or statements, from the fourth to the ninth, six in all, are the versions by the Tribunal, i.e., they were accepted and confirmed by the Tribunal. Why are there six versions? Which is the final conclusion? In dealing with a key issue, the Tribunal presents various versions. That is not in line with the basic principle: "An award must be clear, consistent and certain."[18]

Are there any other versions or statements concerning the time and the main cause of the dispute? Yes, there are indeed more versions about the issue. "The contract arrangement proceeded relatively well for the first 18 months of the relationship."[19] The Agreement was concluded on June 51,988,and the 18-month period ran from June 1988 to December 1989. It is stated that the aforesaid is by one of the attorneys of Revpower. He also stated:

> Revpower's problems with SFAIC (Far-East)started in December 1989 when SFAIC informed Revpower that the battery prices would have to be increased substantially and the Bank of China could not issue the required performance guarantee. Each of these notifications constituted a material breach of the Agreement.[20]

The aforesaid two versions are identical in terms of time. I number them as the Tenth Version. May I draw your attention to the Third Version? The Claim-ant at the oral hearing says that the Respondent demanded substantial increases of the agreed fixed prices in November 1989.

The Claimant almost succeeded in all its claims. Nevertheless, I could not get any impression that the claims were automatically satisfied due to the default of the Respondent.

5 Price and Lesson

It is said that pursuant to the Award, Far-East was ordered to pay Revpower US$6,500,000, which was more or less equivalent to 20 times the contract value.[21] The former SI Court did not accept the application for enforcement of the Award by Revpower due to the pending jurisdiction issue before it.[22] Later, Revpower, on February 29, 1996, submitted its application to the Shanghai No.2 Intermediate People's Court. On March 1, 1996, the Court ruled to recognize the Award. On April 2, 1996, the Court enforced the Award, freezing and allotting a certain amount from Far-East's account. If the sum was inadequate, the balance should be made from selling and auctioning the properties of the Respondent.

Far-East went bankrupt.

Professionals at CIETAC observed the case.[23] Some say that the SIC had wrongfully accepted Far-East's application for commencing legal proceeding concurrently in relation to the same dispute which was pending at the SCC Institute.

One CIETAC professional believes that the arbitration clause in the Agreement at issue was valid and Far-East's action at the SI Court was nothing but a dilatory tactic to interrupt the arbitration proceedings. Furthermore, he holds that the SI Court made another mistake by erroneously applying Chinese law to interpret the validity of the arbitration agreement. In the instant case, it should have been governed by the Swedish law, the lexarbitri. Lastly, he thinks that the SI Court had delayed the enforcement proceedings, which had unnecessarily made justice time-consuming.24[24] And he is of the following view:

> The Revpower case has brought about serious and negative effect on China's reputation with regards to recognition and enforcement of foreign arbitral awards.[25]

In fact, our international counterparts in the commercial arbitration circle are familiar with the tactics repeatedly adopted by some parties from the main-land of China and some courts. A Geneva Professional says:

> When confronted with a Request against a Mainland China party sometimes seizes the Chinese courts claiming that no valid arbitration agreement exist. It used to occur sometimes that in such situations the Chinese courts held that there was no valid arbitration agreement as the ICC was allegedly not an arbitration commission as defined by the Chinese Arbitration Law.[26]

In addition, another foreign professional observes:

> Sometimes you see that a losing party may challenge an award only in order to gain time. This survey has also proven that such methods in principle do not pay.[27]

6 Some Similar Cases

1. Brief Arbitration Clause and Art 16 of the Arbitration Law of PRC

In the practice, the author of this article often comes across a brief arbitration clause that is not tailor-made to fit the kinds of disputes that the parties think will most likely arise between them. On the contrary, it only provides that the parties will refer all disputes in connection with or arising out of their contracts to arbitration. As a professional says:

> It says nothing about how the arbitration is to proceed, where, before whom or when. That leaves the resolution of those things to whatever statute governs. The statutes, however, are usually sketchy and rarely say much, if anything, about those things. The upshot is that the parties are left to fight over them after their dispute arises.
>
> The arbitration clause can resolve all those things, and should. If it does, there will be no fight about them. And if the clause is well-tailored, the arbitration will likely go forward smoothly and exactly as the parties wanted it go.[28]

An arbitration clause could be very simple; still it is valid and workable. For instance, parties could have the clause state, "Arbitration in Hong Kong." When there is a dispute, either party could refer the dispute to the Hong Kong International Arbitration Centre (HKIAC). If the counterpart refuses to observe it, the HKIAC would, according to the stipulations of the Hong Kong Arbitration Ordinance, push the proceedings forward and serve as the channel for the communication of the parties and provide the procedure with administrative services, etc.[29]

Art 16 of the Arbitration Law of the PRC ('the Arbitration Law') provides that three items of contents shall be included in an arbitration clause: the expression of the parties' wish to submit to arbitration; the matters to be arbitrated; and the arbitration institution selected by the parties. Arbitration institutes could be established in the municipalities directly under the Central Government, in the municipalities where the governments of provinces and autonomous regions are located or cities of 'prefecture level'0.[30] There are many cities of "prefecture level" and above in China. Since the Arbitration Law entered into force on September 1, 1995, there have been 185 arbitration commissions established up to now. As there are so many arbitration institutions, there would be more and more issues relating to jurisdiction. But the 'criteria' established in Art 16 of the Arbitration Law is not a standard of globalization. Businessmen should not, in their deals with their counterparts of other countries or regions, determine the validity of an arbitration agreement in light of the criteria contained in the Arbitration Law only.

Furthermore, it is the common understanding in the judicial and arbitral circles of China that rigid adherence to Art 16 of the Arbitration Law would result in the violation of the basic principle—the autonomy of will. A fact that highlights the common understanding and trend in this regard is the Draft Judicial Interpretation Of Some Issues About the Arbitration Law for Seeking Opinions by the Supreme People's Court (issued on July 22,2004).[31] As the parties have commonly expressed to have their future or existing dispute referred to arbitration, any party that unilaterally denies the effect of the agreement or withdraws the commitment or consent, would get no support from a court or an arbitral institution.

2. **A Case Relating to Parties in Guangzhou, China and Singapore**

A lawyer located in Guangzhou told me of a situation involving a sales agreement between a foreign company and a Chinese company where the agreement's arbitration clause stated:

> Any dispute, controversy or difference which may arise between the parties hereto in relation to this Agreement, or the breach thereof, which may not be settled by mutual accord without undue delay, shall be settled by arbitration in Singapore in the English language in accordance with the rules of procedures of the Singapore Arbitration Association. The award thereof shall bind both parties hereto.[32]

In accordance with the aforesaid arbitration clause, the Singapore party submitted a request for arbitration to the Singapore International Arbitration Center. The Guangzhou lawyer wrote me, asking:

> As there was no such an arbitral institution(the Singapore Arbitration Association)in Singapore, was the clause valid according to the arbitration law of Singapore? It is provided in the clause that the arbitration rules of the Singapore Arbitration Association apply, could the Singapore International Arbitration Center accept the case?[33]

In addition, he told me that the Chinese party had brought an action against the Singapore party in a Chinese court and the latter had accepted it and fixed the time for opening a court session.

In my response, I said that the clause was valid and the Singapore International Arbitration Center had the jurisdiction over the case. It was unwise for the Chinese party to institute an action at a court in China. Instead, it would be only reasonable for the Chinese company to accept the cognizance of the Singapore International Arbitration Center and submit a defense or adopt any other proper measures.

I asked advice from a Singapore lawyer, thinking his opinion would be more convincing. The response from Singapore was:

> Although the clause is a pathological arbitration clause—in the sense that there is no such institution as the Singapore Arbitration Association, I believe it is nevertheless valid and the Singapore International Arbitration Center will regard itself as having jurisdiction.[34]

If the Chinese party insisted on the action in China, it might result in great trouble. If you say that the parties incorrectly wrote the name of the Singapore International Arbitration Center and there is only one permanent arbitration institution, it therefore had the jurisdiction over the case. People would accept that explanation.

3. A Case Relating to Parties in Shenzhen, China and America

A report relating a story of the twists and turns of the course of an American corporation purchasing shares of a Shenzhen bank was carried in Nanfan Weekend. It revealed that the negotiation between the Newbridge Asia AIV III L.P.an investment vehicle of Newbridge Investment Group with the Shenzhen Development Bank Co. Ltd. (SZ Development), located in Shenzhen, China for the purpose of the former becoming a heavy(or principle)shareholder which I was still not very sure of after reading the report. Later, some competitor appeared, and there was a serious setback in the negotiation. It was said in the report:

> On September 9, 2003, the Newbridge submitted to the ICC a request for arbitration against the SZ Development and its shareholders in accordance with the "exclusivity" of the parties in the negotiation of reorganization. The SZ Development and its shareholders later submitted a counterclaim. Simultaneously Shenzhen Municipality Investment Management Corporation and other shareholders of the SZ Development (on November 25,2003)brought an action in the Shenzhen Intermediate People's Court, requesting the court to confirm that the arbitration clause, in the framework agreement among the Newbridge and the SZ Development and them, was invalid.[35]

Judging by my professional experience, I guess the framework agreement was between the Newbridge as one side and the SZ Development and its shareholders on the other side; otherwise, one could not say that the SZ Development and its shareholders were in breach of the contract and that they were the respondents of the arbitration application.

Out of professional sensitivity, I believed that it was not wise and not good for the shareholders of the SZ Development to institute an action for the purpose of denying the validity of the arbitration clause. It was beyond my imagination that the American lawyers with the Newbridge would have drafted an invalid arbitration clause referring future disputes to the ICC. But I am not very sure that what some journalists said in the report reflected all the truth or details of the agreement. As no party concerned has made any reaction, such as clarifying some facts, etc., I might be in a position to accept it as roughly true. If I had gotten access to the case, I would have aired some ideas relating to validity of the arbitration clause.

Over one year after reading this report, in July 2005, I got the arbitration cause of the Agreement:

'Article 14 Governing Law and Dispute resolution:

> 14.1 This Agreement shall be governed by and interpreted in accordance with the laws of the People's Republic of China. In the event that there is no provision under Chinese laws with respect of a specific matter of this Agreement, then the international customs shall be applied.
>
> 14.2 any and disputes("Dispute") relating to or arising from the performance of this Agreement shall be first be settled by the Parties through amicable consultation.
>
> If the Parties fail to resolve the Dispute by amicable consultation within thirty (30)days after its occurrence, any of the Parties may submit the Dispute to the Court of Arbitration of the

> International Chamber of Commerce for arbitration to be conducted in a developed country or area to be selected by Seller(including Hong Kong)and under the auspice of the Conciliation and Arbitration Rules of the International Chamber of Commerce. The arbitration manner and proceedings shall be guided by related international customs.
>
> The arbitration award shall be final and binding over all Parties. The arbitration costs shall be borne by the Party/Parties that lost the case.
>
> The Parties shall, except for the Dispute under arbitration, continue to perform all other terms under this Agreement.

This was a valid arbitration clause, though not a good one. I guess it was done with benefit of counsel of both sides. There were some faults in it. A particular permanent arbitral institution was chosen but without a fixed arbitration place yet, therefore lawyers of both sides and their respective principals were not prepared and even were unable to answer the following question:

> Do you know the interaction between the Institutional Rules and the lexarbitri, i.e., the Arbitration Act at the proposed/contemplated place of arbitration?[36]

Furthermore, the parties and their lawyers should have been familiar or sure of that question and a number of derived questions which 'are the most essential areas of concern where you may check for harmony (or conflict) between provisions of Institutional Arbitration Rules and the provisions of the lex arbitri(i.e., the Arbitration Act at the place of arbitration) as far as such latter provisions are of a mandatory character or pertaining to public policy at the place of arbitration.[37] For example,

(g) Does the lex arbitri contain specific pro-visions of a mandatory character regarding proceedings in the absence of the defendant party(see, e.g., Austria and the Netherlands Arbitration Act, Article 1040)?
(h) Does the lex arbitri contain special re-quirements regarding the arbitrators deliberations?
  - For instance, does the lex arbitri recognize the authority of a "truncated arbitral tribunal"? Does it recognize a provision such as Article 11 of the International Rules of the AAA, or(the less clear) Article 16.2 of the LCIA Rules?
  - Does it recognize an authority given to the chairman to decide alone if no majority can be obtained (see, e.g., Article 19 of the ICC Rules and Article 16.3 of the LCIA Rules)?

(i) What is the time-limit for filing a challenge (strictly limited, e.g., 30 days in Switzerland, 3 months or even unlimited as under other national arbitration laws)?[38]

The aforesaid questions are closely related to, inter alia, the efficiency of the arbitration proceedings.

So huge the sum of the transaction was. It is said in the report that Newbridge was to pay RMB1,235,000,000.00 to four principal shareholders of the SZ Development for their shares, the whole share proportion of the three, respectively making up

7.08%, 4.02%, and 1.32% of the whole share of the SZ Development and part of one heavy shareholder's share ownership. That last heavy shareholder's share makes up 5.77% of the whole share ownership of the SZ Development. Parties and their lawyers should have done pre-drafting and drafting checks for arbitration clause.[39]

Nevertheless, I do believe that the lawyers of the heavy shareholders of the SZ Development must know or should have known the validity and enforceability of the arbitration clause. Was denying the validity of it one of the tactics adopted by some parties in the course of the negotiations?

Fortunately, sometime later, the report reveals that the parties reopened their negotiation. On March 19,2004, parties respectively withdrew their requests for arbitration and counterclaim. Though the report does not mention the development and result of the lawsuit at the Shenzhen Intermediate People's Court, it does show that there was a happy ending of the negotiation.

4. **Interpretation of 'An Arbitration Trap'**

There was a brief introduction to an arbitration case, authored by the China Export & Credit Insurance Corporation Shenzhen Branch (the "Insurance Corp") carried in Shenzhen Special Zone Daily entitled as An Arbitration Trap.[40]

Company A (a Chinese company, seller) and Company B (A French company, buyer) concluded a trade agreement. The subject matter was magnesium (Mg) powder, the total price was US$736,000, the terms of payment was T/T 75 days. Company A insured all-risks insurance of short-term export credit insurance with the Insurance Corp., and it obtained a written grant that the credit quota of Company B was US$1,500,000 and subject to O/A 75 days. According to the agreement, from April to July 2003 Company A delivered the goods in five installments.

When the payment was due, Company B, after paying part of the price, required that the payment be rearranged. Thereafter, according to a new repayment arrangement, Company B paid a further part of the debt and the outstanding balance (arrears in contribution) was US$244,000. CompanyA pressed for the repayment of the debt, Company B asked for a grace period of one week. But after the lapse of the week, Company B, to the surprise of Company A, said that it had got a stop-payment order from a court and the sum for the outstanding balance was frozen and it was unable to pay the balance. Company A nevertheless requested Company B to execute the repayment arrangement. Company B refused to pay on the ground of the stop-payment order of the court. Therefore Company A submitted a claim notice to the Insurance Corp.

With the authorization of Company A, the Insurance Corp. got in touch with the debtor Company B, inquiring into the matter of the stop-payment order, finding out that the stop-payment order was a legal document. Further inquiry revealed that there had been a sales contract between Company A and Company C (a British company, buyer)relating to the deal of purchasing Mg Ingot. As Company A had not executed the contract, Company C had referred the dispute to a British arbitration institution. Company A, after receiving arbitration notice from the arbitration institution, defended that there had only been an intention between it and Company C, there had been no valid contract; furthermore, there had been no arbitration clause, therefore the arbitration institution enjoyed no competent jurisdiction; but stated that anyway it would be willing to accept an arbitration within China.

A sole arbitrator decided to rule on his/her jurisdiction. And taking into account the costs that Company A might have to bear and for reasons of economy, the arbitrator decided to hold a teleconference.

In view of the completely different arguments of both parties and their supporting evidence, the arbitrator decided in his/her interim award to deal with two preliminary issues the effectiveness of the contract between Company A and Company C and the jurisdictional objection. With regard to the effectiveness of the contract, the arbitrator, in accordance with the principle of the closest and most real connection, concluded that the applicable law was Chinese law. Based on the provisions of Chinese law and the relevant supporting evidence, the arbitrator ruled that the contract entered by Company A and Company C was effective.

As to the application of law concerning the standard terms, on the one hand Company C insisted on the application of British law, Company A, on the other, did not furnish the arbitrator with any evidence about related provisions of Chinese law; in the end the tribunal applied the law of England.

After ruling that he/she had jurisdiction to adjudicate upon the claim made by Company C, the arbitrator decided in the final award that because of the failure of Company A in discharging its obligations of delivering goods under the contract, it should pay for the damages and related losses of Company C.

Company A with Company C concluded a contract with an arbitration clause. But it seems to me that Company A knew little about arbitration. Company A, after Company C referred the dispute arising from the contract to arbitration, denied that there was an arbitration clause. Judging from the message title, I do believe there was an arbitration clause in the contract. But Company A and the Insurance Corp. could not properly face the arbitration case, making good presentation during the oral hearing on the phone and providing the arbitrator with relative provisions of Chinese law. In the mind of the executives of Company A and the Insurance Corp. as well, the stipulation of referring disputes to arbitration was not the common will of Company A and Company C but a trap made by Company C for deceiving and tricking the seller. It was ridiculous. The title of the message itself shows that Company A and its insurer, in facing the case could not handle the somewhat difficult situation properly.

It should be pointed out that the Insurance Corp. or its staff might have no sufficient legal and arbitration knowledge or be short of experience, and therefore that it is understandable for failing to give its readers a clear picture of the process of the case. For example, strictly speaking about the issue of application of law, the English arbitrator might have said it in this way: Under the rules of English private international law, foreign law is a question of fact, to be established by expert evidence; failing evidence to the contrary, English private international law compels me to assume that any foreign law is the same as English domestic law. Neither party has furnished me with any evidence about the Chinese substantive law of contract. Accordingly, I am bound to assume that it does not differ from the law of England.

But on the teleconference and without any guidance of any lawyers or any previous advice or reminding from the arbitrator, how could Company A be able to have an expert present and accepted by the arbitrator?

Furthermore a legal expert would have to show his/her qualification.

Without proper knowledge of arbitration and without asking advice of qualified lawyers, being a merchant or insurer on the platform of international trade, Company A and its insurer should make up for that deficiency. Otherwise, you would have to pay a price but still have no idea what was the root of the problem.

7 Final Award in Case No. 5460 Under the Jurisdiction of ICCA[41]

1. Arbitrator And Related Information of the Case

Arbitrator: There was a tribunal consisting of sole arbitrator.[42]

Parties: Claimant: Austrian franchisor Defendant: South African franchisee.

Place of Arbitration: London, United Kingdom (fixed by the ICC Court of Arbitration).

2. Background

In August/September 1979, an Austrian Mr. X concluded a franchise contract with a South African Company relating to the manufacture by the South African Company (SA Company) of certain equipment of Mr. X's design and the payment by the company to Mr.X of certain royalties thereon (the 'Contract'). It was provided in a clause that parties submitted to the jurisdiction of the International Chamber of Commerce, as the arbitration court.

When the SA Company failed to pay the minimum royalties under the Contract, Mr. X started court proceedings on January 25, 1983, in the Supreme Court of South Africa (SASC), claiming from the SA company SA Rand 288,000 together with interest thereon at 11%.

> On October 11,1983,the SA Company entered a Special Plea, stating that the Contract contained the aforesaid arbitration clause, that the said action was in respect of disputes which were covered by the arbitration clause, and that it was and remained ready and willing to do all things necessary to the proper conduct of an arbitration in terms of the said arbitration cause; accordingly, *it prayed that the action be stayed pending the arbitration proceedings*, and that the claimant be ordered to pay the costs of the action (emphasis added).

The action was stayed but not dismissed, pending the arbitration proceedings. Were the arbitral proceedings of solid ground at that time?

> *By a request for arbitration of November 12, 1985, Mr. X there upon instituted ICC proceedings (emphasis added), claiming* from the SA company the sum of A$4,896,000 (being the equipment of the sum of SA Rand 288,000 referred above), together with interest thereon at the rate of 11%per annum, and the costs of the arbitration.

The claimant turned on arbitration in the ICC International Arbitration Court but not officially withdrew the lawsuit in the SASC.

By its reply to the said request of December 13, 1985, the defendant contended that:

(a) *because proceedings in respect of the same claim were pending in the SASC, 'it was not competent for the claimant to institute the arbitration proceedings.'*(emphasis added)—Was this argument without any reason?
(b) 'The claimant's claim 'might have become prescribed;
(c) 'The claimant had failed to perform his obligations under the Contract;'—Why not exhaust this argument with some evidence at the oral hearing in the arbitration?
(d) Accordingly, the claimant was not entitled to the payment of the sum claimed, or of any sum, from the defendant.

Despite repeated reminders and extensions of time and duly invited, the SA Company refused to sign the Terms of Reference and refused to participate in the arbitral proceedings. (emphasis added).

'In the course of 1987 the sole arbitrator (appointed by the ICC Court of Arbitration) rendered an award, ordering the defendant to pay Mr.X AS 4,896,000 together with interest from January 25, 1983, at the rate of11%per annum and costs.'

2. Excerpt of the Principal Part of the Award

A. Applicable Law

[1] "The place of this arbitration is London, and on any question of choice of law I must therefore apply the relevant rules of the private international law of England. Under those rules, questions of performance or breach of a contract fall to be determined in accordance with what we call the "proper law" of the Contract. Unlike the laws of some other countries, the principal consideration here is not the lex loci contract us, but rather the law of the place with which the contract has its closest connection—which, in practice, means the place on which the principal obligations under the Contract are to be performed."

[2] 'In the present case, virtually all the obligations of both parties fell to be performed in South Africa. It was there that the claimant's drawings and other documents were to be delivered; it was there that the defendant had to obtain the appropriate exchange control consent before dispatching the royalties to claimant; above all, it was there that the equipment was to be made and sold. On any commercial view, the principal place of performance of this Contract, and the place with which it had its closest connection, was South Africa. Insofar as it may be necessary for the purposes of this award, I therefore hold that the proper law of the Contract was South Africa law.

[3] 'Under the rules of English private international law, foreign law is question of fact, to be established by expert evidence; failing evidence to the contrary, English private international law compels me to assume that any foreign law

is the same as English domestic law. Neither party has furnished me with any evidence about the South African substantive law of contract. Accordingly, I am bound to assume that it does not differ from the law of England.'

B. Competence to Institute Arbitration Proceedings

[4] '...When the claimant instituted his action in the SASC...he had a choice of two action, or the institution of arbitration ings under the Rules of the ICC. He chose the first. Thereupon, the defendant too had a choice: to let the dispute be decided in the action or to rely on the arbitration clause in the Contract and apply for a stay of the action pending the institution of arbitration proceedings. Having considered the matter for several months, it chose the second course by entering *their Special Plea On the claimants motion, the SASC on 23 October 1983 ordered that this Special Plea should be decided separately, and prior to the trial of the matter, and that the action should meanwhile be* stayed (emphases added). There upon, the claimant instituted the present arbitration proceedings'.

[5] 'Having submitted a voluminous reply to the request for arbitration and conducted a good deal of correspondence with me—in the course of which it sought more than once, and received, an assurance from me that its clients would be entitled to be heard in arbitration even if they failed to pay their share of the advance for costs to the ICC—the defendants *representatives in this arbitration, under cover of a brief letter dated 18 August 1986,sent me a copy of a document purporting to be a Notice of Withdrawal of the Special Plea, prepared by the attorneys acting for the defendant in the action before the SASC (who are* not the same as the defendant's representatives in this arbitration), and dated "...day of August 1986." (emphases added).

[6] 'Even on the assumption that a dated original of this copy has been duly submitted to the Supreme Court, it cannot retrospectively affect the competence of the present arbitration. Were it otherwise, a defendant in similar circumstances could send a claimant from pillar to post in perpetuity, by calling for arbitration if the claimant chooses litigation and thereupon, reversing his position, calling for litigation if the claimant accepts that invitation and chooses arbitration. In my judgment, once the defendant has elected to claim arbitration(as it was perfectly entitled to do),and once the claimant, in response to that election, has instituted arbitration proceedings, it is no longer open to the defendant to resile from it.

Accordingly, I conclude that it was competent for the claimant to institute the present arbitration proceedings, and that it is competent for me to determine them.

The arbitrator found that Mr. X had not committed any of the breaches of the obligations under the Contract that the SA Company alleged. The claim of the claimant was fully sustained except for the claim of compound interest.

3. Observations

As there was an explicit arbitration clause in the Contract, the defendant was perfectly entitled to choose arbitration under the jurisdiction of ICC,and deny the litigation in the SASC, though accepting the litigation would have given the defendant advantage over the claimant in terms of travel cost and or in addition to governing law, etc. The defendant could make only one choice. When the claimant, in response to the defendant's election, instituted arbitration proceedings, in terms of good faith and estoppel, the defendant should not change its mind. The SASC on October 23, 1984, stated:

> On the claimant's motion ordered that the Special Plea should be decided separately, and prior to the trial of the matter, and the action should meanwhile be stayed.

No concrete request in Mr. X's motion was mentioned.

I suppose the approach adopted by the SASC rendering that order was normal in South Africa and was in line with the law and the request of the defendant contained in the Special Plea and the request in the motion of the claimant as well. But viewing it from the angle of a Chinese professional, it would be better if the action would have been dismissed instead of having been stayed if it was judged from the angle of the claimant. I have little knowledge of common law. I know once it is dismissed, no litigation should be re-filed relating to the Contract. But as there was so obvious an explicit arbitration clause in the Contract, once the defendant challenged the competence of the SASC, the claimant and the court as well should recognize the validity of the arbitration agreement. And the court should refer the parties to arbitration, believing that it had the effect of excluding the court's jurisdiction, i.e., the arbitration clause excluded the SASC's competence in the present case. Could we say that having the action been stayed did not completely clear the obstacle for the claimant to institute the arbitration? Otherwise the defendant was not in a position to say that the proceedings in respect of the same claim were pending in the SASC and it was not competent for the claimant to institute the arbitration proceedings. According to prima facie evidence, I could not completely deny the contention of the defendant though it was the defendant that '[I]t prayed that the *action be stayed pending the arbitration proceedings.*' In this connection, the SASC had not rendered a final decision yet.

If I had been in Mr. X's shoes, I would have officially withdrawn the lawsuit from the SASC prior to submitting the request for arbitration to the ICC's International Court of Arbitration.

Nevertheless, more importantly and for safety's sake, the defendant should have exhausted its contention to the tribunal and should have been present at the hearing, arguing with some supporting evidence that the claimant had failed to perform his obligations under the Contract. But there was no proof mentioned in the award showing that argument of the defendant was well grounded. The defendant did engage some representatives for the arbitration. And previously it had engaged some attorneys in the action before the SASC. That showed that it spent money on the dispute. It seems to me that the South African company's executives, attorneys, and representatives did not focus on the settlement of the dispute but tried their best to delay the matter. What a pity! They had got lost.

Now I am discussing the matters of place of arbitration fixed by the ICC Court of Arbitration and the selection of the sole arbitrator. It is said:

> If the agreement is silent, the Court of Arbitration determines the place of arbitration(Article 14 of the Rules). In doing so, it takes account of the logistical convenience of the parties, the language and applicable law of the contract, political neutrality, the likelihood of excessive intervention of state courts during the arbitral process, costs of the arbitration in a certain venue, and the legal framework ensuring the award's enforceability.[43]

One could find out little logistical convenience for the parties in fixing London as the place of arbitration. If logistical convenience for the parties was the factor which the ICC Arbitration Court had taken account of, I suppose Cairo, Egypt, or Lagos, Nigeria, might be more suitable.

About selecting an arbitrator, a former Secretary General of the ICC International Court of Arbitration once said in one of his articles:

> [W]here an institution is to select the chairman or sole arbitrator, as a practical matter it is far easier to appoint the best possible person when it is known in what country's law the arbitrator should be most expert.[44]

I do believe that the arbitrator in the case was qualified. He wrote a very good award. But in terms of the applicable law, the principle or the good idea or practice referred above was not embodied in the selecting of the sole arbitrator.

The consequence of that was that the place of arbitration and the applicable law of the case were man-made factors by the Institution (though that is normal). Originally England and its law had little connection with the case.

Now let me return to my subject. What the defendant did in the arbitral proceedings was to submit the arbitrator a replay of December 13, 1985 (it was said that was a voluminous one),holding proceedings in respect of the same claim were pending in the SASC and the claimant was not competent to institute the arbitral proceedings; to send a brief letter of August 18,1986 with a copy of a document purporting to be a Notice of Withdrawal of the Special Plea and conduct a good deal of correspondence with the arbitrator. That had nothing to do with substantive matter. I dare not say if the SA Company had been following the advice of the arbitrator and was present at the oral hearing, it might have got somewhere. But as the defendant refused to participate in the arbitral proceedings, the defendant missed its last chance.

8 Conclusion

A party to a case, if without proper competence in determining the existence or validity of an arbitration clause, should consult some experienced lawyers but should not take liberties with the arbitration clause, denying its existence or validity and enforceability.

If the claimant's viewpoint pertaining to the existence or validity is initially accepted by the tribunal, the respondent should seriously face the situation, reserving his viewpoint but not giving up his rights to defense, appointing arbitrator etc., and in all, not refusing to participate in the proceedings. Grasping all the opportunities to present his least, the respondent would find out that all his reasonable countermeasures are worthwhile even if he is in breach of contract.

Notes

1. See Art 6.1 of the CIETAC Arbitration Rules (effective as from May 1,2005). Chinese arbitrators hold that the parties to a case first of all have the jurisdiction of an arbitration institution provided in their arbitration agreement and when an arbitration tribunal is formed, the jurisdiction over the case is under the tribunal.
2. Advokat Lars Rahmn, chairman(Swedish); Dr. J. Gillis Wetter (designated by the Claimant); Prof. Jereme A. Cohen(U.S., designated by the Respondent).
3. See Zhao Xiuwen, Examining the Principles of the Arbitration Jurisdiction with the Revpower Case as an Example (the note in p. 5), pp. 4-16,Arbitration and Law (sponsored by CIETAC and other institutes), Issue 6, 1996 thereafter it was divided into as No.1 and No.2 Shanghai Intermediate People's Courts.
4. See the Award of Revpower Ltd.V.Shanghai Far-East Aero-Technology Import & Export Corporation, and Alberto Moro(Holland & Knight Washington, D.C), Case Study 5: The Revpower Dispute: China's Breach of the New York Convention? It is carried in the Dispute Resolution in the PRCed by Dominic Carman and Christopher Brown (managing directors), Asia Law & Practice Ltd, pp. 151-154.
5. Id,p. 221.
6. See Revpower Case Award, Paragraph 19, II. Factual Backgrounds and the Basic Submissions by the Parties.
7. There was only one intermediate people's court in Shanghai under the jurisdiction the Shanghai Higher People's Court before July 1, 1995.
8. See Wang Shengchang, Enforcement of Foreign Arbitral Awards in the Peoples Republic of China ICCA Congress Series No.9 Improving the Efficiency of Arbitration Agreements and Awards:40 Years of Application of the New York Convention, Kluwer, 1999, p. 222.
9. Id., Paragraph 6, II. Factual Background and the Basic Submissions by the Parties, the Award.
10. Id., Paragraph 7.
11. Id.
12. Id., Paragraph 1, VI-2. Breach of Contract Liabilities, the Award.
13. Id.
14. Id, Paragraph 5, IV-2.
15. Id, Paragraph 6, IV-2.
16. Id.
17. Id., Paragraph 1, 3. Termination of the Agreement, VI. Opinion, the Award.
18. See Michasel O'Reilly and Eleni Sfakianaki, Arbitral Awards: Contents, Requirements and Layout, Arbitration,the Chartered Institute of Arbitrators, Volume 66, No.2, May 2000,p.80.
19. Alberto Moro (Holland & Knight, Washington, D.C), Case Study 5: The Revpower Dispute: China's Breach of the New York Convention? It is carried in the Dispute Resolution in the PRCed by Dominic Carman and Christopher Brown(man- aging directors), Asia Law & Practice Ltd, p. 153.
20. Id.
21. See super Note 8, p. 222.
22. Id.
23. See supra Notes 3 and 8.
24. See super Note 8, pp. 223-224.
25. Id., p. 223.

26. Robert Briner, Arbitration in China Seen from the Viewpoint of the International Court of Arbitration of the International Chamber of Commerce, Albert Jan Den Berg(General Editor),New Horizons in International Commercial Arbitration and Beyond, International Council for Commercial Arbitration, 2005, Kluwer Law International, p. 22.
27. John Gernandt, The Swedish Perspective on Arbitration and Conciliation Concerning China, Id., p. 52.
28. David M.Heilbron, The Arbitration Clause, the Preliminary Conference, and the Big Case, Arbitration Journal, American Arbitration Association, June 1990, Vol.45, No.2, pp. 38-39.
29. Michael J.Moser, Teresa Cheng, Hong Kong Arbitration, Law Press, China, May 2004, p. 9.
30. See Art 10 of the Arbitration Law.
31. See Issue 1 of that Draft Interpretation subtitled About the validity of an arbitration agreement.' It has not been formerly issued yet.
32. Gao Guosheng, A Note to Yanming Huang by email, October 15, 2004.
33. Id.
34. Yang Ing Loong, Response to Yanming Huang by email, October 17, 2004.
35. Wang Yuan, Tian Jiantong and Hu Huimin, The Twisted Course of the New bridge in Purchasing SE Development, Nanfang Weekend (a weekly of Guangdong Province, China, has been the most popular weekly in China), June 3, 2004, C21.
36. Marce Blessing, Drafting Arbitration Clauses, trans-quoting from Marcus S Jacobs, International Commercial Arbitration In Australia Law and Practice, The Law Book Company Limited, Vol. 2, p. 29424, The Law Book Company Limited.
37. Id.
38. Id., pp. 29429-29434.
39. Id.
40. An Arbitration Trap, Shenzhen Special Zone Daily D8, April 27, 2005.
41. Collection of ICC Arbitral Awards, 1986-1990, ICC publishing S.A. Paris—New York, Kluwer Law and Taxation Publishers, Deventer Boston, pp. 136-142.
42. Paul Sieghart(UK)appointed by the ICC Court of Arbitration.
43. W. Laurence Craig, William W. Park and Jan Pauls-son, International Chamber of Commerce Arbitration, 3ed Edition Oceana Publications, Inc, p. 186.
44. Stephen R.Bond, How to Draft An ICC Arbitration Clause(Revised),ICSID, Foreign Investment Law Journal, Volume 7, Number 1, Spring 1992, p. 162.

Part IV
Some Basic Ability and Skills of an Arbitrator

Outlines

Although the commentaries in this chapter are categorized under "**The Basic Abilities and Skills of an Arbitrator,**" the cases analyzed inherently involve multiple dimensions of international commercial arbitration. It is **impossible to isolate a single issue** in such disputes, as they often **intersect with the question of applicable law**. The **application of law is rarely singular**, as the governing law of a contract often encompasses **the CISG (United Nations Convention on Contracts for the International Sale of Goods)** alongside the **domestic law of a party and the arbitration seat or the jurisdiction of the arbitral institution**.

All the cases reviewed in this chapter **fall under the jurisdiction of CIETAC Shenzhen**.

Commentary 1: Grasp the Key to the Case

The author in this commentary examines an international trade dispute involving a **Chinese buyer** and a **Singaporean seller** over the purchase of **Indonesian Merbau Round Logs**. The dispute was referred to **CIETAC Shenzhen** under the arbitration clause in the contract.

The case unfolded as follows:

- The **Chinese buyer inspected the goods upon arrival** and informed the **Singaporean seller** of the results.
- The *seller promptly responded*, expressing willingness to **accept the rejection of goods and refund the payment**.

- However, after receiving the seller's response, the **buyer proceeded to dispose of part of the goods** and later sold even more—without providing any formal reply to the seller's proposed resolution.
- Eventually, the **buyer raised claims** on the grounds of **shortages and defects in the goods**.

In this commentary, the **author recalls the arbitration process**, analyzing **what constituted the key issue of the case and how to grasp it**. The discussion also explores the **application of law and the CISG**, shedding light on the legal complexities inherent in international trade disputes.

Commentary 2: Find Out Some Key Detail to a Case

The author in second commentary examines a dispute arising from an **external sale contract** between a **Hong Kong buyer** and **sellers located in Hunan Province, China**.

Key details under **Section III A of the Commentary** reveal that:

- The contract in question was **concluded via fax**, following **preliminary telephone negotiations**.
- The **sellers, though absent from the oral hearing**, made every effort to **deny that they were parties to the contract**.

Despite the absence of the **respondent**, the **sole arbitrator proceeded** with the case, strictly adhering to the **principle of natural justice**. The **arbitral award was rendered based on the available evidence**, with a particular emphasis on a **key detail that became the deciding factor**.

The **commentary highlights how the arbitrator meticulously examined all available evidence**, treating the process **as if a full hearing had taken place**. However, in reflecting on the case, the **sole arbitrator admits to some uncertainty** regarding whether his approach—identifying the key detail as the determining factor—was entirely appropriate.

Revisiting Past Cases: A Broader Perspective

Upon revisiting this case, the author is inevitably reminded of **two cases previously discussed in this book**:

- **Foshan Jiadian Lighting Co., Ltd vs. Prestige Lighting Co., Ltd**
- **Revpower Ltd. vs. the Shanghai Far-East Aero-Technology Import and Export Corporation**

These cases, though distinct, share common themes of **contractual obligations, arbitration procedures, and the consequences with a defaulting party**. They serve as **powerful lessons** on the importance of **contract clarity, participation in arbitration, and the careful examination of evidence by arbitrators.**

Commentary 3: Application of General Terms and Conditions Provided in a Contract Which Has Been Concluded—The Long and Twisted Course of Shen M200 3099 Arbitration Case at CIETAC South China

A British buyer refers disputes arising from deals in 2002 to CIETA, South China, believing that the deals were carried out on the bases of the general terms and conditions included in a contract of 1998. The Chinese counterpart challenges the validity of the arbitration clause in the contract and the jurisdiction of CIETAC and so that three intermediate court (including the one enjoying jurisdiction of the enforcement of the final award). Two higher courts of different administration regions and even the supreme people's court of China are involved. The tribunal in its award analyzing the close connection between the deals under the first contract of 1998 and the subsequent deals in the following years, discussing the reasons and come to the conclusion that the general clause in the first contract apply to the subsequent deals.

Commentary 4: An Arbitrator Examines: None Replaceable Goods of a Specified Trademark by a Some Manufacturer

It is provided in a sales contract between two corporations located in Hong Kong that the governing law is the law (of the mainland) of PRC. The subject matter of the contract is of a special trademark and the sole manufacturer, on that point the attorney of the respondent briefly touched in his written closing statement but did not present his argument at the only one oral hearing conducted.

The application of the law in this particular case mainly involves *the issue of* ***force majeure*** and the standard terms inconsistent with non-standard terms, etc.

The author discusses the application of the Chinese contract Law, especially some provisions closely related to the issues of the case, reveals and analyzes some defects in the award, in his opinion, by the tribunal, of which he himself is one of the three members, failing to deal with the special question that the attorney of the respondent raises in his closing statement.

Commentary 5: Whether the Tribunal Should Confirm That the Consideration Has Been Paid Up?—An Arbitrator's Note On a Case

Both Parties to some share transfer agreements are of Indian nationality. The 90% of the share of the transfer or transfers in a subsidiary of his (or their) own to the Transferee. The deal has been approved by the board of the company and then by some competent authority of the local government in China with an official written replay and a new certificate of approval to the company recoding that the total investment unchanged and the two investors' names and their respect contributions. It is explicitly recorded in the agreements of bilingual versions (Chinese and English) that the consideration for share transfer has been paid. The two shareholders have an amended articles of association signed and approved as well. But registration with a local bureau of industrial and commercial administration could not be gone through due to short assistance from the transfer(s). Disputes arise, in the course of the arbitration proceedings, the transfer denies that he has been in receipt of the consideration. How the arbitrators construe the wording of some particular provisions in the agreements and the deal between the parties?

Commentary 6: Claims Based on a Replaced Contract Unacceptable—Comparing Two Proposals of Award to a Case

This article deals with some issues relating to an arbitration case arising from some sales contracts. The Buyer in his Request for Arbitration claims that the Seller did not perform contract and therefore was in breach of it. In the Defense the Seller reveals that after the conclusion of Contract A, based on the consensus in idem that the parties entered into Contract B Series and the latter were the attachments or the amendments to or even the replacements for the former, the Seller's substantial part of obligations were fulfilled. The Buyer insists that Contact A and Contract B series were in dependent to each other. The contentions advanced by the Seller were basically accepted by the Tribunal. Therefore the claims of the claimant and should be wholly rejected. There were three proposals of award drafted respectively by arbitrators. Two were presented herewith. The CISG applies to the case.

Grasp The Key To The Case

1 Introduction

With the help or following the advice of some attorney, a party to a contract intends to lodge some claims against the other party with an arbitration institution, the attorney and his/her principal must be convinced that the other party is in breach of the contract and their party is in an advantage position.

An attorney could not be ever victorious. His competency, experience, skills, etc., could not be only judged from some isolated cases. But being an attorney to a claimant, if you advice and even incite your principal to initiate arbitration proceedings, you should have a deep and through understanding of the case at least within the scope of the documents and comparatively detailed and objective account provided by your principal. Your knowledge and experience would enable you to make a judgment whether the account is objective or reasonable. If you are not sure, or you have no certainty of success, you should not rashly urge your principal to refer the dispute to arbitration. But I have now and then come across such lawyers who do not study cases care-fully from the beginning to the end of arbitrations.[1]

It is provided in the United Nations Convention on Contracts for the International Sale of Goods ("CISG") that a buyer has the right to re-examine the goods or cause them to be re-examined at the destination of the goods within as short a period as is practicable in the circumstances! Then within a reasonable time after he has

This commentary was published in Mealey's International Arbitration Report, Vol. 17, # 8, August 2002, pp. 39–62.

Thanks are due to Mr. Marcus S. Jacobs, one of her Majesty's Council for the State of New South Wales of Australia, Senior Advocate of the Supreme Court of South Africa, Mr. Robert Margan, assistant professor with the Faculty of Law, City University of Hong Kong and Dr. John Shijian Mo, associate profee or with the Faculty of Law, City University of Hong Kong, for the books and reference materials given me as gifts or sent to me which enable me to have a better understanding of some issues in relation with this article.

Y. Huang, *Commentaries on Commercial Arbitration in Modern China*, Modern China and International Economic Law, https://doi.org/10.1007/978-981-95-0168-7_6

discovered a lack of conformity of the goods, he should give notice to the seller specifying the nature of the lack of conformity.[2]

What principle should an international commercial arbitrator abide by when applying law and the CISG?

Is the result or conclusion of the examination at destination final, no matter how quick a response the seller makes and what suggestion or way of remedy he puts forward? Does the buyer have the last say when he has got an inspection certificate showing that the goods are not in conformity with the provisions in the contract, though the seller challenges the accuracy of the inspection and at the same time explicitly states that he would accept the rejection of the goods and promises to return the payment he has received? What option does the buyer have after he has informed the seller of the inspection result?

Professionals or practitioners in the field of international trade and commercial arbitration might think that what silly questions I have raised. Let's study the following case.

2 The Parties and Terms & Conditions

A. The Parties to the Sales Contract

On November 11, 1998, a light (industry products) import and export corporation located in G city as buyer entered into a sales contract (hereinafter referred to as "the Sales Contract" or "the Contract") numbered XXCLI-053 in G city with a trading PTE LTD is, on and from the October X, 1983,incorporated under the Companies Act, Cap.185 (of Singapore), as seller. The Contract was in Chinese. The buyer was a company in the line of commodities of light industry.

The goods were Indonesian Merbau Round Logs of 7000m^3 (10% more or less allowed).

B. Some Terms And Conditions That Closely Related to the Dispute

The terms and conditions closely related to the dispute are as follows:

Specification: Diameter: 60 cm–79 cm 30%or less; 80 cm &up 70%or more.

Length: 6 m & up, 4 m–5.9 m less than 5%.[3]

Price: USD200/M^{3}CIF Huangpu, China.[4]

Total Price: USD1420000.00.[5]

Package: Bulk packing.[6]

Shipping Mark: Decided by the seller.[7] Shipment: Before December 1998.[8]

Loading Port and Discharging Port: From an Indonesia main port to Huangpu Port.[9]

Insurance: The insurance shall be effected by the seller for 110%of invoice value covering all risks, war risk, strike risk.[10]

Payment: The buyer shall before December 15, 1998, with the China Construction Bank, G Branch open an irrevocable Letter of Credit in favor of the seller.[11]

Quality: Fresh cut, no rot, no visible bending, free from insects decay, no dead knots, no big holes and large splits. The diameter of big holes must not excess 10%of the surface, depth does not over10%of the length.

The Calculation of the Log Volume: Diameter Measurement: Cross method, measuring the diameters of both ends, plus the two figures and then divide it by four and take an average.

The calculation formula: V = 0.7854D2XLXI/10000.

D=Diameter CM L = Length M.

V=Volume M^3.

1/1000...Conversion coefficient.[12]

Inspection: The buyer has right to make a re-inspection at the destination port. The species, quality, specifications and quantity will be determined by the China Commodity Inspection Bureau(CCIB).Should any discrepancies arise, the buyer would deliver the inspection certificate issued by the CCIB to the seller for compensation.[13]

Compensation period: within 45 days after arrival at the destination port.[14]

Force Majeure: omitted.[15]

Arbitration: All disputes arising from the execution of this contract shall be settled through amicable negotiation. In case no settlement can be reached, the case shall then be submitted to the China International Economic and Trade Arbitration Commission for arbitration which shall be conducted in accordance with the Commission's arbitration rules. The arbitral award is final and binding upon both parties. The arbitration fees shall be borne by the losing party (16).[16]

3 The Claims and Grounds of the Buyer

The buyer referred the dispute arising from the Sales Contract to the China International Economic and Trade Arbitration Commission, Shenzhen Commission (CIETAC, Shenzhen) in June 1999.And the latter took cognizance of the case on June 29 by issuing a Notice of Arbitration numbered SHEN R990XX.3 The 1998 Arbitration Rules of CIETAC (effective as from May 10, 1998) applied to the procedures of the case.

A. The Main Contents of the Application for Arbitration

The Application for Arbitration was very brief, consisting of two pages (A4) leaving great margin.

The Claimant requested that the Respondent be arbitrated: to pay the damages of USD143186.80; to bear the arbitration fees and all the expenses incurred relating to the arbitration.

The Claimant stated that after the conclusion of the Contract, it on schedule had a L/C opened in favor of the seller. The seller delayed in discharging the Contract, the goods arrived at Huangpu on February 10, 1999.The inspection by CCIB, G revealed that the quantity (the volume of the logs) of the goods was short and there were grave defects in quality. The losses of that amounted to USD143186.80 (please refer to Attachment 2). The Claimant by letter to the Respondent claimed the damages on March 8, 1999 (please refer to Attachment 3). The Respondent made a reply on the next day, lacking sincerity in compensation (please refer to Attachment 4). So the dispute could not be settled. Therefore, pursuant to the arbitration clause in the Contract, the Claimant submitted the Application for Arbitration to CIETAC, Shenzhen.

B. **The Three Attachments to the Application for Arbitration**

Attachment 2 was an Inspection Certificate ("the Inspection Certificate") dated March 2, 1999, and numbered XX0000/ZZ80092 by CCIB, G. As the Contract was in Chinese, so CCIB, G issued it in Chinese. I have the main contents of the Inspection Certificate turned into English:

The Quantity and Volume of the Logs: 830 Piece of logs 6727.163M^3.

Shipment: From Babo, Indonesia loaded on the Mv. PT(the name of a ship)to Huangpu.

(G city, China)	
Unloading date:February 14,1999	Invoice no:CXX990117
Contract no:XXCLI-053	Mark and number:N/M

Result of Inspection: Following the provisions of the Contract and the stipulations of Indonesia relating to hard logs, the inspection is conducted and the results are of the following:

Commodity: The goods are Indonesia Merbau Logs.

Quantity:832 pieces(parts).Among them the No 537,No 539 and No 540 are cut into two parts. There is No.537B part missing (the volume is 8.925M^3).

Specifications: Length 4 meter and up, diameter 60 cm and up that are in conformity with the stipulations of the Contract.

Volume: The inspection is conducted on random sampling of 262 pieces of logs and the volume is 2137.810M^3.The volume of the logs sampling in the Log List[4] is 2239.544M^3,the volume inspected is short of 101.734M^{3}and the shortage rate is 4.54%.

Quality: Not less than 15%of the logs' surfaces and inner parts are rotten and with splits(the serious splits with length 1–2.5 meter).These defects are not allowed according to the Contract.

Opinions: The shortage of above logs is because of the inaccurate of the inspection before consigning; the defects have been existed at the loading.

Remarks: (1) Attached there are nine photos.

(2) Inspection Fee:RMB31214.00.

Attachment 3 was a letter dated March 8, 1999 by the buyer to the seller("the Letter of March 8").It was sent to the seller together with the Inspection Certificate initially by fax. The main contents were as follows:

In accordance with the Inspection Certificate, we raise the following claiming opinions:

(1) Shortage of quantity. The real volume is short of 8.925M^3.
(2) Shortage of Volume. The Inspection Certificate was conducted on random sampling 262 pieces of logs and the shortage rate was 4.54%.Calculating on the rate, the real volume of the lot is short of 305.413 M3.
(3) The Grave Defects of the Goods. More than 15%of the logs are rotten or with splits, etc. That would seriously infect the marketing of the goods. We have to sell then at 30%discount.The losses of volume would be 302.722M^3.
(4) The above items added up, the losses of the log volume would be 617.06$M^3$and that would amount to USD123412.00.
(5) To convert the inspection fee RMB31214.00 and that equals USD3774.36.
(6) The value added tax RMB215.22/M^3multiplied 617.06(M^3)is RMB132803.65. To convert the figure into US currency, the figure is USD16000.44.

To sum up, your company should compensate us for the losses above, amounting to USD143186.80. Wish that you reply soon and send some representative to talk the matter over.

Attachment 4 was a reply in Chinese by hand dated March 9, 1999(Letter of March 9)by the seller to the buyer. The main ideas are as follows:

Referring to your fax of today, I believe that Mr. L has called you up. We could not accept your opinions. If you think that the quantity and quality are not in conformity with the stipulations in the Contract, we are willing to take back the goods and return you the payment. Mr. L of our company is nowadays in Hong Kong. He will talk with you over the details of taking back the goods. His mobile phone is 96xxxxxx. Please directly contact him on the phone.

4 The Actions and Measures Taken by the Seller upon Receiving the Inspection Certificate and the Letter of March 8 of the Buyer

A. Some Facts

The Respondent stated in the Defense, saying that they had delivered 830 pieces of Merbau Round Logs to the Claimant, the net volume was 6727.163 m^3 and the gross volume was 6738.793 M3.

Upon receiving the letter (the aforesaid Attachment 3, the Letter of March 8) and the Inspection Certificate (the aforesaid Attachment 2), the seller immediately made a reply (the aforesaid Attachment 4, the Letter of March 9), stating its stance: unable to accept the conclusion of the inspection and the claims of the Claimant, willing to take back the goods and returning the payment. Furthermore the seller on March 18,1999 sent two experts, qualified Indonesian Merbau Graders, to G city to check the goods. The goods were stored at a log yard of YZ Timber Mill in G city. There were only 556 pieces at that time. The Claimant had sold out 270 pieces.

B. Two Merbau Graders Checked the Goods at the Destination

The two experts spent one week over there, checking the 556 pieces of logs one by one, recording the measurement of every piece in the Log List attached to the Invoice and comparing that with the measurement marked on the logs by YZ Timber Mill on behalf of the Claimant. In addition, they had each piece of the log photographed with its log number and the log measurement on length and diameter clearly marked.

C. About the Quantity

Based on the data collected by the two experts, the seller made another Log List with the Invoice Measurement (length, diameter, volume of the 556 pieces) and the Measurement (length,diameter and volume of the 556 pieces) made by the YZ Timber Mill coded as G Measurement. The contrast between the two measurements showed that, calculating the measurement of the 556 pieces of logs made by the buyer, the volume was 4840.976 m^3. Originally, the volume of the 556 pieces of logs calculated on the measurement in the Log List to the Invoice made by the seller was only 4474.804 M3.The difference of the two figures of volume was 366.172 M3.The difference showed that the seller had dispatched 8.18% more than the figure of the volume (of the 556 pieces), of which the price had been calculated.

D. About the Quality

The Respondent holds that the nine photos attached to the Inspection Certificate could not reflect the real quality. The two reasons the Respondent adduced in the Defense are as follows:

1. With regard to the 556 pieces of logs, there is an extra volume of 366.1712M^3. At the time of dispatching the goods, the Respondent had deducted the volume of the nature defects(please refer to the Log List Nos 31,87,105,289,65,398,415, 418,423,432,506,533,546..0.821 pieces—26 pieces in all, the recording of the deducted volume).The Respondent had deducted total volume 11.629M^3.
2. The volume of the defective part shown in the nine photos had been deducted, i.e. that volume had not been included in the net volume.

The Inspection Certificate mentioned that 262 pieces of logs had been sampled but without referring to the numbers in the Log List. So that could not be checked against the original data recorded in the Log List and confirmed. Nine photos of nine pieces of logs were 1.08%of the total 830 pieces. That amount should not lead to the conclusion that 15%of the total were of grave defects. Therefore the Respondent believed that the Claimant had not provided the inspection institute with enough information, such as the Log List. Without sufficient information, the institute could not get a correct conclusion. Therefore the Respondent requested the Tribunal:

To turn down the claims of the Claimant; the arbitration fees be borne by the Claimant and the Claimant compensate the Respondent for the expenses incurred in dealing with the case including the legal fees paid for the lawyer.

The Respondent never provided to the Tribunal any information such as the concrete amount, the calculation method, etc., with the third request.

5 Some Other/Issues Raised or Argued by the Parties

The parties argued over the issues of measuring methods, proper law. At the oral hearing on October 20, 1999, the three-member tribunal inquired into some matters.

A. About the Proper Law

The attorney of the Claimant held that as the Contract was concluded in G city, China, the venue of arbitration was in China as well; the proper law should be Chinese law.

The attorney of the Respondent was of the following view:

> There was no stipulation of proper law in the Contract; the Con-tract was of international trade. China and Singapore were Contracting States to the CISG; hence the CISG should apply to the case.

B. About Inspections of the Goods

At the oral hearing the attorney of the Claimant could not tell whether the Log List and the Commercial Invoice(CXX990117)had been provided to the inspector with CCIB, stressing that the Claimant took the Inspection Certificate as the conclusion, which should be accept by the parties. After the oral hearing, in her brief written submission, around 300 Chinese characters, she said that the numbers of the 262 pieces of logs and other relating information had been on file at the inspection bureau, if they were needed, the Tribunal might directly ask the bureau for that.

A shareholder of the Respondent Mr.L, who was the representative to sign the Contract, at the hearing said that the Claimant had not be informed of the inspection by the two Indonesian Merbau Graders at the log-yard of YZ Timber Mill in G city.

The Respondent submitted a copy of a letter dated April 20,1999 to the Respondent titled Indonesian Merbau Logs Loaded on Mv.PT January 28, 1999, rendered by a timber company of Indonesia PT.AGODA RIMBA IRIAN ("PARI")[5] to whom the Respondent had bought the batch of the logs, recalling the inspection of that lot of 830 pieces of logs conducted by their team of log graders and two of the graders from the Respondent (the buyer to the timber company) four weeks prior loading; stating Deduction on volume was made on certain pieces thus compensating the buyer's recovery loss on wood defects bound to exist from trees, many grown for more than a century in the Tropical Rain Forest; confirming that documents of the Indonesian Forestry were prepared for their inspections to obtain approval from the Indonesian Authority to load and the Merbau Logs had been classified on the Mv.PT as Grade A or Prime Quality.

The last two paragraphs of the letter also revealed that two experts of PART were sent to check the goods in G city. The paragraph reads:

> "To dispel false allegations from your buyers, we have on the March, 18,1999 sent two qualified Indonesian Merbau Graders Mr.T and Mr.Z to G city, China to check altogether a total of 556 pieces of Merbau Logs which could be found in YZ's log-yard. Each peach of log was photograph(ed)with its log number and YZ's log measurement on length and diameter clearly marked. Both graders confirmed there was no shortage in our measurement to them. Appropriate volume deduction was compensated for log defects on certain pieces.
>
> "Relevant information found on 556 photos taken by them was self-explanatory."

C. About the Proposal of Returning the Goods

The attorney of the Claimant commented on the Letter of March 9, holding there were no details for the return of the goods reflecting no sincerity of the Respondent. As the Claimant had paid the total price of the Contract, there was no guarantee that there would be no loss if we accepted the proposal of return of the goods. Moreover, it would be complicated, as the Claimant had paid some interest for the sum in the L/C, the goods had been declared, and duties on them paid.

At the hearing the attorney of the Claimant could not confirm that her principal had made any response to the Letter of March 9.

The shareholder of the Respondent Mr. L said that the Claimant did not make any response to the letter of March 9. The Respondent proposed that the goods be returned. The seller could resell the goods to some other clients. Therefore, neither party would suffer any losses.

B. About the Selling of the Goods by the Buyer

The attorney of the Claimant said that before March 11, 1999(ten days after the issuing of the Inspection Certificate by CCIB, G, and three days after it had informed the seller of the inspection result by fax and two days after it received the Letter of March 9 by fax)it had sold 81 pieces of the logs;around the oral hearing it had sold 470 pieces, the remainder figure was 362.

6 Points the Parties Emphasized in the Course of the Arbitration

A. The Points the Claimant Emphasized

The attorney at the oral hearing stated that the Claimant had kept control over the goods and it had got the right to dispose of the goods. It was unnecessary for it to sell the goods until the claims were settled. It was provided in the Contract that the result of the inspection certificate issued by the CCIB should be taken as conclusion and the buyer could make claims based on it.6 In the written statement(submission)of the attorney? she reiterated that as both parties had had that provided in the Contract that the result of the Inspection Certificate issued by the CCIB would be taken as the conclusion, and the CCIB conducted the inspection under the Law of PRC On Import and Export Commodity Inspection("the Commodity Inspection Law").Therefore the Chinese law was lex fori, the Chinese law should apply to the instant case. She did not quote any provisions of Chinese law.

B. **The Points the Respondent Emphasized**

To counter to the aforesaid viewpoints of the attorney of the Claimant, the attorney of the Respondent claimed that the Inspection Certificate of the CCIB did not reflected the real conditions of the goods. There was no shortage of quantity and no problem in quality.8 In the additional statement of the attorney,9 he stressed that the seller even had a certificate, issued by the Forestry Administration of Indonesia, which confirmed that the cargo of the Merbau Logs during the loading had been checked, the quality as Grade A Export Quality in accordance with Indonesia Forestry Regulations.10 The attorney emphasized the significance of the PARI's letter, showing that there was no such problem as shortage of volume and poor quality. About the proper law, he repeated what he had said at the oral hearing, holding, as both China and Singapore were Contracting States to the CISG, so the CISG should apply to the instant case. But he stated without elaboration, i.e. without referring to any provision of the CISG.

7 The Opinions of the Tribunal

A. **About the Proper Law**

There was no provision of law in the Contract. It is provided in Article 5 of the Law of P.R. C. on Economic Contracts Involving Foreign Interest("the Foreign Contracts Law")that in the absence of such a choice by the parties, the law of the country which has the closest connection with the contract shall apply. The Contract was concluded and performed in Guangdong Province, China. Pursuant to the principle of closest connection, the law of the People's Republic of China should first apply. And the Tribunal is aware of that the parties whose places of business are in the two Contracting States of the CISG, they did not exclude the application of the convention, therefore the CIAG applies to the instant case too.

B. **Quantity And Quality of the Goods**

There are two main issues in the case: whether the volume and the quality of the goods were in conformity with the stipulations of the Contract.

The Claimant held that according to the Contract, after the goods arrived at the destination, the result of the inspection of CCIB should be taken as final. If it revealed that there was non-conformity, the buyer had the right to make claims. The Inspection Certificate by the CCIB, G proved that there was a shortage of volume and grave defects in quality. So the Respondent should compensate the Claimant for the losses it suffered.

However, the Respondent held that the Inspection Certificate "was unable to reflect the real conditions of the goods", challenging the objectivity of the contents of the Inspection Certificate; and declared in the Letter of March 9 that it could not accept the claims.

The Tribunal confirms that in line with the stipulations in the Contract, the Claimant timely applied to the CCIB, G for conducting the inspection of the goods and then promptly informed the Respondent of the result of the inspection and made claims. All those acts themselves of the Claimant were reasonable. However, the Tribunal is aware that the Respondent made response by fax, stating that it could not accept the claims and would accept the return of the goods and it would return the Claimant the payment. When there was divergence over the quality and quality of the goods, the Claimant was aware of that but failed to properly execute its right. That led to the unsettlement of the dispute. The Tribunal holds that the Claimant was responsible for the dispute. The Tribunal has further analyses and opinions in the following:

1. Upon receiving the reply(the Letter of March 9)in which the Respondent turned down the compensation claims but expressed to accept the return of the goods and to return the payment to the Claimant, the Claimant never made further response. In international trade, "silence" would be regarded as "approval." Article 48(2) of the CISG reads:

   > "If the seller request the buyer to make known whether he will accept performance and the buyer does not comply with the request within a reasonable time, the seller may perform within the time indicated in his request. The buyer may not, during that period of time, resort to any remedy which is inconsistent with performance by the seller".

   That provision also indicates what would be the result if the seller explicitly puts forward some way of remedy but meet with no response from the buyer. The Claimant received the goods and held that there were defects in them, therefore claimed damages. But the Respondent believed that there was no shortage in volume and defects in quality and at the same time expressed to accept the rejection of the goods, i.e. the remedy was to accept the return of the goods. If the Claim- ant did not make response within a reasonable time, the seller might perform the obligations as it requested previously. When the Respondent put forward different remedy, the Claimant should have made prompt replay, expressing to accept it or not. The Claimant made no response, the act of omission, meant that it gave up its rights to claim.

2. When the batch of logs reached the destination, the Claimant had the logs carried from the Huangpu Port to the log-yard of YZ Timber Mill. YZ Timber Mill, upon accepting the store of the goods, did measure the logs. For some reason which the Tribunal has no idea, the Claimant did not ask YZ Timber Mill to follow the stipulation in the Contract, the latter adopted another measurement method other then the "Cross Method." The different measurement method adopted by YZ Timber Mill led to a different result. So the result of the inspection by the CCIB was not in conformity with the result of the inspection before loading.

3. When there was divergence over the quantity and quality of the goods, the Claimant disposed of the goods. The Claimant sold 270 pieces of logs before March 11 1999.When the Respondent sent two experts to re-examined the goods on March 18,there were 556 pieces of logs. At the oral hearing, the Tribunal requested that the attorney of the Claimant to provide the arbitrators with the information of the selling of the logs. The attorney was unable to do so, but excused herself, saying that some clerk of the buyer in handling of the affairs was not available abroad. The Secretariat of CIETAC, Shenzhen, urged it for the second time that the attorney had to state in writing that 470 pieces of logs, the volume of $3724.89M^3$,had been sold. But she still failed to hand any copies of sales contracts or invoices. She did not submit any log list and related materials connecting to the random sampling logs in the inspection by the CCIB.

   Article 21 of the Regulations for the Implementation of the Law of the PRC on Import and Export Commodity Inspection("Regulations on Commodity Inspection")reads:

> "For import commodities found substandard upon inspection or random and follow-up inspection by the commodity inspection authorities with a claim already lodged with the foreign party for compensation, a sufficient quantity of the goods or samples shall be retained by the consignees provided that the commodities are not to be replaced or returned; while the commodities intended for replacement by or return to the foreign party must be appropriately taken care of and may not be used until the settlement of the compensation case."

Similar provision could be found in Article 86(1) of the CISG, which reads:

> "If the buyer has received the goods and intends to exercise any right under the contract or this Convention to reject them, he must take such steps to preserve them as are reasonable in the circumstance. He is entitled to retain them until he has been reimbursed his reasonable expenses by the seller."

In the instant case, the Respondent explicitly expressed to accept the rejection of the goods. Without making any response, the Claimant unilaterally disposed of most part of the goods. That was not only against the provision concerned in the CISG but also the international practice. What the Claimant had done should be regarded as accepting the goods and giving up the rights to compensation. Moreover, the logs were not perished goods. Even if they were perished goods, according to the CISG, a party must take reasonable measures to sell them and meanwhile to the extent possible he must give notice to the other party of his intention to sell.

Based on the analyses and opinions aforesaid, the Tribunal holds that in the period after receiving the goods and then to turning the dispute to arbitration, excepting for applying for inspection of the goods according to the provision of the Contract, what the Claimant had done was against the international commercial practice, the provisions of the CISG and the Commodity Inspection Law. The Tribunal denies the Claimant's claims as they are supported by no sufficient facts and based on no law grounds. All the arbitration fees shall be borne by the Claimant.

8 Brief Comments on Some Issues

A. The Contract Itself

According to the Respondent, the Contract was a form contract provided by the Claimant, the Claimant didn't deny the fact. The Contract was very brief, with only 16 short terms and conditions in all, in two pieces of paper of A4. I do hold that this kind of contract should be more detailed or with some terms and conditions more. For instance, as the payment was by L/C, then it should have provided what documents were required, as the duties of a seller under CIF contract are, inter alia, to make out an invoice of the goods, to tender, within a reasonable time after shipment, the bill of lading, the policy or certificate of insurance and the invoice to the buyer would enable the buyer to obtain delivery of the goods, if the goods arrive at the destination, or recover for the loss of the goods, if they are lost on the voyage. People might argue that those documents should have been included in the obligations of the seller under a CIF contract. I have no objection in this regard. But I still persist that, as this was the first deal between the parties, parties should have been more cautious. In this particular case some certificate of origin, some certificate of phytosanitary issued in Indonesia should have been included. What is more, a deal of importing logs is a trading under license. The buyer should have shown its seller that it had been authorized to deal with such transactions. I had doubt whether the buyer had got the license. Being a member of the three-member tribunal, I did not find any of them, and the parties did mention those certificates and license, and certificate of phytosanitary, though they might have nothing to do with the merits of this case. We all know that plant quarantine is very important; authorities concerned of the country to which the logs are imported would always pay great attention to that imported goods including the wooden packing materials. The bill of lading tendered must correctly state the date of shipment; otherwise the buyer can reject the good. Under a CIF contract, the buyer has a right to reject the documents and also a right to reject the goods; later delivery and penalty should not have been omitted, as they would enable the buyer to have more reliable protection. A clause of notice would facilitate the burden of proving that what the parties had properly done. The clause of inspection should have been more detailed; at least it should have provided that an inspection certificate issued by some authorities before the shipment, showing that following the stipulation in the Contract the seller had the "cross method" adopted and the goods were in conformity with the provision of the Contract. Then at the destination, an inspection institute should conduct the re-inspection with the "cross method." It would be better to have it provided that the CIF the terms in the Contract were based on INCOTERMS 1990 of the Inter-national Chamber of Commerce, etc.

B. About the Professional Knowledge of the Persons in Handling the Deal

As this matter had no relationship with the factors in deciding the merits of the instant case, I did not inquire into it. But I did believe it was one of the reasons that led to the result of the deal.

The form contract was provided by the Claimant, I suppose it might have been copied by someone with the Claimant from another company. From the name of the Claimant, one could judge that its staff members were familiar with the deals of light industry products. But a question remained unsettled. If the person handling the deal was a qualified and experienced one in international trade, why didn't s/he see to it that the prompt response, the Letter of March 9 of the Respondent, met with timely reply? I thought that she/he should have kept an eye on the deal from the beginning to the end, following the development of it, having all the questions related to it handled properly. Disputes, especially the small or initial ones, might have been removed or settled by and between the parties themselves.

At the hearing, the respondent impressed me that the merchants of it cherished their credit, they were eager to settle the case by prompt response to accept the rejection. I had no idea of the operation of the claimant and should not be too arbitrary to say more. Something that I did know or even could not imagine that might have prevented some staff member from handling the deal properly.

C. About the Regular Functioning of the Respondent

I have written down my thoughts on some issues of this case relating to the Claimant as it has been my habit or also one of the small aspects in the commercial arbitration that have attracted my attention, focusing on some issues emerged in the practice and reflections on them.

I have mention that the Respondent's business integrity, their ability to meet their obligations impressed me. They did say and provided with some written document that they had had the inspection conducted before shipment at Indonesia, stating that the "Documents of the Indonesian Forestry were prepared for their inspections to obtain approval from the Indonesian Authority to load. They have classified out Merbau Logs On Mv.PT as Grade A or Prime Quality".But they did not confirm with evidence that they had sent the inspection certificate to the Claimant, though this certificate itself after the Claimant accepted the goods would be of no significance in deciding the case by the arbitrators. But still, I felt puzzled over the irregular ways that the businessmen of it adopted in handling the "dispute." They did promptly make a response to the letter of March 8 by the Claimant. As they did send the letter of March 9 to the Claimant, inter alia, suggesting that the buyer return the goods back and they return the payment. Thereafter they could wait for further response form the Claimant before taking any measure. They on March 28, 1999 sent two qualified Indonesian Merbau Graders to G city to check the logs in YZ's log yard. But it was strange that they had neither officially informed the Claimant of it beforehand and nor had formerly informed the Claimant of the result of the re-check thereafter. What on earth the purpose, meaning and value of that act were? As they did re-checked the goods, normally they should have informed the Claimant of the result and simultaneously expressed their viewpoint, for instance, saying that in fact the Claimant had accept the goods as there were only 556 pieces over there, 274 pieces of logs had been sold, etc.

9 Re-Examining the Key Issue from Different Angles

A. From the Angle And Stand of the Claimant And Its Attorney

The Claimant is a state-operated enterprise, a legal entity in the line of import and export, mainly in light industry products in China.

Its professional staff members should have known what was to receive goods and what was to accept goods.

The Claimant did, within the period of 45 days, inform the Respondent of the result of the re-inspection at the destination. But the staff members with the Claimant in handling the transaction should have known that there was divergence over the volume and quality of the goods. Under such conditions, they were not in a position to dispose of the goods.

Dealing with acceptance, a scholar said:

> Acceptance of delivery: the buyer may accept goods by express statement, or express or implicit conduct of acceptance. An act of acceptance can be established when the buyer exercise the right of an owner over the goods in question, or when he or she fails to reject the goods within a reasonable time after delivery. Acceptance has legal implications under the sale of goods legislation, which are often associated with the performance of contract and the passing of property and risk.1

Without further steps forward in dealing with the divergence, instead, the Claimant sold part of the goods. People might think that the buyer changed its mind or gave up its ideas formerly expressed in the Letter of March 8. The buyer did exercise the right of an owner over the goods in question. If I had been in the shoes of the manager of the buyer, I would have asked the staff members in handling the transaction to give an account of it to the attorney and then asked her to analyze the case: what the key issue was, what claims we could raise, what reasons we would be based on and what advantage we would have over the seller. In a word, I would have asked the attorney to estimate the result based on the objective analysis of case.

The attorney of the Claimant should have been aware of the nature and consequence of the act by the buyer in disposing of the goods just some days after it sent the Letter of March 8.If I had been her, I would have enlighten the buyer, telling its executives and the persons in handling the deal that they had no advantage over the seller. I would have inquired into the matter whether markets for the Merbau Logs were coming down. Even if that was the case, I, as a professional should have advised the executives not to refer the case to arbitration.

If the attorney was retained after the Respondent had referred the case to CIETAC, it was not a bad tactic to draw the attention of the Tribunal and the opponent to the stipulation of the Clause 13 of the Contract and the result of the inspection conducted at the destination as she got little room to maneuver. Though her arguments could not bring some arbitrator over, it doesn't mean that that would not work under any circumstances, or influence the decision of any arbitrators. Anyway the question of having the remains of the goods re-inspected according to the Commodity Inspection Law and its Regulations for the Commodity Inspection was raised in the discussion within the three members of the Tribunal. In fact, the attorney of the Respondent had to passively cope with her arguments. Or on the whole, the attorney of the Respondent fell under the Claimant's influence.

When I was appointed as an arbitrator and had access to the file of the case, reading it, my initial impression was that the claims of the Claimant might not gain support from the Tribunal. It was quite strange, the attorney at the oral hearing argued that as the buyer had kept control of the goods, so it had got the right to dispose of the goods. It was unnecessary for the buyer to sell the goods until the claims were settled. Did she get no option?

B. From the Angel And Stand of the Respondent And Its Attorney

I have mentioned the points the Respondent emphasized. Its attorney stressed that the points of quality and volume were in conformity with the stipulations of the Contract. For that purpose, he even explained it in detail, saying that by checking the original Log List the two experts (Merbau Graders)had found out that the No.537 piece of log was cut into two parts at the destination, it was in the log-yard of the YZ Timber Mill.

Moreover, he suggested that the three arbitrators visit the site of the log-yard of the YZ Timber Mill in G city or another log-yard at a wharf of the Shenzhen Port, as some clients of the Respondent had Merbau Logs stored there, wishing that the arbitrators would familiarize themselves with the distinguishing features of the Merbau Logs. Then the Tribunal would be aware that the Inspection Certificate did not mirror the real conditions of the goods. He said if the Tribunal held that it was necessary, the Respondent would dispatch the two Merbau Graders who had re-checked the logs in the log-yard of YZ Timber Mill to appear at the second oral hearing to give testimony.

It was understandable to have one's submission cover as many points and issues as possible. It would at least be more reliable not to omit or miss some points that the Claimant had raised and the Tribunal might think important.

If I had been in the position of the attorney of the Respondent, I should first have coped with the questions and arguments raised by the opponent and then actively dealt with the key issue to the case, focusing on the point and elaborating that the Claimant had accepted the goods. The Latter of March 9 from the seller had met with no response. Selling part of the goods on March 11, 1999 showed that the buyer accepted the goods and it did exercised the right as an owner over the goods. In a word, I would have tried to draw the attention of the Tribunal to it.

If the attorney had grasped the key to the case and if he had been sure that the claims of the Claimant would be denied, he would have stressed the third request of the Respondent by providing to the Tribunal with some data, showing the amount of the travel expenses and fees for employing a lawyer.12 The expenses of the Respondent in this case mainly consisted of two sums of money, one was the fees it paid to the attorney it retained and the other was the travel and boarding expenses the attorney and the representative, who signed the Contract on behalf of the seller, appeared at the oral hearing.

10 Review some Issues of the Case from the Angel of an Arbitrator

A. Grasp the Key of the Case

What was the key of this case? I suppose that I have made it clear. Now recalling the course of the case, I won't say I was wise then. In the files,1[3]written record shows that at the discussion of the Tribunal on November 18,1999,I said that the Respondent had a right to challenge the result of the Inspection Certificate, namely the result was not final yet. The Claimant should have known about that. But without coming to a conclusion on the matter, the Claimant had sold 220 pieces of logs, that should be regarded that it had accept the goods, i.e., the quality and the volume of the goods. On the one hand the Claimant should tell us the facts of the selling with somewhat elaboration upon request; on the other hand, when the facts was confirmed that the Claimant had disposed of part of the goods, the case could be decided.

At the second discussion of the three arbitrators on December 13,1999,I stressed that there was a distinction between "receiving" and "acceptance." The parties diverged over the matter of the quality and volume of the goods; the Claimant had sold part of the goods without the consent of the Respondent. The act of acceptance could be established when the buyer exercises the right of an owner over the goods in question, that is to say that act should be regarded as the acceptance of the goods, it had lost the right to claim on the shortage and defects in quality of the goods. What is more, when the seller had received the Letter of March 8 concerning the shortage and defects in quality of the goods, in the prompt reply the Letter of March 9, the seller explicitly expressed that it would accept the rejection of the goods. The Claimant had made no response; instead, it had sold most part of the logs. No doubt that act should be regarded that it had accept the goods, thus it would enjoy no right to damages at all.14.

I know what I copy down above is not well organized but quite redundant. But I have to be faithful to the original records by the secretary who was assigned to help the Tribunal with arbitration affairs. Anyway, I believe the main idea is clear. So, briefly, confirming or not the establishment of acceptance of the goods by the Claimant was the key to the instant case. So the attorneys of both parties should have focused on it, trying to bring home to the arbitrators their respective views or arguments on the establishment or not of the acceptance of goods. Finding it out and focusing on it, the Tribunal could decide the case.

B. Law Application

I have quoted the opinion about the matter of proper law. Frankly, when the opinion was put forward by one of my co-arbitrators, the presiding arbitrator at the discussion on December 13, 1999, I did second it.15 But on second thoughts, I changed my mind and had my idea written with red ink on page 10 of the draft of the award,[16] explaining as follows:

> We had better first apply the CISG to the case. The reason is that among the many connecting factors of this Contract, the characteristic performance is clearly that of the delivery of goods by the seller, the act of payment by the buyer is not the characteristic performance. Therefore, usually under such circumstances, that a contract is governed by the law of the state with which it is most closely connected which in turn is determined by the habitual residence of the party providing the 'characteristic performance.[17]
>
> That was to say that it might be more appropriate to apply the law of Singapore but not that of China because of 'characteristic performance'.

My formal opinion on this matter was:

> China and Singapore are the Contracting States to CISG, the par-ties did not exclude the application of this Convention, and so the CISG applies to the Contract.[18]

That idea of mine was not accepted by my co-arbitrators.

About the characteristic performance, a distinguished arbitrator dealt with the methods of determination of the proper law, inter alia, he expounded the determination of the proper law without reference to any national law:[19]

> This method is becoming increasingly commonplace. By its application, the arbitrators determine which country is most closely connected to the transaction and then directly apply that country's substantive laws.[20]
>
> In ICC case No.4237,reported in S Jarvin &Y Derains supra, 167,it is stated:
>
> > In view of the international character of the present arbitration, the arbitrator deemed it appropriate to apply those conflict rules which are generally followed in international arbitration of this kind under consideration. The decided international awards published so far show a preference for the conflict rule according to which the contract is governed by the law of the country with which it had the closest connection. The country with which it has its closest connection is the country where the party who has to carry out the most characteristic performance has its head office.
>
> A similar approach was taken in Saudi Arabia v American Oil Co (Aramco) (1963)27 ILR. Chukwumerjie, at 309, not 24, with reference to this method says:
>
> > The direct approach is best suited for eradicating the con-fusion the confusion which this area of arbitration has become. If generally accepted, it would enable arbitrators to directly select the applicable law without the rigours of deciding which conflict rule to apply. An arbitrator faced with a problem of determining the governing law in the absence of the parties' agreement would directly apply the law most closely connected to the contract. It is to be hoped that the next international project on arbitration will adopt this straight-forward approach to choice of law by arbitrators.[21]

I guess by adopting the direct approach, the CISG should be applied in the instant case, otherwise the Singapore law would be chosen as the proper law out of the most characteristic performance.

I in the course of reviewing the case and writing this article consult some books by my colleagues. The following expression is quite good:

> Even before the adoption of the most recent ICC rules, ICC arbi*trators had taken the position that an arbitrator should not be compared to a state court judge in the choice of law process since arbitrators have no obligation to apply the law of the seat as an assimilated lex fori (em*phasis added). For example, an ICC arbitral award of 1970 held:
>
>> The Rules determining the applicable law vary from one country to the next. State judges derive them from their own national legislation, the lex fori. But an arbitral tribunal has no lex fori in the strict sense of the word, particularly when the arbitration case is of an international nature by virtue of the object of the dispute, the choice of the arbitrators, and the organization itself which supervises the arbitration(emphasis added), In this instance the international Chamber of commerce.[22]

We arbitrators at CIETAC, though claim that CIETAC has been an international commercial arbitration organ, in practice some of us have not been free from the influence of the factors relating to the seat of arbitration yet. Ideology is closely related to practice. I believe most of the arbitrators in the international commercial circle would accept this idea after they know more about the modern trend in this regard, having some chances more to exchange ideas with counterparts the world over, handling cases of both foreign parties and co-arbitrating cases with foreign arbitrators rather than only those of the same nationalities of the parties, abandoning the sense that CIETAC as a Chinese Arbitration institution chosen by the parties but not mainly for its credit and repudiation established in its long history. An arbitration institution chosen by parties not mainly for its nationality, even the advantageous geography, speedy transportation and convenient communication are not the most important factors involving the determination of choice by parties, as now, most arbitration institutions are located in those cities enjoying those conditions.

Some scholar said:

> In the past, the arbitrators would probably have felt bound to apply the conflicts rules of the forum. It now appears that arbitrators, like parties, are possessed of free will. They are not even required to reconstruct a fictitious 'common intention of the parties.

Re-examining the opinions of my co-arbitrators and mine on the matter of choice of substantive law in the award, I think it was not as appropriate as it should have been, though it was not wrong, i.e., the rights of the parties were not deprived or damaged. Though there were some defects in the discussion and applying governing laws, the decisions were not incorrect in this particular case.[23]

Some of our colleagues with the International Chamber of Commerce (ICC) dealing with the matter of free choice by arbitrator without reference to any system of conflicts, i.e., direct choice, said:

> [I]n the absence of party choice, the arbitral tribunal may apply the rules of law 'which it determines to be appropriate' is the choice by the arbitrator of the applicable law (or rules of law)without passing through any system of conflicts whatsoever. This possibility of direct choice of the applicable law permits arbitrators to choose rules of law appropriate for the very case before them, without concern for whether the same principles could be applied in another case. One of the factors which weighs on whether a law would be deemed appropriate

is whether it would recognize and give force to the agreement between the parties. Where parties have entered into an agreement and entrusted its interpretation and enforcement to arbitrators it goes without saying that the arbitrators will favor the application of a law which permits its enforcement over one that will invalidated it.[24]

C. Some Comments about the Applying the CISG by Chinese Arbitrators And Lawyers

I had better review the CISG, in case I am not so familiar with it as I should be. Article 1 of it does provide the basic rules of applicability. Under it, the CISG should apply to an international sale of goods contract when the parties have their places of business in different states.

and: (a) each party's respective state is a signatory to the CISG, or (b) the conflict rules of private international law would lead to the application of the law of a state that is a signatory to the CISG. Frankly I did not try to persuade my co-arbitrators by invoking this provision of the CISG.I did not draw the attention of my co-operation to the fact that China has made Article 95 reservation and, based on that and the 'characteristic performance' of the instant case, hence we had more reason to have the case governed by the CISG. If I had done so, the opinion in this regard in the award might have been more appropriate.

In fact, quite a few foreign colleagues, who are interested in the CIETAC arbitration, have paid great attention to the development or trend of CIETAC and been keen on the materials of it. One of them, an American scholar, pointed out similar mistakes or shortcomings in the application of the CISG.[25] He got access to some CIETAC awards translated from an official collection of CIETAC awards published by CIETAC itself.[26] He mentioned two cases and analyzed them in his article. He said the translation was completed by some one,a member of the bar(Association of Lawyers) of China, while participating in the international L.L.M. program at the University of.

Pittsburgh School of Law during the 1998–1999 academic year.[27] The data about the cases he furnished in his article:

> Case 1 is an arbitration award from China's international commercial arbitration organ, China International Economic and Trade Arbitration Commission(CIETAC),date October 31, 1991, translated from an official collection of CIETAC awards published by CIETAC itself. Case 2 concerns an arbitration under China's fore-runner of CIETAC and consists of an arbitration award dated March 2,1988,the seller's statement of defense, a supplementary submission by the buyer in answer to seller's statement of defense, and commentary by an officer of the China Legal Affairs Center.[28]

According to the above data, if I have not made any mistake, I believe I have located the cases. Case 1 is as Case 75 in the Selected Arbitration Awards of CIETAC (1989–1995)0.[29] In the original, the date of the award is October 31, 1991. Case 2 is as Case 44 in the Selected Arbitration of CIETAC (1963–1988).[30]

In the Introduction, the scholar argued:

> [T]hat Chinese arbitrators and lawyers are applying the CISG in an idiosyncratic way, out of step with the plain meaning of the CISG's provisions, and thus poses a threat to a uniform international practice.[31]

I have to quote some paragraphs from the article, so that people might be better aware of his arguments.

> Case I involves a dispute arising from contracts for the sale of aluminum materials to be used in the manufacture of aluminum cans. The first contract was partially performed in that a portion of the goods were shipped and they arrived in China, but were at that time found to be non-conforming. Buyer then requested that seller take back that portion of the goods. Subsequently, the seller failed to deliver a second portion of the goods, and, after a failed attempt at resolution through friendly negotiations, seller attempted to cancel the contract applicable to the undelivered goods. The buyer then brought the case before CIETAC in accordance with an arbitration clause in both contracts.
>
> Case 1 was chosen for translation because, although the identities of the parties and their nationalities have been concealed, the goods relating to the contract in dispute are certain aluminum materials manufactured in the United States, shipped from a United states port to a Chinese port for use in the manufacture of aluminum can by a Chinese manufacturer. This, combined with the arbitration tribunal's application of the CISG, leads to the inference that the buyer was a Chinese company and the seller a U.S. company, both from nations that are Contracting States under the CISG. This reasoning is admittedly circular in that any conclusion that the CISG should apply to the contract in dispute must be based on the fact that the parties are from Contracting States under the CISG, and that such a conclusion in this case is based on an inference partially informed by the fact that the CIETAC arbitrators applied the CISG. Nevertheless, the inference is a strong one because in this case the arbitration tribunal applied the CISG according to Article 6 of the FECL(the Foreign Contract Law of China—the author), which only requires the application of an international treaty which China has participated in if such international treaty 'relates' to the contract in dispute. Therefore, it seems to be safe to infer that the parties are from Contracting States because there would otherwise be no legitimate reason for the arbitrators to conclude that the CISG relates to their contract.[32]

The seller was an American company and the buyer was a Chinese company. The identities of the parties were concealed in the original but their nationalities were not.[33] I have no idea why the scholar had to draw this inference from the data of the case.[34] Did the translators omit or miss some lines?

The scholar held that a dispute arising from a contract for the international sale of goods between parties from different Contract States should be governed by the CISG.[35]

Pertaining to Case 1, I believe the parties did not specify the applicable law in their contracts as the scholar inferred.[36]

The tribunal in the Part of the Arbitrators' Opinions of the award concluded:

> Because the contracts in dispute were all signed in Beijing, and because the material problems related to the disputes are connected with China, hence the Chinese law applies to the instant case.
>
> According to Article 6 of the Law of the People's Republic of China on Economic Contracts Involving Foreign Interest the Foreign Contracts Law (the Foreign Contract Law—the author), there-fore the United Nations Convention on Contracts for the International Sale of Goods is also applicable.[37]

The American scholar believed that the conclusion was totally untenable according to the terms of CISG Article 1.38 He argued:

> Nowhere in CISG Article 1 is there a provision for the combined use of the CISG and any nation's domestic law (emphasis added).Only CISG[38]
>
> Article 7, which covers matters not expressly settled by the CISG would give an arbitral tribunal the authority to apply the domes-tic law of the place in which it sits, and this only if the matter is not covered by the CISG, it cannot be settled in conformity with the CISG's general principles, and the rules of private international law point to the domestic law of the place where the tribunal sits. In contrast, The CIETAC tribunal in Case 1 is applying the CISG to a dispute between parties from Contracting States, but only to the extent that the CISG's provisions 'different from the law of the People's Republic of China.[39]

That scholar said:

> The tribunal does not elaborate on the reasoning behind its decision to apply the CISG and the FECL(Foreign Contract Law—the author)in tandem, but the questions raised by such a decision are numerous. For instance, just how does a tribunal decide when CISG's provisions differ from China's domestic laws? After our discussion concerning the need for uniformity in application of the CISG, it seems impracticable that a tribunal would or could do the research necessary to discover how the CISG is being applied around the globe, compare it to China's domestic law, and then use CISG's provisions only when they would lead to a different outcome than would occur under China's domestic law.[40]

He put forward many questions:

> Should the tribunal rely on the lawyers appearing before it to point out the differences? Is it possible for a lawyer to predict which provisions of the CISG a tribunal find different? How is the tribunal to decide between differing interpretations of the CISG? Should it interpret the CISG without regard to international practice, interpreting it anew each case? Or should it follow a strictly Chinese interpretation, giving a unique interpretation to the official Mandarin version of the CISG? If Chinese arbitrators follow a strict Chinese construction of the official Mandarin version of the CISG (after all, who else is going to interpret it?),how will it affect international uniformity?[41] The scholar was of the view that:
>
> For practitioners, predictability of application was the key consideration and arguing form the general principle of uniformity in international trade embodied in CISG Article 7,and therefore in *sisted that the CISG be applied without reference to any nation's domes*tic contract law (emphasis added).[42]

As for Case 2, I suppose that I have located it. But what the information I get from reading the original is different from that contained in that scholar's article. For example, he said:

> For our discussion, the pertinent aspect of this case concerns the application, or lack thereof, of the CISG. It is quite clear that the seller in Case 2 was from the People's Republic of China. However, we are left without a clue, other than the final shipping destination of Saudi Arabia, as to the nationality of the buyer. Saudi Arabia is not a Contracting State under the CISG. If the buyer was indeed a Saudi national, then there would be no reason to apply the CISG. If the buyer was not a Saudi national, and was in fact from a Contracting State, then only the CISG should have been applied. Unfortunately, the arbitration award itself does not cite to either the FECL (the Foreign Contract Law—the author) of the CISG. To determine the law on which the tribunal relied, we must look to the statement of defense of the seller and the reply made by the buyer.[43]

In the Chinese original, it is quite clear that the buyer was a company coded GSO from Lebanon. So far as I know, Lebanon was not a member country of CISG before July 1999. The transaction was concluded in September 1985.[44] And what is more, I could not find the facts he retold about the case in the original.[45] If I did not made any mistake in locating Case 2, then the cause for the different information in the original and in the article of that scholar might shows the gap of two languages could not be easy to bridge over.

Though it seems to me that the discussion of the colleague was somewhat satirical, I suppose sometimes a satirical comment is more vivid but does no harm. I could see that the American scholar meant no harm to CIETAC and its arbitrators. I have been enlightened from reading this article. Re-examining this case, as I have often done, has led me to peruse the files of the case and read more. Consulting some books and articles by my colleague enabled me to have a deeper understanding of the CISG and the application of law.

Now apart from the main work of administrating the arbitrations, CIETAC has been engaged in many jobs. One of them is to compile the awards in the past years and have them published by the Law Publishing House, Beijing, China as it has done in the last two decades of the twentieth century.

Why not summarize our experience, including finding mistakes and analyzing their causes, so that our capacity might be improved? That would be at least as valuable as publishing awards. On the road, we had better stop occasionally for a while to look back upon what we have done. If we find some mistakes, errors, or even serious blunders we made in the past, that would show we have gained some progress now. I don't think that we should cover up our errors or deficiency if there are some. "I believe mistakes are the cost on the road forward."[46] We should try not to have the mistakes repeated too many times or have the cost doubled or tripled.

D. Could the Commodity Inspection Law Apply to the Instant Case Together with the CISG

The America colleague I have mentioned above said that CISG be applied without reference to any nation's domestic law except for the matter not covered by CISG. He insisted at the end of his article, "that the CISG be applied without reference to any nation's domestic contract law."

I am not sure whether what he first said "national domestic law" is equally to "national domestic contract law." One of my colleagues said in one of his books:

> *[2.7] Whether or not the application of the Convention is compulsory in a member country, once the conditions for its application are satisfied,* is an issue subject to debate (emphasis added).On one hand, previsions of the Convention imply that the application of the Convention is compulsory, unless any restriction or deviation from the whole or part of the Convention has been agreed expressly by the parties to a contract,in pursuance of art 6 of the Convention. On the other hand, there is nothing in the Convention decides that the Convention is not applicable, for whatever reasons justified under the relevant domestic law.
>
> In GPI. Treatment Ltd v Louisiana-Pacific Corp 914 Pacific Reports
>
> (2nd Series)682;323 Oregon Reports 116,the Canadian sellers sued the US buyer for breach of the contract for the sale of cedar shakes. The sellers commenced their case under the

Uniform Commercial Code (UCC)of US. During the trial, the sellers attempted to raise the issue of whether the Convention, rather than UCC, should apply.

The trial judge denied the motion on the ground that it was too late for the sellers to rely on the Convention to proceed with their case. The sellers won their case all the way against the buyer, and thus whether the Convention should apply appeared to be only a technical question. A dissenting judge of the intermediate appellate court questioned the rationale of the trial judge's denial of the application of the Convention, but the Supreme Court did not ad- dress this issue at all.

Though this case decided largely on the basis of UCC, it may suggest that the application of the Convention may be denied by the implied agreement of the parties, which can be inferred from the acquiescence of the parties to proceed with proceedings at the beginning of a trial without raising the issue of Convention. This proposition, if it were what the trial judge meant in GPI. Treatment Ltd o Louisiana-Pacific Corp, is inconsistent with art 6 of the Convention. In addition, the court of each member of the Convention must answer the question as to whether or not its country has an international obligation to implement the Convention within its own territory. In light of these arguments, the scale will learn heavily towards the conclusion that the court of a member of the Convention probably has an obligation to apply the Convention, once the condition for its application have been established, and its application has not been excluded in pursuance of the provisions of the Convention.[47]

My impressions of reading this quotation are that, on the whole, the conclusion of this scholar is the same as that of the American scholar except for some lines I have underlined: (1) The court of a member of the CISG has an obligation to apply it once the conditions for the application have been established. (2) Sometimes whether the CISG should apply appeared to be only a technical question, not always so serious as someone held. (3) The case GPI. Treatment Ltd. v Louisiana-Pacific Corp is an eye-opener for me. If I had been one of the judges in handling the case, if the parties had not excluded the application of the CISG, when the sellers raised the issue of the application of the CISG, I might not have denied it on the ground it was too late because under such circumstances, no matter what the opinions of the two I, as an arbitrator, believed the CISG should apply, I would decide. It has been my practice. (4) If the American scholar takes notice of this case, he might have different opinions from the judges of the case, his countrymen?

I have to quote some paragraph more from the book:

The application of the Convention in any particular circumstance has been inevitably affected by the legal tradition concerned(emphasis added).

In a French case, Societe Sacovini v SARI, Les Files de Henri Ramel, decided on 23 January 1996 by the Court of Cassation(1st Civil Division),the Montpellier Court of Appear of France applied the Convention, in particular art 35,to dismiss an appeal by the Italian wine seller against a decision of the Sete Commercial Court in favor of the French buyers, despite the fact that the trial court did not apply the Convention to adjudicate the dispute in the first in-stance. This case is interesting, in the sense that at the trial the dispute was settled under the French domestic law, but at the appeal, the Court of Appeal brought in the Convention by its own initiative to dismiss a claim formulated on the basis of the French domestic law."[48]

France and Italy both are the Contracting States of the CISG. The judges of France did not apply the CISG in dealing with a case arising from an international sale of goods. Instead, they applied the domestic law of France. Was it a serious problem? Just now I have mentioned no matter what the parties' opinions were on the matter of the application law, if I were a private judge in handling a case, I would decide if I believe the application of the CISG is correct. I have no idea how many claims were put forward by the parties in the case, as I have got access to the case second-hand. I guess there must be more than one claim. The Court of Appeal brought in the CISG by its own initiative. Our views happened to coincide. Furthermore, it seems to me the judges with the Court of Appeal did not deny the application of the French national domestic law combined with the application of the CISG, did they?

In my opinion, different from my co-arbitrators mentioned above, "We had better first apply CISG to the case." And in fact, "shouxian" that means "first of all" or "firstly" was used in the Opinion of the Tribunal of the award.

In the award, we did apply the Commodity Inspection Law in the case. Was it wrong? Is the *application of law a question of simple substance(I am not sure whether it is a correct collocation and* whether my colleagues could guess what I mean)? Is any domestic law excluded when CISG applies?

Let me recall the consideration in the application of Commodity Inspection Law in the instant case. The CISG does provide that the buyer has the right to re-examine the goods at the destination. Does it mean that the result of the inspection at the destination is final? It seems to me that the issue is not dealt with in the CISG. For the purpose of safeguarding the smooth international transactions, in this particular case, we the three arbitrators did believe that judging the particular matter of the inspection at the destination, the Commodity Inspection Law, including the Regulations on Commodity Inspection, should be applied. It is provided in the Regulations on Commodity Inspection Article 49, the result of the inspection is not final; party concerned could apply to the higher inspection authority for re-inspection.49 And what is more, we do believe that Article 21 of the Regulations on Commodity Inspection is in conformity with that of CISG Article 86(2) and is even more explicit.

11 Conclusion

Any party with his/her attorneys to a case should try to grasp the key to a case if they want to have their claims sustained. The defense of the other party with his/her attorneys should be directed against the claims and the grounds the claims are on. But what the respondent and his/her attorneys should not do is follow the claimant step by step. They should, from their stance and angle, grasp the key to the case.

Arbitrators should be able to quickly find out the key to a case. That is the crux of the matter. Experienced arbitrators could, with less time, grasp the key to a case. Being an attorney or an arbitrator in handling dispute of international sale of goods, some basic qualifications you should have. You should be able to read the English versions of INCOTERNS and the CISG and have read some articles on various aspects of international trade including on the application of law and the CISG.

Though nowhere in CISG Article 1 is there a provision for the combined use of the CISG and any national domestic law, I don't think that the application of the CISG would absolutely exclude the application of any national domestic law. I prefer to accept the view that, as the CISG is a contract law in nature, it should be applied without reference to any national domestic contract law.

Notes

1. See Article 38(1) of CISG.
2. See Article 39(1) of CISG.
3. See Files of CIETAC, Shenzhen, No.1138–1, p. 022.
4. The Log List consists of 11 pages, carrying the log number, length, diameter, gross volume, defect volume and net volume of every log and part.
5. See supra note 3, p. 180.
6. See supra note 3, p. 040, the recording of the oral hearing.
7. See supra note 3, p. 080.
8. See supra note 3, p. 041, the recording of the oral hearing.
9. See supra note 3, pp. 173–175.
10. See supra note 3, p. 179.
11. Mo, John Shijian, International Commercial Law, 2nd ed, Butterworths, 2000, p. 49.
12. Please refer to Article 59 of the 1998 Arbitration Rules of CIETAC.
13. See supra note 3, p. 011 of the supplement.
14. Id., p. 014.
15. Id., p. 013.
16. Id., p. 026.
17. Please refer to Article 117 of the Swiss Private International Act.
18. See supra note 13, p. 026 of the supplement.
19. Marcus S Jacobs, International Commercial Arbitration in Arbitration Law and Practice, The Law Book Company Limited, 2001, Vol.1, p. 2819.
20. Id.
21. Id., pp. 2819–2820.
22. W. Laurence Craig, William W. Park, Jan Paulsson, International Chamber of Commerce Arbitration, 3rd ed., Ocean Publications Inc/Dobbs Ferry, NY, pp. 322–323.
23. Stephen J Toope, Mixed International Arbitration: Studies in Arbitration between States and Private Persons, Jrotius Publications Limited, 1990, p. 49.
24. W. Laurence Craig, William W.Park, Jan Paulsson, International Chamber of Commerce Arbitration, 3rd ed.,Ocean Publications Inc/Dobbs Ferry, NY, p. 329.
25. Frank N.Fisanich, Note & Comment: Application of the U.N.Sales Convention in Chinese International Commercial Arbitration: Implications for International Uniformity,10 Am.Rev. Int'l Arb.1999.
26. Id., p.116.

27. Id. See note 90 to the text.
28. Id., see supra note 25, p.116.
29. Selected Awards of the China International Economic and Trade Arbitration Commission(1989–1995), China Foreign Economic and Trade Publishing House, September, 1997,pp.429–438.
30. Selected Awards of the China International Economic and Trade Arbitration Commission(1963–1988), The Publishing House of the Renmin University of China, May, 1993, pp.144–148.
31. See supra note 25, p. 102.
32. Id., p. 117.
33. See supra note 29, p. 430. 34. See supra note 25, p.117. 35. Id., p. 118.
34. See Paragraph of the Witness statement of Christopher Brown,p.9,Case No.2000 F1188.
35. Id.
36. Id., pp. 117–118.
37. See supra note 29, p. 434.My translation is in line with the literal meaning, taken literally. Mr Fisanich's reflects the real meaning in p.118 of his article.
38. See supra note 25, pp. 118.
39. Id.
40. Id.
41. Id., pp. 118–119.
42. Id., pp. 122–123.
43. Id., pp. 119–120.
44. See supra note 30, pp. 144–145.
45. See supra note 25, p. 120; supra note 331, pp.145–146.
46. Yanming Huang, An Arbitrator Looks Back: Did CIETAC Have Jurisdiction Over Foshan Jiadian Lighting Co.,Ltd and Prestige Lighting Co.,Ltd? Mealey's: International Arbitration Report, Vol.16, Issue 9(9/01) at p. 52.
47. See supra note 11, pp. 5 9–60.
48. Id., p. 60.

Find Out Some Key Detail to a Case

1 Introduction

On April 11, 1980, the United Nations Convention on Contracts for the International Sale of Goods ("CISG") was approved in Vienna unanimously by 62 states and China was one of them. The CISG entered into force in 1988.China signed the CISG on September 30, 1981, and on December 11, 1986, deposited an approval with the Secretary-General of the United Nations. The CISG entered into force to China on December 12, 1987.

People in the circle of law know that before the Contract Law of the P.R.C, the uniform contract law of China, came into force on October 1, 1999, there were quite a few contract laws in China, such as the Economic Contract Law, Law on Economic Contracts Involving Foreign Interest (conveniently abbreviated it as Foreign Contract Law), Law on Technology Contracts, etc.

The Foreign Contract Law was effective as of July 1, 1985, before the date when CISG entered into force in China. But it was known that it did use the CISG as a guide. I am not going to deal with the application of the CISG in this article. What I am going to write down are some of my reflections in the course of an arbitration and thereafter. They might be ideas on trifles relating to some provisions of the CISG but not accepted or even strongly rejected by some party to a case under the jurisdiction of the China International Economic and Trade Arbitration Commission (CIETAC).

Being an arbitrator, a practitioner, when handling a case, usually I would study the files, analyzing the issues and trying to find out the main contradiction or the

☆ This commentary was published in Mealey's International Arbitration Report, Vol. 18, # 1, January 2003, pp. 21–45.

Thanks are due to Ms Mao/Yin, lawyer with Huanan Jiaoyang Law Firm for the feedback and all the materials sent to me relating to the case expecially those involving the events which happened after the award was issued.

Y. Huang, *Commentaries on Commercial Arbitration in Modern China*, Modern China and International Economic Law, https://doi.org/10.1007/978-981-95-0168-7_7

most important respect of the main contradiction of the issues, i.e., the key to the case. Once the key to a case is grasped, the hard nut might be consequently cracked.

Sometimes I have to pay close attention to details in handling cases, as I believed under certain circumstances a detail would be a key to the merits of a case or leading you to tell the right and wrong or bringing light to the responsibility of parties to a dispute.

2 The Status of a Fax Document as Documentary Evidence

It is provided in the CISG that for businessmen, who do not have face-to-face negotiation, a contract could be concluded by means of letter, telephone, telegram, telex or other means of *instantaneous communication.*[1]

So far as I know, at the beginning of the 1980s, the most convenient and instantaneous communications in business were telegram and telex in addition to the most commonly used mails (including the most reliable registered letters by air). Who would have thought that there would be electronic data interchange (EDI) and email emerged and quickly popularized around the 1990s? But the drafters of the CISG did have foresight by wording "or other means of instantaneous communication," so the gradually popular means of facsimile and other more instantaneous and less expensive but more reliable communication means were implied, including all the future means which would appear along with the speed of development of science and technology.

At the end of twentieth century, though people were astonished at the forging ahead at a tremendous pace of science and technology, it was unimaginable for us that we could communicate with anyone in any corner of the world with a portable computer. It is said that any computer we use in our offices or daily life is much better than that used by the American scientists and engineers in their Apollo Project more than one score and ten years ago. You can see people, even teenagers, carrying small and exquisite mobile phones everywhere.

It was stipulated in the Foreign Contract Law for businessmen, who did not have face-to-face negotiation, "an agreement was reached by means of letters, telegrams or telex (emphasis added) and one party requested a signed letter of confirmation, (and) the contract shall be formed only after the letter of confirmation is signed."[2]

It could be presumed that the drafters of the Foreign Contract Law made use of the similar provision in the CISG. But the fault was obvious. It seems to me, when making use of the similar provision of the CISG, the drafters of the Foreign Contract Law were not foresighted enough. They missed, in my mind, the most important terms and expressions in the similar provision, the *"or other means of instantaneous communication."*

In the period of the effectiveness and existence of the Foreign Contract Law (July 1, 1985—October 1, 1999), most of us professionals or practitioners in the commercial arbitration circle always, so far as I know, equated a fax message or note with a letter, telegram or a telex in handling cases. But the status of a fax or its effectiveness was without the explicit and direct support of Chinese law, especially when the proper law of a contract was Chinese law that would be to some extent a question. At the end of 1980s, airmail was regarded as too slow. Telegram and telex as means of communication were gradually stepping down the stage of history. In the community of international trade, fax as communication means were popular. Even many people had fax sets at home.

Initially the old fax sets used specially made fax paper. A certain lapse of time, the words and contents including the recording showing where they came from and who were the receivers on the pieces of paper became dim and even disappeared.

Now laser fax sets are one of the most popular. Words in the documents communicated by a laser fax set would not become dim. As the documents of this kind are lasting, people could clearly see the details showing the senders and the receivers, the dates and moments. Fax documents are so reliable that they could show the existence, the process, and changes of deals.

It is explicitly provided in the Contract Law that the parties may, when making a contract, use written form, verbal form, or any other form.[3] It is provided in the Contract Law Article 11:

> "'Written form' as used herein means any form which renders the information contained in a contract capable of being reproduced intangible form such as (emphasis added)a written agreement, a letter or electronic text (including telegram, telex, facsimile, electronic data interchange and email)."[4]

I use fax to substitute facsimile in this article.

Now fax, EDI, and emails are the most popular and instantaneous communication means employed by businessmen. Telegram and telex have been disappearing. Would there be any more instantaneous, more reliable, convenient, and cheaper means of communication in the future? The *expression of "other means of instantaneous communication" in the CISG is of so big* a *capacity.* Quite a few means are enumerated. But who dare say that it has been the end of the enumeration? So "such as" is used in the new Contract Law.[5]

I suppose a fax message as one of the documentary evidence, its status, is established in the CISG and the law of China as well. I am going to present some cases under the jurisdiction of CIETAC; some issues in them are related to the effectiveness of some pieces of faxes.

3 Pieces of Fax Documents in the Case of SHEN R 200,106

A. *The Conclusion of the Disputed Contract*

In October 2000, through telephone negotiations, the Whole China Investments Ltd. ("WCIL") registered in Hong Kong as buyers with the agent HUNAN HUILIPU ("Huilipu") registered in Changsha, capital city of Hunan Province on behalf of their principal Hunan Provincial Imp. & Exp. Group Corp. ("Hunan I & E Group") as sellers made a deal on zinc ingots and then on October 23 by fax concluded a Sales Contract numbered TX2000-14 ("Sales Contract" or "Contract"). On the Page 1, it was recorded that the Date of Conclusion: October 18, 2000 (my emphasis). The form contract was provided by Hunan I & E Group.

The Sales Contract was in English. The subject was 120MT zinc ingots of 99.5% zinc content, the price was USD1025/MT FOB Huangpu (Guangzhou), the total price as USD123.000.00. The terms and conditions, which are more closely related to the dispute, are as follows:

> Country of Original and the manufactures: China (5).
>
> Time of Shipment: Before November 15,2000 (6).
>
> Place of Loading: Guangchou (Huangpu), China; Partial shipment prohibited, transshipment allowed (7).
>
> Port of Destination: Gaoxiong, Taiwan (8).
>
> Terms of Payment: Irrevocable L/C at sight (10).
>
> Some general terms are on page 2 of the Contract. There are Quality/Quantity Discrepancy, Force Majeure, Arbitration, Documents, Penalty, Additional Clauses and Terms (6). It must be the reverse side of the one-piece contract. As the Contract was concluded by fax, it should have been duplicated and then sent and exchanged by fax in two pages. I am copying down some terms.
>
> Arbitration: All disputes in connection with this Contract or the execution thereof shall be settled through friendly negotiation between two parties. In case no settlement can be reached, the case under dispute shall then be submitted for arbitration to the Foreign Trade Arbitration Commission of the China Council for the Promotion of International Trade (the formal name of the CIETAC before 1988—the author) accordance with the Provisional Rules of procedure of the Foreign Trade Arbitration Commission. The decision of the Commission shall be accepted as final and binding upon both parties (3).
>
> Penalty: In case of the non-shipment, seller(s) shall pay 5% of the contract amount to the buyer(s) for breach of contract (5).
>
> Your company (the seller—the author) must send staff to the factory to inspect the goods and must have evidence to prove the goods exist to the buyer(s). Then the buyer(s) will open L/C to your company (the seller—the author) immediately (6).
>
> Additional Clause: This contract is effective since signed/sealed by both parties (7).

I have to make an explanation here that while copying down the above clauses, I do not correct the parties' slips or grammatical errors.

A lady Ms C on behalf of the WCIL and a lady Ms L (she declared herself to be) the authorized representative of the Huilipu in the name of the Hunan I&E Group signed on the Contract.

Below the signature of Ms L, were some words in handwriting: Oct.23, 2000 (my emphasis). Obviously it was the actual date of conclusion and Ms L's handwriting.

B. *The Buyers Refer the Dispute to Arbitration*

Pursuant to the Arbitration Clause in the Sales Contract the buyers WCIL on June 4, 2001 submit- ted an application for arbitration to CIETAC, Shenzhen, not against Hunan I&E Group but against Huilipu only.[6]

Usually when we receive an application for arbitration and its attachments, the Secretariat would right away issue a Notice of Receiving the Application for Arbitration. A rough translation of the contents and wording of the Notice is as follows:

> Regarding your application for arbitration submitted on (the date), we deem, after a preliminary examination, that it satisfies the accepting requirements. Please pay in advance, according to Articles 14(3)and 78 of the Arbitration Rules of CIETAC, a sum of arbitration fee RMB/USD/HK$, the registration fee RMB10.000 and other expenses prepaid required RMB/USD/HK$. The amount is to be remitted to the following account. Please do mark the names of the Claimant(s) for our check when remitting.
>
> (The bank accounts of CIETAC, Shenzhen for various currencies).
>
> Please remit the above amount to us within 20 days after the issuance of this Notice. Your materials are not to be kept beyond the specified time limit.
>
> A receipt is to be issued as the Secretariat of CIETAC, Shenzhen, receives the amount.

And the CIETAC, Shenzhen, took cognizance of the case on June 29, 2001.[7] That is the date No. SHEN R2001060 Notice of Arbitration was issued.

The 2000 Arbitration Rules ("Arbitration Rules"), which came into force as form October 1, 2000, applied to the case.

According to the Arbitration Rules, as the amount of claims was less than RMB500000, the Summary Procedure applied to the case.[8]

C. *The Procedure of the Arbitration*

On June 29, 2001, the Secretariat of CIETAC, Shenzhen, sent the Respondent by EMS the Notice of Arbitration, a copy of the Application for Arbitration by the Claimant and the appendices thereto a copy of the Arbitration Rules with Arbitration Fee Schedule, a copy of the Panel of Arbitrators of CIETAC.

It is provided in Article 65 of the Arbitration Rules that when a case the summary procedure applies, a sole-arbitrator tribunal would be formed to hear the case. And the parties shall jointly appoint a sole arbitrator from among the Panel or jointly entrust the Chairman of the CIETAC to appoint one within 15 days from the date on which the Notice of Arbitration is received by the Respondent. Otherwise the Chairman shall appoint one sole arbitrator on the parties' behalf. This provision is to ensure the smooth and fast procedure.

On July 17, 2000, the author of this article was appointed as the sole arbitrator to from a tribunal to hear the case.

Handling affairs without delay had been my work style. On the day when I was appointed I immediately went through the file of the case and then consulted with the Secretariat and we decided that an oral hearing would be held on August 3, 2001.

The Secretariat on July 17 sent the notice of that to the Respondent and the attorney of the Claimant a lawyer Ms M with a law firm in Changsha, Hunan Province respectively by EMS and registered mail.

The Respondent did receive all the notices and materials relating to the case. The executives of the Respondent submitted a written defense, and it was transferred to the Claimant.

On the date of the oral hearing, the legal representative of the Claimant and the representative signing the Contract and her attorney were present. The Respondent failed to appear.

At first I, the sole arbitrator, inquired about the two representatives' opinion of the formation of the tribunal, i.e. asking whether they had any challenge against me. Though I had never known them before that hearing and therefore had no interest in the case.

Though the evidence and then give a formal award. That should not be regarded as making an award by default.[9]

The English version of the Article 42 of the CIETAC Arbitration Rules, which goes:

> Should one of the parties fail to appear at the hearing, the arbitration tribunal may proceed with the hearing and make an award by default.

The original meaning of it, I suppose, is that a tribunal may proceed with the hearings and render an award in ex parte proceedings on the basis of the facts and evidence before it. Because of the cultural gaps, the obstacle reflected in that provision has not been overcome or I should say that we have not been aware of it yet, therefore misunderstanding exists.

At the oral hearing, I listened to the statement of the Claimant and inquired into some matters. The lawyer made a last statement.

At the end of the oral hearing, I required that if the Claimant wanted to submit any additional submission or have its oral statement made at the hearing written that should be handed over before August 4, 2001. The Claimant agreed.

But the claimant failed to submit a submission with some additional materials before the deadline. Instead, on August 14 Ms M called a secretary with the Secretariat, saying that she had been ill after the oral hearing and she would submit the additional submission and materials in a week. Having got the information, I said to the secretary, as the deadline was beyond, the delay would cause trouble to the tribunal as all the materials provided should be transferred to the other party for examination; then the tribunal might not be able to render the award within 30 days from the date of the oral hearing if only one hearing was to be held.[10] Moreover she should have requested for a delay before the deadline we agreed, otherwise it would be unfair to the Respondent.

I drafted the award and had it rendered on August 27, 2001. The attorney of the Claimant submitted her additional submission with some attachments around August 20. I asked the secretary to have that turned back because of the aforesaid reason. Frankly I had the additional submission and its attachments copied but made no reference of them. I duplicated them for the purpose of later study or I expected that I might find them useful in my future research.

D. *Claims, Facts and Reasons of the Claimant*

In the application for arbitration in Chinese, the Claimant stated that after the conclusion of the Contract, the Respondent asked it to open an L/C and proposed that the unit price increase USD5 and the time of shipment was delayed to November 25,

2000. The Claimant agreed and had its Taiwan client open an L/C through a bank. But the Respondent did not perform the obligations of the Contract, even though the Claimant urged it quite a few times.

The Claimant referred to Article 402 of the Contract Law,[11] saying according to the stipulation in it where the agent entered into a contract with a third party under the agent's name within the scope of authorization by the principal, and if the third party was aware of the proxy relationship between the agent and the principal, the said contract should directly bind the principal and the third party. The Contract directly bound the WCIL and the Respondent.

The Claimant said that as breach of contract by the Respondent caused losses to the Claimant, it claimed a penal sum USD6180 plus interest in light of Article 114 of the Contract Law.[12]

The calculation formula was:

(USD1030 × 120/MT) × 5% = USD6180 plus interest.

Obviously the application for arbitration was drafted by the attorney of the claimant. She didn't deal with the reason for the law application but directly quoted some articles of the Contract Law. She was a Chinese lawyer, I guess, she might not have much experience of foreign and external commercial arbitration yet.

E. ***The Points of the Defense by the Respondent***

The Respondent submitted a brief Defense.[13] The substance content was less than 100 Chinese characters consisting of three points as follows:

(1) No.TX200-14 Sales Contract was signed by and between the Claimant and Hunan I & E Group. The Claimant and Hunan I & E Group were parties to the Contract. The Contract had nothing to do with the pleader (Respondent).
(2) The pleader (Respondent) had never signed any agency contract with Hunan I & E Group.
(3) The act without written authorization of the pleader was of no legal effect.

The executives of Respondent on July 26, 2001 wrote to the executives of CIETAC, Shenzhen, claiming that they had no idea of the transaction.[14] They put forward some views, saying that there was no agent relation between Huilipu and Hunan I & E Group; the Contract between Hunan I & E Group and the WCIL had nothing to do with Huilipu and the terms and conditions of it could not bind upon Huilipu, and you could not invoke Article 402 of the Contract Law and have Huilipu undertake the responsibility of breach of contract. Furthermore, they declared that Mr. H was not a staff member of Hunan I & E Group but a clerk of XHJT company of Changsha; XHJT company was an independent legal entity; Ms L was not a staff member of Hunan I & E Group, she signed the Contract in both Chinese and English was invalid and additionally Hunan I & E Group had not entrusted her with that. The last point they confirmed was that Hunan I & E Group had never endorse the Contract.

The letter of July 26 was sent both by mail and fax. I am to mention it in the late part of this article.

F. ***The Points I Took Notice Before the Oral Hearing***

Reading the attachments to the Application for Arbitration before the oral hearing, I dropped down some points:

(1) The status of Ms L who signed on behalf of the Respondent in the name of the Hunan I&E Group
(2) Did Ms L produce any power of attorney and which was issued by whom?
(3) How could the Claimant show that Ms L was authorized by the Respondent?
(4) The process of the negotiation and conclusion of the Contract.
(5) What happened after the conclusion of the Contract?
(6) Are there any communications between the parties after the Claimant referred to arbitration?

G. ***The Facts I Confirmed at the Oral Hearing***

At the hearing I got to know that it was the first contract signed by Ms Con behalf of the WCIL with Ms L. Ms L had got to know the WCIL and called them up. The deal was not made through face-to-face negotiation. Before the Autumn Fair of Guangzhou Export Commodities Fair,[15] on the phone they talked and reached the agreement. Originally they intended to formally sign the Contract at the Guangzhou Fair. Ms C was unable to go to the Fair because of illness. Therefore, by means of fax Ms L supplied the form contract. C was not aware whether Ms L had got an official authorization by Hunan I & E Group and Hulipu. After the conclusion of the Contract, the WCIL had their Taiwan client on October 26, 2001 open a L/C with Hunan I&E Group as beneficiary. After the WCIL accepted the increased price from USD1025/MT to USD1030/MT, they had their Taiwan client amend the credit. Ms L sent the WCIL a copy of contract dated November 7, 2001 between Huilipu and Hunan I & E Group as purchasers and a company in Baoji, Shanxi Province as suppliers. The subject matter of it was 120 MTS of ZINC INGOT ZC 99.5 PCT MIN, AT RMB9000/MT; the total price of it was RMB1080000.

I made inquiries about the status of Ms L and her authorization while signing the Contract. The attorney of the Claimant answered, saying that Ms L was the director of the trading section of Huilipu but without any written evidence to show her official status for the time being. Ms M did not know whether Ms L had got any official authorization.

Ms C with the WCIL said at the oral hearing that Ms L after Huilipu received the Notice of Arbitration asked Ms C to withdraw the case and Ms L promised to make up for the loss the WCIL suffered.

At this stage, did I suppose that the terms and conditions of the Contract were binding upon the Claimant and Huilipu as well? Did I hold that the claim of the Claimant was of reasonable or without foundation? Could I decide to turn down or sustain the claim?

Though it was a small case involving a tiny amount, I the sole arbitrator should do justice to both parties. The amount in a dispute might show the importance of it, but the nature of a case does not depend on the amount it involves. If the amount is small or even too small, for the gaining and enjoying one's rights under a contract the expenses or cost should be taken into account by the party himself/herself and s/he would decide whether to turn the case to arbitration. An arbitrator shall form a judgment upon facts.

Shenzhen is adjacent to Hong Kong, with a narrow boundary river in between, enjoying speedy transportation and convenient communication. Traveling from the city proper of Hong Kong to Shenzhen proper would only cost a Hong Kong resident less than HKD100. If he/she is afraid of no trouble, he/she could come to Shenzhen four times in a single day.

H. *The Details that Attracted the Attention of the Sole Arbitrator After the Oral Hearing*

After the oral hearing, I re-examined the file of the case. Before signing the Contract, Ms L on October 19, 2001 wrote to Ms C with a form contract of Hunan I & E Group. It could be regarded as the draft Contract, as some standard terms and conditions and some terms and conditions for this particular deal were in it for the consideration and approval of the buyer. The content of the letter written by Ms L of Huilipu to Ms C with WCIL was focusing on the transaction and the faxing of the draft Contract. It was written in a piece of letter paper of Huilipu, that is to say the header of the letter paper contained all the communication information of Hilipu, including their email-address: huilipu@public.cs.xx.yy.[16] The letter and the two-page Contract (in all it was a three-page fax including the one-page letter and two-page draft Contract) were sent to the WCIL by fax. I fond that the line as the fax imprint at the head of the letter as follows:

> 19-OCT-200015:45 FROM: HUI LI PU 07315311129 TO:0085228933213 P:1

On the two pages of the draft Contract submitted by the WCIL, one line as the fax imprint at the head of each page was as follows:

> 19-OCT-200015:45 FROM:HUI LI PU 07315311129 TO:0085228933213 P:2
> 19-OCT-200015:45 FROM:HUI LI PU 07315311129 TO:0085228933213 P:3

"P:2" was recorded on Page 1 of the first page of the draft Contract, "P:3" was recorded on Page 2 of the second page of the draft Contract.

In the proceeding part of this article, I have mentioned that the contract as a form contract of two pages, some terms and conditions were on the right side and some general terms were on the reverse side. In that draft contract, the blanks on the right side for the names of the parties, quantities of goods, price terms, place of shipment, port of destination, and shipping terms, etc. were filled. On the reverse side, the blanks in the documents terms and additional clause remained empty.

On the two pages of the Contract submitted by the WCIL, two lines as the fax imprint at the head of each page were as follows:

> 23 OCT-200017:16 FROM: HUI LI PU 07315311129 TO:0085228933213 P:2 19-OCT-200015:45 FROM: HUI LI PU 07315311129 TO:0085228933213 P:2 23-OCT-200017:16 FROM: HUI LI PU 07315311129 TO:0085228933213 P:3 19-OCT-200015:45 FROM: HUI LI PU 07315311129 TO:0085228933213 P:3

"P:2" was recorded on Page 1 of the first page of the Contract, "P:3" was recorded on Page 2 of the second page of the Contract. The reason for the existence and formalization of this fax of the Contract must be exactly the same as the above, i.e., a short note or letter of one page by Ms L to Ms C together with the two-page Contract was faxed from Huilipu to WCIL. In addition, the Contract was first signed by Ms L with Huilipu and then she faxed it to Ms C of WCIL.

The first fax number was in conformity with the fax number recorded in the letter paper of Huilipu. The second fax number was exactly the fax number of the WCIL recorded in the header of its letter paper.

In the proceeding part of this article, I have also mentioned that the executives of Huilipu submitted a brief defense; besides, sent a letter, the Letter of July 26, to the executives of CIETAC, Shenzhen. They had it first sent by fax. Thereof I did find a line as the fax imprint at the head as follows:

26-07-200111:46 FROM: HUI LI PU 07315204022 TO:1790907552500573 PAGE:1

The first fax number was Huilipu's, though it was different from that recorded in the documents mentioned above. I did not think that Huilipu had got only one fax set and one fax number. The second fax number was one of the CIETAC, Shenzhn's. We had got more than three fax sets and fax numbers.

Now the details contained in the header of the letters revealed that Ms L from Huilipu communicated with Ms C of the WCIL. The lines as the fax imprints at the head of the two-page Contract and the Letter of July 26 all betrayed the status of Ms L. She had been an employee of Huilipu. You might let someone who is not your staff member use your fax set. But how can you provide a stranger or an outsider with your fax set for days or even months running to fax notes or letters and all the contents of the notes, letters by fax relating to and concentrating on a deal between you and your clients. To think that an outsider would know your commercial secret or she made some deal in your name without the awareness of you! That would be absolutely ridiculous.

Moreover, the views in the Letter of July 26 strengthened my analysis and inference. Huilipu claimed that Ms L was not an employee of Hunan I&E Group and she had not been authorized by Hunan I&E Group. But Huilipu did not deny that Ms L had not been an employee of them; it was Hunan I&E Group that had never (but not Huilipu) endorse the Contract.

4 The Opinions of the Sole Arbitrator

This sub-topic is generally used by the arbitrators at CIETAC. I believe it could be regard as "My Findings of Fact and Reasons for This Award." I would like to extract the main points:

A. *The Proper Law of the Contract*

It is provided in the Contract that any dispute shall then be submitted for arbitration to CIETAC in inland China. The place of discharging the Contract is inland China. In the Application for Arbitration, the Claimant invokes the provisions of the Contract Law of inland China to support its claim and the Respondent makes no objection to that invoking. Therefore, the law of inland China applies to this case.

B. *The Status And Authorization of Ms L as Signature Representative*

Ms L on October 19, 2001 from Huilipu faxed a letter (the letter of one-page sent by Ms L together with the draft Contract of two-page) to the Claimant, saying that as an export license for zinc ingots is provided by Hunan I & E Group, so the Contract should be signed in the name of Hunan I & E Group with the WCIL. Hunan I & E Group was the export argent of Huilip. The funding for this deal and all the responsibility relating to it are undertaken by Huilip. If you have any problem, please do not hesitate to contact me.

The Respondent's executives stated that Ms L was not a staff member of Hunan I & E Group and she had got no authorization from the Group. But the executives did not deny that Ms L was their staff member and I believe they could not deny that. In the course of the deal, all the documents relating to the deal were faxed from Huilipu to the Claimant. Huilipu is the Chinese Phonetic Writing of the name of the Respondent.

C. *The Export Agency Contract*

The Client: Huilipu
The Agents: Hunan I&E Group

Changsha XHJT Trading Company(XHJT)

The obligations and responsibilities of the agents and client were provided in it. It was signed by Ms L with the Client Huilipu and a Mr. H in the name of the Agents.

D. *Some Points of Export Agency Contract*

The Export Agency Contract was sent to the Claimant. The line as the fax imprint at the head of the copy of the agency contract submitted by the Claimant shows that the Export Agency Con- tract was fax from Hunan I & E Group-After the award was issued I got to know that it was not directly faxed from Hunan I&E Group to WCIL, I made a mistake in confirming that fact.

E. *Ms L Signed the Contract in the Name of Hunan I & E Group*

The draft Contract was first faxed to the Claimant from Huilipu on October 19, 2000. The final version of it was again faxed to the Claimant on October 23. Beneath the signature of Ms L was the date of Oct.23, 2000 written down by Ms L. On page 2 of the Contract, the original Terms (5) Additional Clause was amended as Terms (7)and a new Terms(5)Penalty and a Terms(6)—about sending a staff member by the sellers to their goods-providers' factory to inspect the goods to make certain that there were goods ready, etc., were added to the Contract.

When the disputed Contract was concluded, Ms L signed it in the name of Hunan I & E Group The name Hunan I & E Group was printed in the Contract. And the two words: "Authorized signature" was also printed below the printed name Hunan I&E Group and Ms L signed by the right of the two words.

F. ***The Beneficiary of the L/C***

The beneficiary of the L/C was Hunan I & E Group. I have mentioned that the Export Agency Contract was faxed to the Claimant from Hunan I & E Group. Based on that fact, as I see it, that the executives of Hunan I & E Group were aware that Ms L signed the Contract in the name of them but they had got no objection, i.e., Ms L herself acted as the authorized representative of Hunan I & E Group to sign the Contract with the Claimant, the disputed Contract was valid and binding upon the parties.

It is provided in the Contract Law Article 402:

> Where the agent enters into a contract with a third party under the agent's name within the scope of authorization by the principal, and if the third party is aware of the proxy relationship between the agent and the principal, the said contract shall directly bind the principal and the third party, unless truthful evidence proves that the said contract binds only the agent and the third party.

The (assigned) agent (Hunan I & E Group) signed the contract in its own name and within the scope of authority by the client (assigner or principal Huilipu). While concluding the contract, the claimant was aware of the agent relationship between the agents (Hunan I & E Group and XHJT) and the principal (client), therefore the contract was directly binding upon the principal Huilipu and the claimant.

G. ***The Contract Between the Respondent And Hunan I & E Group as Buyers And Their Goods-Provider***

The subject matter, the price, the quantity, and shipping date were coinciding with those of the disputed Contract. The copy of that contract was produced by the Respondent to the Claimant to show that the former could perform the Contract.

H. ***Breach of Contract***

The Claimant urged the Respondent to discharge the Contract by delivering the goods. But the latter failed and was in breach of contract.

Therefore, I find accordingly that the claimant is entitled to the penalty, i.e., that the claim of the claimant shall be sustained.

For the reasons above, I make my award as shown hereafter.

I. ***The Decisions of the Tribunal***

(1) Within 20 days from the date this award is rendered, the Respondent shall pay the Claimant the penalty USD6180 and plus interest incurred from the last date of shipment (November 25, 2001) to the date the Respondent pays the sum. An interest at the rate of 5% per annum shall be calculated.

(2) The arbitration fee RMB10000 shall entirely be borne by the Respondent. The Claimant has paid the sum in advance as a deposit and hence the Respondent shall pay that sum to the Claimant together with the sum provided in the above item.

5 Additional Words to the Award

A. ***Some Omitted Details***

I have not presented every detail of the case, though I have focused on some details which I did think, when they were revealed or brought to light, the whole truth or the merits of the case would come out. I have omitted the details about the date of the amendment to the price and the date of shipment delayed to November 25, 2000, etc. As I proceeded with the hearing in default of the Respondent, I could not say that I had all the details correctly confirmed.

B. ***Some Contents in the Additional Statement of the Claimant***

At the oral hearing, the representatives of the Claimant at the oral hearing promised to submit additional submission and materials before August 8, 2000. But they failed. When the additional submission with attachments reached Shenzhen, it was around August 20. Before that I had my draft award finished and submitted it to the scrutiny group. The scrutiny was finished on August 17 and the draft was faxed to the headquarters of CIETAC for further scrutiny.[17]

The Additional Statement was signed by the attorney of the Claimant Ms M. She went into the detail of the course of the negotiation and conclusion of the Contract. She said that all the faxes to the Claimant were "From: Hui Li Pu 0731–5,311,129," and Ms L sent emails from the email address: hulipu@public.cs.xx.yy. Ms M submitted more than 20 communications between the parties.

Ms M quoted Article 49 of the Contract Law:

> Where an actor enters, without the right of agency, in excess of the right of agency or beyond the expiration of the right of agency, into a contract in the name of a principal, and where the counterpart has grounds to believe that the actor has the right of agency, the act of agency shall be deemed as effective.

According to that provision, all the letters sent from Huilipu and the Respondent could not deny that Ms L was not a staff member of it; the contract was valid and binding upon the parties.

The Respondent was in breach of the Contract.

The Claimant added a claim, requiring that the Respondent compensate the expenses incurred by the Claimant in dealing with the case. The sum was RMB 7179 consisting of the lawyer fee RMB6000 and travel expenses, etc.

C. *Comments on the Additional Submission of the Claimant*

Usually before closing an oral hearing, I would require the parties to have their presentations submitted in written form; if necessary, they should have their submissions handed over with additional materials. I do that for the purpose that I might not miss their views and arguments. I would always inquire how many days they could have the job done. The deadline would be established by the parties and the Tribunal. If the attorney of the Claimant could have the Additional Submission submitted before the deadline I would have her viewpoints in it adopted in the award and the added claim would have be listed in the award and might have been sustained if I thought it was in line with the stipulation of the Arbitration Rules. The amendment was not too late.[18] What is more, it should be subject to the examination of the Respondent. The description of the case would have been more accurate.

6 After the Award Reached the Parties

A. *The First Response of the Respondent*

The award was issued on August 27, 2001. It was on the same day that a letter rendered by CIETAC, Shenzhen, to the parties together with each original of the award to each party requiring the parties to automatically execute the decisions of the award.

The Respondent wrote a letter dated September 15, 2001 to the executives of CIETAC, Shenzhen, by mail and fax. The faxed copy reached the receiver on September 17. I had better have the line as the fax imprint at the head copied down:

17-09-200108:07 FROM: HUILIPU 07315204022 TO:1790907552500573 PAGE:1

The main contents are as follows:

[2001]Shen Guo zhong Jie Zhi No.61 Award reached us. We could hardly understand why the award is made in this way. May we request it re-arbitrated based on the facts and reasons as follows?

(1) Our company had never had any transactions with the Claimant. There is no document or contract of legality.
(2) Our company is different form the Huilipu Group the Claimant referred to. Our fax number is 0371-5204022 and our telephone number and address all are different from those of the so-called Huilipu Group.
(3) Ms L is a staff member of Huilipu Science and Technology Ltd. She has nothing to do with our company.

(4) There was never any agency contract between our company and Hunan I&E Group and we had never entrusted any one to sign such an agency contract.
(5) The Claimant signed the Contract with Hunan I & E Group and that the beneficiary of the L/C was that Group. Why the arbitration was not against the Group? We doubt that there was joint fraud. CIETAC, Shenzhen, only listened to the one- sided statement of the Claimant, did not make any investigation. The award was made on the base of guess and inference.
(6) The deal contained in the contract between us and Hunan I & E Group as one side and a company in Baoji, Shaanxi Province as another side was a domestic transaction. We undertook the responsibility of it only. We would not undertake any responsibility in any other links of it. CIETAC, Shenzhen, made inference from only that transaction. The award was done without legal evidence and the arbitrator was not aware of the whole set of links. It was so rash. We do not think that you respect law.
(7) An award equals to a judgment. It should be a very well knitted document with validity of law. "The Claimant states..." and "the Respondent states" are repeated quite a few times in the award (in the Part of the Facts of the award—the author) of your institution. But we could not find out expressions such as "it has been established..." in it. That shows you did not make any investigation. We would like to ask, what is the arbitration fees RMB10000 you have collected for?

The executives said in the last part of the letter:

China would soon be a member of the World Trade Organization (WTO). Your institution should see to it that your arbitrators have a consciousness of legal responsibility, capacity being improved, and that they should be devoted to their duty. No matter whether an enterprise is from inland China or outside, whether or not you have some "connection" with it or its employee, the principle of "fairness, justice and openness" should be abided by.

Let's work hard to build up the law system of China, and don't abuse (your) authority!

The aforesaid is the wish of all the staff members of Huilipi. Wish that you would have the case re-arbitrated!

B. ***Some Impressions of Reading the Letter***

I have said "I am fond of collecting feedback after an award is issued especially when the award is the focus of enforcing proceedings."[19] I would like to add that I am eager to get some response from a loser of a case. Though most of the responses from losers are negative. This response mainly contained criticisms, complaints, or even attacks. No doubt it was not positive. We would now and then receive such kind of response. That kind of feedback, in my mind, is valuable. At least this kind of response would remind us of not making mistakes in handling cases. Furthermore, this kind of response would remind me to review, for instance, "Fair and justice for resolving disputes are indispensable in our society. Commercial arbitration is an important method for deciding many types of disputes. In order for commercial arbitration to be effective, there must be broad public confidence in the integrity and fairness of the process. Therefore, an arbitrator has a responsibility not only to the parties but also to the process of arbitration itself, and must observe high standards of conduct so that the integrity and fairness of the process will be preserved. Accordingly, an arbitrator should recognize a responsibility to the public, to the par- ties whose right will be decided, and to all other participants in the proceeding..."[20]

The following Code relating to the conduct of members of the Chartered Institute of Arbitrators is instructive:

> An arbitrator shall not permit outside pressure, fear of criticism or any from of self interest to affect his decisions. An arbitrator shall decide all the issues sub- mitted for determination after careful deliberation and the exercise of his own impartial judgment.[21]

This Code, I believe, also applies after an arbitration is closed. A case should stand the test of time. For the purpose of winning broad public confidence, an arbitrator should first be confident. That kind of response was first-hand information, to me was no less valuable than some praise of empty words and much more valuable than some indirect information or hearsay.

It was interesting to have direct comments of laymen. A proverb goes that sometimes you could find some inspiration in the words of some laymen. Some people even say that occasionally you would be enlightened in listening to some rubbish.

It did give me an insight into the real thinking of the executives of the Respondent. Many businessmen still know little about arbitration. While approaching some strange or not familiar matter, they would naturally make inferences from their experience or what they had known better from some frequent occurrence or phenomena in life.

We, being professionals, might be able to do something more, such as conducting some publicity in this regard.

And the executives of the Respondent should first make sure what arbitration is. They should have consulted some lawyer, come and seen with their own eyes, made their conclusion with first-hand materials, directly dealt with their private judge. They should draw some lessons. If they came across a dispute arising from an unsuccessful transaction later, an ostrich policy should not be adopted. I do wish businessmen would realize some rights, such as to prevent a dispute from worsening, you had better consult your lawyer, and should adopt tactics properly; some chance should be cherished.

If the Respondent had been at the oral hearing, there would have been cross-examination and I would have known the case better. I must face the pressure of the criticism by myself, though I don't think there was something wrong with me in dealing with the case. I do think I was prudent and devoted to my duty.

About the Item (7) in the letter, I believe the expressions they mentioned were in the Part of the Facts of the award. We usually objectively list the views or arguments relating to the dispute in that part.

About WTO, for quite a few years, it has been one of the fashions in the public opinion and the daily life of the citizens of China. People, especially officials and business executives, would mention it on some occasions. It is not bad. On the one hand, that shows the result of publicity of WTO. But on the other hand, that phenomenon also reflects that the tradition in China that some people prefer to chant some slogans when they have only superficial understanding of something. For example, if the executives of the Respondent had asked some lawyer for advice, they might have known something more about commercial arbitration. They had got no idea what due process and natural justice in arbitration were. Instead, they naturally and lazily pick up the slogan "Abiding by the principle of 'fairness, justice and openness.'"

It is reported that the famous historian, the later president of Beijing Normal University Mr. Chen Yuan once said to his students earnestly:

> The development of a nation relies on many aspects. The lifting of its status is the accumulation of all respects (all walks of life or all industries).Once the chairman of the Chamber of Beiping (the former name of Beijing before 1949-the author) Commerce visited Japan. The hosts specially dispatched some leaders of the commercial community to receive him and his party. In talk the Chinese merchants understood nothing. These merchants were even short of qualifications to exchange ideas with their hosts. How could these businessmen compete with their counterparts? By what means do they win the respect of their counterparts? All of us should do our bit, trying our best in competition with our counterparts in other countries...[22]

We Chinese and businessmen in the new era should have a down-to-earth style of work and work harder.

C. ***A Phone Call from the Respondent***

Some months later, after the letter reached CIETAC, Shenzhen, one day a gentleman called me up, inquiring whether I had seen the letter. I told him I had read it but I was not in a position to make a response. At that time, the claimant in fact had applied to the Immediate People's Court of Changsha ("Changsha Court") for enforcing the award.

I said it was unimaginable that you should provide an outsider with your fax set to communicate with the Claimant to talk about the transaction in your name for quite a few months running. Anyway, if you had any opinions, you were welcome to put forward.

D. ***Brief Looking Back***

I, as the sole arbitrator, was assigned on July 17, immediately glanced over the file of the case, and on the same day consulted with the secretariat of CIETAC, Shenzhen to decide to have an oral hearing on August 3. From July 17 to August 27, 2001, the day I rendered the award, in 41 days I had the case settled.

7 Events Happened After the Award Rendered

A. ***The Claimant Applied for the Enforcement of the Award***

The Respondent should have automatically executed the decisions before September 16, 2001.

On September 26, the claimant wrote to CIETAC, Shenzhen, asking for a certificate of service to the respondent of the award.

On October 9, Ms M on behalf of the Claimant submitted an application for enforcing the award to the Changsha Court.

B. ***The Respondent Applied for the Ruling to Refusing Enforcement***

The Respondent applied to the Changsha Court for the ruling refusing enforcement of the award. This request was dated October 23, 2001, saying that there had not been any arbitration agreement between it and the WCIL and the concreting facts and reasons were formed under two suptopics. The first subtopic was that Huilipu had never signed any commission agency contract with Hunan I & E Group; the contract signed by and between Hunan I & E Group and WCIL had got nothing to do with Huilipu and therefore the contract was not binding upon Huilipu. Some main points under the subtopic are as follows:

(1) In the course of the arbitration, Hulipu got to know that Ms L on behalf of the Hunan I & E Group signed the Contract with WCIL, on October 23, 2000, Ms Lin the name of Huilipu signed the entrustment of agency contract (the Export Agency Contract mentioned above—the author) with a subordinate company under Hunan I & E Group, the XHJT company. The entrustment was not established, as it is provided in Paragraph 2 of Article 65 of the General Principles of the Civil Law of the PRC that "Where the entrustment of agency is in writing, the power of attorney shall clearly state the agent's name, the entrusted tasks and the scope and the duration of the power of agency, and it shall be signed or sealed by the principle." Huilipu neither chopped its seal on the Contract and the entrustment of agency contract, nor its legal representative signed on them and nor it authorized any one on its behalf to sign the contracts.
(2) Ms L was a staff member of Huilipu Science and Technology Ltd. but not Huilipu and what was more she was not authorized by Huilipu. The signing of the two contracts had nothing to do with Huilipu.
(3) The Contract was concluded on October 18, 2000.The entrustment of agency contract was signed on October 23, 2000. Obviously the latter was forged.

C. ***The Submission of the Attorney of the Claimant***

A submission dated October 31, 2001, by the attorney of the WCIL was submitted to the Changsha Court, rejecting what the Huilipu said in its request. Her opinions were under two subtopics. The first one was that the confirmation made in the award was correct and explicit. The main ideas of the attorney are:

(1) It was proved that Ms L was the very staff member of Huilipu in handling the deal of the Contract.
(2) The Contract was signed on October 23, 2000 not as it was printed the date of conclusion was October 18, 2000.
(3) The subject matter, the price, the delivery point, the quantity and shipping date of the contract between the Respondent and its goods-provider were coinciding with those of the disputed Contract. It was signed for the purpose of discharging the obligations of Huilipu in the disputed Contract

The attorney under second sub-topic stressed that the Contract was binding upon Huilipu and the arbitration was in line with the procedure rules. Her conclusion was that the award was legal and effective, and therefore she requested that the Court enforce it.

D. *Huilipu Report A Case to a Security Bureau—A Farce*

I have got a copy of the Receipt for Receiving A Case numbered as (2001) No. 6 issued by the Criminal Investigation Detachment under the Public Security Bureau of Tianxin District, Changsha *City. Deception Relating to a Contract was recorded in the Classification of Case Column in the* Receipt. It reveals that a Mr. Z on behalf of Huilipu on November 20, 2001, went to the Security Bureau to report a case, he autographed in the Column of the Person Coming to Report the Case of the Receipt. The contents of the report by Mr. Z recorded, stating:

> On October 23, 2000, Ms L with the said company(emphasis added)signed the Contract with WCIL; the total amount was USD123600.00; later they with Huilipu timely realized ("shipo" in Chinese—taken literally 'to see through the opponent or see through the fraud by the opponent'-the author)that the opponent might be practicing on Huilipu by means of forging signature and in the name of Huilipu, hence Huilipu terminated (according to the characters or terms used in the re- cording it was not "suspended"—the author)the performance of the Contract and come to report the case to the Public Security Bureau.

The Receipt also plays the role of showing someone has come to report a case, the receiver writs down the gist the visitor repots and then gives the visitor a duplicate of the receipt carrying both telephone numbers of the visitor and the Public Security Bureau for further contacts.

The normal transaction was unsuccessful because of rising price according to a letter from Ms L to WCIL. In that letter dated December 13, 2000, Ms L said that she had been to a factory in Baoji City but only to find that the zinc ingots ex factory were RMB9750/MT. That figure plus freight RMB250/MT, dock charges RMB50/MT, license fee RMB70/MT and traveling expense would amount to RMB10200/MT at Huangpu Port.[23]

What Ms L said in the letter might be true. But it did not mean that her company could shirk its responsibility. For the sake of saving her company's credit, her company should have paid the cost incurred from her or including some of her colleagues' miscalculation. That was the regular way her company should have chosen in handling the transaction. Otherwise there would be bigger cost that her company had to pay.

The case was closed on August 27, 2001.The winning claimant had applied for the enforcement of the award. It had submitted the application on October 31, 2001.Unexpectedly on November 20, 2001, the executives of the Respondent dared to report the case to the Public Security Bureau, making up a most fantastic tale, saying that they had timely seen through the fraud. What a brilliant performance! What a wonderful and colorful world we have!

No matter what the cock-and-bull story Huilipu had made up, the executives could not conceal the fact but confessed that Ms L had been a staff member of "the said company." It is very interesting that they had spent too much energy in the matter of the status of Ms L. They might not have thought that someone else would get a copy of the Receipt. It is said that MiL went to the Public Security Bureau with some documents to show her status on behalf of Hulipu in handling the transaction with WCIL. Sometime later "the case of fraud" was withdrawn.

Ms M even got a copy of the (2000) No 9 Document of Huilipu Group (in fact it is the name of Huilipu used in advertisement or the Group might be underway of establishing—the author) concerning the appointing of Ms L and some of her colleagues to some positions within the company. Reading it, I could not help laughing. It turned out that the very person whose name was recorded in the Receipt issued by the Public Security Bureau as he came to report the case signed and issued that document. Ms L was forced to defend herself by producing some documents to the Public Security Bureau.

E. *The Respondent Applying for Setting Aside the Award*

The Respondent submitted an application to the Intermediate People's Court of Shenzhen, Guandong Province ("Shenzhen Court"), applying for setting aside the award. The application was dated January 21, 2002, stating that it did not agree with the decisions in the award; there was no arbitration clause beforehand and no arbitration agreement afterwards; the award was not in line with Article 260(1) of the Civil Procedure Law of PRC "Civil Procedure Law"); therefore applied to the court for setting aside the award.

On the whole the Respondent repeated what it had said and stressed that it and the Hunan I & E Group had never delegated Ms L to sign the Contract, and furthermore had not chopped on the Contract. In a word, the two companies had known nothing about the deal, hence the Contract was not binding upon the Respondent and the Hunan I & E Group. The Contract was null and void and the arbitration clause in it subsequently invalid.

I won't summarize more points from it, repeating too much makes a reader dull. But I would like to draw your attention to what the Respondent emphasized over here and compare this with what its representative, the person with the family name Zhou, said when reporting the case to the Security Bureau, stating that Ms L with "the said company" had signed the Contract with WCIL. The Respondent terminated the performance of the Contract because it had seen through the fraud by WCIL.

I have mentioned that the executives of Huilipu preferred chanting some slogans than learning some knowledge relating to their industry and consulting lawyers. They knew little about arbitration. It is provided in Article 5 of the 2000 Rules:

> An arbitration clause contained in a contract shall be regarded as existing independently and separately from the other clauses of the contract, and an arbitration agreement attached to a contract shall be treated as a part of the contract. The validity of an arbitration clause or an arbitration agreement shall not be affected by any modification, rescission, termination, expiry, invalidity, or non-existence of the contract.

Our colleagues dealt with the autonomy of the arbitration clause:

> Normally, the arbitration agreement is to be deemed separate from and independent of the contract in which it is contained. This autonomy (or severability) of the arbitration clause is a conceptual cornerstone of international arbitration. It is often confused with notion of competence-competence, which relates to the authority of an arbitral tribunal itself to decide, although generally only in the first instance, whether it has jurisdiction. But unlike competence-competence, which in most situations is a matter of procedure, the autonomy of the arbitration clause is a substantive principle. Thus, in a legal system which did not accept competence- competence but upheld the autonomy principle, a contention that a contractual claim could not be heard in arbitration because the entire contract was void would have to be decided by a judge, but the latter would then send the matter to arbitration if it appeared that the autonomous arbitration clause itself was not necessarily affected by the invalidity of the contract.[24]

I might be naive in requesting the executives of the Respondent to know the above-mentioned procedural matter and substantive principle of arbitration.

The Secretariat of CIETAC, Shenzhen did send the Respondent a copy of the 2000 Arbitration Rules with other arbitration documents. I guess few of the executives of Respondent would read them carefully. As they were laymen, they could hardly understand the Rules thoroughly. But they should realize that at current times, when China is a member of WTO, they should consult lawyers before they take important action.

F. ***About the Legal Provisions Relating to the Refusing Enforcement and Setting Aside of an Award Involving Foreign Elements***

It is provided in the Arbitration Law Article 58:

"A party may apply for setting aside an arbitration award to the intermediate people's court in the place where the arbitration commission is located if he can produce evidence which proves that the arbitration award involves one of the following circumstances:

(1) there is no arbitration agreement;
(2) the matters decided in the award exceed the scope of the arbitration agreement or are beyond the arbitral authority of the arbitration commission;
(3) the formation of the arbitration tribunal or the arbitration procedure was not in conformity with statutory procedure;
(4) the evidence on which the award is based was forged;
(5) the other party has withheld evidence sufficient to affect the impartiality of the arbitration; or
(6) while arbitrating the case, the arbitrators committed embezzlement accepted bribe, practiced graft or made an award that perverted the law.

The People's Court shall rule to set aside the arbitration award if a collegial bench formed by the People's Court verifies upon examination that the award involves one of the circumstance set forth in the preceding paragraph.

If the People's court determines that the arbitration award is contrary to the public interest, it shall rule to set aside the award."

G. *The Submission of the Attorney of WCIL to the Shenzhen Court*

A collegial bench formed in the Shenzhen Court held an oral hearing in May, 2002. Ms M submitted a written submission dated May 13. She reiterated that there was an effective agreement between WCIL and Huilipu and the contract was binding upon WCIL and Huilipu.

She stressed that in the course of the hearing the Huilipu confirmed that Ms L had been its staff member. Furthermore, it was explicitly printed in the fax messages relating to the deal to WCIL: From: Hui Li Pu 0731-5311129. What was more, when the parties communicated by email, the email from the opponent was: huilipu@public.cs.xx.yy. That was exactly in conformity with that printed in the Defense in the letter paper of the Respondent submitted to the CIETAC, Shenzhen. In the Submission, Ms M dealt with other matters including rejecting the Huilipu's allegation of the joining deception of WCIL and Ms L. She was of the view that the material breach of contract by Huilipu was against the Contract Law; its act should not be supported. On the contrary, it should be punished.

8 Comments on Some Issues Reflected in the Documents of the Respondent and in the Events of the Award Issued

A. *About the Status of Ms L*

The executives of the Respondent adopted all means to deny the existence of the Contract and the arbitration agreement. They tried their best to distort and cover facts or truth.

Let us examine what they talked about the status of Ms L. It should be a simple question.

In their first document the first letter (dated July 16, 2001) to the executives of CIETAC, Shenzhen, the matter of the status of Ms L was initially mentioned, saying that she was a staff member of Huilipu Science and Technology Co.

In their second document the Defense (dated July 26, 2001), they did not mention the status of Ms L.

In their third document the second letter (dated September 15, 2001) to the executives of CIETAC, Shenzhen, they said Huilipu had no connection with Huilipu Group; Huilipu was an independent entity (my emphasis).They repeated that Ms L was a staff member with Huilipu Science and Technology Co. I wish to draw your attention to the (2000) No 9 Document of Huilipu Group (Ms M said this is the name of Huilipu used in advertisement or the Group might be under way of establishing—the author) concerning the appointing Ms L and some of her colleagues to some positions within the company. It was signed and issued by Mr. Z, who was the very person that went to the Public Security Buriau to report the case on behalf of Huilip recorded in the receipt, of Huilipu Group.

In their fourth document (dated October 23, 2001) applying (the Changsha Court) to refuse the enforcement of the award, they said for the third time that Ms Li was a staff member of Huilipu Science and Technology Co.

In their fifth "document" the Receipt (dated November 20, 2001) relating to the reporting of the case by Mr. Z on behalf of Huilipu revealed that Ms L was of "the said company," the company of which the person came to report the case, i.e., Huilipu. The executives of the Respondent might have not imagined that Ms M would get a copy of the Receipt.

In their sixth document (dated January 11, 2002) applying (the Shenzhen Court) for setting aside the award, they did not deny that Ms L was an employee of Huilipu. Instead, they stressed that Huilipu and Hunan I & E Group had neither authorized Ms L to sign the Contract nor had set their seals to the Contract. It turned out that they failed in the attempt.[25]

Was the small sum of penalty sustained by the Tribunal in the award so dear and valuable in the mind of the executives of Huilipu? Was the dignity and reputation of Ms L nothing? When they were lying for the purpose to cover the truth, I suppose, that was done at the cost of the dignity and reputation of Ms L, their colleague, and their business integrity and credit as well. They tried to cover up the facts, only to make them more conspicuous. A Chinese old saying goes: Lift a rock only to drop on one's feet.

The executives of Huilipu, a private enterprise, knew about WTO, could utter some terms or expressions, and chant some slogans relating to it. But I incline to another matter that they should be aware that the principle of bona fide or the word of credit had been one of the most used terms or words in the press. More and more businessmen have realized that a lack of credibility had been and would be costing their business dearly. Without business integrity, in the end your business could hardly be flourishing.

Credit is the unity of a norm, a system, and character of a person.[26]

B. ***On Whom the Claim of WCIL Should Be Put Forward***

In accordance with Article 402 of the Contract Law, as a third party to the so-called principal Huilipi and so-called agent Hunan I & E Group, WCIL could refer the dispute to arbitration against the principal Huilipu as respondent or against the principal Huilipu and its so-called agent Hunan I & E Group as two respondents.

WCIL did refer to Article 402 in its application for arbitration but omit the proviso "[U]nless there are conclusive evidences to prove that the said contract only binds the agent and the third party." Did it mean that the Claimant and its attorney held that the situation reflected in the proviso was excluded, i.e. the Contract did not only bind the so-called agent Hunan I & E Group and the third party WCIL? Did WCIL and its attorney believe that the Claimant had got alternative else?

In their third document the second letter (dated September 15, 2001) to the executives of CIETAC, Shenzhen, the executives of Huilipu said that "The Claimant signed the Contract with Hunan I & E Group and that the beneficiary of the L/C was that Group. Why the arbitration was not against the Group?"

In her letter dated July 6, 2001 to M C, Ms L request WCIL to withdraw the application for arbitration or have the Hunan I & E Group as respondent to substitute Huilipu.

I believe the attorney of WCIL Ms M was wise to have had Huilipu as the respondent. It was more reliable. Otherwise WCIL and Ms M would have had to prove that Huilipu had officially authorized Hunan I & E Group and then the agent Hunan I & E Group had formally delegated Ms L herself as its representative to sign the Contract.

Now without dealing with the validity of the agent relation or the existence of the Export Agency Contract between the principal Huilipu and agent Hunan I & E Group and or and the other one else and the authentication of the authorization to sign the Contract by Ms L in the name of Hunan I & E Group, the tribunal could determine the merits of the case once the key detail was established. Hunan I & E Group had kept silence, though it had been the beneficiary of the L/C and I did say in the sixth item of the Opinions of the Tribunal in the award:

> "The beneficiary of the L/C was Hunan I & E Group. I have mentioned that the Export Agency Contract was faxed to the Claimant from Hunan I & E Group.
>
> Based on that facts, as I see it, that the executives of Hunan I & E Group were aware that Ms L signed the Contract in the name of them but had no objection, i.e., Ms L herself acted as the authorized representative of Hunan I & E Group to sign the Contract with the Claimant, the disputed Contract was valid and binding upon the parties.
>
> "...
>
> "The (assigned) agent (Hunan I & E Group) signed the Contract in its own name and within the scope of authorization by the client (assigner or principal Huilipu) While concluding the Contract, the Claimant was aware of the agent relationship between the agents (Hunan I & E Group and XHJT) and the principal (client), therefore the Contract was directly binding upon the principal Huilipu and the Claimant."

Frankly, if the Claimant had had the so-called agent as the only respondent or one of the respondents, on the grounds of the evidence submitted by the WCIL, I would not have come to that conclusion and had Hunan I & E Group undertake the responsibility based on the evidence provided by the Claimant. Because being the beneficiary of the L/C didn't mean it would certainly be a party to the Contract. Furthermore, I could not neglect the following stipulation:

> "A contract that is entered into by an actor without the right of agency, in excess of the right of agency or beyond the expiration of the right of agency, in the name of a principal and without ratification by the principal, shall have no binding force on the principal, and the actor shall bear the responsibility therefore."
>
> "The counterpart may urge the principal to give ratification of the contract within one month. Where the principal does not respond, the nor-response shall be deemed a refusal of ratification. Pending the ratification, the bona fide counterpart has the right to rescind. The rescission shall be made by a notice."[27]

The aforesaid opinion of mine in the award was not a decision. The so-called agent, in fact, was not forced to take any responsibility. I know it might be better for me to have expressed my opinion of that in another way.

In addition, it was reasonable for the attorney of WCIL not to deny the existence and validity of the Export Agency Contract; otherwise, it might be more trouble.

Because the current foreign trade policy, which has been executed for several decades, states that only those specially authorized state-owned foreign trade companies have licenses to deal with foreign trade, including the trade with Hong Kong SAR. Only those companies have the capacity to sign a foreign trade contract. Therefore, if Huilipu as a private enterprise in its own name had signed the Contract with WCIL, it would have been void ab initio. The Huilipu might have held this stance, though it could not side-step responsibility.

9 Conclusion

All the documents or communications relating to the Contract or the deal exchanged between the seller and the buyer, by fax, were from WCIL to Hulipu or vice versa. Once the fact was established, the Respondent could not evade responsibility as the seller to the deal. Huilipu could not directly make deal with foreign companies and companies in Hong Kong SAR etc. It has been the policy of inland China that a foreign trade license should have been specially approved and vested. So it could only make deals of that kind through a state-owned foreign trade company.

The key, though it might be only a particular detail, could not be concealed and denied. In handling a case you, as an attorney or an arbitrator, should try to find out the key and grasp it.

Sometimes an important issue is the key to a case. But on some occasion, a particular detail might be the key to a case.

If the attorney of WCIL had perused the materials of the case and found out the important detail of its role or the significance in the instant case before the dispute was referred to arbitration, it would be better. But it was reasonable that she did not pay enough attention to that point, namely, the executives and their attorney might have not appreciated that they would have to prove the existence of the contract and Huilip was the other party to the contract.

Considering that factor, the attorney should not be blamed. But after she got access to the Defense of the Respondent, she should have been aware of that. If she had dealt with that detail at the oral hearing, it would have been more convincing.

The Respondent should have been a little wise or realistic, should not have tried to save a little (the small sum of penalty provided in the Contract and then confirmed by the tribunal) only to lose a lot (the time, energy, the cost spent in denying the Contract, etc., damages to its credit or business integrity).

As an attorney to a party or the party itself, when they are not sure of the existence of a relationship of agent contract between a so-called agent and its principal, being a so-called third person to the so-called principal, it would be much more reliable to file a case against the so-called agent but not the so-called principal.

This article should be ended here. But when the draft of it was done, I, on some tribunal with two co-arbitrators, was engaged in handling some case of which the respondent was absent from the arbitration proceedings. I consulted a colleague in Stockholm, Sweden. He said under such circumstance, "The tribunal will assure itself that the claims are well based. However, in doing so" *"the tribunal will not act as counsel for the non-appearing respondent* (emphasis added)."[28] I accepted his advice. But I have to reflect on the other side of this matter. In the instant case, if the claimant did not mention the key, should I have ignored it?

Notes

1. Please refer to Article 20-(1) of CISG.
2. See Paragraph 1 of Article 7 of the Foreign Contract Law. The English version was quoted from the Handbook of Foreign Economic Law, Publishing House of Law composed by the Finance, Money and Trade Division of the Research Office under the State Council of PRC, 1997, p.224. So far as I know, it had been the model translation of the Law.
3. See Paragraph 1 of Article 10 of the Contract Law, the English version is quoted from that English Loose-leaf Edition of Laws and Regulations of the People's Republic of China compiled by the Legislative Affairs Office of the State Council, China, Legal Publishing House, Beijing, China, Volume 3, II. Civil and Commercial Law, II-04-00-101, p.3.
4. Id.
5. Id.
6. See Files of CIETAC, Shenzhen, No. 1365–1, p.15.
7. See id., p.17.
8. See Article 64 of the 2000 Arbitration Rules.
9. Id., Article 42.
10. Id., Article 73.
11. Article 402 of the Contract Law: "Where the agent enters into a contract with a third party under the agent's name within the scope of authorization by the principal, and if the third party is aware of the proxy relationship between the agent and the principal, the said contract shall directly bind the principal and the third party, unless there are conclusive evidences to prove that the said contract only binds the agent and the third party."
12. Article 114 of the Contract Law:

    "The parties to a contract may agree that one party shall, when violating the contract, pay breach of contract damages of a certain amount in light of the breach, or may agree upon the calculating method of compensation for losses resulting from the breach of contract."

    "If the agreed breach of contract damages are lower than the losses caused, any party may request the people's court or an arbitration institution to increase it; if it is excessively higher than the losses caused, any party may request the people's court or an arbitration institution to make an appropriate reduction."

    "If the parties to a contract agree upon breach of contract damages in respect to the delay in performance, the party in breach shall perform the debt obligations after paying the breach of contract damages."
13. See supra note 7, p.67.
14. Id., p.58.

15. The Guangzhou Fair was held twice in a year. The Spring Fair is held from May16 to 30.The Autumn Fair is held from October 16–30.
16. For some reasons I have "xx" and "yy" cover some real information relating to Huilipu in this regard.
17. See supra note 7, p.39 of the additional File 1.
18. See Article 19 of the 2000 Arbitration Rules.
19. Yanming Huang, An Arbitrator Looks Back: Did CIETAC Have Turisdiction Over Foshan liandian Lighting Co., Ltd and Prestige Lighting Co., Ltd? Mealev's International Arbitration Report, Vol.16, #9, September 2001.
20. See Canon 1 of the Code of Ethics for arbitrators in Commercial Disputes, The America Arbitration Association.
21. Paragraph 2 of Rule 2 of Part 2, the Chartered Institute of Arbitrators Code of Professional and Ethical Conduct, Arbitrator (the Journal of the Chartered Institute of arbitrators), Vol. 67, No. 3, August 2001, p.274.
22. Wang Mingzhe, Chen Yuan, An Outstanding Patriot—The Later President of Beijing Normal University, Guangming Daily, Beijing, May 23, 2002, p.B1.
23. That was one of the additional materials submitted by the attorney of the Claimant. I have mentioned she failed to hand up within the time limit.
24. W. Laurence Craig, William W. Park, Jan Paulsson, International Chamber if Commerce Arbitration (3rd ed.), Oceana Publications, Inc./Bobbs Ferry, NY, 2000, pp.48–49.
25. See the Shenzhen People's Intermediate Court, Guangdong Province, (2002) Shen Zhong Fa Jin Er Chu Zhe No.17 Civil Ruling.
26. Please refer to Zhu Shaohua, An Assay About Credit, Guangming Daily (Beijing), June 6, 2002, p.B1.
27. Article 48 of the Contract Law.
28. See Johan Gernandt's replay of November 12, 2002, to Yanming Huang. ■

Application of General Terms and Conditions Provided in a Contract Which Has Been Concluded—The Long and Twisted Course of Shen M2003099 Arbitration Case at CIETAC

1 Introduction

It is common sense that once the obligations of both parties to a sales contract have been performed, i.e., that the seller has delivered the goods and the buyer has paid money for the goods, both parties have enjoyed their corresponding rights; thereafter, the rights and obligations of the contract are terminated except for some clauses such as clauses of guarantee of quality, inspection, settlement claims, and arbitration, etc. In a word, once the deal is finished, most of the general conditions in a sales contract are no longer with any effectiveness.

But under particular circumstances, could the parties imply by actions that all or most of the general conditions contained in a previous sales contract are valid and apply to the subsequent transactions between the parties? Could the general conditions of a previous sales contract in fact consist of part of the terms and conditions (clauses) of the subsequent transactions? Or, in other words, for the subsequent deals, the parties could only agree on some new concrete terms and conditions: the specifications, quantity, time of shipment, price term, unit price, and total amount, etc. And all the deals are carried out in light with both the general conditions in the previous sales contract(s) and the concrete terms and conditions of particular subsequent deals.

☆ This commentary was published in Mealey's International Arbitration Report, Vol. 22, # 4, April 2007, pp. 35–46.

The author is grateful to his co-arbitrator Porfessor Chengbi Zhao, as he was the main drafter of the Award and to Mr. T.C. Foo, solicitor of Hong Kong for his advice on the English expression of the title of the article and Dr. Xingping Liu's feedback information relating to the enforcement of the Award. Translated documents referred to in the commentary are available. CIETAC award. Document #05-070427-001A. Civil ruling; Document #05-070427 002Z, Civil ruling; Document #05-070427-003Z; CIETAC decision; Civil ruling, Document #05-070427-004Z.

Y. Huang, *Commentaries on Commercial Arbitration in Modern China*, Modern China and International Economic Law, https://doi.org/10.1007/978-981-95-0168-7_8

When there is some dispute arising from the subsequent deals relating to the quality of the goods, the seller tries its best to deny the validity of the arbitration clause in the previous sales contract, insisting that the arbitration clause could not apply to the subsequent deals. Is there any advantage to be gained by the seller from denying the validity of the arbitration clause: How to weigh up the advantages and disadvantages in adopting some denying tactic: should the objection to the jurisdiction of an arbitration institution be viewed from the angle of law only? should the parties take account of the long-standing trade relationship and cherish it, safeguarding their commercial secret from being revealed by some lawsuits and protecting their own reputation against being ruined? Should the parties cherish the access to some markets and market share?

In the course of handling a case, now and then I thought of the aforesaid questions. It seemed to me that some part neglected the aforesaid issues.

I am exploring a case under the jurisdiction of CIETAC to that I Was a member of the three-arbitrator tribunal, showing that a long and twisted course and various proceedings the parties to the case experienced and endured in dealing with the issue of jurisdiction enjoyed or not by CIETAC. The issue of validity of the arbitration clause at last ruled by a people's court in China, the delayed and clumsy tricks or tactics adopted by some party though resulted in a long and tortuous process. In the end do thus methods in principle pay?

In this article, an arbitration clause is synonymous with an arbitration agreement; in a sales contract 'clause,' 'terms' and 'condition' are synonyms; 'fridge' is with the meaning of "refrigerator," 'freezer' and 'larder' etc.; 'a deal' is of the same meaning with 'a transaction'; 'a set' is equal to 'a unit.'

2 Main Clauses in the No.HYELE-030398 Sales Contract

The seller was Jingdezhen Huayi Electrical Appliance General company ('Huayi'), located in Jianxi Province, China. The buyer was Naiko UK Limited ('Naiko'), located in Leeds, England. Since March 1998 to October 2000, there were some sales con- tracts entered by and between the parties. On March 3, 1998, the parties entered into NO. HYE LE-030398 sales contract ("First contract") in which all the standard clauses were provided by the seller. It was a bilingual Chinese-English contract.

But Terms 1 to 5 (Name of Goods and specifications, Quantity, price Term, unit price and Amount) were mainly in English. It was provided in it that the seller sold 44,280 units of refrigerators and freezers of four models; the unit prices were USD81–97.95/set of different models FOB SHANGHAI; the total price was USD3,904,740.00. The general conditions are as follows:

6. Packing: As per seller's export standard.
7. Shipment: to be made as above schedule from April to December of 1998 from China port to UK port, with partial shipments and trans-shipment to be allowed.

8. Insurance: To be effected by the buyer.
9. Payment: BY 100% confirmed irrevocable letter of credit to be available by sight draft, to remain valid for negotiation in China until the 21st day after the aforesaid time of shipment, and to be opened by the ex-one month before each shipment.
10. Shipment Marks: N/M.
11. (relating to L/c, omitted).
12. Quality discrepancy: If any, it shall be respectively raised by the buyer within 50days after the arrival of goods at the port of destination, and quantity discrepancy, if any, shall be raised by the buyer within15 days after the arrival of good at the port of destination. It is mutually understood that the sellers hall not assume any responsibility for any discrepancy(ies) of the goods shipped owing to causes for which the insurance company, shipping company s, other transportation organization or post office are to be liable for.
13. Force Majeure: (omitted).
14. Arbitration clause: All disputes arising from the execution of or in connection with this contract shall be settled amicably through negotiation. In case no settlement can be reached through negotiation, the case s hall then be submitted to the Foreign Economic & Arbitration Commission of the China council for the promotion of International Trade Beijing for arbitration in accordance with its provisional rules of procedure. The arbitrator's decision is final and binding upon both parties.[1]

When a dispute relating to the quality of the goods arising from the deals between the parties and they could not settle it through amicable negotiation, Naiko as claimant on November 3, 2003 referred the case to the China International Economic and Trade Arbitration commission, south China Sub-Commission (CUETAC, South China).

In the Application for Arbitration, Naiko states that after the conclusion of the First contract, the parties established long term and stable relationship. On october 17, 2000, the parties concluded a Memorandum ('Memo'). There were some amendments to the unit price terms in the First contract and the Memo was a supplement to the First contract. Since then to June 2002, the parties had kept on good terms. In the past years, Huayi in all had sold 150,000 sets of various brands and models of fridges to Naiko.

3 The Contents of the Memo

On October 17, 2000, the representatives of both parties in Guangzhou, China after friendly discussion signed the Memo. Party A is Naiko and Party B Huayi. The concrete contents are as follows:

1. **A Review of Past Cooperation**

To review the cooperation in the past few months between the two sides, both parties are very much satisfied by the outstanding achievement made So far. Starting from this April to September nearly 60,000 sets worth of five million us dollars have already been exported to UK via (so and so) company Limited based in Hong Kong. General speaking a solid and good foundation has been laid, while as a seller Party B has developed some new product range specially for European Market Style and supplied Party A with qualified products (emphasis added), and as a buyer party A ensured party B a trustful and in time payment. In short, the business has been ease and trustful as well as successful.

2. **Quality Problem**

Unfortunately, there are also some quality problem occurred on Model NO. LRI. A detailed laboratory report soon will be feedback by party A to party B to enable party B to improve the design and overcome such problem again in the future. Party B Confirms that the entire problem shall be solved within a short period of time.

3. **Order(S) in November and December**

Though the peak season for fridge and freezer passed and the outstanding devaluation of British pound against Us Dollar, party A Confirm that an order for the last three months of this year will be placed within this month, in order to continue the business between two parties. Details of this order read as follows:

Model NO	Quantity
LR1	2115 sets
FR1	2350 sets
UF1	0 sets
BFR1	1104 sets
Total	5569 sets

4. **Order(S) for the Year of 2001**

Through many suppliers including two Chinese Manufactures approached many times Party A who have NOT given any commitment so far, still Party A would like(to) cooperate with Party B closely as usual (emphasis added). After dedicated and friendly discussion twice in China, both parties finally agreed upon the following price:

> Based on the annual purchasing quantity of minimum 150,000 sets for existing Model NO. LR1/FR1/UFl plus BFR1 (50L) Party B agrees to try the best to offering party A an unique preferential price, I.E. for the existing LR11 FR1 USD3.50 is to be deducted based on the previous price, and USD4.00is to be deducted from the formal price

Now the new price of FOB Shanghai l Ningbo reads as:

> LR1: USD65.80; FR1:USD66.00; UF1: USD78.50; BFR1(50L): USD55.00.

However whenever the exchange rate between GBP and USD return to 1:1.62 from current rate of1:1.44 Party A should accept the previous price and amend any new L/C accordingly.

5. **New Products Range**

In order to expand the export quantity (that) Party A requires more products like 'A' rated of existing three models and chest freezer. Party B has already sent Party A two samples of 'A' rated products for evaluation. Currently Party B agrees to offer a preferential price of both LRI 'A' and FRI 'A' by increasing only USD5.00 based on the above agreed price, i.e., price for LRI 'A' is USD70.80 and the price for FRI 'A' is USD71.00. Party A agrees to send Party B within one week a sample of chest freezer which could be popular in UK and European Market (emphasis added). Both parties agree upon the price of USD62.00 FOB shanghai/ Ningbo for a chest freezer of about 85 liters.

Any uncertain points shall be discussed friendly by both parties later.

4 Arising of the Dispute and Referred to Arbitration

According to the arbitration clause contained in the First contract, Naiko on November 3, 2003, referred the case to CIE TAC, south China, stating that in the Memo there were some additional provisions for the matters of price, etc., provided in the First contract, and therefore the Memo was the requisite supplement to the First contract. Until June2002, both parties had been on good terms. In the past years, Huayi sold 150,000 sets of fridges to Naiko. On June 30, July 31 and August 20, 2002, Huayi respectively delivered fridges of LR39 and uF40 totally 10,340.when the shipment of June30 reached British, the distributor comet of Naikoinics routine inspection (selecting 10 to 12 sets in a container) found out dented doors of the fridges and the goods failed to pass the in section. Naiko on July 13 informed Huayi of the quality problem. But there were similar problems in the goods of subsequent shipments. In those shipments of goods, there were 4225 sets with den cs in the doors and rejected by comet. Huayi admitted the problem but without timely giving solution.

Naiko was forced to have a company inspect all the sets of the fridges and had to restore the dented fridges. Huayi refused to bear the extra costs or expenses incurred in the inspection, storage and transportation. It was at the end of october 2002 that Huayi sent a director Mr Luo and a chief engineer Mryu to British to inspect the fridges. They confirmed the problem relating to the dents in the doors of the fridges but refused to pay for the loss.

As the quality problem could not be settled but persisted, thereby the costs relating to it were increasing. After repeated representations and requests, Huayi agreed co have 1000 pcs doors air-freighted from shanghai to London and another 3225 pcs by sea, so that the problem dented doors would be replaced. But part of the air-freighted shipment of doors was damaged due to poor packing. Accordingly, 3835 pcs doors hall base on the ruling to decide co resume the proceedings or set aside the arbitration case." Therefore, Huayi applies to your arbitration institution for suspending the arbitration proceedings.

The request was attached with a case acceptance notice dated December 18,2003rendered by Nanchang Municipality Intermediate people's court, Jian xi province and a receipt of fee, showing that the case had been indeed accepted by the court and the case acceptance fee as a deposit was RMB500.

9 Notice to CIETAC, South China from Nanchang Municipality Intermediate People's Court

On January 8, 2004 a notice of January 2, 2004 issued by the Nanchang Municipality Intermediate people's court was handed to CIETAC, south China by a judge from that court, repeating the aforesaid matter, informing the addressee that according to the Response Relating to some Issues about confirming the validity of an Arbitration Agreement by the Supreme People's Court[2] it is hereby to notify your institution that the arbitration proceedings of the case between Naiko and Huayi should be suspended.

10 Naiko's Object Against the Jurisdiction of Nanchang Municipality Intermediate People's Court and the Latter's Ruling

On December 24, 2003, Naiko fled an objection against the jurisdiction of the Nanchang Municipality Intermediate People's court, holding that according to the provisions in the Response Relating to the Jurisdiction Enjoyed by which Level of a people's court over a Dispute concerning the validity of an Arbitration Agreement [Fashi (2005) No 25],[3] the jurisdiction of the present case should be enjoyed by the Shenzhen Municipality Intermediate people's court.

But the Nanchang Municipality Intermediate people's court on March 16, 2004 rendered a civil Ruling [see (2004) Hong Min Si Chu Zi NO 2 Civil Ruling, the Appendix 2) to overrule the objection made by Naiko against the jurisdiction of the instant case.

Nevertheless, the Nanchang Municipality Intermediate People's Court did not touch on the issue whether the arbitration clause in the First contract was valid and could apply to the arbitration case between Naiko and Huayi yet. It only ruled that it had the juris diction over the validity of the arbitration clause.

11 Petition for Appeal by Naiko and the Final Ruling of Beijing Municipality No 2 Intermediate People's Court

On March22, 2004, Naiko fled a Petition for Appeal to the Higher people's court of Jian xi province, requesting the Higher court that it should set aside the aforesaid civil Ruling and refer the case to the Shenzhen Municipality Intermediate People's Court. Naiko in the petition for Appeal stressed, inter alia, that the concrete and explicit provision in the Response Relating to the Jurisdiction Enjoyed by which Level of a People's Court over a Dispute Concerning the validity of an Arbitration Agreement should be abide by. That provision reads: 'when the parties have agreed on a domestic arbitration institution, a party disputes the validity of the arbitration agreement and applies to a people's court for ruling on the validity, the jurisdiction should be enjoyed by the intermediate people's court of the location of the arbitration commission.'

As CIETAC, South China is located in Shenzhen, so that Naiko was of the above-mentioned view.

On May 17, the Higher court of Jianxi Province ruled to set aside the Civil Ruling of the Nanchang Municipality Intermediate People's Court and referred the case to Beijing Municipality NO.2 Intermediate People's Court. The reasons must have been that the headquarters of CIETAC is based in Beijing and sub-commissions are an integral part of it[4] and according to the division of the labor between the two intermediate people's courts in Beijing that has been known by the professionals in the legal circle in China.

Beijing Municipality NO. 2 Intermediate court referred the case per the higher people's court of Beijing Municipality to the supreme People's Court of China. I suppose it must have been of the view that it did not enjoy the jurisdiction over the case. After a lapse of about seven months, the Supreme Court decided to designate the NO.2 Intermediate court to exercise the jurisdiction.

On May 13, 2005, the NO. 2 Intermediate Court rendered a Civil Ruling ((2005) Er Zhong MinTe zi NO. 03211, see Appendix 3) after an oral hearing by a collegiate bench consisted of three judges. The judges in the civil Ruling hold that:

> The arbitration clause contained in the sales contract entered by and between Naiko and Huayi on March 3, 1998, is with the expression of the parties' wish to submit to arbitration, the matters to be arbitrated, and the arbitration institution selected by the parties. That arbitration clause is in line with the stipulations of the law and it is valid.
>
> About the dispute arising from the deals in the period of June 26 to August 14, 2002, that Naiko has referred to the arbitration tribunal for arbitration, Huayi is of the argument that it is not within the scope of the arbitration clause in the sales contract of March 3, 1998, that matter should be inquired and then decided by the arbitration tribunal, but not within the inquiring and deciding scope of this court in dealing with the validity of the arbitration clause. Therefore, Huayi's claim requiring this court to confirm that the arbitration clause in the sales contract by and between it and Naiko on March 3, 1998, is no valid shall be rejected. The second claim of Huayi, requesting that Naiko should pay the sum of USD51,700, converting it into RMB427,024 and the overdue interest is not within the inquiring and deciding scope

> of this court in dealing with the validity of the arbitration clause and therefore it shall be rejected, too.
>
> According to Art 16 of the Arbitration Law of the People's Republic of China and Art 140.1.11 of the Civil Procedure Law of the People's Republic of China, it is hereby rendering the following ruling:
>
> Reject the application of Jingdezhen Huayi Electrical Appliance General company.
>
> ...
>
> This ruling is final ·

At this point, the process relating to the validity of the arbitration clause in the First contract and issue of jurisdiction over the arbitration case should have been settled. But Huayi did not give up yet, returning to the CIETAC and raised an objection to jurisdiction before its submission of the first substantive defense.[5]

12 Pleading About the Arbitration Clause Not Applying to the Dispute Arising from the Deals Between Naiko And Huayi

On June 27, 2005, CIETAC, South China received this written document of June 21, 2005, reiterating Huayi's arguments presented before and going over the same old ground:

> The deals in June to August 2002 were not under the First contract and therefore, the arbitration clause in the First contract does not apply to the instant case.
>
> The deals of the instant case were not under the memo either, and the memo has nothing to do with the arbitration clause.
>
> The deals of goods between the parties during the period of June to August 2002 were not based on the First contract or its amendment either, but based on some new contracts (electric contracts) concluded by email or fax. They were independent ones and had nothing to do with the First Contact. In those electric contracts, there was no arbitration clause.

13 No. 98HYELE-1016 and No. 00HYELE-0303 Sales Contracts—The Second and Third Sales Contracts

It turned out that in fact within the period between the conclusion of the First contract and the execution of the Memo, there were some written sales contracts in between (see the Appendix 1—the Award). Naiko did not submit the two sales contracts to the arbitration tribunal through the secretariat of CIETAC, South China until May 27, 2005. The interval between November 3, 2003, to May 27, 2005, is 18-month long.

In the course of the oral hearing on July 5, 2005, the attorney of Naiko said that he his principal recently provided him with the copies of the two sales contracts. And the attorney of Huayi said that he had previously got no access to the two contracts.

The delayed submission of the two sales contracts are of some negative effect on the arbitration proceedings and the author would deal with it in the later part of this article. Now the facts concerning the sales contracts should be introduced according to the sequence.

Following the suit of the First Contract, on October 16, 1998, the parties signed NO. 98HYE IE-1016 sales contract (the second contract). In it, there were no different clauses except for the models, quantity, unit price and the total price of the goods. All the general conditions were exactly the same as they were the standard ones provided by Huayi.

On March 3, 2000, NO. 00HYE LE—0303 sales contract (Third contract) was concluded by and between the parties. It was provided in it, the seller sold to the buyer 34,228 sets of pro line brand refrigerator, larder and upright freezers of three models; unit price respectively USD81.10, 80.98 and 95.00/ser, CFR SHANGHAI/ NINGBO, CHINA, the total price was USD3,003,497.36. There was no difference between the general terms and conditions and those in the previous two contracts.

With the submission of the two contracts or the fact existed and established, the gap is bridged over.

14 Decision on the Jurisdiction by CIETAC

CIETAC did render a decision—the Decision on Jurisdiction of SHEN M2003099 Case (see the Attached 4) in this regard. It or the secretary of the Arbitration Tribunal or someone at the secretariat in charge might have worried that there would be some obstacle in the way of the arbitration proceedings, I guess, so the obstacle must be cleared.

On June 30, 2005, only five days before the scheduled oral hearing, CIETAC rendered the Decision. In the Decision, CIETAC quoted the arguments of Huayi and came to a conclusion:

> It was in accordance with the arbitration clause contained in NO. HYE LE-030398 sales contract that CIETAC, South China accepted the instant case. According co the arbitration clause in NO. HYE LE-030398 sales contract that CIETAC enjoys the jurisdiction over all disputes arising from the execution or in connection with the contract. As to the argument of the Respondent that the deals in dispute of the instant case were not carried out under NO. HYE LE-030398 sales contract, that matter should be established by the Arbitration Tribunal after the hearing and inquiry into the matter. Therefore the objection to the Jurisdiction is untenable, the arbitration proceedings shall continue.

But in the course of writing this article, I have been pondering over the matter of whether the decision was necessary: If the answer is affirmative, what the significance of the final nature of the Civil Ruling of the Beijing Municipality NO. 2 Intermediate people's court or any court in the mainland China? What CIETAC should have done with regard to the plea to Jurisdiction of CIETAC and the Arbitration clause not Applying to the Dispute Arising from the Deals between Naiko and Huayi? I suppose what CIETAC should have done was to remind the Respondent of the final

Civil Ruling of the NO. 2 Intermediate court, stressing that CIETAC and the Tribunal of the case should observer the civil Ruling and informing the Respondent of the continuation of the arbitration proceedings. It is explicitly provided in Art 4 of the aforesaid Response Relating to some Issues about conforming the Validity of an Arbitration Agreement by the supreme people's court that after receiving a copy of the ruling in this regard of a court, 'the arbitration institutions hall base on the ruling to decide to resume the proceedings or set aside the arbitration case.'

People all know that a final civil ruling just like a judgment, or order or the like precludes further litigation or non-appealable.[6] In the Decision of CIETAC the civil Ruling from Beijing was mentioned, though the word of 'final,' was not. The Decision was in fact not in line with the basic principle of law—principle of finality. That principle is so serious that I suppose it was by accident violated. I have no idea why the inner controlling system or screening system within CIETAC, South China and the headquarters in Beijing as well did not work in dealing with the matter. All the staff members and persons in charge involving the matter neglected the fact that there had previous been a final civil ruling.

Generally speaking, there have been three links in dispatching a document within CIETAC. The first link was that a staff member or secretary to the Tribunal thought that a document relating to that matter of arbitration procedure should be rendered, he/she would draft it. In the instant case, if he/she due some reason neglected the existence of the Ruling of the Beijing Municipality Intermediate People's Court or the finality (but in fact the Ruling was mention in the Decision) or the provision of Art 4 in the document titled Relating to some Issues about conforming the Validity of an Arbitration Agreement by the supreme people's court that after receiving a copy of the ruling in this regard from a court, believing that there should be a decision by CIETAC to counter the last pleading by Huayi, he/she was no doubt actively making a draft; then there was the second link, his/her supervisor might have not perused the Ruling, missing the key the word 'final,' in the Ruling. At last came the third link, the mistake was repeated by a superior or anyone in charge this kind of affairs at the headquarters located in Beijing.

A Chinese proverb goes: draw a snake and add feet to it ruin the effect by adding something.

I had no idea about the matter until a copy of the Decision was handled tome. And frankly I did not pay attention to it at that time, unaware of any problem relating to the Decision. I believe there might have been staff at CIETAC reviewing the case, finding out the problem and trying to dig out the roots of the matter so that there would be no repetition in this regard.

15 Expositions of the Tribunal in Award on Some Issues

The Tribunal, after inquiry at the oral hearing and examining the written materials submitted by the parties, holds that it enjoys jurisdiction over the instant case and the arbitration clause in the First contract applies.

The Tribunal is of the view that the First contract was not relating to one deal only built of basic nature. The deals and the subsequent deals from March 3, 1998, to the year of 2002 were carried out on the basis of the "general terms and conditions" of it (clauses G to 14).Therefore, in most cases, deals were made when the parties agreed on the quantity and unit price. And only in a few cases, the parties entered into some new contracts and the arbitration clause in the First contract was followed.

The Tribunal, in comparing with the terms and conditions of the second and Third contracts and the First contract, believes that there are no substantial different clauses except for provisions of the quantity and unit price. The Third contract and the Memo dovetail with each other. All the basic clauses including the arbitration clauses in the preceding contracts were implied and actually to apply to the Memo.

The three arbitrators discuss some aspects of matters concerning an international sales contract, saying that the main body usually consists of two parts: concrete terms and general conditions. In the instant case, the aforesaid three contracts are exactly the same. The first part consists of Terms 1 to Terms 5 (Name of Goods and specifications, quantity, price terms, unit price, currency and amount) as concrete terms. Those concrete terms vary according to each deal. The second part is made up of clauses 6 to 14 (packing, shipment, insurance, payment, shipping marks, claim and disputes settlement, force Majeure and arbitration clauses etc.) as general conditions. They are established through negotiation between the two parties and fixed as standards. The parties needn't negotiate on the terms and conditions for each deal. That is the practice in the international trade. Obviously, the transactions in 2002 under the contracts in the instant case could not be carried out only on the bases of the first part concrete terms, namely the terms of the new contracts reached by email or fax claimed by the Respondent could not be performed without role of the second part general conditions without a combination of the two parts of terms and conditions, one could not have a transaction performed. Furthermore, the Respondent fails to submit to the Tribunal any agreement with general conditions that are different from those in the three preceding contracts. Thereby the arbitrators infer from the aforesaid facts that transactions under the contracts in 2002 of which the general conditions are those including the arbitration clauses in the previous three contracts.

Most parts of the claims of Naiko were tenable. And the Tribunal rendered its Award on October 21, 2005.

16 Random Remarks on Some Matters of the Arbitration Case

About the dented doors of the fridges, I would like to quote some lines from the communications between the parties by email from my case file. Mr. LUO, the director of Huayi by email of August 2, 2002, replied Mr. Goldman of Naiko, saying:

> Respondents larder, maybe you are right. But considering cost, I have to find (out) the lowest way to solve the problem.

There had been opportunities for the parties to settle the quality problem by themselves.

According to the copies of communications between the parties submitted to the arbitrators by Naiko, the first one regarding to the quality problem was of July 13, 2002, from Mr. Martin Goldman to Mr. Luo of Huayi. Mr. Goldman said:

> Upon routine incoming Q. C it was found that a large number of unit s had dents and ripples in the doors. We don't really know the extent of the problem but I would suggest that you send somebody(ies) from your company to see for themselves.
>
> "The shipment of uF 40 there seems to be no problem.
>
> ...I don't know what has happened to your quality control within the factory but actually we are experiencing problems not with the actual working of your products, which are ok, but the cosmetic side of production..."

It reveals that the problem was not very serious but relating to the cosmetic of the products. On August 11, 2002, Mr. Goldman and Mr. Luo met in Shenzhen, China. According to themes age of that day from the former to the latter, both parties agreed that Huayi would solve the problem by sending doors by air and by sea to UK.

On August 14, Mr. Goldman in his message told Mr. Luo that anew customer had placed and order for 3 x 40' HQ containers (732 pcs) of Naiko N BF-130 same colours as previous.

Mr. Luo on September 2, 2002, write to Mr. Goldman, telling his counterpart that: "Yesterday, I also reported this matter to Mr. Fu, our president, about you, your, and the factory's opinion. Mr. Fu said that he requested the factory to arrange some technician and quality person (inspector) to UK for inspection and counting. If the fact is realistic, we will bear all of the loss."

Mr. Luo on September 5 informed Mr. Goldman of the decision that Huayi was to send Luo and his colleague a chief engineer to UK for checking the dented fridges.

Naiko, in my mind, was out of goodwill analyzing the cause of the dents problem for Huayi. Mr. Johnson of Naiko on September 5 wrote co MY LUO, celling his Chinese counterpart that:

> "This morning, I made a further visit to one of the comet warehouses to have a further detailed look at some of the rejected fridges, along with the chief Technical officer of comet. We fee 90% sure that this problem is caused by the container loading process. All the dint s are between 45 and 52cms from the bottom, and mostly they are in the center of the door(s). When your workers are loading the container, does one worker carry one fridge on his own? I am asking you this question because it seems to us that, if you imagine a situation where a worker lifts up a fridge and then pushes his knee into the front to keep it steady, then approximately 45 to 52 cms is exactly where the worker's knee would be! we cannot, of course, be 100% sure, but it seems to us the most likely cause and, therefore, it is just bad handling...'

This was one of the some messages among the great number of communications by email between the parties that impressed me most deeply. If that was the case, the quality problem should have easily and timely been settled without as an obstacle in the way of the continuation of trade relations between the parties. But in his replay of september6, 2002, Mr LUO of Huayi said:

> 'However, I believe that the problem happened is not caused by the container loading process. If so, the quantity is few not big... since the problem mentioned by you, the factory (has) pay (paid) more attention to it in July's production..."

I have no idea whether Huayi had finally found out the root cause of the dented doors of its fridges. Never the less, it turned out that the dispute could not be settled through amicable negotiation between the parties due to some reasons. One of them was that reflected in the message of November 19, 2002, from Mr. LUO to Mr. Goldman, saying that:

> '...we may confirm the problem but we cannot accept so high charges happened while JTM inspected, one side you didn't inform Huayi before inspected, another side so high inspection charges didn't be informed Huayi and confirmed by Huayi... Naiko should share (the) change(s).."

In the end that the parties had chosen the most expensive approach to have it settled, wasting great energy, time and money. Furthermore, the good relationship between the parties might not be restored for a long period. Huayi might have lost its market share in UK and Europe as well for a long period. And in addition Huayi as a listed company in Hong Kong, the case itself and the applying by Naiko to the Shenzhen Municipality Intermediate people's court after 45 days specified in the Award countdown form the date of october 21, 2005 for the enforcement of the Award would cost Huayi even more. Indeed, Naiko through its attorney-at-law of China has submitted an application for enforcement of the Award to the Shenzhen Municipality Intermediate people's court and the court according to the information provided by the lawyer has adopted some measures. Naiko would also lose some channel and chances in OEM deals in China.

We the arbitrators by nature were sorry for the parties who had in fact broken off their commercial relationships. We did try to mediate between them and the attorneys of both parties were reasonable. Nevertheless, we failed to narrow the gap.

I have little idea whether OEM is one of the approaches that a manufacturer has to adopt in its developing course. Though many professionals have no positive comment on it, nevertheless, as it exists it must be of some value to some enterprises in its developing.

About the submission of the copies of the second and third contracts, there was a long interval of 18 months between November 3, 2003, the date Naiko's agent went to CIE TAC, south China with the Application for Arbitration and attachment, to May 17, 2005. Naiko did submit a rather great number of written documents, including copies of Chinese versions of the messages originally in English of communications between the parties, copies of L/C in English original and the Chinese versions, etc. Naiko's attorney said that the courts required all the pieces of evidence turned into Chinese. But without the second and third contracts, one could not say that it was beyond doubt that all the subsequent deals were carried out in line with the general clauses in the first contract, as there was a gap between the deals under the first contract and under the Memo. Naiko did not present any documents showing the subsequent deals under the Memo, and the deals in the period from June to August 2002 were exactly following the general terms and conditions of the first contract.

I suppose Naiko should have produced some documents such as invoices, bills of lading, showing the shipping marks N/M and packing, etc., exactly as those under the first contract.

In the course of the oral hearing, the attorney of Huayi gave me the impression that he had been familiar with the general concepts of commercial arbitration and inclined to respect the jurisdiction of CIE TAC. I was not sure why he or his principal after the receiving the final civil Ruling by the Beijing Municipality NO. 2 Intermediate people's court did not change his mind; it was decided that the arbitration proceeds resumed on May 24, 2005, and Naiko thereafter submitted the copies of the second and Third contracts, he would repeated the tactic by submitting a pleading. His principal might have decided to adopt the approach, but the action itself was against the basic law principle. A final civil ruling should be respected and abided by. General speaking no one could act against a final civil ruling. One can see, in fact, the tribunal was only given a few months in handling the case.

I would like to say the analysis in the final civil ruling is simple but sound, showing the courts' attitude toward commercial arbitration in China.

17 Conclusion

I might be in a position to say that the exposition of the Tribunal in the Award on the whole are very sound and convincing, though I could not say they are perfect. I believe that in fact that the general terms and conditions established in the First contract and then repeated in the second and Third contracts apply to the deals under the Memo and logically those carried out in the year of 2002, though on cursory examination the Memo that it originally was only covering the orders for the year of 2001.

Notes

1. The former name of CIETAC before June 21, 1988 and the first set of rules of it (1956 Rules).
2. see the Document of Fashi [1998] NO. 27, October 21, 1998 of the supreme people's court, China.
3. Issued by the supreme people's court of China on July 20, 2000.
4. see Art 11 of the 2000 Rules of CIETAC.
5. see Art 6 of the 2000 Rules of CIETAC.
6. Please refer to James E. clapp, Dictionary of the Law, Random House, New york, 2000, p.187.

An Arbitrator Examines: None Replaceable Goods of a Specified Trademark by a Sole Manufacturer

1 Introduction

People know that the people's Republic of China and her Hong Kong special Administrative Regio (HKSAR) are of two different jurisdictions.

Many businessmen in East Asia and the world over are somewhat familiar with the Hong Kong International Arbitration center (HK LAC) and the China International Economic and Trade Arbitration commission (CIETAC) with its south China sub-commission (CIETAC, south China). CIETAC, HKIAC and over 180 newly established local arbitrational institutions in the China over provide businessmen of mainland, Hong Kong and other regions or countries with arbitration service. But to tell the truth, among the newly established arbitration institutions only a few, say about five, have been comparatively frequently chosen by foreign-related parties. The parties located in Hong Kong to some contracts or transactions incline to choose CIETAC to deal with their disputes and choose the law of the mainland of PRC as the governing law to their contracts and dispute.

This commentary was published in Mealey's International Arbitration Report, Vol. 23, #3, March 2008, pp. 31–46.

The viewpoints in the article are the author's own in his self-examination without necessarily representing that of his co-arbitrators, except for those contained in the original award. The author wishes to acknowledge the advice of Mr Hancai Deng, a lawyer located in Guanzhou on some issues of the case.

Y. Huang, *Commentaries on Commercial Arbitration in Modern China*, Modern China and International Economic Law, https://doi.org/10.1007/978-981-95-0168-7_9

2 Briefs of the Case[1]

The Buyer and the seller, both incorporated under the laws of Hong Kong, have their principle offices there on August 3, 2004, the parties in Hong Kong entered into a sales contract, standard terms supplied by the seller and the contract consists of two pages namely a front and overleaf, and a supplement as well.

The subject matter is addressed as "commodity" PETL IN LDPE PRIME "GRADEC450Y" (in original bags). The concrete clauses expressed in a mixture of Chinese and English, i.e. part in Chinese, part in English and part is bilingual on the upper part of the frontpage areas follows:

> Quantity: 192 x 20'APPR.3264MTS (10% more or less in quantity and total amount is acceptable);
>
> Shipping information: ETD SEP 2004 TO AUG. 2005; 16 x 20', APPR. 272MTS/ monthly; partial shipment allowed;
>
> Unit price: CIF Hong Kong and details in the supplement:
>
> Payment Term: payments hall be made in cash in full... in exchange for the Bill of Lading and the Buyer agrees to pay HKD255,000.00 as security deposit.

Twelve bilingual general terms in English and Chinese under the sub-title other Terms and conditions ("other Terms") on the lower part of the frontpage, and the following are re laced to the dispute:

1. The Buyer shall pay security deposit on or before4 Aug 2004…
4. CIETAC arbitration at Shenzhen.
6. 1% interest per month will be charged against the Buyer on any overdue payment.
7. The Buyer has to complete the transaction within 3days from the date of notification by the seller that the seller is ready to deliver the Goods, otherwise the seller is entitled to terminate this contract and the Buyers hall com pens are the seller for all loss incurred.
8. In the event of breach of any terms here of on the part of the Buyer and the seller exercises its right of termination of this contract, the security deposit s hall be forfeited by the seller and the Buyer shall be liable to the seller for all losses and costs there by incurred.
9. The conditions of this contract overleaf and the supplement forms part here of and is legally binding on both parties.
10. This contract and any modification or amendment to or waiver of the same shall only be valid if chopped and signed by (some representative) of the seller.
11. In case of conflict between the Chinese and English versions of this contract, the English version shall prevail.
12. This contract shall be governed by and construed in accordance with the laws of the PRC.

Overleaf there are eight clauses under the sub-title conditions (the "conditions") in English only, respectively titled Terms of payment, Delivery, Risk and property,

Insolvency of Buyer, Liability, Description and sample etc. The "5 Liability" is closely related to the disputes:

5.5 The seller shall not be liable to the Buyer or be deemed in breach of the contract by reason of any delay in performing, or any failure to perform, any of the seller's obligation in relation to the Goods, if the delay or failure was due to any cause beyond the seller's reasonable control without prejudice to the generality of the forging, the following shall be regarded as causes beyond the seller's reasonable control:

5.5.1 Act of God, explosion, flood, tempest, fire or accident;
5.5.2 War or threat of war, sabotage, insurrection, civil disturbance or requisition;
5.5.3 Acts, restrictions, regulations, by-laws, prohibitions or measures of any kind on the part of any governmental, parliamentary or local authority;
5.5.4 Import or export regulations or embargoes;
5.5.5 Strikes, lock-out s or other industrial actions or trade disputes (whether involving employees of the seller or of a third party);
5.5.6 Difficulties in obtaining raw materials, labor, fuel, parts or machinery;
5.5.7 Power failure or breakdown in machinery;
5.5.8 Any delay caused by the shipping company in the transit of the Goods.

The translation of the supplement in Chinese only is as follows:

1. The price clause(unit: MT):

1.1. The price of the raw material: The unit price of the next month should be based on the information about the price of the raw material of current month, Hong Kong region carried in the IC IS-LOR issued on every Fridays, the (average) medium price of LDPE FILM GRADE plus usD5/MT is the unit price of the coming month;
1.2. (Omitted).

2. Other Conditions:

2.1. The seller shall deliver the agreed monthly quantity where there is any *force majeure* event and that would prevent the seller from delivering the agreed quantity on time, the seller should be relieved from responsibility, and the Buyer could not claim on it.
2.2. If there is any non-compliance not arising from *force majeure* event or without any pre-consensus of the two parties and the seller in fact has received the security deposit, the matter s hall be settled as the following:
2.2.1. Failing delivery of a monthly quantity, the seller s hall refund the Buyer the security deposit HKD255,000 and compensate the Buyer for the loss a sum equal to the amount of the security deposit, i.e. HKD255,000. The contract s hall be automatically cancelled. The Buyer s hall not claim further damages from the seller or request the delivery of the shortage of goods or further performance of the contract.

2.2.2. If the Buyer refuses to receive the monthly quantity or part of the goods or is not in line with the provision in the payment terms, that is the breach of contract, the seller shall forfeit the security deposit HKD255,000 and is entitled co resell the goods to any third party. In the circumstance, the contract is automatically terminated.

3 Main Communications Between the Parties and Delivery of Some Containers of Goods

Letter One of 2004-9-14 is in a mixture of two languages from the seller to the Buyer (the successive ones are of the same model or following this precedent t, except as is noted—the author), relating to goods of 16 x 20' (APPT272MTS) of the September quantity. It is based on the agreement of both parties to alter the shipment of the September quantity "ETD in sep.2004" to "ETD sep. to Mid. oct.2004."

This letter is signed and chopped by the Buyer according to clause 10 of the other Terms and later confirmed by the tribunal as the First Amendment to the contract. And there are four similar letters from the seller to the Buyer based on the agreements of both parties to alter the shipment and are regarded as amendments to the contracts. All are acknowledged and confirmed by the Buyer.

On September 23, eight containers of goods were delivered by the seller to the Buyer.

Letter Two Of 2004-10-06 from the seller to the Buyer relates to the remaining goods of the September quantity as the seller on Sep.23 delivered goods of eight (standard) containers. It focuses on the date of shipping delayed co "ETD OCT. to Mid. NOV. 2004."

It is the second Amendment to the contract.

On October 18 and November 24, two and six containers of goods, respectively, were delivered.

Letter Three of 2004-10-11 from the seller to the Buyer in Chinese tells the addressee that "Due to the serious production accidents with PETL IN [Petlin (Malaysia) Sdn Bhd—here in after referred to as 'PETLIN'—the author], and the normal production has not been restored yet. In addition, the information relating to the technical difficulties from the plant of raw materials of last week has not reached us yet under such circumstances, we estimate that the state of the production interruption might last for a week. No further information is available at the moment. But it could be expected that would affect the shipment...."

Letter Four of 2004-10-14 from the seller to the Buyer refers to the October quantity, changing the shipment from "ETD Oct.2004" to "ETD Oct. to Nov.2004."

This is the Third Amendment to the contract.

Letter Five of 2004-11-10 from the seller to the Buyer also refers to the October quantity altering the shipment of "ETD Oct. to Nov.2004" to "ETD Nov. to Early Dec.2004."

This is the Fourth Amendment to the contract.

Letter Six of 2004-11-10from the seller to the Buyer is about changing the shipment of the quantity of that November from "ETD Nov.2004" to "ETD Nov. to Early Dec.2004." It is the Fifth Amendment to the contract. As Letters Five and six are on the same day, so the two could be combined as the fourth amendment as the parties do.

On November 24, five containers of goods were delivered.

Letters Seven of 2004-12-03 from the Buyer to the seller is in English, saying "... Regarding the Oct./Nov.HK." arrival ***material*** (emphasis added), the estimated losses incurred is USD72,080 instead of making decent profit. In this case, costs prefer to reduce monthly quantity to 34MTS (2 x 20'). Incidentally, appreciate if ultimate manufacturer can provide a light discount for Oct./Nov ***Contracts*** (emphasis added)..."—why the word of "contract" is used in lieu of "quantity"?

Letter Eight of 2004-12-08 from the seller to the Buyer in Chinese pertains to the remaining goods of the ETD October and November quantity, telling its counterpart that due to serious production problems with the factory of the raw materials, the shipment could not be made; wishing that it would be forgiven and it would be without delay in providing any information.

The Attached Letter of 2004-12-03 to Letter Eight from PETL IN to the seller refers to the delayed shipment, saying that: "...the shipment of above mentioned grades cannot meet your shipment requirement due to the shortage of ethylene. We must update you on the latest solution by middle of next week. We are sorry for the inconvenience that we have caused."

Letter Nine of 2004-12-09 from the Buyer to the seller is in English saying in the first paragraph that "...We received the Letter of Dated 3rd December 2004 (the Attached Letter—the author) from (the) ***manufacture*** (emphasis added) stating that shipment will be delayed again without a definite schedule..." And in the last paragraph of the same letter the Buyer asks "...why PETLIN did not extend same courtesy but asked ultimate buyers to suffer tremendous losses for PETLIN's mistakes? It is absolutely not fair at all!"

Letter Ten of 2004-12-13 from the Buyer to the seller is in English saying that "the Custs felt extremely disappointed with attitude adopted by (the) ***ultimate manufacture*** (emphasis added). According to the contract, ***supplier*** (emphasis added) has to compensate us HKD225,000 due to non-performance of timely shipment which was not caused by *force majeure*. We are not asking for such explicit compensation but refuse to take further concession in this down market." supplier "here means the seller, I guess, but the tribunal did not ask the parties to confirm, I am to deal with it in the ensuing part of the article."

Letter Eleven of 2004-12-15 from the seller to the Buyer in forms the addressee of the price of the 16 containers of the December shipment.

Letter Twelve of 2004-12-21 from the seller to the Buyer is mainly in Chinese regarding to the balance of goods 171 containers, saying that due to the shortage of the materials, the shipment could not be made according to the schedule, though it has tried its best to assist the **yuanliaochang** (factory of the raw materials) with the problem, the accident is beyond the control and is unexpected; "with regard to your company's requests for canceling the order, after consultation with our **gong ying shang** (supplier), we have the following arrangements: the goods (on hand) of 16 containers produced in December with unit price CIF USD1,381.25/MT Hong Kong, hoping that the Buyer would accept; about canceling the balance of last Oct. and Nov. quantity and the balance of the contract quantity of 155 x 20 (2635MTS), the seller has no objection when the goods produced in December is delivered, the seller would refund the security deposit."

The seller asks the Buyer to confirm the arrangements on or before December 22.

Letter Thirteen of 2004-12-22 from the seller to the Buyer is in English saying that: "[t]he Contract has clearly stipulated that in the case of *force majeure* and circumstances beyond the our reasonable control, we shouldn't be regarded in breach if we cannot deliver; we have already, by our fax dated 11 october 2004, indicated to you that due to the production failure and technical problems of the supplier, delivery for the October, November and December shipments could not be made.

"We will agree to cancel the contract as from January 2005, but must remind you of your legal obligation to take delivery of those goods delivered by us prior to the aforesaid cancellation."

Letter Fourteen of 2004-12-24 from the seller to the Buyer is in English reiterates its arguments: "the original October and November shipments could not be made because of *force majeure*... regarding the December shipment which was made strictly in accordance with the contract terms, you have a legal obligation to take delivery, which we hereby urge you so to do and give us a positive reply before 31 Dec. 2004, otherwise you shall be in breach of contract and we will have no alternative but to exercise our right to terminate and forfeit the deposits..."

Letter Fifteen of 2005-01-06 from the seller to the Buyer in English except quoting those clauses in Chinese in the supplement, mentioning the Buyer's letter of 2005-01-04, says that "First we disagree with you that we have never mentioned the *force majeure* incident occurred in October 2004. In fact we have as earlier as on 11th october 2004 informed you that our ***supplier*** (emphasis added) was unable to ship us the goods as scheduled due to *plant outage*, such notice was given to you once we were informed by our supplier"

And the seller reiterates that, inter alia, since the Buyer has failed to take delivery of the December shipment, in breach of clause 7 of the other Terms, "we therefore have already exercised our right under clause 2.2.2 of the supplement (and) on 3 January 2005 terminated the contract, for feited the deposit... and reserve our right to recover from the you any deficiency arising from the resale of goods."

Another Attached Letter of 2004-10-18 from PETL IN to the seller states "regret to in form that the shipment of the mentioned grades has to be differed due to *plant outage*."

4 Claims

The Buyer, in its Request for Arbitration, states that after conclusion of the contract it paid the seller the security deposit HKD255,000; the seller, at the initial stage of performance in September 2004, demanded to postpone the shipment; the shipment of the planned quantity of September was delayed until November 24; after several delays to early December, the seller could only deliver 5 containers of the goods totaling 85MT relating to the October and November quota and thus was in breach of contract. Therefore the Buyer requires the following:

1. to rescind the Contract;
2. the Respondent refunds the security deposit HKD225,000 and pay the li quidated damage HKD255,000 and;
3. the arbitration fees, legal fees of the Buyer and the expenses that would be incurred in the enforcement of the award borne by the Respondent.

IV. **Issues and Arguments of the Parties**

The main points of the Buyer in its Request for Arbitration are:

1. **The Seller unable to discharge its duty of delivering goods, in breach of contract, in early December 2004, the Contract automatically terminated.**

After several delays the seller still was unable to discharge its duty of delivering goods amount to a breach of contract and it should undertake the responsibility. Furthermore, as the seller failed to deliver the goods in early December 2004, the contract should be terminated automatically and without any effectiveness.

If failing code liver the monthly quantity, the seller shall according to clause 2.2.1 of the supplement refund the Buyer the security deposit HKD255,000 and compensate the Buyer for the loss a sum equal to the amount of the security deposit, i.e. HKD255,000.

The contract shall automatically terminate. *Therefore, the contract should be rescinded as of December 8, 2004*, the date respondent, after four delays, was still unable to deliver the goods of the October and November.

2. **The Seller respectively in Letters Three and Eight mentions some accidents, technical problems and a shortage of raw materials occurring at the factory of raw material**

These matters could not constitute *force majeure* provided in clause 5.5 of the conditions. Hence, they could not be regarded as reasons for exemption from liability.

According to clause 5.5, those accidents or technical problems with the factory of raw material were not within the provided scope because they were not "beyond the seller's reasonable control" Therefore the seller could not be exempted from liability.

What is provided in clause 5.5.6 should be of the seller's own but not of any third party. Additionally, the "difficulties" should mean that the seller could not obtain raw materials by all means and from any channels or resources including all the available

Exceptions in the contract should include Acts of God and any accidents provided therein. The key is how the parties have agreed to address such situations. Clause 5 of the Condition is not a clause of *force majeure* only but also an exception clause. The scope of an exception clause is wider than that of a clause of *force majeure*.

4. **Even if there is some act in breach of contract with the Seller, the Buyer is not in a position to claim a refund of the security deposit HKD255, 000.00 and the liquidated damages of HKD255, 000.00 as well.**

The security deposit is for the whole contract. The contract has been partly performed. According to it and the amendments, the seller has executed the obligation of delivering the quantity of September, and part of the quantity of October. It would be unfair if the Buyer is in a position to claim liquidated damages and requires the refunding of the security deposit for the whole contract on the grounds of the seller's failure in shipping some lots of the product.

"Baozhen jin" (the aforesaid security deposit) and "dingiin" are of two different concepts.[2] It is provided in clause 12 of the other terms that the governing law is the law of the PRC. According to the law, only if a party that receives the deposit fails to perform a contract, it shall return twice the amount of the deposit. As to the security deposit, there is no provision in the law.

As the aforesaid security deposit HKD255, 000.00 is for the performance of the whole contract, if there is some breach of contract, the seller has partly performed its obligation under the contract. The Buyer could at most claim part of the security deposit as compensation. Based on the same facts, the seller believes that the liquidated damages are too big a sum; according to the law the seller is in a position to request it be reduced.

After the oral hearing, attorneys of both sides submit their closing statements

The arguments of the Buyer's attorney:

1. **The Buyer since November 10, 2004, has never agreed to amend the Contract. Letter Eight by the Seller is an act of breach of contract.**

The Buyer does not deny that there have been four amendments to the contract. For the purpose of performing the contract and out of understanding, the Buyer has several times consented to the postponing of the shipment. On November 10, for the fourth time, the claimant agreed that the standing order relating to the lots of October and November could be extended to December. Nevertheless, the seller has not made any shipments. In Letter Eight the seller says that due to serious production problems with the factory of raw materials, the shipments originally ETD in October and November could not be made; there is no concrete date yet and no mention of altering the shipment date. Therefore the date of December 8 should be regarded as the starting point on which the seller has been in breach of contract.

2. **"Serious production problem with the factory of the raw materials" is not within the scope of the exception clause, and this matter is not proved by any piece of evidence.**

It is due to the too wide a scope of the exception clause 5.5 of the conditions as the standard terms provided by the seller, itis obviously unfair. In clause 2 of the supplement, exceptions are limited within the catalog of "Act of God." As for the other accidents, whether or not they are beyond the seller's reasonable control that should be confirmed by the parties.

About the catalog of exceptions in the instant case, clause 2 of the supplement should be applied but not clause 5.5 of the conditions.

"Serious production problem with the factory of the raw material" is doubtful.

First, the Attached Letter carries the explanation, saying that is due to the shortage of ethylene. Secondly, Letter Three mentions that there have been some technical problems with the factory of the raw materials and the production must be interrupted for about a week; Letter Eight contains the explanation of serious problem of production, the state lasts so long a period and that is unbelievable. Thirdly, on receipt of Letter Eight, the claimant responded that it intended to rescind the contract and claim damages, the seller in Letter Eleven states the shipment would be made and there would be 16 containers of goods. There is only a gap of 7 days. That raises great doubt!

Even if there has been a "serious production problem" with the factory of the raw materials, the seller is not in a position to invoke the exception clause. It is provided in Art 121 of the contract Law: "one party that violates the contract because of a third party shall be liable for the breach of contract to the other party. The disputes between the said party and the third party shall be settled according to law or their agreement."

3. **Claiming liquidated damages HKD255, 000.00 is in accord with the provisions of the Contract**

The claim is based on the provision of the contract and the equal principle and that is fair. The provisions in the supplement that compensating the Buyer for the loss a sum equal to the amount of the security deposit, i.e. HKD255, 000.00 shows its nature—liquidated damages. There should be no misunderstanding. As for the argument of the seller, saying that it is too big a sum, it is without good grounds.

The main viewpoints of the seller's attorney:

1. **The meaning of ETD in the Contract**

The ETD is the abbreviation of Estimated Time of Departure. It is not the real and fixed date of departure. That is to say the date of shipment is to be fixed later, i.e. that could be before the ETD or after it. Every postponement is based on an amendment to the contract. The Buyer is not in a position to condemn the violation of contract by the seller. It is groundless. Actually there has been no delayed shipment as ETD is provided in the contract. There is no fixed date of shipment. The practice of the seller is to complete a transaction within 3 days from the date of notification when the goods arrive at the destination. That is provided in clause 7 of the other Terms.

2. **The breach of contract by the Buyer in the course of performance**

According to the amendment (Letter six) relating to the standing order concerning the quantity of November, the date of shipment was extending to early December. That should be the first 10 days of the month. In the amendment the ETD Was extended to early December which was not the fixed date of shipment. Furthermore the seller on December 8 informed the claimant of the production problem with the *supplier* with the Attached Letter to prove the fact. According to clause 5 of the conditions and clause 2 of the supplement, difficulties in obtaining raw materials, power failure or breakdown in machinery, etc., with the supplier are within the exceptions. Therefore at that time there was no breach of contract with the seller under the circumstances, the contract remained effective; the Buyer was obligated to receive the goods. The Buyer claimed that the contract on December 3 automatically terminated and it refused to accept the goods delivered in December which was a breach of contract. The seller was entitled to terminate the contract.

3. **About the CIF.**

The terms in the instant case have nothing to do with fixing the date of shipment. It relates to the factors of the price. It means the components of price, i.e., cost, insurance and freight. It means sales conditions seller would get the goods from its supplier. As both parties are located in Hong Kong, the deals have no connection with transportation insurance. The date of shipment should be that provided in clause 7 of the other Terms.

4. **About the relationship between the exception clause and the force majeure clause.**

The exception clause of the Conditions and clause 2.2 the *force majeure* clause in the Supplement are not in contradiction with each other. First of all, *force majeure* means the objective circumstances that are unforeseeable, unavoidable and insurmountable. ***The object matter of the contract is low-density polyethylene of PETLN trademark. That is to say the goods are of specified trademark and produced by a specified corporation. PETLN is located in Malaysia. If there had been production problem PETLIN encountered and it could not deliver goods to the seller and subsequently the seller could not get the goods of PETLIN made mark produced by another PETLIN through other channels***.

Secondly, when PETLIN had encountered problems and failed to perform the contract between it and the seller, the seller could not deliver the goods of PETLIN trademark. That was unavoidable. ***To the best of the knowledge of the seller, there is the world over only a corporation named PETLIN located in Malaysia. The trademark PETELIN is owned by that corporation named PETLIN. The Seller through other channel could not get goods of the same trademark and same corporation as provided in the contract***. At the oral hearing the seller said it could get replacements from another corporation which is non-realistic, unless the parties had amended the trademark of the goods and the manufacturer as well.

Thirdly, when the parties entered into the contract in August 2004, no party would have expected that PETLIN would experience such troubles.

The international authoritative LCIS[3] in its Report of October 8, 2004, revealed that PETL IN shut the 255,000-my/yr line(s) on Thursday after encountering technical difficulties. It expected that the problem would be settled in a week. But in the Report there was no further information in this regard.

In Letters Three and Eight, the Seller informs the Buyer of the event. The Attached Letter reveals that PETL IN could not make shipment of the goods due to production problem. Examining the concrete situations in the instant case, such an event is not only within the limits of the exceptions of the conditions, but also, in the strict sense of *force majeure*, could be regarded as within the scope of clause 2.2 of the supplement.

5 Opinion of the Tribunal

1. Application of Law

Both the claimant and the Respondent are legal entities incorporated in the HKSAR. It is provided in the contract that it shall be governed by and construed in accordance with the law of the PRC. In their respective Request for Arbitration and Defense and in the course of the arbitration proceedings, both parties invoke legal provisions of the law of PRC. Therefore the law of the PRC applies in the instant case.

2. Effect of the Contract

Both sides have proper capacity as the contractual parties, and true declaration of will is reflected in the contract. Furthermore, there are no circumstances provided in Art 52 of the Contract Law that lead to the voidance of a contract. In accordance with Art 44 of the Contract Law, the contract established according to law becomes effective when it is established. Thereafter, the amendments to the contract are effective too. Both parties should abide by the provisions in it and its amendments, discharging one's obligations and enjoying one's rights.

3. Performance of the Contract

The tribunal has confirmed the following facts:

After the conclusion of the Contract, the claimant paid the security deposit HKD255,000.00 to the Respondent.

Five amendments to the contract have been reached by the parties and certain number of containers of goods have been delivered.

The contents of the letters show the course of performance of the Contract confirmed by the tribunal.

4. Is There Any Delay in Lots of Shipment by the Respondent?

The five amendments are the real expression of both parties' will. A party discharging its duty according to the amendments is not in breach of contract.

The problem is whether the Respondent discharges its obligations in line with the five amendments.

The tribunal is aware that the Contract of the instant case is of one-year duration relating to monthly quantity shipment of 16 standard containers. The above-confirmed performance facts show that there is breach of Contract relating to the first lot of shipment. Among the quantity of September, goods of 6 containers were delivered later than the date altered by the parties. The claimant forgave the Respondent's responsibility for that delay in delivery. Thereafter, regarding the balance of the October quantity 11 containers and the November quantity of 16 containers, the Respondent was still unable to deliver in November and early December as altered by the parties. Letter Eight shows this fact. Therefore, the Respondent is liable for that.

In its defense, the Respondent deals with the meaning of ETD, the abbreviation of Estimated Time of Departure, saying that the date of shipment was to be fixed later, i.e. that could be before or after the ETD. Therefore the Respondent denies that there was any delay in shipment and any breach of contract.

The tribunal holds that as the contract is of one-year term and the goods are to be shipped in lots of 16 containers monthly, the Respondent could deliver the goods on any day of a month. In this regard, the time window is fixed but not decided later. When the Respondent failed in making shipment and therefore the fact that it entered into five amendments with the claimant shows that. As a result, the tribunal does not accept the plea.

5. **Are There Any Factors of Force Majeure Or Exceptions?**

Being aware that the parties are of great divergence in this regard, the tribunal deals with the two aspect of this issue as follows:

a. **The Relationship Between Clause 5.5 of the Conditions and the Clause 2 of the Supplement**

It is provided in clause 9 under the other Terms that conditions overleaf (of the principal part) and the supplement of the contract form part hereof and are legally binding on both parties. Therefore it looks like that validity of clause 5.5 under the conditions is equal to that of clause 2 of the supplement. But it must be noticed that all the terms and conditions on the frontpage and the clauses under the sub-title of conditions overleaf of the contract are the standard terms supplied by the Respondent. There are 8 items listed in clause 5.5 under the conditions covering so wide a sphere. Under such circumstances the seller shall not be liable to the Buyer or not be deemed in breach of contract by reason of any delay in performing, or any failure to perform, any of the seller's obligations. Simultaneously, provisions regarding the price of the raw material, exceptions and breach of contract are provided in the supplement. According to clause 2 of the supplement, only when there is a *force majeure* event and that prevents the seller from delivering the agreed quantity of the goods on time, the seller could be relieved from responsibility. And if there is any non-compliance not due *force majeure* or without pre-consensus of the parties, the seller has to bear responsibility.

It is provided in Art 41 of the contract Law that "...Where the standard terms are inconsistent with nonstandard terms, the latter shall be adopted."[4] The last sentence in the quotation, in the author's opinion, should be construed as that "the latter shall prevail."

The provisions in the supplement are not the terms prepared in advance by any party. Instead, they are clauses specifically agreed by the parties, namely special clauses. Within a contract, special clauses prevail over standard terms. Therefore, in determining whether or not the delaying performance by the Respondent is in breach of contract, it is the exceptions of the supplement that should be applied.

6. **Are There Any Circumstances in the Course of Executing the Contract Within the Coverage of the Exemption Clause?**

The tribunal noticed that there are three letters from the Seller's side in the course of executing the contract mentioning the cause of delay in shipment to the Buyer. Letters Three, Eight, and the Attached Letter show why the Respondent and its supplier could not make delivery.

Further, Letter Fifteen reveals that the seller had as early as October 11, 2004, informed the Buyer that the seller's supplier was unable to ship the seller the goods as scheduled due to a plant outage. The incident was of *force majeure.*

According to another attached letter with Letter 15 and Letter Three, the seller and its supplier listed the causes concerning the postponement of shipment: "due to serious production accident," "due to serious production problems" and "technical difficulties," "due to the shortage of ethylene" and "due to plant outage."

In fact, when Letter Three arrived, the Buyer and the parties, respectively, on October 14 and November 10 agreed on the delay in the shipment of the goods of 16 containers of the October quantity and agreed on the postponing of the shipment of the November quantity. At last, the parties agreed on the shipment in early December and within the period the seller could only deliver five containers of the October quantity. Therefore when the period was drawing to an end, whether or not the course referred to in Letter Eight and in the Attached Letter is *force majeure* is the key. According to Art 117 of the contract Law, *force majeure* means "the objective circumstances that are unforeseeable, unavoidable and insurmountable." In the Attached Letter, PETLIN says the shipment could not be satisfied due to the shortage of ethylene and it would update the seller on the latest situation by middle of the next week, i.e. before December 8. But in Letter Eight (December 8), the excuse for the further delay was still due to serious production problems with the plant of the raw materials. The tribunal holds that what the seller and its supplier state could not be regarded *force majeure.* In the provisions contained in the exception clause of the supplement, the parties did not agree on the excuse mentioned in the aforesaid letters respectively by the seller and its supplier, namely that it is not within the exceptions as a reasonable excuse exempting the seller from any responsibility.

7. **About the Claims of the Claimant**

a. **Does the Claimant Have Right to Rescind the Contract?**

It is provided in Art 94 of the contract Law:

> "The parties to a contract may rescind the contract under any of the following circumstances"

> "…
>
> "(2) one party to the contract expresses explicitly or indicates through its acts, before expiry of the performance period, that it will not perform the principle debt obligations..."

And it is provided in Art 166 of the Contract Law:

> "Where the seller delivers the object in batches, if the seller fails to deliver one batch of the object or the delivery fails to satisfy the terms of the contract so that the said batch cannot realize the contract purpose, the buyer may rescind the contract with respect to such batch of object…."

Based on the aforesaid legal provisions and clause 2.2.2 of the supplement, and as the seller in Letter Eight tells the claimant that it could not deliver the goods of the October and November quantity by December 10, the Buyer could rescind the contract with respect to these batches and the subsequent batches of objects.

b. The Date on Which the Contract is Rescinded

The claimant maintains that the contract was automatically rescinded on the date when the Respondent violated it, i.e. on December 8, 2004.

Pieces of evidence show that upon receipt of Letter Eight, the claimant in Letters Nine and Ten (on December 9 and 13), expresses disappointment about the delayed shipment and no definite new schedule, but without mentioning rescinding the contract. What the claimant says in Letter Ten seems to remind the Respondent only of the relative provisions in the contract but does not deal with the problem of the provisions concerning the liabilities of a defaulting party. Hence when the claimant argues that the contract was rescinded on December 8, which was the date the Respondent violated the contract could hardly hold water. Nevertheless, the tribunal also notices that while there is no letter from the claimant referencing the problem of rescinding the contract, the Respondent notes the new arrangement in Letter Twelve, so a conclusion could be reached that at the latest the claimant raised the question of rescinding the contract to the Respondent on December 21, 2004.The Respondent in the aforesaid letter requested the claimant accept the goods of the December quantity and the Respondent would agree to rescind the contract and refund the security deposit.

The tribunal holds that the Respondent did not deliver the balance of the quantity for October and the whole quantity for November but requests the claimant accept the quantity delivered in December. That would enable the claimant to refuse to accept the goods of the December quantity and rescind the Contract. Thus, December 21, 2004, could be regarded as the date of rescinding the Sales Contract.

c. Liabilities of the Respondent as Defaulting Party

According to clause 2 of the supplement, the claimant reclaims the security deposit HKD255,000.00 and claims the liquidated damages HKD255,000.00. The tribunal sustains the claim.

Respondent argues that as the security deposit is for the performance of the whole contract and not for some lot or several lots of the shipment, it would be unfair to claim liquidated damages and refund the security deposit on the grounds of failure to deliver some lots of the shipment. Furthermore the Respondent believes that the liquidated damages are too big a sum, and requests a reduction of the sum.

The tribunal finds that it is explicitly stipulated in the Contract that as long as the Seller fails to deliver a monthly quantity, the Buyer has the right to act according to the provisions in the contract and make a claim against the Seller. The liabilities and consequences of breach of contract are also explicitly provided for in the contract. The tribunal found that the liquidated damages HKD255,000.00 is too big a sum, but that the Respondent has not produced any acceptable evidence showing that there are grounds for adjusting the liquidated damages.

The tribunal holds that clause 2 of the supplement reflects that the costs of both parties in violation of the contract is equal.

d. **About the Arbitration Fees, Legal Fees and the Expenses that Would Be Incurred in the Enforcement of the Award**

Based on the aforesaid reasons, the arbitration fees and the lawyer's fee of the claimant should be borne by the Respondent.

The tribunal did not accept the claimant's request for expenses that would be incurred in enforcing the award, as the enforcement has not yet occurred.

6 Reflections on Some Issues Overlooked by the Tribunal or the Parties as Well

1. **PETLIN Is the Special Trademark of the Subject Matter and the Only Manufacturer of It as Well**

About the subject matter of the disputed contract: It is provided that the commodity is **PETLIN LADE PRIME GRADE C450Y. That contains the trademark and the manufacturer, standard and specifications of the goods or the subject matter PETLIN—the trademark, the trademarks owner and the manufacturer of the subject matter of the contract; LDPE—the standard, low-density polyethylene; PRIME C450Y—the specifications** and in the course of performing the contract were once altered as C225Y.

Respondent's attorney argued in a written closing statement after the oral hearing, that PETLIN is located in Malaysia, and if there was a production problem, the Respondent would have not been able to get delivery from PETLIN and would not have been able to obtain goods of the PETLIN brand to deliver to the Claimant.

I should add that the first two questions put forward by the seller's attorney under the subtitle "About the relationship between the exception clause and the *force majeure* clause" in his closing statement could be regarded as one question.

It might be proper to say the viewpoint or argument is only briefly touched upon.

The tribunal does include the argument in its award, but without commenting on whether it is true or false. After rendering the award, I re-read the files of the instant case. I realize that the argument of the Respondent's attorney should have been regarded as one of the key issues of the case.

Should the tribunal have required the claimant res pond to the argument after the oral hearing when this issue was first put forward? And even under such circumstance should the tribunal have inquired into the matter, requesting the claimant make an observation on it, trying to make certain whether or not the seller had explained to the Buyer when concluding the contract that PETLIN was not only the trademark of the goods but also the name of the manufacturer?

I am now certain that we, the arbitrators, should have dealt with this matter no matter whether we would have accepted or denied it in the award. The problem is that the tribunal should not have neglected the issue. That is to say that the tribunal should have made sure whether the Buyer had been aware of the matter even though the tribunal might not need to conduct another oral hearing. The simplest way to deal with the matter is that we, as arbitrators, should have said, that the Respondent provided no evidence to support its argument.

In the course of writing of this article, I, on a social occasion exchanged ideas with the attorney of the seller, inquiring how he had constructed such a good argument. Interestingly enough his response was that in the process of drafting the closing statement, he figured it out. The attorney is experienced and quite wise in this regard, but what a pity as he expressly revealed he did not consult with his principal—the seller—to discuss the argument and ask whether there was any ground and any pieces of evidence to support the viewpoint. If there was any proof relating to the argument, what would have been the ending of the case? At least some reasons should be added and discussed in the award under the subtitle "The Tribunal's opinion."

The communications between the parties, for instance Letter Nine, reveal the Buyer was aware that PETLIN was the manufacturer of the goods.

If the above-mentioned special argument of the seller's attorney could be established, would the claims of the claimant have been accepted or the points contained in the defence of the Respondent have been sustained?

Up to now, I am not sure whether PETLIN is the specified trademark, the sole manufacturer of the subject matter of the Contract.

2. A Piece of Evidence Submitted and not Properly Employed by the Seller

In the preceding part of this article, the main points contained in the Respondent's defense and the closing statement by its attorney are mentioned and dealt with by the tribunal.

What about what the LCIs polyethylene (Asia pacific) in its Report of October 8, 2004? I quote the second and third paragraphs on page 4 (of the photocopy) as follows:

> "Production News: The poly olefin Co. (T PC) and chevron Philips in Singapore was forced to shut down their 180,000-mt/yr plus 70,000-m tl yr LDPE and 190,000-mt HDPE lines respectively on Monday due to an outage at upstream ethylene supplier pcs no. 1 cracker (460,000-my/yr). production at the TPC plant is expected to resume on 12 October, with full operating rates expected on 14 October, a market source said. PCS I is expected to restart over the weekend."

> "Malaysia's Petlin, which operates the world's largest low-density polyethylene (LDPE) train, has shut the 255,000-mt/yr line of Thursday after encountering technical difficulties, a market source close to the company said. The plant will be down for almost a week, but no further details were available at press time. petl in is a joint venture owned by Malaysia Petronas, Saudi Arabia's Sabic and south Africa is Sasol polymers."

The Respondent's attorney produced this document at the oral hearing, but in his closing statement draws the attention of the arbitrators and the Buyer's attorney to the third paragraph only, without touching on the above-quoted second paragraph. I guess that ethylene is the material for low-density polyethylene (LDPE).

Is there any connection between the two paragraphs? Is there any relation between the TPC located in Singapore or the pcs with PETL IN in Malaysia: IS TPC or pcs the supplier of PETLIN? Are the answers to these questions a formative or negative?

Some more questions. If without the supply of ethylene, could PETLIN be expected to restart the normal production, namely could PETLIN produce low-density polyethylene without ethylene? If the answer to this question was negative, then the responses to the questions in last paragraph would be affirmative. Then could Respondent's argument of *force majeure* be established, and the result of the case be somewhat different?

On the above mentioned social occasion, I, seeking feedback on the case from the seller's attorney, had to confess that there were some faults in the award, such as the arbitrators did quote his arguments on the product of special trademark and sole manufacturer in the award, but made no observation on it. Then I drew his attention to the connection between the two paragraphs, inquiring why he had not viewed it from this angle without hesitation, he said he had overlooked it and his principal had not reminded him of that relationship. The attorney admitted that if he had not missed that point and had combined it with his argument relating to the special trademark and sole manufacturer, the ending of the story might be different.

I went further, asking whether or not his principal could produce any proof so that his contentions could survive the examination of the Buyer and the analysis and examination of the arbitrators. He said he was not sure.

3. **Parties Involved in the Transaction and Different Names Used to Address Them but Without Clarification**

The Respondent is the seller and the claimant is the Buyer in the relationship between them. There was a relationship between PETLIN as supplier or manufacturer of the Seller. There was a customer, the end user of the Buyer. That should be clear.

But in the course of the transaction and during the arbitration proceedings, the parties to the instant case addressed PETL IN as "yuanliao chang"—the factory of raw mace rial, "gonyin shang"—supplier, manufacturer and the ultimate manufacturer. In Letter Ten the Buyer said, "According to the contract, supplier has to compensate us HKD255,000 due to non-performance of timely shipment...." I conclude, in the aforesaid, that the "supplier" means the "Seller" not PETLIN. And in the communications between the Buyer and the seller, some names were used such as ultimate buyers (in Letter Nine) and customers (in some letter of December from the Buyer to the seller) to address the end user of the Buyer.

Whether the Tribunal Should Confirm That the Consideration Has Been Paid Up?—An Arbitrator's Notes on a Case

1 Introduction

This case is relating to a share transfer and it will accept in 2007 by the China International Economic and Trade Arbitration Commission, South China Sub-Commission (CIETAC, South China), numbered as SHEN T2007006 case and the final decision numbered as CIETAC SHEN No. 101 Award.

The claimant Mr. Rajiv Rakyan resides in Belgium. The Respondent Mr. Vijay P. Nahata is a resident of the United States of America and with permanent address in New York. Both hold Indian passports.

Mr. Nahata owns the Real oriental Diamond Product s Co., Ltd. incorporated under the laws of People's Republic of China on November 19, 1998, located in Panyu District of Guangzhou Municipality, Guangdong Province; he is the sole shareholder and the legal representative of the company before and upon the share transfer.

The registered capital of the Diamond Ltd is USD 2,127,500.00 and its total investment is USD2,200,000.00.

In the first quarter of 2005, Mr. Nahata as Transferor and Mr. Rakyan as Transferee made a deal of the share transfer of the company.

In March, the two gentlemen, respectively or jointly signed various documents for the purpose, particularly entered into a Share Transfer Agreement and a Shareholding Agreement.

Centering on the key issues as whether the consideration for the share transfer has been paid up and whether the STA has come into force and remains as effective,

---

This commentary was published in Mealey's International Arbitration Report, Vol. 24, #1, January 2009, pp. 37–49.

The author is grateful to his co-arbitrator Mr. Xiaochun Liu (chairman of the tribunal, who is the main drafter of the principal part of the Award) and Mr. Yue Zhang, to Mr. Linyon Fu the secretary to the tribunal and to Mr. Gorden Lin and Ms. Kelly Lo, lawyer with the Sino-West Law Associate located in Guangzhou for their feedback.

Y. Huang, *Commentaries on Commercial Arbitration in Modern China*, Modern China and International Economic Law, https://doi.org/10.1007/978-981-95-0168-7_10

there are various views derived therefrom. But this article is mainly devoted to the discussion and analysis of the main issues of the case and comments about some points and introspection of the author as one of the three-member tribunals.

In the two agreements, it is explicitly recorded that consideration for the share transfer has been paid upon the conclusion. Related documents reveal that some formalities relating to the share transfer have been gone through; namely the deal has been approved by the board of the company and according to the governing law and administration regulations of China approved by the Foreign Trade and Economic Bureau of Panyu District with an Office Written Replay and a New Business License issued to the company. The Revised Articles of Association recording the share transfer have also been filed with the competent authority and approved. But registration with the local bureau of industrial and commercial administration could not be gone through without the assistance from the Transferor, and so are the registrations with some other local competent authorities.

Disputes arise, in the defense, an attorney employed by the Transferor presented at the oral hearing holds, inter alia, that the Transferee has to prove that he has actually paid the consideration for the share transfer. How should the arbitrators construe the wording of certain provisions in the two agreements and the effectiveness of the related documents? Should the Transferee be required to provide further evidence to prove that the consideration has been paid out?

The Transferee and the Transferor were not personally present at the oral hearing. The latter engaged first two attorneys but only one was present making presentation at the oral haring and that he thereafter submitted a written statement. After that and before the tribunal rendering the Award, the Transferor discharged the first two attorneys and engaged some other Chinese attorneys and all their names are recorded in the Award, but the tribunal has no idea of what the arguments or the ideas about the case of those follow-up attorneys engaged by the Transferor. In this article when the propositions or arguments of the Respondent are mentioned, that means those expressed by the attorney presented at the oral hearing and in his written statement and then of the Respondent's own.

For easy memory and avoiding confusion and in a pithy style, please see the following abbreviations:

Mr. Rajiv Rakyan—Mr. Ra

Mr. Vijay P. Nahata—Mr. Na

Real Oriental Diamond Products Co., Ltd—the Diamond Ltd., or the Company

The Share Transfer Agreement—STA

The Shareholding Agreement—SA

The Foreign Trade and Economic Bureau of Panyu District Government—the Foreign Economic Bureau

The Office Written Replay by the Foreign Economic Bureau—OWR

The New Certificate of Approval—NCA

2 Claims in the Request for Arbitration by the Transferee

Mr. Ra as claimant employs some attorneys-at-law of China files a Request for Arbitration to CIETAC, South China. There are four claims in the request:

1. The Respondent shall execute the STA, in line with clause 4 of it going through formalities with the local bureau for industrial and commercial administration, the taxation bureau, the exchange control authority and the customs, etc.;
2. The Respondent shall handle all the registration affairs relating to the claimant as the new legal representative of the Diamond Ltd with local bureau for industrial and commercial administration, the taxation bureau, the exchange control authority and the customs;
3. The Respondent shall pay the legal fee of RMB150,000 to the claimant;
4. The Respondent shall bear all the arbitration fees.

3 Documents Showing the Steps of the Conclusion of the Share Transfer

A. Letter of Appointment

On March 28, 2005, for the deal, Mr. Na as the chairman of the board and sole shareholder of the Diamond Ltd first of all reshuffled the board. That reveals that Mr.Ra has been and remains a member of the board. Mr. Na personally signed the letter carrying the seal of the company as follows:

> I, Vijay P. Nahata, am the sole shareholder of the Diamond Ltd. I have received and approved the resignation of MS. M.O. as director of the Diamond Ltd. I hereby withdraw her nomination as the director and at the same time appoint Mr. Avd Agar as the new director of the Diamond Ltd. I and Mr. Ra remain at the board.[1]

A board members list is attached to the letter with some information of the three directors and their signatures.

B. Minutes of a Meeting of the Board of Directors of the Diamond Ltd. Pursuant to Provisions of the Articles of Association of the Company

On March 9, 2005, Mr. Na chaired a meeting of the board of directors of the company. The other two directors were present. The main item on the agenda was to discuss whether it was proper to approve the share transfer of the company from Mr. Na to Mr. Ra and the amendments to the Articles of Association.

The minutes record that:

> 4. This matter was duly discussed and it was unanimously resolved that: Ninety percent of the shares of the company are transferred, at the value of $1,913,750.00, from Mr. Na to Mr. Ra; The Articles of Association shall be amended. The shareholders, Mr. Na and Mr. Ra jointly make anew Articles of Association of the company and that shall be submitted to the Approving Authority for approval and registration.[2]

The three directors signed on the minutes.

C. Clauses in the STA Closely Related to the Disputes

On March 9, 2005, Mr. Na as the Transferor and Mr. Ra as the Transferee signed the STA and it was chopped with the company's seal. It contains the information about the parties' status and permanent addresses of both parties and the address of the Transferor in Guangzhou. A Chinese attorney-at-law signed on it as a witness. The following clauses are closely related to the disputes.

> 1. Share Transfer and the consideration: The Transferor ... hereby transfers 90 percent of the share ... to the Transferee, and the Transferee hereby accepts this share transfer. The Transferor reserves the rights to buy back 40 percent of the share upon a consideration to be agreed by the parties.
>
> The consideration for this share transfer is USD1,914,750.00 only. ***The Transferee has already paid up the consideration of USD1,914,750.00 only to the Transferor and the Transferor hereby acknowledges receipt of such payment.*** (Emphasis added)
>
> 3. Approving procedures of the share Transfer: The share transfer shall be proceeded in according with approval of some approving authorities of the PRC. This STA Will come into effect upon being approved by an approving authority.
>
> 4. Handling of the procedures of the share Transfer: After 7 days from obtaining the approval as mentioned in clause 3, the Transferor and Transferee will proceed with relevant authorities to carry out the completion of the share transfer.
>
> 7. Governing Law: This STA Shall be interpreted and shall be governed by the laws of the PRC.

Any questions or disputes arising out of the STA shall be referred to CIETAC, South China.

> 8. Rights and Liabilities of the Transferee: upon execution of the STA, the Transferor and the Transferee shall sign new Articles of Association of the Diamond Ltd, which will be submitted for approval.[3]

The Chinese version of the STA, as well as all other documents mentioned in this case, must be prepared for the purpose of being duly filed with the local approving or administrative authorities concerned.

The author is to mention and discuss the clause 1. 2 of the English version of the STA in some ensuing paragraph.

D. Clauses in the SA Closely Related to the Dispute

The bilingual versions of the SA were signed by the two parties simultaneously with the STA and chopped with the seal of the company. The information relating to the various addresses of the parties in the STA is repeated. The clauses closely related to the disputed areas are as follows:

> 1. The share Transfer and consideration: Party A (Mr. Na) has entered into the STA with Party B (Mr. Ra) and transferred go percent share s to Party B on entering into this SA. The rights and interests arising from the 90 percent of shares shall be transferred to Party B with the share transfer. ***Party B has already paid up USD1,914750.00 to Party A for the share transfer.*** (Emphasis added)
>
> 2. Operation of the Diamond Ltd.: Two parties will operate the company in accordance with the already signed Revised Articles of Associations of it.

Clause 3 is subtitled as Governing Law consisting of two paragraphs exactly as clause 7 in the STA, playing the role of an arbitration as well.[4]

E. **The Deal Recorded in the Revised Articles of Association of the Company**

Also on March 9, 2005, the two parties signed the Revised Articles of Association of the company to replace the former ones and their revisions that have been duly filed with the approving authority. It is recorded in the Chapter I "Preface" the deal of share transfer.[5]

One can see that all the documents concerned were prepared in the course of the negotiation between the two parties.

4 Other Acts Adopted and Other Documents Amended Showing the Approve of the Share Transfer

A. **The Main Contents in the OWR and NCA by the Foreign Economic Bureau**

On June 8, 2005, the Foreign Economic Bureau rendered the OWR to the Diamond Ltd, approving the STA and the Revised Articles of Associations; directing the company the Transferor and the Transferee to go through procedures with some other competent departments of the local government.[6]

The NCA is issued on December 20, 2005, by the Foreign Economic Bureau in the name of the Guangzhou Municipality Government, recording that the two investors' related information an respective capital contribution: Mr. Na's $212,750.00 and Mr. Ra's $1,914,750.00.[7]

5 Some Main Propositions in the Defense of the Respondent

The main propositions in the Respondent's attorney's written statement, which are closely related to the main issues under discussion and the Claimant's first claim, are as follows:

A. **About a Proper Party**

The Respondent is not a proper party to this arbitration but the company is.

It is the company that should shoulder the responsibility to hand the former business certificate together with the OWR and the NCA to the local bureau for industrial and commercial administration, so the bureau would issue a new business certificate to the company, carrying the new information of Mr. Raas the legal representative, etc.

B. **About Evidence Showing the Payment of the Consideration for the Share Transfer**

The evidence produced by the claimant could not prove that he has paid up the consideration provided in the STA.

The STA and SA actually have been in the state of in-execution. Judging it from a legal angel, the conclusion of the two agreements only shows that the consensus in idem of the both parties or their common will. Conclusion and performance are of two different actions.

The claimant must produce receipts and vouchers to show that he has paid up the sum. He has failed to do so, so he has to bear the adverse result and verdict.

Further, in going through formalities regarding to the moderation of registration about any share transfer at a bureau of industrial and commercial administration, in the practice, the bureau would require both parties to show the consideration for the share transfer has been paid up. Without evidence in this regard, the moderation registration could not be done. Therefore, the first claim is obviously without grounds.

C. **The Connotation of the Provision of 'Buy-Back'**

In clause 1.1 of the STA, it is explicitly provided that the Transferor reserves the right to buy back 40% of the share. That provision shows that whether or not the claimant has made the payment of the consideration is uncertain.

D. **The OWR Has Been Void and so Has Been the STA Itself**

As the registering moderation of the share transfer has not been done within a reasonable time limit, the OWR with regard to the STA has been void without any effectiveness now. As a result, the first claim of the claimant should be rejected.

6 Main Points of the Tribunal Relating to the Issues Under Discussion

A. **Proper Law**

The parties' disputes are out of the share transfer with the company of foreign investment located in Guangzhou, PRC. In addition, it is explicitly provided in the two agreements that they shall be interpreted and governed by the laws of PRC, so the law of PRC is the proper law of this case.

B. **The Main Issues**

There are nine issues in the case. The author is to discuss the main and most closed ones: the effectiveness of the STA and the SA; the state of performance of the STA; whether the tribunal should confirm that the consideration has been paid up; the effectiveness of the Revised Articles of Association; the status of the Respondent as a proper party.

C. **The Effectiveness of the STA and Some Related Documents**

The STA was concluded by the parties. Art 44 of the Contract Law of PRC:

> The contract established according to law becomes effective when it is established.
>
> With regard to contracts which are subject to approval or registration as provided for by the laws or administrative regulations, the provisions there of shall be followed."

Art 10 of the Law on Foreign Wholly-owned Enterprise (PRC):

> The splitting-up, merge of changes of other important matters of a foreign wholly-owned enterprise s hall be reported to an examination and approval authority for approval and the enterprise shall go through procedures for the modification of registration at an administration authority for industry and commerce.

In the instant case, the STA has been approved by the approving authority—the Foreign Economic Bureau and it rendered the OWR of June 8, 2005, and the NCA Of December 20, 2005, in the name of the Guangzhou Municipality Government to the company. Consequently, the STA came into force on December20, 2005.

The Foreign Economic Bureau by issuing the OWR in fact approves the Revised Articles of Association of the company.

But as the company has not gone through procedures for the modification of registration at the local administration bureau for industry and commerce due to the omission of the Respondent, does the NCA remains effective?

Art 33 of the company Law of PRC provides that where any of the registered items of a company is changed, it shall handle the modification of the registration; if the company fails to do so, it shall not, on the basis of the unregistered or unmodified registration item, stand up to any third party.

The NCA remains effect and so is the STA. The latter is binding upon the parties. The two parties shall enjoy the rights provided in it and shoulder the correspondent obligations.

D. The Payment of the Consideration of the Share Transfer

It is explicitly provided in clause 1.2 of the STA the exact figure of the consideration for the share transfer and the Transferee has paid the total amount and the Transferor acknowledges receipt of the payment.

The wording clearly shows that before or upon the conclusion of the STA, the claimant had paid the consideration $1,914,750. 00 and that was confirmed by the Respondent upon the conclusion of and in the STA. That fact was further affirmed by the parties in clause 1 of the SA simultaneously entered into by the two parties with the STA.

It is unnecessary for the claimant to produce any evidence more to prove the fact and the claimant is under no obligation to pay the consideration once more.

For that fact recorded in the STA, actually the claimant has produced the two agreements as two pieces of evidence. The Respondent could challenge them with some counter-evidence or evidence in rebuttal to prove that the Transferor hereby acknowledges receipt of such payment is not true.

E. The Provision of the Reserved Rights of 'Buy-Back'

The parties agree on that "The Transferor reserves the rights to buy back 40% of the share upon a consideration to be agreed by the parties' in clause 1.1 of the STA."

The provision or the wording does not have any connotation that the Transferee has not paid the consideration up yet.

F. The Status of the Respondent as a Proper Party

The tribunal believes that judging whether or not the Transferor is a proper party to the arbitration or whether or not he is of the status as the Respondent to the instant case, first of all one shall see if there are any arbitration clauses in the two agreements.

No doubt, the answer is affirmative. Obviously, the two arbitration clauses bind upon the two parties.

The Respondent raises the question that he is not the proper party to the instant case, holding that he has no obligation to go through the formalities regarding to the modification registration; that is the obligation of the company. In nature that is an issue of substance.

In the instant case, the status of Respondent is not only the Transferor to the STA, but also the sole shareholder of the company before and upon the conclusion of the two agreements. The tribunal confirms that up to now, the Respondent is still the legal representative of the Diamond Ltd, and the Respondent does not deny the fact. He has been controlling the stamp of the company. without the cooperation or assistance from the Respondent, concretely without his signature and chopping with the stamp on the application forms (being filing in by an applicant enterprise) designed by the General Bureau of Industrial and commercial Administration of PRC for the modification registration, the formalities for the share transfer could not be finally gone through. So the Respondent is in breach of the STA.

G. The Decisions of Tribunal in Its Award

The Award in favor of the claimant was issued on September 17, 2007.

In the Award, the first claim of the claimant is sustained. About the third and fourth claims, the tribunal decides that the two parties share the legal fee occurred to the claimant in this case and the arbitration fee, the claimant bears a quarter, and the Respondent the other three quarters. The two sums added are RMB240,000.00.

The second claim is close connected with the first claim, but the tribunal rejects it, accepting one of the arguments in the written statement by the attorney of the Respondent and confirming that the claimant has failed to produce direct evidence to show that he had according to the relevant articles of the Revised Articles of Association of the company holding a shareholder meeting by and via telephone conversation mode about the topic of replacing the formal legal representative of the company on the agenda. Put it in a briefest way that Mr. Ra has been unable to submit any direct evidence—any video, showing that he did convene a shareholder meeting by and via telephone conversation mode on March6, 2006. Namely that the tribunal does not accept the truth and effectiveness of the Minutes (in bilingual) of shareholders Meeting of the Diamond Ltd Held via Telephone conversation Mode on this 6th Day of March 2006 pursuant to Arts 7.4, 7.5 and 7.6 of the (Revised) Articles of Association. The piece of evidence is only with Mr. Ra's signature, recording that:

> 2. All these two shareholders discussed to appoint Mr. Ra as the legal Representative of the company to remove (substitute) Mr. Na as current (new) legal representative.

> 3. This matter was duly discussed, but the two shareholders were unable to reach unanimous decision. Pursuant to Arts 7.5 and 7.6 of the (Revised)Articles of Association, Mr. Ra, as the major shareholder of the company exercised the casting vote and decided to remove Mr. Na as the current legal representative and appoint himself as the legal Representative.[8]

The tribunal holds that without a proper meeting of the shareholders, officially appointing the claimant as the new legal representative, his second claim could not be sustained.[9]

7 Further Pondering Over and Comments About Some Points of the Case After the Award Rendered

The Award in original is of somewhat long, over 32,500 Chinese characters. The author has only touched some of the issues above and would be pondering over some points more.

A. **The Tribunal Should Have Revealed That the Two Agreements and Some Other Related Documents Are of Bilingual**

In the course of drafting the Award, being a member of the tribunal, the author did in writing formerly suggest that the tribunal should make clear that all the main documents of the case are of bilingual Chinese-English versions. It is a fact, and that is pertaining to the foreign nationality of the parties, showing the basic character of the arbitration. The author believes that mentioning that face would enable the potential informed readers of the Award to understand that actually the tribunal took account of that that the two Indian gentlemen might not be good at Chinese; the documents in Chinese were drafted by some Chinese lawyers respectively or jointly engaged by them or by one party only. The two parties though are absolutely clear about the main ideas and purpose of the documents might have limited knowledge of the concrete provisions or language of the Chinese versions. English is their official and working language, but Chinese is not. But as the deal is made and the company is located in China, all the main documents have to be held to some competent authorities of the local government of China for approval or kept on file. So documents must be in Chinese as it is the official language in China. Further, some Chinese lawyer(s) must also prepare the English versions of documents. The most important point is that the two gentlemen not only sign on the Chinese versions of the documents but also on the English versions as well, some documents are witnessed by a Chinese lawyer. Therefore, the two versions of a document concerned in this regard are of equal validity. The fact that the tribunal does not reveal that the main documents are of bilingual versions and expresses the idea that two versions of the document are of equal effect, the author holds that is a fault.

If what the author holds is tenable, the author is also liable, liable jointly and severally with his co-arbitrations. That at least shows that the author has failed to persuade his co-arbitrators because of his argument and explanation is want of persuasiveness. Are the arguments and explanations of the author lack of logical or he is still short the consideration for share transfer has been paid up and the Transferor acknowledges receipt of such payment. As to the matter of application of law, it should beat his engaged lawyers' disposal.

A reader might feel puzzled over or be curious about the explicit and exact wording relating to the payment of the consideration in the four documents of bilingual versions of the two agreements. One might be inclined to search out the root. Actually the Respondent had got sufficient time and chance to produce counter-evidence to set the effect of the two clauses, if he really wanted he could. He could even tell the story why the claimant had been a member of the board of his subsidiary before the conclusion of the two agreements.

One might ask without receiving the payment of the consideration, why the Transferor would have accepted the language explicitly showing that such payment had been made upon the conclusion of the two agreements. That might be beyond the imagination of a normal person. Without any piece of evidence in rebuttal, would the tribunal have any alternative or other conclusion?

The author peruses the aforesaid letter and its attachments. Mr. Na stresses in the third page of the letter that the consideration is not a small amount. Mr. Rakyan must have the proof. He says:

> As far as I have signed the agreement saying, that I have received the payment, is a very day normal situation.
>
> If you think, when every month (a) worker get(s) paid his or her salary, he or she sign(s) and then(a)cashier give(s) the money s, what happen if(the) worker sign(s) and (the) cashier do(es) not pay, then what happen? Her or she will not get paid? Or police cannot check again or just say to (the) worker, you have already signed.
>
> And there was also more reason than this:
>
> Plaintiff is my personnel friend for almost 20 years. He is associated with this company almost 8years.The lawyer, who made the contract, and also witness, is a personnel friend of mine for more thang years, I was the one who introduce the plaintiff the lawyer.
>
> So looking to all above it was very obvious that I have to trust and sign the paper, but why your office (all the three arbitrators) do not want to ask for payment receipt:? Because they know that Mr. Ra do(es) not have and your office wants to favor Mr. Ra.[12]

I could not say what his arguments above by analogy with the way of a worker gets his/her monthly salary would never stand up. But no matter a worker signs on a payroll before or after getting an amount of cash as his/her monthly salary from a casher with a company, the two actions almost simultaneously take place. Further, if a worker signs a payroll but without getting his/her salary, and if there is some witness around, what measure he would immediately take? Could he/she claim after a lapse of several months or in a couple of years?

At this moment, may the author repeats that the two agreements were concluded on March 9, 2005, and the OWR by the Foreign Economic Bureau was on June 8, 2005. May the author point out that there is a period of almost three months in between? If the Transferee had not paid the consideration then what measures or actions the Transferor could adopt to inform the competent authority of the failure of the Transferee in paying the consideration and had he engaged any Chinese lawyers to try to stop the Transferee from obtaining the OWR? Could the author draw the attention of any readers to the Award and to the case files and to this article to the fact that the NCA issued on December 20, 2005, by the Foreign Economic Bureau in the name of the Guangzhou.

Municipality Government. There is another longer period of more than 6 months in between. The NCA issued to the Diamond Ltd records the names of the two investors (shareholders), Mr. Na and Mr. Ra, their respect capital contributions to the Diamond Ltd. Doesn't it mean that the competent authority on behalf of the local government has by means of rendering it confirmed that the consideration of the share transfer had been paid up when the NCA was issued? Then from June to December of 2005, what action or measure could Mr. Na take or did he take for the purpose to prevent the deal from being confirmed and approved or require the Foreign Economic Bureau not to approve the deal as the Transferee had not paid the consideration up: Further, what had he done in denying the payment of the consideration since then to the inception of the arbitration proceedings? Could that fact actually confirmed in the NCA by the local government based on the documents submitted by the party (or parties in the name of the company) be denied by the tribunal without any powerful counter-evidence from the Respondent?

In the course of reviewing the case file and writing this article, the author supposes that if he had suggested that the analysis and comments above should have been added to the part under the subtitle "the Tribunal's opinion" in the Award, it would be somewhat more persuasive.

D. **The Long Interval Between the Date of the OWR and the Date of the NCA**

In the course of the arbitration proceedings, that point caught the author's attention. It might have nothing to do with the issues of the instant case, but such a point sometimes might lead to a dispute of some parties to a similar contract ordeal. No doubt it would prevent a smooth deal between parties.

Just looking back again, on June 8, 2005, the Foreign Economic Bureau rendered the OWR to the Diamond Ltd, approving the STA and the Revised Articles of Association; on December 20, 2005, in the name of the Guangzhou Municipality Government the Foreign Economic Bureau issued the NCA to the Diamond Ltd. The tribunal in the Award discusses the matter, saying rendering the OWR is one of the links or one of the steps within the operation of the Foreign Economic Bureau, the STA came into effect after the issuance of the NCA of December 20, 2005. That is to say there are two links or two steps relating to the approving of that matter. The interval between the two steps is too long. The legal professionals—the lawyers of the Transferee believed that according to the clause 4 of the STA, the parties should be within seven days, counting from June 8 to 15, 2005, to jointly apply to some other competent departments of the local government for registration of the share transfer. The parties have to wait for six months more after getting the OWR. Who should be blamed? What the poor efficiency of the competent authority of the local government—the government of Panyu District of Guangzhou Municipality!

8 The Respondent Applies for Not Enforcing the Award

A. An Outline of Current Situation Relating to the Award

According to feedback from the Claimant's attorneys, they obtained from CIETAC South China a certification of the effectiveness of the Award on October 22, 2007. The tribunal's first decision in the Award requires—without specifying an exact date—that the Respondent execute the decision, i.e., to execute the STA and, in accordance with its provisions and applicable law, handle the registration of the share modification in the company.

Then the claimant's attorney applied for enforcement of the Award to the Guangzhou Municipality Intermediate people's court of the Guangdong Province (the "Guangzhou Court") the next day, October 23, 2007, mainly applying for the execution of the first decision in the Award and the payment of RMB240,000.00 as legal fee and arbitration fee—the portion that the Respondents hall bear.

Several weeks later, the attorney was informed by the Guangzhou court that Mr. Na had submitted an application for not executing the Award before his application for the enforcement of the Award to the Guangzhou court.

It turned out that Mr. Na has engaged some legal worker as an attorney with the Guangdong Mediation center associated with the China council for the promotion of International Trade, on October 8, 2007, applied for not executing the Award to the Guangzhou court.

On December 10, 2007, the Guangzhou court rendered a civil order, suspending the enforcement of the Award, transforming the application of Mr. Na for examination; the enforcement of the Award is to wait for the finishing of the examination.

On the same day, the attorney of the claimant submitted an application to the Guangzhou court urging an immediate rejection to Mr. Na's application.

The attorney of the claimant holds that the reasons given in the Award are so convincing that he has no doubt that it would be enforced.

The author has got no access to the attorney of the Respondent, the staff member of the Mediation Centre.

B. The Main Reasons in the Application Submitted by the Respondent to the Guangzhou Court

Mr. Na's main reasons in the application for not enforcing the Award are respectively under two subtitles:

1. **The Respondent Unable to Present His Case due to Causes for Which He No responsible**

All the arbitration notices were serviced to his residence in China and were signed and received by his housekeeper, an illiterate woman. He was not available in China and the housekeeper did not forward those notices to him. He got to know that case after his assistant had got access to the notices from CIETAC, South China about the formation of the tribunal, etc. Therefore, he failed to appoint an arbitrator.

When he returned to China but only to find that his attorneys before presenting at the oral hearing failed to sufficiently communicate with him, the author tries to be faithful to the original Chinese, and he has got no access to Mr. Na and has no idea whether he could express himself in Chinese, so that in the oral hearing the attorney(s) insufficiently revealed the truth; his application for a second oral hearing and examining some supplement pieces of evidence was turned down by the tribunal; the conclusion of the tribunal is false.

It is provided in Art 260 of the Civil Procedure Law of PRC:

> A people's court shall, after examination and certification by a collegial panel of the court, make a written order not to allow the enforcement of the award rendered by an arbitral organ of the PRC handling cases involving foreign element, if the party against whom the application for enforcement is made furnish proof that;
>
> (2) the party against who the application for enforcement is made was not given notice for the appointment of an arbitrator or for the inception of the arbitrator proceedings or was unable to present his case due to causes for which he is not responsible.

According to the provision, the Respondent requests the Guangzhou court not to enforce the Award.

2. **The claimant Has Not paid the consideration, the Respondent Enjoys the Right Not to Deal with the Formatives Regarding to the Modification of Registration**

The consideration is a big sum that could not be paid in cash.

Art 66 of the Contract Law of PRC:

> If both parties have obligations towards each other and there is no order of priority in respect of the performance of obligations, the parties shall perform the obligations simultaneously. one party has the right to reject the other party's request for performance before the other party's performance. one party has the right to reject the other party's corresponding request for performance if the other party's performance does not meet the terms of the contract.

Art 217 of the Civil Procedure Law:

> If a party fails to comply with an award of an arbitral organ (panel— the author) established according to the law, the other party may apply for execution to a people's court which has jurisdiction over the case. The people's court applied shall enforce the award. If the party against whom the application is made furnishes proof that the arbitral award involves any of the following circumstances, the people's court shall, after examination and verification by a collegial panel, make a written order not to allow the enforcement:
>
> ...
>
> (4) the main evidence for ascertaining the facts is insufficient.

Claims Based on a Replaced Contact Unacceptable—Comparing Two Proposals of Award to a Case

1 Introduction

The parties to the case:

> The claimant—a trade corporation located in the Hong Kong Special Administration Region (HK SAR) of the People's Republic of China Hong Kong, as the Buyer to some sales contracts.

The Respondent—a group corporation located in Chengdu, Sichuan Province, the mainland of China, as the seller to some sales contracts.

The arbitration institution—China Arbitration Commission (CAC) in May 2007 accepted the case.

In the end, the arguments and grounds of the claimant were not substantiated. The Tribunal basically accepted the contentions and reasons advanced by the Respondent. So in the nature of things, the decisions rendered by the Tribunal should have been closely connected with claims and the contractual grounds advanced by the claimant, that is, as his grounds and arguments were not accepted by the Tribunal, the claims could not be sustained; as the basic facts, contentions and reasons in the statement by the Respondent were confirmed and accepted by the Tribunal, the claims of the claimant could not be sustained; or as the Respondent admitted that he had once intended to deliver the last installment of goods, so the main claim of the claimant could be adjusted and then partly sustained or met.

The author of this article was one of the three members of the Tribunal. In the course of the proceedings, I first based on the common understanding of the Tribunal drafted a proposal of award, trying to reflect the principles that as the claims of the claimant were lack of reasonable grounds (unfounded, unestablished) and the facts and arguments that the claims based on were dismissed by the Tribunal, therefore all his claims could not be acceptable.

This commentary was published in Mealey's International Arbitration Report, Vol. 24, #9, September 2009, pp.27–45.

Y. Huang, *Commentaries on Commercial Arbitration in Modern China*, Modern China and International Economic Law, https://doi.org/10.1007/978-981-95-0168-7_11

After reading the proposal by me, the other two arbitrators drew up their own respective proposals. The views of the two arbitrators were identical on main issues and the proposed decisions were of great similarity between the two. In addition, the proposal by the presiding arbitrator unexpectedly for a certain period had been prevailing.

Thereafter, the principals involved or reflected in the formation of the decisions or the course of decision- making have been lingering in my mind and I could not get rid of them, So I have got this article done. I would like to introduce to the one by the presiding arbitrator and the one by me and make some comparison between them.

All the events concerning the transaction between the parties to the case were happened in 2006, so for the purpose of simplicity, when an event is referred, the calendar year might not be mentioned or when the calendar year of an event is omitted, it does mean that it happened in 2006.

The terms and conditions specified in contract A are identical with those terms and conditions of some immediate following contracts (collectively as contract B series) except for the provisions for payment of the goods. If you overlook some little details reflected in some documents relating to the procedures of clearance through customs, you might hold that they were the principal obligations and correspondent rights provided in contract B series but not those in contract A had been performed and enjoyed by the parties. Thus contract A could be said to have been actually replaced by contract B Series, and ceased to be of legal effect separately or I could say that actually details of the aforesaid documents revealed that it should be regarded that contract A and the contract B series were merged. Therefore, it follows that any claims by the Buyer in relation to contract A would not be acceptable.

2 Briefs of the Case

A. The Main Contents in the Request for Arbitration of the Buyer and His Claims Based on Contract A

The Buyer as claimant in his Request for Arbitration submitted on March X, 2007, states:

> On May23, 2006, the parties entered into contract (No. XX10627002A,[1] hereinafter referred to as 'Contract A,' so that it could be distinguished from and connecting to the subsequent contracts). The subject matter is 720MT silicon metal of specified specifications of China origin.

After the conclusion of contract A, on June 7, he received a letter from the seller, demanding that the last delivery should be delayed to August 20 and the expiry date extended to September 4. The parties modified the last dates of shipment of the three installments respectively as on June 30, July 30 and August 20.

Upon the application of the seller, a bank located in Chengdu (the capital of Sichuan Province) on June 9 rendered a Letter of Guarantee in favor of the Buyer for the sum specified therein as security for compliance with the seller's obligations in accordance with Contract A and it remained valid until September 4.

Upon the application of the Buyer, a bank located in Xiamen (formally named as Amoy in Fujian Province) on June 12 rendered an irrevocable L/C in favor of the seller for the sum specified in contract A.

On June 27, the Buyer wrote to the seller, demanding the addressee to have a batch of goods of 120MT prepared by June 30 in Huangpu (Guangzhou) Port.

But to the Buyer's disappointment that up to the date of referring the dispute to arbitration, the seller had not performed his obligations under contract A.

Further, on September19, a lawyer located in Xiamen engaged by the Buyer wrote to the seller, demanding the addressee to have the goods of 720MT under contract A delivered, but the seller did not discharge his duties under contract A and the Buyer on November 11 in a letter by post rescinded contract A.

According to Art 76 of the United Nations Convention on Contracts for the International Sales of Goods ('CIGS') *['(1) If the contract is avoided and there is a current price for the goods, the party claiming damages may, if he has not made a purchase of resale under Art 75, recover the difference between the price fixed by the contract and the current price at the time of avoidance as well as any further damages recoverable under Art 74…'*] and making reference to the information at: www.sie.cn on the date of rescinding Contract A, saying that he is in a position to claim that the seller was in breach of contract as he failed to perform his obligations under Contract A, requesting the arbitrators to decide that the Respondent shall:

1. Indemnify the claimant the loss of expected profit USD136, 800. 00;
2. Indemnify the claimant the expenditures occurred in handling this case the legal fees and arbitration fees, respectively, as RMB10,000.00 and USD13,680.00.

B. Terms and Conditions (Collectively Addressed as Clauses) Closely Relating to the Disputes in Contract A

Clause 2 Specifications: Size: 10–100MM 90% MIN; SI: 98.5%MIN; FE: 0.5%MAX; AL:0.5%MAX; CA: 0.3%MAX.

Clause 5 Terms of Delivery: FOB Huangpu (Guangzhou), Shanghai or Tianjin at the Buyer's option.

Clauses 6–7 unit price and Total Amount: USD915/MT and the total amount is USD658, 900.00 and ±5% tolerance in both quantity and amount to be allowed at the seller's option.

Clause 8 Loading port: Huangpu (Guangzhou), Shanghai or Tianjin at the Buyer's option.

Clause 9 Discharge Port: At Buyer's option, Japan.

Clause 12 Latest ship men Date: 240MT before June 30, 240MT before July 30 and 240MT before August 20, 2006 (both parties particularly stamped over here in the contract A—the author).

Clause 14 payment: The Buyer should open an irrevocable letter of credit at sight covering full value of the contract within 5 working days upon receiving a letter of performance guarantee issued by a first class bank covering the amount of 10% of the total value of the L/C under the present contract.

Clause 20 Arbitration: Any disputes shall then be referred to the CAC for arbitration under INCOTERMS 2000 and the CISG.

C. The Defense of the Seller Revealing the Existence of Contract B Series[2]

As the process proceeded, the Defense submitted by the seller and the inquiry by the Tribunal revealed that contract A was materially replaced by contract B Series.

1. About Contact A

In the Defense, the seller confirms what the Buyer says in his Request for Arbitration about the formation of contract A, the amendments to the latest shipment dates of contract A and the expiry dates of the Letter of Guarantee and the L/C.

2. About the Cause of the Conclusion of Contract B Series and the Modification of the Terms of Payment

After the conclusion of contract A, the price of silicon metal was soaring and the seller was worrying that he might not be able to obtain the prescribed quantity of the goods in stock as agreed; he communicated with the Buyer, suggesting that all the terms and conditions except for the terms of payment remain unchanged allowing sale by installment; the parties entered into some installment contracts; the seller promised to deliver the total quantity of goods agreed in contract A by September 15.

As September 15 was beyond the expiry dates of the Letter of Guarantee and the L/C, for the purpose of being free from any trouble and fees for applying for the issuance of any Letter of Guarantee and any credit letter, the parties agreed that the seller would deliver the goods by installment before September 20 and that the parties would enter into some separate contracts based on the actual deliverable quantity of goods and the terms of payment were by Telegraphic Transfer—T/T (within 7working days after the shipment).

Thereafter, the parties, according to the quantity of goods purchased by the seller in stock, respectively, on July 5, August 4 and 21 by fax entered into purchase contracts NO. XX10627003A, NO. XX10627004A and NO. xx10627002c (herein after referred to as contract B series, so that it could be distinguished from and connecting to the aforesaid contract A).

D. The Seller Holds: The Accusation of the Buyer Against the Seller That the Latter Un-Discharging His Duties Under Contract A Being Contrary to the Facts

Comparing the provisions in contract A with those in contract B Series, the only difference is that in the former the terms of payment were by L/C and the latter by T/ r: Therefore, with regard to contract A, Contract B series were the ones with changed terms of payment only and were supplements to the former.

According to Clause 5 of Contract A "Terms of Deliver: FOB Huangpu, Shanghai or Tianjin at Buyer's option," the Buyer should have informed the seller of his appointed port, concrete date for shipment and the name of the carrier. But after the conclusion of contract B series, the Buyer had never executed his informing obligation to enable the seller to deliver the goods of 720MT. Further, the communications between the parties on August 22 regarding the transport, clearance through customs, and delivery of the goods reflected a common understanding between them. The goods of 240MT were the last batch (or installment) of the total quantity of 720MT originally intended to deliver before September 20. As the Buyer's lawyer in his letter to the seller denied the fact that after the amendments to the manner of the deal and then under contract B series the seller had already delivered goods of 480MT and that led to the undeliverable of the last installment of the goods.

The seller had actually delivered goods of 480MT. All the documents or certificates relating to the commercial inspections, the clearance through customs and other procedures had carried the title of contract A, namely that the contract A had been the legal base of all the separate installments.

The Buyer is wrong by declaring that the deals under contract B series had not got any connections with contract A. If the contract B series were fully separated from contract A, there would not have had any recordings about the clearance through customs under contract A.

In the course of delivering the goods of 480MT by the seller in July and August, the Buyer never mentioned or reminded the seller that the latter had not yet performed his obligations under contract A. If the claims and their facts as base relied by the Buyer could be established or sustained, it would not be logical. The seller, about the goods of same specifications and same unit price, would have never fulfilled the obligations under a former contract with payment by credit letter—more reliable.

And what is more that under the circumstances that the Buyer had regarded the seller in breach of contract, the seller would have had with the Buyer entered into contract B Series relating to the same goods of same specifications, same unit price and same destination(s), and the terms of payment of the latter ones were TIT obviously less reliable than that by L/C. The seller would have delivered the goods under the latter contracts.

The Buyer, during the course of performing the Contract B Series by the parties, would have even forgotten that the seller having been in material breach of contract A, and would have waived all claims to the guaranty money in the Letter of Guarantee [in the Letter of Guarantee, the bank pledges the Buyer: *We hereby affirm that we are the guarantor and responsible to you, on behalf (of) the Seller, up to a total amount of USD65,000.00 and we undertake to pay you, upon receipt of your first written demand stating that the Seller fails of his obligations under the contract (Contract A—the author), any sum or sums within the limits as aforesaid without your needing to prove or to show grounds of reasons for your demand for the sum specified therein*]. And the valid date fell on September 4. In a word, having Contract B Series replace contract A was the common understanding of both parties.

E. **The Seller Analyses and Stresses: About the Dispute Over the Performance of Contract and the Real Purpose of the Buyer's Applying for Arbitration**[3]

While the Seller was engaged in purchasing the last portion of the goods, 240MT, he on September 10 got a sudden notice by telephone from the Buyer demanding that seller must deliver goods of 720MT by September 25. On that date, the L/C, Letter of Guarantee and last shipment of contract A had expired.

On September 19, the lawyer of the Buyer rendered a letter to the seller requiring that the seller must deliver the goods of 720MT on September 25, otherwise the Buyer would have resorted to law.

When the whole transaction between the parties was almost completed, out of malicious intention, the Buyer would have claimed the full rights under Contract A; actually he had enjoyed substantial part of the rights under it. The act of the Buyer was without sound grounds and it was against the principle of good faith, what is more, that put the seller in a dilemma as to whether or not to deliver the last installment—the 240MT goods. The Seller worried that the Buyer, as he completely denied that there had been amendments to the manner of the transaction, would not enter into a further one of contract B Series with the seller about the last installment of goods. If the seller would deliver the goods of the last installment, the Buyer might detain the goods on the pretext that the seller had been in breach of contract and make no repayment.

In timely response to the above-mentioned demand, the Seller safeguarding his own interests stated his arguments and opinions: He had already delivered goods of 480MT according to the new common understanding of the parties; for the purpose of avoiding losing payment, if the Buyer persisted in the performance of contract A (as a separate deal), the 240MT goods should be paid by L/C and the seller would be willing to correspondingly apply to some bank to act as his guarantor to render a Letter of Guarantee in favor of the Buyer; as the Buyer acted without good faith and the soaring price for the goods, the price of the 240MT should be increased properly, anyway a most favorable price would be offered.

The Buyer made a response to the aforesaid arguments and opinions, reiterating that contract B series and Contract A were separate from each other, definitely refusing to accept only the last installment of 240MT goods.

The seller stresses that contract A and contract B Series were involving in the same transaction of goods. The latter was an adaptation by the parties in light of the changed objective conditions.

F. **The Tribunal's Findings**

1. The Tribunal ascertains the facts, inter alia, that the conclusion of contract A and the related matters; the L/C issued by a bank in favor of the seller and performance guarantee in favor of the Buyer issued by another bank; and some more facts confirmed are as follows;
2. On July 5, the parties entered the first of contract B series (NO. XXI0627003A), the quantity being 240MT of silicon metal, payment by T/T, the latest shipment date being before July 30, 2006;
3. On August 4, the parties entered into the second of contract B series (NO. XXI0627004A), the quantity being 120MT of silicon metal, payment by T/T, the latest shipment date being before August 8;

4. On August 21, the parties entered into the third of Contract B (NO. XXI0627002C), the quantity being 120MT of silicon metal, payment by T/T; and the latest shipment being by August 30;
5. The goods of contract B Series aforesaid totaling 480MT of silicon metal and that consisting of the quantity of the first and second installments of Contract A were delivered and the consideration was paid up;
6. About the goods of 240MT of silicon metal under third installment of contract A, the seller by fax on August 22 informed the Buyer, saying:

> Concerning the goods of 240MT of Silicon Metal under Contract A third installment and under the L/C, we inform you of the following concrete affairs.
>
> From August 26 to 31 goods of 120 MT in total would be delivered respectively from XX and XX factories, Sichuan province, expecting that they would probably arrive at Shanghai Huangpu (Guangzhou) Ports on September 5 and customs clearance might be dome on around September 10.
>
> Another installment of 120MT would be delivered on September 5 from XX factory, Sichuan province, expecting that it would probably arrive at Huangpu (Guangzhou)/Shanghai Ports on September 15, and customs clearance might be done around September 20.

7. The message by fax reached the Buyer and his officer (or employee) in charge responded by writing on the same piece of paper re-faxed to the seller, requesting the receiver to have the 240MT of goods respectively delivered or customs clearance done: 120MT by September 5; 60MT by September 10; and 60MT by September 15;
8. On August 22, the Respondent by fax wrote claimant informing the addressee about the third installment of 240MT, saying that he would deliver the goods in installments by September 20;
9. In response by fax to the above, the claimant on the same day demanded that all the 240MT should be delivered in installments by September 15 and the addressee should confirm in writing. But the Respondent made no response;
10. On September 19, the lawyer engaged by the claimant rendered a letter to the Respondent, claiming that the addressee had not yet delivered 720MT under contract A and demanding him to deliver the whole quantity to the appointed port by September 25;
11. On September 21, the Respondent made response to the aforesaid letter, confirming that under Contract A he should deliver the last installment of 240MT and requiring the claimant to have a credit letter rendered and the unit price should be in line with the present market price;
12. In a letter of September 25, the claimant responded that he could not accept any price rise;
13. Thereafter, the parties had been engaged in consultation. On October 10, the Respondent drafted an Agreement of Canceling the Contract: '*The parties through amicable negotiation agree to cancel Contract No.10627002A (Contract A). Upon the conclusion of a new contract by the parties to sell and buy 240MT Silicon Mental (553#) at the unit price of USD915/MT and the total*

price being as USD219600, this Agreement would come into effect' (Emphasis added).

The Respondent sent the Agreement draft to the claimant by fax.

14. On the same day, someone with the claimant faxed back the above-mentioned draft with some amendment to the Respondent. 'Upon the conclusion of a new contract' was varied as 'upon the performance of a new contract.' On October 17, the Claimant wrote to the Respondent urging him to finalize the said Agreement by signing on it but the latter did not make any response;
15. Consequently, the claimant by sending a letter of November 6 to the Respondent officially rescinded Contract A.

3 Proposal One of Award—The Opinions of the Tribunal

This one was drafted by the presiding arbitrator, though it was done after the proposal two by me, I prefer to have it first presented.

It summarizes the respective arguments, viewpoints of the parties and their divergence of views, especially quotes the different views and arguments in the last statement or final submission by the attorneys of the two sides.

A. About the Application Law of the Instant Case

The Claimant to the instant is a corporation incorporated under the law of and registered in the HK SAR; the Respondent is established under the law of and located in the mainland of PR China. The dispute arising from the contracts between the two parties should be treated as foreign-related contracts for sale of goods. It is explicitly provided in the contracts that CISG shall be applied. Based on the principle of party autonomy, CISG shall be applied in this settlement of the dispute. The business place of the seller, the place of goods delivery and the place of arbitration are all in the mainland of China. The main land of China should be regarded as the closest connecting factor, in light of the general principles of conflict of laws, the Tribunal holds, concerning the matter about which there is no provision in CISG, and the relevant provisions of the law of the mainland of China should apply.

The parties also agree that INCOTERMS 2000 shall apply; this choice as applying international practice is in line with the principle of party autonomy. INCOTERMS2000 shall apply.

B. About the Effectiveness of Contract A

According to the facts confirmed based on the written materials, Tribunal is aware that the parties entered into Contract A on May 23. Art 23 of CISG provides:

> '*A contract is concluded at the moment when an acceptance of an offer becomes effective in accordance with the provisions of the Convention.*' Therefore, Contract A was established upon the conclusion by the parties.

As there is no such concrete provision in CISG as to the effectiveness of a contract, the Tribunal determines the validity according to the law of the main land of China. The Tribunal has noticed that the contents of contract A do not conflict to the mandatory norms of the present law.

Art 44 of Contract Law (Act) of the PRC ('Contract Law')[4]: '*A contract formed according to law shall take effect when it is formed.*'[5] According to it, Contract A was effective and binding upon to the parties, and the parties should under it perform their respective obligations and enjoy their respective rights.

C. About the Performance of the Involved Contracts and Dispute

1. Performance of the Involved Contracts

Based on the written materials submitted by the parties and their statements, the Tribunal confirms:

> After the conclusion of contract A, on June 7, the Respondent wrote to the claimant, demanding the delivery date be extended 10 days, that is, the last deliver was delayed to August 20, the valid period of the L/C extended to September 4. And the parties varied contract A; that is, the latest shipment dates were respectively on June 30, July 30 and August 20.
>
> The Chengdu branch of a Shanghai bank upon an application of the seller on June 9 issued the Letter of Guarantee in favor of the Buyer.
>
> A bank upon an application of the Buyer on July 13 rendered the L/C in favor of the seller. The expiry dates of both the Letter of Guarantee and the L/C were on September 4.
>
> Within the validity of the Letter of Guarantee, the Buyer did not claim from the bank guarantor; within the validity of the L/c, the seller did not apply to honor.
>
> On July 5, August 4 and 21, the parties separately entered contracts NO. XX10627003A, NO.XX 10627004A and NO. XX100627002C (they are the Contract B Series), specifying that the Buyer purchases, at the unit price of USD915/MT from the seller, respectively 240MT, 120MT and 120MT silicon metal of same specifications, the latest dates of shipment respectively July 30, August 8 and 25. The terms of payment of the three contracts are the same: T/T after 7 working days after shipment. And all the other clauses are exactly the same with those corresponding ones in Contract A. All the three contracts were performed.

About the performance of contract, the claimant holds that contract A and contract B Series were separate from each other; the Respondent did not discharge his duties under contract A.

The Respondent on the contrary holds that Contract A was the main contract and the contract B Series should be regarded as the supplementary or accessory ones with the only varied terms of payment.

2. The Relationship Between Contract A and Contract B Series

The Tribunal is aware:

> In the course of performing contract B series, contract A was not simultaneously put into effect. The Respondent says after the conclusion of contract A, owing to the soaring of the silicon mental on international market, and the supply of the goods in China was very tight. Under such circumstances, he was unable to get enough stock of the goods. For the purpose of avoiding that the Respondent might fail to deliver the prescribed quantity of goods, and in

> addition the varied dates of deliver were beyond the expiry dates of the L/C and the Letter of Guarantee, and for the purpose of saving the trouble and fees in applying the issuance further credit letter and Letter of Guarantee, the parties therefore specially agreed that a separate contract should be concluded according to the actual quantity of goods in stock and could be delivered.

The claimant holds that there was no wording in contract B series to the effect that they would substitute or vary or supplement to contract A; therefore contract B series were neither the supplementary nor the substitutions of contract A. But instead Contract B series were separate from contract A.

The Tribunal confirms:

> The correspondent clauses in contract B Series, except the ones relating to the quantity of goods, dates of delivery and payment, were identical to the ones of contract A.

According to contract A, the three installments should respectively be done by June 30, July 30 and August 20. On June 7, the claimant wrote the Respondent with some information about the booking space to the schedule of a carrier, urging the addressee to deliver the first installment of goods. There was no similar letter from the claimant to the Respondent relating to the second and third installments. Further, within the validity of the L/C under contract A, the L/C remained without playing any role.

After the conclusion of contract A, the parties on July 5, August 4 and 21 entered into three contracts of contract B series, specifying that by July 30, August 8 and 25 the respective delivery of 240MT, 120MT and 120MT of silicon mental and all the duties under the contract B series were discharged.

On August 22, the Respondent wrote to the claimant by fax about delivery of the third installment under contract A.

All the aforesaid facts prove that the arguments of the Respondent that the parties entered into contracts according to the goods in stock, that is, Contract B series substituted Contract A.

Though the claimant holds that contract B Series were separate from contract A, he has not submitted any evidence to show after July 5 that the parties entered into the first of Contract B series until the expiry date of the L/C, that he had once demanded the Respondent to fulfill obligations under Contract B series and simultaneously discharge his duties under contract A as well.

In accordance with the terms of FOB in contract A, the Buyer must give the seller sufficient notice of the vessel name, loading port and required delivery time. The claimant claims that he by telephone gave notice of the name of a carrier, loading port and concrete delivery date, but the Respondent denies that the claimant had once given him such notice. The claimant is unable to produce any evidence to show there had been such a notice. The claim of the claimant is lack of evidence.

The Tribunal is also aware that contract B Series were concluded after the last date of the first installment under Contract A. If Contract B series were separate from Contract A, that means that under the circumstance that the seller had failed to deliver goods under Contract A, the parties would have entered into a series of contract on the same subject matter with same unit price and all the same terms (except terms of payment). That means that the Respondent had paid no notice to his obligations under Contract A, and would rather enter into Contract B Series and then deliver the goods there of—the same as those under contract A to the claimant. And the deal manner would remain unchanged, and the parties would have paid little notice to the validity of the Letter of Guarantee and the L/C. That was no normal at all and the claimant has produced no cogent evidence or given some valid reasons.

Based on the confirmed facts and the submitted evidences, the Tribunal accepts the viewpoint of the Respondent that Contract A was the main contract and the concrete performance was under Contract B series and they substituted or varied Contract A. That is, after the conclusion of Contract A, as the Respondent was unable to get sufficient goods in stock, for the purpose of avoiding that the prescribed quantity of goods could not be delivered in time, the parties entered into contracts of contract B Series in accordance with the goods in stock, the terms of payment was varied from L/C to T/T and all the other terms remained unchanged.

Therefore, the Tribunal holds that after the conclusion of Contract A, the parties, according to the situation of the goods purchased in stock by the Respondent, agreed to sign a single contract with terms of payment of T/T and fulfill their respective obligations and enjoyed their corresponding rights under Contract A. The three ones of Contract B Series signed by the parties substituted the obligations of delivering goods of 480MT under contract A. Nevertheless, the Respondent was still obligated to perform the obligations relating to the third installment of 240MT under contract A.

3. The Responsibility of Non-performance Relating to the Third Installment Under Contract A

Under previous Item 2, the Tribunal confirms that parties fulfilled their respective obligations and enjoyed corresponding rights under Contract B series. Therefore, the Respondent, after delivering 480MT of goods under contract B series, was still obligated to discharge the duties pertaining to the third installment of 240MT under Contract A.

(The Tribunal after the oral hearings confirms the following facts: The facts of Items 8 to 15 under II. F aforesaid are listed.)

The Tribunal has noticed that on November 6 the claimant declared to rescind Contract A because the Respondent did not execute his duties under it. On receipt of the letter of November G from the claimant, the Respondent made no response as to discharge his duties relating to the third installment of 240MT. Therefore, the Tribunal confirms the deal relating to the third installment of 240MT goods under Contract A was cancelled.

Pertaining to the failure of performance relating to the third installment under contract A, the claimant holds that within the period of August and September, the price had been soaring, the Respondent was to chase bigger benefit and that was the reason that he did not perform the Contract A.

The Respondent insists that as the claimant completely overturned the fact that manner of deal had been varied and totally was without any good faith, he had to suggest and persist that the payment manner relating to the third installment under Contract A should be through credit letter.

Based on the evidence submitted by the parties and the facts confirmed, the Tribunal is of the following opinions:

> First, the Respondent wrote to the claimant saying that he intended to deliver the goods of third installment 240MT by September 20. It was proper for the claimant in his response demanded the delivery be done before September 15. But the Respondent should but actually did not make response to the claimant's demand.
>
> Second, on September 19 the lawyer of the claimant rendered a letter, demanding the Respondent to deliver goods of 720MT under contract A, this act was not in line with the principle of good faith. The Tribunal has confirmed that the Respondent already delivered the goods of 480MT under contract B series and that was actually under Contract A; therefore, the claimant had no more rights to require that the Respondent deliver the goods of 720MT under Contract A.
>
> Third, though on the one hand the claimant was in no position to demand that the Respondent deliver the goods of 720MT under Contract A, on the other hand the Respondent should not have demanded the terms of payment be restored to by means of credit letter and required price rise as that would result in the variation of the former agreement and arrangement, that is, the payment of T/T under Contract B series replaced the terms of payment in Contract A.
>
> Fourth, the claimant urged the Respondent to finalize the Agreement of canceling the Contract A. The Respondent did not make any response and that was one of the reasons leading to the failure of fulfilling obligations relating to the third installment under Contract A. In addition, the amendment made or suggested by the claimant to the draft of the said Agreement was not improper, and that was in line with the performance of Contract B series to substitute the performance of Contract A.

The Tribunal, according to the aforesaid analyses, holds that the obligations relating to the third installment under Contract A were not fulfilled and that resulted in the cancellation of the deal relating to the third installment under contract A, both parties were responsible for that. And for that reason, the damages or losses arising from the cancellations hall be shared by the parties.

D. About the Claims of the Claimant

1. The First Claim: Indemnifying the Claimant the Losses of Expected Profit USD136,800.00

The Tribunal is aware that the losses of the expected profit calculated by the Claimant based on the claimed fact that the Respondent did not fulfill any obligations under Contract A. As the Tribunal has confirmed that the performance of Contract A was replaced by the performance of Contract B Series, though not completely, that is, the Respondent delivered goods of 480MT under contract A. The Claimant does not have the rights to claim on the damages or losses relating to the already delivered goods of 480MT.

Art 75 of CISG '*If the contract is avoided and if, in a reasonable manner and within a reasonable time after avoidance, the buyer has bought goods in replacement to the seller has resold the goods, the party claiming damages may recover the difference between the contract price and the price in the substitute transaction as well as any further damages recoverable under Art 74.*'

And Art 76(1) of CISG '*If the contract is avoided and there is a current price for the goods, the party claiming damages, may, if he has not made a purchase or resale under Art 75, recover the difference between the price fined by the contract and the current price at the time of avoidance as well as further damages recoverable under Art 74. If, however, the party claiming damages had avoided the contract after taking over the goods, the current price at the time of such taking over shall be applied instead of the current price at the time of avoidance.*'

According to the provisions above and the materials submitted by the claimant and refer to the fixed price of the contracts, about the current price of the third installment of 240MT under Contract A at the time of rescinding, the Tribunal accepts the viewpoint of the claimant that goods of the instant case at the time of rescinding the deal relating to the third installment under Contract A were FOB in (main)ports of China USD1,080.00 to 1,130.00/MT; and the middle price was USD1,105 . 00/ MT as the current price. Therefore, the difference between the contract price and the current price of the 240MT is USD45,600.00 (the formula:USD1,105.00x240 - USD45,600.00).

As the Tribunal believes that both parties were equally liable for the consequence, so the Respondent shall compensate the loses USD22,500.00 (the formula: USD45,600.00 × 50% = USD22,800.00).

2. **The Second Claim: Compensate the Claimant the Expenditures Occurred in Handling This Case the Legal Fees and Arbitration Fees**

Taking account of the claimant's claims being only partly sustained, the Tribunal decides that the legal fee of the claimant is on the claimant and he shall bear 70% of the arbitration fee.

4 Proposal Two of Award—The Opinions of the Tribunal

Being an arbitrator of the three-member Tribunal, the author of this article after the first oral hearing (there were two oral hearings) drafted this proposal.

After the examining all the written materials submitted and inquiring into all the related matters at the oral hearing, the Tribunal confirms the facts and is of the opinions as follows:

1. **About the Proper Law of the Instant Case**

> The claimant is incorporated under the law and registered in the HK SAR; the Respondent is established under the law of the mainland of PRC. The Tribunal notices that the parties to the instant case in the contracts specify that CISG shall be applied in the settlement of any disputes. Under the principle of party autonomy, the Tribunal thinks that CISG shall be applied.

As the Seller's place of business, the place of delivering goods and the place of arbitration are all in the mainland of China; the mainland of China is the closest connected place.

The main land of China should be regarded as the closest connecting factor, in light of the general principles of conflict of laws, the Tribunal holds, concerning the matter about which there is no provision in CISG, the relevant provisions of the law of the mainland of China should apply. And that is in conformity with the doctrine the characteristic performance.

2. **About Contract A**

On May 23, the Claimant as Buyer and the Respondent as seller entered into International Purchase Contract NO. XX10627002A by fax; it was based on the standard terms in English provided by the claimant. It bore a number of the serial number within the Claimant. The terms of payment were of by credit letter.

3. **The Origin and Performance of Contract B Series**

The claimant as Buyer and the Respondent as seller on July 5 entered into International Purchase Contract NO. XX10627003A with silicon Mental of 240MT as the subject matter; on August 4 and 21 they respectively entered into International Purchase Contracts NO. XX10627004A and NO. xx10627002X, both with silicon mental of 120MT as the subject matter. The three ones of Contract B series were all based on the standard terms in English provided by the claimant. Each bore a number of the serial number within the claimant. All the terms, except for the ones for quant it, payment, date of shipment (delivery), were exactly the same as the corresponding terms of Contract A. The delivery date of contract NO. XX10627003A was on July 30; the delivery date of contract NO. XX10627003A was on August 8; the delivery date of contract NO. XX10627002C was on August 25.

The terms of payment provided in the three contracts were by T/T, within 7 working days after shipment. All the three ones of Contract B were performed. In the course of the performance of them, outwardly Contract A was not simultaneously put into effect.

4. **The Relationship Between Contract A and Contract B Series**

The claimant is of the view that Contract A and Contract B series were separate from each other; the former was not performed owing to the main reason that during August and September of that year the price of silicon mental had been soaring and the Respondent chased bigger commercial interest; the failure to fulfill his obligations under contract A has caused actual economic losses to the claimant.

Whereas the Respondent is of different view, holding that Contract A was the main contract and concrete performance was under its substitution of Contract B Series as the subject matter, specifications, unit price and manner of delivery of the two were exactly the same except for the terms of payment, the quantity and date of delivery; the actual delivered quantity under Contract B Series was 480MT and that was done through a series of trade procedures, the documents submitted by the Respondent relating to the clearance through customs for export (all customs formalities for the export), commercial inspection and all the other documents (such as commercial in voice, packing list l weight memo, slip in exchange for cargo Export permit issued by China Entry and Exist Inspection and Quarantine Administration) bore the title and the series number of Contract A, that is, contract NO. XX10627002A was recorded in all the foresaid document s. If Contract B Series were treated as independent ones from Contract A, no one could find out any records relating to the seller under contract B series to clear the goods for export at any China customs; according to the obligations under the terms of FOB, the buyer must obtain at his own risk and expense any import license or other official authorization and carry out, where applicable, all customs formalities for the import of the goods and, where necessary, for their transit through any country; if the claimant had not consulted with the Respondent for the purpose of confirming related data and accepting related documents, certificates, he would have not been able to go through all customs formalities for the import of the goods at the destination(s).

The Tribunal notices that the claimant stresses that the Respondent didn't fulfill his obligations under Contract A owing to the soaring price of the subject matter and he was seeking a bigger commercial interest.

In examining the terms of Contract A and Contract B Series, the Tribunal as certain that except for the terms of quantity, payment and date of delivery, all the corresponding terms in the contracts were without any difference. In respect of terms of payment, generally speaking, the manner of payment in Contract A was more reliable or safer than that in contract B series to the Respondent.

The Tribunal believes that there was no reason for the Respondent to readily accept a manner of payment which was less reliable. Contract B Series must have been concluded by the parties under the changed circumstances and after consultation they reached a compromise. The fact of keeping on the performance of Contract A and enjoying the rights under it in the manner of Contract B Series is in conformity with the general rule and the practice of international trade. It would be unimaginable that merchants would have a transaction divided into several smaller deals under same set of terms and then they would have first performed the contracts concluded later and then would perform the contract concluded previously. Further, usually a merchant would prefer to have more reliable terms of payment, if not under changed circumstances, he would not accept a less reliable manner of payment.

The time of delivery of Contract B Series was roughly the same with that of Contract A, apart from the date of delivery in the third of Contract B series was five days later than that of the third installment of Contract A. The dates of conclusion and time of performing of the first and second of contract B Series were in the period that the claimant claims that the price of the goods was soaring. The Respondent did not demand to vary and increase the price provided in Contract A.

On June 27, the claimant sent to the Respondent a notice with initial information relating to some booked space of a vessel, urging the addressee to have the goods ready, deliver the first installment of goods of 240MT under Contract A and have the goods clear for export in Huangpu Port by June 30; in forming the addressee that a vessel (without giving the name yet) would reach Huangpu Port according to her schedule. This written notice sent to the Respondent by the claim and in line with his obligations under FOB. That showed actually the claimant had once informed his counterpart of some information in written not as he declares that all the notices were sent orally by phone.

After sending the notice of June 27, on July 5 the claimant entering into the first of contract B Series with the Respondent and then in respect of the period to August to deny the fact that contract A had been substantially replaced by contract B series and that was not in line with the real situation and the common understanding of the parties. As the claimant during that period repeatedly laid stress on the delivery of the 720MT goods under Contract A, it was understandable that the Respondent failed to deliver the last installment of 240MT.

6. **About the Claims of the Claimant**

Art 29 (1) of CISG: '*A Contract may be modified or terminated by the mere agreement of the parties.*'

Art 72 of CISG: *(1) "If prior to the date for performance of the contract, it is clear that one of the parties will commit a fundamental breach of contract, the other party may declare the contract avoided. (2) If time allows, the party intending to declare the contract avoided must give reasonable notice to the other party in order to permit him to provide adequate assurance of his performance."*

The Claimant, in the validity of Contract A, did not say that Contract A and Contract B Series were separate from each other, demanding the Respondent to simultaneously discharge his duties under Contract A together with the duties under Contract B series, or the claimant should inform the Respondent that as the Respondent did not perform Contract A and therefore declare Contract A avoided or rescinded. Instead, the Claimant in his letter of November 6 to the Respondent declared the rescinding of Contract A and on that date, it was a lapse of two and half a months after the date of last delivery on August 20.

It might be due to the reason that neither the claimant (including to his any officers or staff members, clerks or employees in charge of the transaction) had clearly related the backgrounds of the conclusion of Contract B series to the lawyer who rendered the letter of September 21 nor had they completely and objectively described the evolution of the trans action to the attorney in the arbitration proceedings. The attorney has not been very clear that in coping with the changed situations on the market, Contract B Series were concluded on the base of contract A and every one of contract B series was to be concluded according to the purchased goods in stock by the seller and therefore to deliver every batch or installment of goods under each one of Contract B Series. The claimant could not claim on the basis of the whole contract A, condemning that the Respondent did not fulfill his obligations under Contract A, demanding the price difference between the fix price and the market price of the total quantity of 720MT.

The attorney on behalf of her principal quotes Arts 74–76 of CISG, they are not applied to the situations of the instant case; the Tribunal thinks that the first claim of the claimant is unacceptable.

As the grounds of and reasons for the first claim of the claimant are not proper, his second claim could not be sustained by the Tribunal.

5 Reflections and Comments

A. The Viewpoints That the Claimant Upholds

1. Contract B Series were neither the supplementary nor the substitution to Contract A; in the Contract B Series there was no word relating to the substitution or variation or supplementary to Contract A, so Contract A and Contract B series were separate from each other.
2. Contract A was not performed mainly owing to the soaring price of the goods, the seller was chasing a bigger commercial interest but not fulfill his obligations under Contract A and that caused great losses to the Buyer.

B. The Main Points in the Defense and Arguments of the Respondent

1. Contract B series, concluded on the common consent of the parties, with main variation of the terms of payment, were the supplements to or ones replacing Contract A.
2. Within the validity of Contract A and in the course of performing contract B series, the Buyer had never mentioned the necessary of discharging the obligations by the seller under Contract A or required the seller to perform Contract A.
3. About the goods of same specifications and same unit price, there had previously been a contract concluded with terms of payment by L/C, but the parties would have it shelved. Furthermore, the Buyer holds that the seller had committed fundamental breach of contract; however, the seller would then enter into contracts with the Buyer accepting the less reliable manner of payment by T/T, and would deliver goods under those subsequent contracts. The Buyer would under such circumstances have forgotten that the seller had committed fundamental breach of contract and in addition the Buyer had given up the rights to claims on the Letter of Guarantee (remaining valid until September 4) demanding the sum of USD65,880.00 from the bank guarantor. It was illogical.
4. Contract A and Contract B series were involving the same transaction of goods; the latter was an appropriate adaptation in light of the changed situations.
5. While the seller was in purchasing the last installment of 240MT goods, the Buyer on September 10 on the phone informed the seller demanding that the addressee deliver the goods of 720MT under Contract A by September 25. In the letter of September 19, the Buyer's lawyer reiterated the same demand. The seller was in a dilemma as to whether to deliver the goods of 240MT as intended. As the Buyer denied that the manner of transaction had been varied, he would no longer accept the 240MT by means of Contract B Series, so the seller worried that the Buyer might detain the goods on the pretext that the seller had been in breach of contract A and not make any repayment. For safeguarding his own interest, the seller in his response said, inter alia,

if the Buyer insisted that Contract A should be performed, he had to pay for the 240MT by L/C and the seller would correspondingly apply a bank to act as guarantor to render a Letter of Guarantee; the price of the silicon mental was soaring and out of fairness, the price of the 240MT should be increased but a most preferential price would be offered.

In his last submission, the lawyer of the seller stresses that if judging only by the contents of Contract A and Contract B Series, you might not tell the substitution relationship of the two; but if you would take all the pieces of evidence as a complete chain relating to the instance case and combining them to the normal commercial practice, the substitution relationship of the contracts would be obvious or beyond doubt.

The lawyer of the seller emphasizes the substitution relationship between Contract A and Contract B Series as the focus in his defense statement, holding if his argument of substitution could be established, the validity of contract A would have vanished as the L/C under Contract A expired, the Buyer did not pay by it; and the Letter of Guarantee also expired and the Buyer did claim on it. There was only an interpretation to all the facts aforesaid, after the conclusion of contract B series based on the consensus (common understanding), the parties had Contract B Series replace Contract A, as an independent contract, the performance of contract A had lost all the conditions. Hence as to the contract in the instant case, there was only one alternative. Contract A and Contract B Series could not separately exist. Since Contract A was replaced by Contract B Series, parties should not afterward fuss over the cause of the substitution and who was first to suggest. After all it was the common understanding of the parties to have a replacement.

Art 80 of CISG provides that *'A party may not rely on a failure of the other party to perform, to the extent that such failure was caused by the first party's act or omission.'* Therefore, the liabilities of the Seller pertaining to the last installment of 240MT could be exempted, as the undelivered of the goods was not the seller's intention. On the contrary, it was due to the act by the Buyer as he officially rescinded the contract. After Contract A was replaced, the goods of 720MT could not be completely delivered; it was the fault of the Buyer.

The author believes that the statements and argument s of the seller's lawyer were so good and to the point, he has firmly grasped the key to the case.

After August 20, the last date of delivery expired; on September 4, the validity of the L/C and Letter of Guarantee expired. The validity of Contract A and that of Contract B Series were roughly the same or overlapped. All the terms, except for the terms of quantity, delivery and payment, were exactly the same and relating to the same transaction. A subsequently concluded contractor contracts replaced the previously concluded one about the same subject matter. This contention could be established, especially in the instance case. Commercial arbitrators and merchants of the same trade with the parties to the instant case could understand the points and accept the contentions of the seller and the conclusion of the Tribunal. Otherwise it would be ridiculous. What is more, the Respondent once rebutted, stating that the Buyer in the course of performing Contract B Series, roughly in the validity of

Contract A (since June 27 to September 9), had never mentioned the matter or urged the seller to fulfill his obligations under Contract A.

The attorney of the Buyer upholds that in the contents of Contract B Series, there were no terms or words relating to the substitution or variation or supplementary to Contract A. The two were separate from each other. That mechanical or rigid viewpoint should not have been from an experienced lawyer. In many books or papers on contract, one could find out similar exposition *'A promise is an undertaking to act or refrain from acting in a specified way at some future time. This promise may be made in clear and express words, or it could be implied, that is, inferred from conduct or from the circumstances of the transaction.'*[6] The variation of consensus performance should be treated in the same way. While there is no counter-evidence, the Tribunal should accept that the parties intended to have Contract B series replace Contract A.

If you would demand perfection from the lawyer of the seller, you might suggest him to have all the numbers of the contracts listed together—'NO. XX10627002A, NO. XX10627003A, No. XX10627004A, and No. XX10627002C.' Then people could easily workout that they are the numbers in sequence within the Buyer. The relationships between them were explicitly reflected in the numbers in sequence.

I, the author, am not in a position to say that I am somewhat superior to the lawyer of the seller about this matter. I have to be frank, as one of the three arbitrators and the author of proposal Two of Award, I didn't stress on that relationships between the contracts reflecting in the numbers in sequence in my proposal. I only realize that I should have dealt with that detail properly while I am engaged in writing this article, regarding it as one of the critical details to the case.

If we assume that Contract A and Contract B series were separate from each other, within the validity of the former, the Buyer would no doubt have urged or demanded the seller to discharge his duties. Further if the seller would have dare to commit breach of the former, the Buyer's rights and interests would have been secure. First of all the Buyer could claim on the bank as the guarantor rendered the Letter of Guarantee, as easy as falling off a log. Because in the Letter of Guarantee, the bank affirms that, upon receipt of the Buyer's first written demand stating that the Seller "fails to perform his obligation under Contract A," it would pay any sum or sums within the aforesaid limits, without the Buyer needing to prove or show grounds or reasons, up to USD65,880.00.

An international trade company would have neglected the validity of a contract and a Letter of Guarantee, missing the chance to gain the secured claim. Unimaginable!

On September 10 and 19, the Buyer respectively on the phone and by post sending a letter in the name of an engaged lawyer demanded the seller to deliver the goods under Contract A, after the expiry of the validity of the contract, was the Buyer entitled to do so?

If, after the expiration of the validity of contract A, the seller made no response to the urge and demand of the Buyer or explicitly pointed out the expiry of validity, would the letter of November 6 of the Buyer declared the rescinding of contract A be any effect?

The Seller was willing to deliver the last installment of goods subject to some conditions. 'That should have been regarded as the concrete display of his good faith. In the face of the changed situations especially the Buyer's attitude, it was normal for the seller to worry about, so he suggested that the original manner of paying by L/C be re scored, and correspondingly he would apply a bank to be his guarantor to render a guarantee in favor of the Buyer. It was fair. If I had been consulted under such circumstances, I would have suggested that the seller should take such preventive measures.'

If examining the Proposal One of Award from the angle of the convention on the Recognition and Enforcement of Foreign Arbitration Awards ('New York Convention'), there might be uncertainty for the enforcement. In the circle of international commercial arbitration, if my understanding is not wrong, Art VI (c) is about the concrete scope of authority relating to the submission to arbitration.

> *(c) The award deals with a difference not contemplated by or not falling within the* ***terms of the submission to arbitration****. Or it contains decisions on matters beyond the scope of the submission to arbitration...* (emphasis added)

The meaning of 'the terms of the submission to arbitration' is different from that of 'arbitration clause or agreement.' The latter is the base or grounds on which an arbitration institution or a tribunal accepts the jurisdiction over some disputes or some cases arising from some contract. That is '*A contractual provision mandating arbitration—thereby avoiding litigation—of disputes about the contracting parties' rights, duties, and liabilities.*'[7] 'Terms' in the former means the scope of arbitration and the whole phrase of the former means '*(3) the action of allowing, or agreement to allow, an authority to decide an issue (The voluntary submission of parties to the jurisdiction of courts) or (4) the referring of a matter to arbitration (submission to arbitration by consent).*'[8] '*Under the Federal Arbitration Act (FAA) (9 U.S.C. Sect.1 et seq.) an award may be vacated when the award is procured by corruption, fraud, or undue means... and when the arbitrators exceed their powers, decide a matter not submitted, or fail to hear a matter that was submitted. (Id. At Section 10.)*'[9]

The first claim of the Buyer was that as the seller did not at all fulfill his obligations under Contract A and that led to the losses of the expected profit of the Buyer. The defense in respect of that by the seller is that Contract A in nature was replaced by Contract B Series.

With some arbitration institution, for instance under Art 18 of the 1998 ICC Rules, a tribunal is required to draw up, on the basis of documents or in the presence of the parties and in light of their most recent submissions, a document defining its Terms of Reference. '*The terms of reference are agreed upon between the parties at the first meeting (preliminary conference—of the arbitral tribunal.*'[10] This document shall include, inter alia, a summary of the parties' respective claims and of the relief sought by each party, with an indication to the extent possible of the amounts claimed or counterclaimed, a list of issues to be determined. The Terms of Reference shall be signed by the parties and the arbitral tribunal. When the Terms of Reference are signed in accordance with Art 18(2) or approved by the Court (of ICC), the arbitration shall proceed.

In the instant case, the Request for Arbitration and the Defense and other submissions of the parties, roughly speaking, consisted of the terms of submission to arbitration.

The Tribunal accepts the arguments or contentions of the seller, believing that Contract B series materially replaced Contract A or actually Contract A and Contract B Series merged into each other, that is, they were merged. But in the proposal one, the Tribunal would have decided that the seller should identify the Buyer for the losses suffered arising from the rescinding of the deal relating to the third installment under Contract A; the formula is USD1105/MT × 240(MT) × 50% = USD22,800.00. The decision of the Tribunal is based on that the seller should still be liable to the third installment under contract A, and both parties were equally liable to the rescinding of the deal relating to the third installment under Contract A; therefore, they shall respectively bear half the losses resulting from that consequence.

Is there any contradictory between the fact or the matter of the Contract B series replacing the Contract A and the factor the matter of the seller still being liable for the third installment under Contract A after the validity of the contractor it being rescinded by the Buyer? or the reasons of their coexistence have been clear expounded?

Won't the Tribunal's decisions in the Proposal One constitute the excess of authority?[11] Therefore, '*Under this ground, enforcement may be refused if the respondent asserts and proves that the award deals with a difference not contemplated by or not falling within the terms of the submission to arbitration or contains decisions on matter beyond the scope of the submission to arbitration.*'[12]

I believe that the principles of modern International Commercial Arbitration reflected in the New York Convention; arbitrators in China should be familiar with, follow or abide by.

If Proposal One is tenable, it might not exclude the room and grounds for the tenability of Proposal Two. After all there might be more than one award proposal to a case and they might all be tenable.[13] As a British colleague says '*...to state with honesty that we all know—that often there is no definitive "right" answer. In many cases, the best we can hope for is that a sensible, fair and enforceable decision be reached. I certainly challenge any five judges—or decision-makers in any field—to reach identical decisions on matters as complex as those set out in the case. To show how unrealistic that might be, one needs only to consider for a moment one of the many House of Lords cases, where there is a split decision and each of the five Law Lords has put forward his own individual reasoning.*'[14]

But frankly, I don't think that the matters or main issues in the instant case are very complex and could go either way as the experiment of that the case was drawn up so that there were issues that could go either way in arbitration.[15]

Until now while I am writing this article, I have a partiality for Proposal Two. It might be due to the reason that I have not become aware of hidden problems of it yet. Actually, there is another proposal submitted by another arbitrator of the Tribunal, as it is roughly the same with proposal one, I would not make any introduction to it.

The arguments and reasons submitted and upheld by the Respondent are on the whole accepted by the Tribunal. Then according to the statement of the Respondent and facts confirmed that originally he would have to deliver the last installment of goods of 240MT by means of performing the forth of Contract B series, that is, that the parties would have concluded the forth of Contract B series.

In Proposal One, actually the Tribunal adjusts the first claim, the claimant claims on all the losses of expected profits of the 720/MT under Contract A, but the Tribunal as a matter of fact adjusts or changes as the difference between the fixed price and the market price of the last installment of 240MT.

I did notice in the arbitration proceedings, the lawyer of the Respondent stresses in his last oral submission (also in writing) the viewpoints by the end of the second and last oral hearing:

> '*According to Art 80 of CIGS that "A party may not rely on a failure of the other party to perform, to the extent that such failure was caused by the first party's act or omission,"*' pertaining to the last installment of 240MT; the seller should be exempted from responsibility, as the part of unfulfilled obligations was due to the changed situation that the Buyer rescinded the Contract (A) and carried out a fraud. That was against the principle of good faith. Stopping the performance was not the seller's original intention. Therefore after Contract A was replaced, the consequence and responsibility relating to the goods of 720MT that could not be completely delivered were caused by the Buyer and that could not put blame on the Seller.

I hold that the first claim of the Buyer is specified. Whether or not it is tenable depends on the preconditions (prerequisites): Contract A and Contract B Series were separate from each other and the latter did replace the former; the seller did not deliver any goods of 720MT committing fundamental breach of contract, and the act of rescinding Contract A was proper and in line with the provisions of CISG.

The Claimant upholds that Contract A and Contract B Series were separate and independent from each other. If the Tribunal makes decision not about a particular claim submitted, it might be interfering in the parties' own substantial rights to disposal of civil Fairstead would be against the applicable arbitration rules and brings about some obstacle to the final fair and justice settlement of the dispute.

The Tribunal does not entertain the claimant's contention. The reasons are not accepted by the Tribunal. Then the Buyer's claims are based on no grounds. It is nature that the Tribunal should completely reject or not sustain the claims. A Chinese proverb goes, with the s king one, what can the hair adheres to—a thing cannot exist without its basis.

I suppose that is a matter of theory and practice. A contract claim find its cause of action in a contract or the claim finds its root in a contract.

6 Conclusion

In the instant case, after the performance of Contract B Series (all the obligations of the concluded contracts were fulfilled), the Buyer still claims independently on Contract A; nevertheless Contract A could be no longer as the independent base for the claims.

The Buyer was aware of or should have been aware of the relationship between Contract A and Contract B Series; however he depended on Contract A as 'cause of action' and exercised 'right of action.' This act of the Buyer, if not as the A seller, holds that the Buyer intentionally evaded the crucial issue that the transaction had been divided into smaller deals under different ones of Contract B Series and the Buyer's purpose was to gain illegal earnings, or was that due to the Buyer's losing his way? Or the lawyer of the Buyer as attorney in the arbitration proceedings did not play the role well as her principal had expected, failing to show how to deal with the case properly. The attorney upholds that Contract A was separate from Contract B Series, the contents in the latter had nothing to do with the substitution of the former; Contract B Series were not supplements to the former. She might have neglected that the acts of the conclusion of Contract B Series by the parties would explicitly show or one could infer from the facts that Contract B Series replaced Contract A or they were merged. It was certain. Or at last the lawyer might realize her mistake, but she could not return to the correct direction after going along distance in the wrong way in the arbitration proceedings.

Claims based on a contract that it was replaced by another one, or performed, lapsed or merged with another one(s) could not be acceptable or substantiated.

Notes

1. It is numbered by the Buyer in its corporation, and the original first two letters are deleted—the author.
2. Summarized or indirectly quoted from the Defense of the Respondent and the other related viewpoints or arguments of the attorneys of both parties would be summarized in the opinion of the Tribunal—in the proposals of Award.
3. *Id.*
4. The author knows that 'ACT' should be used here as it is a synonym for 'statute.' But in PR China when English version is done, 'Law' is used instead.
5. Quoted from the English version of the Harmony consultants Ltd. Art 44. The contract established according to law becomes effective when it is established (quoted from Contract Law, China Legal system publishing House, 1999, p. 21).
6. See Brain A. Blum Contracts (Second Edition), Fangzheng Publication Company, China, April 2004, pp. 5–6.
7. See Bryan A. Garner Editor in chief, Black Law Dictionary, Eighth Edition, 1999 West Group, p. 113.
8. See Bryan A, A Dictionary of Modern Legal Usage, Second Edition, Law Press China, 2003, p. 844.
9. See Richard M Mosk, Comments on Enforceability Awards. The article is in New Horizons. In International Commercial Arbitration and Beyond (Albert Jan van den Berg as the General Editor), 2005 Kluwer Law International, pp. 328–329.
10. See Marcus S Jacobs QC, International Commercial Arbitration in Australia Law and Practice, Thomson Reuters 2009, p. 4431.

11. See Albert Jan van Berg. Why Are Some Awards Not Enforceable? The article is in New Horizons in International commercial Arbitration and Beyond (Albert Jan van den Berg as the General Editor), 2005 Kluwer Law International, p. 301.
12. *Id.*
13. See Arbitration, the Journal of the chartered Institute of Arbitrators, vol. 66, No. 2, May 2000. It contains the fruits of an experiment. Five distinguished arbitrators were invited to write an award based upon the same hypothetical case.
14. *Id.*, Michael O'Reilly, Editor, Editorial, p. 77.
15. *Id.*

Part V
Some Notes on the Application of Law and the CISG

Outlines

The issue of applicable law is ever-present in international commercial arbitration. How should it be addressed?

In one case, a **Hong Kong buyer** purchased goods from a **Mainland Chinese seller**. A dispute arose, and the seller initiated arbitration, claiming unpaid goods under the contract's arbitration clause.

In dealing with the issue of proper law, some of our colleagues as arbitrators in drafting an award, would put it in this way, "**The contract was signed in Mainland China, and the goods were produced there; thus, Mainland Chinese law applies to this case.**"

The author holds that a more precise reasoning would be: **The contract was signed, performed and the goods delivered in Mainland China. According to the doctrine of characteristic performance, the law of the place of performance applies. Since the contract is of foreign-related and no governing law was chosen, therefor, Mainland Chinese law governs. Furthermore, as China is a member to the CISG, the CISG is therefor a composition of the domestic law of PR China, its application should be prevail.**

Commentary 1: A Conditional Contract or Not and Limited Views on the Application of Art 114 of the Chinese Contract Law

A dispute arose from a Sales Contract. The sole arbitrator holds that the disputed contract is conditional one and as the collateral condition is not accomplished , therefore the Contract is not effective and the provision relating to damages, 30% of the total price paid by the defaulting party to the other party, does not work.

It is believed in another draft award that the Contract is effective: accordingly the defaulting party has to pay the innocent party the damages. But Paragraph 2 of Art 114 of the Chinese Contract Law applies; an appropriate reduction of the excessively higher damages should be made.

The author discusses some aspects of the application of Art 114 and briefly mentions some different views on the nature of damages in this regard.

Commentary 2: Notes on the Application of the CISG to Some International Commercial Cases

Case 1: Dispute Between an Australian Company (Victoria) and a Chinese Company

The disputed contract does not specify the applicable law. The author tries with this case to illustrate the correct understanding of the CISG applicability.

Case 2: Dispute Between a Chinese Company and a Singaporean Company

It is provided in the contract that Chinese law as the governing law but without mentioning the CISG. The author argues that this does not necessarily imply exclusion of the CISG, as the CISG in the case is part of Chinese domestic law.

Case 3: Dispute Between a Hong Kong Company and a Vietnamese Company

It is designated in the contract that Chinese law as the governing law. The Vietnamese buyer's Chinese lawyer claims that the CISG does not apply to the dispute. Is this interpretation correct?

Case 4: Dispute Between a Chinese Company and an Australian Company (New South Wales)

It is provided in the disputed contract that the Chinese law as the governing law. Does this mean the CISG is automatically excluded? The author tries to explore the proper interpretation.

Commentary 3: Two Notes on the Application of the CISG to Cases Under the Jurisdiction of the CIETAC South China

The notes taken by the author from his experience as an arbitrator, analyzing the application of the CISG in arbitration proceedings.

Case 1: Dispute Between a Mainland Chinese Seller and a Hong Kong Buyer

The seller's lawyer argues that both Mainland Chinese law and the CISG apply, while the buyer's lawyer contends that the CISG is not applicable. The key legal question is:

Does a transnational trade contract between a seller from Mainland China and a buyer from Hong Kong, with Rotterdam as the destination, and an explicit choice of Chinese Contract Law, exclude the application of the CISG?

The tribunal of three arbitrators is divided on this issue.

Case 2: Dispute Between a Chinese Buyer and an American Seller

The core legal question in this case is:

Does an international trade contract between a Chinese buyer and an American seller, with arbitration in China but no explicit governing law clause, exclude the application of the CISG?

The author reflects on these cases to explore how the CISG interacts with domestic law in arbitration.

A Conditional Contract or Not and Limited Views on the Application of Art 114 of the Chinese Contract Law

1 Briefs of SHEN DM2004118 Case

The case was referred to and officially accepted by CIETAC, South China (former CIETAC, Shenzhen)[1] on October 24, 2004. The author of this article was appointed as the sole arbitrator.

The Respondent Sellers located in H City and the Claimant Buyers located in S City concluded a Sales Contract on October 8, 2004. The subject matter is 10,000 sockets of M501P Model. The unit price is RMB28 and the total price is RMB280,000. Main clauses are as follows:

> Clause 2 Quality: Up-to-date products qualified with a China Compulsory Certification ('3C Certification')...
> Clause 4 Inspection before delivery: The Sellers shall in 5 days after the conclusion of the Contract send 2 qualified samples of the products to the Buyers by express mail with a Test Report and a 3C Certification (that could be duplicates with seal of the Sellers and the Sellers should produce the originals upon request by the Buyers); after inspecting the samples and checking the certifications, the Buyers advance the Sellers 30%of the total price.
> Clause 5 Delivery and Settlement: After receiving the advance contribution, the Sellers make delivery in 15 days at their premises, and the Buyers receive and accept the goods by sample and on the same day pay the balance of the price in full.
> Clause 6 Liabilities for breaking Contract: The party in default shall pay the other party 30% of the total price as damages.
> Clause 7 Settlement of Dispute: All the disputes arising from this Contract shall be referred to the China International Economic and Trade Arbitration Commission, South China Sub-Commission for arbitration, and there will be no oral hearing

This commentary was published in Mealey's International Arbitration Report, Vol. 20, # 7, July 2005, pp. 34–41.

Y. Huang, *Commentaries on Commercial Arbitration in Modern China*, Modern China and International Economic Law, https://doi.org/10.1007/978-981-95-0168-7_12

(the tribunal will deal with the case on the basis of the documents only—the author).

The Buyers filed a request for arbitration with CIETAC, South China, stating that on October 11, 2004, they received 2 samples and a duplicated Test Report and a duplicated 3C Certification. The name and sign and mark were not those of the Sellers. The subject matter in the Test Report and the 3C Certification were not that of the Contract.

On October 13, they informed the Sellers that the samples and documents were not in accord with the provisions of the Contract, requiring explanation.

On October 15, a written response from the Sellers reached them, acknowledging their fault but making no mention of when they could deliver a 3C Certification.

On October 17, they wrote to the Sellers, asking for a 3C Certification of the sockets.

On October 21, a written response reached them from the Sellers, telling them that the Sellers had not got 3C Certification for the sockets yet and the procedure for that certification was under way and it might be finished in 20 working days.

The Buyers state in their request for arbitration that as the sockets are without 3C Certifications, the Sellers are in breach of contract and they on October 21 had demanded to rescind the Contract and asked the Sellers to pay the damages.

The main points of the Buyers' submission:

1. A producer of the sockets is required to have the products tested and obtain a 3C Certification. That is a compulsory requirement.
2. Without a 3C Certification, sockets of M501P Model are not allowed to be on the market and that is provided in the Contract. The failure of the sockets to go through the test for a 3C Certification shows that the Sellers are short of capacity to perform the Contract.
3. Before the conclusion of Contract, the Sellers said that their sockets had passed the test for a 3C Certification and the samples were marked with a 3C Certification symbol. That shows they practiced fraud.
4. The Sellers failed to perform the contract obligations in light with Clauses 2 and 4. They are in breach of contract.
5. The Sellers on the letter of October 20 said that the test for the 3C Certification was underway. But in fact, their breaching act resulted in the failure to achieve the aim of the Contract.
6. According to Art 114 of the Contract Law of the People's Republic of China (the Contract Law) and Clause 6 of the Contract, the Buyers request that the Sellers pay damages RMB84,000 and bear the arbitration fees.

The main points of the Sellers written defense are of the following:

1. The Buyers' purpose of concluding the Contract is not for performing it but for obtaining damages without consideration. It is of fraud, going against the principle of good faith. The course of negotiation was very short. The Sellers told the Buyers that they had got the initial products of the M501P Model sockets and obtaining a 3C Certification would take 20 (working) days. From the signing of

the Contract to rescinding, it was only 15 days (from October 9 to October 21). The Buyers drafted all the documents and they themselves appointed an express delivery company to deliver them. As to some potential dispute, the Buyers drafted the arbitration clause providing that it shall be referred to CIETAC, South China, and there would be no oral hearing for handling a dispute. That is a trap made by the Buyers to provide excessively high damages, tricking the Sellers into paying the amount. As a new company, the Sellers at that time were eager to have orders more and were not on guard against any trap and trick.

2. There is no substantial performance of the Contract yet; therefore, there is in fact no losses suffered by the Buyers. The performance of the Contract is divided into several stages, without taking account of that but demanding 30% of the total price as damages is unreasonable. Even if the Sellers are in breach of contract, at the present stage, 30% damage is obvious excessively higher than the Buyers' losses; therefore the damages should be reduced properly.
3. The performance of the Contract in fact is divided into 6 stages: Stage 1, the Sellers providing samples and relevant certifications; Stage 2, the Buyers confirming the samples; Stage 3, both parties sealing the samples together; Stage 4, the Buyers advancing 30% of the total price; Stage 5, the Sellers commencing the production of the subject matter; Stage 6, the Sellers delivering the goods and the Buyers paying the balance of the price. Now it is in Stage 2, there is no such big a substantial loss. Even if the Sellers were in breach of Contract, there is no actual loss sustained by the Buyers. In addition, the Sellers have the capacity to produce qualified sockets and get a 3C Certification to continue the performance.
4. As it was at the initial stages of the Contract, the Buyers have paid no consideration yet and there is no actual loss. It is obviously unreasonable to require that the Sellers pay damages, 30% of the total price. According to Paragraph 2 of Art 114 of the Contract Law, the Sellers request that the damages be reduced to 5% of the total price. It would be beneficial to the social orders and fair.
5. The initial samples of the Sellers are of JB Mark but not of the Sellers' own. That is due to the authorization of BJ Company. The Sellers originally provided the Buyers with the samples produced by BJ Company, intending to have them improved after soliciting advice from the Buyers, and then providing the Buyers with official samples of the Sellers' own mark. That is not against any law and the Contract.

The Buyers reject the aforesaid points of the Sellers, insisting on that the Sellers are of no capacity in producing qualified sockets of M501P Model.

The author as the sole arbitrator had a draft award done. And the scrutiny group within the arbitral institution initially believed that the principal views and conclusions in the Draft Award 1 were based on no grounds. Namely, one could not regard the disputed Contract as a conditional one. And then it was very kind of one of my colleagues who helped me to work out a second draft—Draft Award 2. It provides the author of this article with a chance to study some aspects relating to the interpretation, understanding and application of Art 114 of the Contract Law and the nature of the damages provided in it. The sole arbitrator was willing to study it. For easy reference, I would like to copy down, a fair English translation of, that Art 114[2]:

The parties may stipulate that in case of breach of *contract by either party a certain amount of penalty shall* be paid to the other party according to the serious of the breach, and may also stipulate the method for calculating the sum of compensation for losses caused by the breach of contract.

If the stipulated penalty for breach of contract is lower than the loss caused by the breach, the party concerned may apply to a people's court or an arbitration institution for an increase. If the stipulated penalty for breach of contract is excessively higher than the loss caused by the breach, the party concerned may apply to a people's court or an arbitration institution for an appropriate reduction.

If the parties agree upon a penalty for the breach of contract by a delayed fulfillment, the breaching party shall, after paying the penalty for breach of contract, discharge the debts notwithstanding. (emphasis added.)

2 Draft Award 1

I, being a sole arbitrator, find as facts that there are no controversy over the existence of the Contract and that the Sellers failed to deliver the goods satisfying the terms and conditions of the Contract.

I find the main divergence of views is that the Buyers hold that according to the Contract the Sellers must deliver qualified samples which passed the test of 3C Certification; otherwise they are in breach of contract and have to undertake the liabilities; the Sellers in breach of contract have resulted in the failure in accomplishing the purpose of the Contract and therefore the Buyers claim to rescind the Contract and in light of Art 114 of the Contact Law and Clause 6 of the Contract, the Sellers under the Contract have to pay damages 30% of the total price to the Buyers.

The Sellers in one of their replying letter to the Buyers said the sockets of M501P Model were under the way of testing for 3C Certification and it would be finished in 20 working days, so they believe that they had and still have the capacity to perform the Contract. The Sellers hold that the purpose of Buyers in concluding the Contract was not for the real performance of it but for the purpose of gaining the sum of breach of contract damages. The Buyers practiced fraud going against the principle of good faith. The Sellers believe that the Contract was not at the substantial performance stage yet; it was at the Stage 2 of inspecting and confirming the samples. Even if the Sellers were of default, there were no substantial losses suffered by the Buyers. The damages should be reduced to 5% of the total price.

I am of the view that the Contract was based on the concurrence of both sides. As who was first making offer or what ways adopted in negotiation and sending documents by express mail, there was nothing to do with the establishment of the Contract. It is provided in Clause 2 "Up-to-date products qualified with a 3C Certification" and in Clause 4 the Sellers shall in 5 days after the conclusion of the Contract send 2 qualified samples of the products to the Buyers with a Test Report and a 3C

Certification; after inspecting the samples and checking the certifications, the Buyers advance the Sellers 30% of the total price.

The above provisions in essence are collateral conditions on the validity of the Contract. The validity of the Contract relies on the 2 samples that the Buyers, after inspecting and checking the related certifications, accept them as up to the requirements. Paying 30%of the total price itself is the concrete action in confirming the samples as qualified. In accordance with the provisions of Clause 5, the Sellers, after receiving the 30% of the total price, would deliver the goods at their premises in 15 days and the balance of the total price would be settled on the same day, without paying the 30%of the total price and refusing the 2 samples are the concrete actions in denying the validity of the Contract.

A collateral condition is a fact but not a duty. Whether a condition is accomplished or not is not illegal. Whether or not a condition could be accomplished might be beyond the expectation of the parties at the time of concluding a contract or they are not very sure. And the condition is an uncertain fact.

For some reasons, such as the Buyers in the instant case were not very sure whether the Sellers could produce new sockets of M501P Model and the products could pass the test of 3C Certification as the Sellers declared at the time of entering into the Contract. The Buyers might have estimated that the Sellers might be unable to have the work done; therefore, they requested to provide in the Contract that the samples and documents should be inspected and checked and when there was necessary the Sellers had to produce the originals of the certifications. When all were confirmed, the Buyers would simply pay 30% of the total price, the condition was accomplished and the Contract would become effect.

Based on the understanding and viewpoints aforesaid. I hold that what the Sellers say about the divided stages of performance of the Contract and the dispute was arising at the Stage 2 of confirming the samples is on the whole grounded. The Buyers did not accept the samples due to its quality problem and did not pay the 30%of the total price and are of the view that the Contact did not become effective yet. At the time of signing the Contract, the Buyers estimated that there might be such situation. Therefore, the first claim of the Claimant could not be sustained.

But the dispute arising from the Contract and referred to arbitration is not simply due to the misunderstanding to the collateral condition by the Buyers. The Sellers declared that they had the capacity to perform the Contract and after October 20, 2004, in 20 working days they would get a 3C Certification for their goods. But in 20 working days their sockets might or might not pass the test, there was no certain answer. And it is provided in the Contract that new products up to standard with a 3C Certification. That is to say at the time of signing the Contract, the sockets were or were about with a 3C Certification and the Sellers could produce it in no time. In the defense, the Sellers say that they are a new company eager to get some orders more. Without proper conditions, the Sellers signed the Contract. That is the reason leading to the dispute. When the dispute arouse, the Sellers still declared that they had the capacity to satisfy the terms and conditions of the Contract and even required that the Contract should be continually performed. They do not know that Clause 4 implies a condition that in 5 days after signing the Contract, the Sellers failed to deliver qualified samples, the Buyers enjoy the rights to rescind the Contract. As a result, the Sellers are obligated to undertake the responsibility to the dispute and have to share the arbitration fees.

Decisions

I award and direct:

That the first claim of the Claimant is rejected.
The Claimant and the Respondent share half of the arbitration fees.

3 Draft Award 2

1. **About the Validity of the Contract**

Both parties were voluntary to enter into the Contract, and it is up to all the effective conditions of a contract; therefore, it is valid and binding upon the parties.

2. **About the Performance of the Liability of the Contract**

…

According to Clause 4, the Respondent should after the signing of the Contract in 5 days by express mail send the Claimant two qualified samples and with a Test Report and a 3C Certification of the product. As on the samples the name and mark of the producer are not those of the Respondent, there are items in the Test Report showing the subject matter is not that of the Contract. In addition, the sockets of M501P Model are without 3C Certification yet; therefore the Tribunal holds that the Respondent is in default and it has to undertake the liability.

It is provided in Clause 6 or the Contract that the defaulting party shall pay 30% of the total price as damages. The Respondent is of the view that as the performance of the Contract was at an early stage, the Claimant has not paid any consideration and there is no substantial losses, for that reason, the Respondent requests upon Paragraph 2 of Art 114 of the Contract Law that the damages be reduced to 5%of the total price. But the Claimant contends that the defaulting action of the Respondent has caused direct economic losses exceeding 30% of the total price.

In accordance with Paragraph 1 of Art 114 of the Contract Law…It is provided in Paragraph 2 of Art 114 that….

The Tribunal in light of the aforesaid provisions holds, on the one hand parties have the rights to provide damages in a contract, but on the other hand, a tribunal has the rights to make appropriate adjustment according to concrete situations upon the request of a party. The Tribunal has taken notice of the concrete figure of the direct loss claimed by the Claimant but without any evidence that could be accepted. Furthermore, in consideration of the situation that it was at the early stage of the performance of the Contract (inspecting the samples and checking the Test Report) and the dispute was arising within this stage. The subsequent rights and duties of payment of an advance contribution, delivering and receiving the goods and the payment of the balance of total price are not performed or enjoyed. The Tribunal is of the view that the agreed damages are excessively higher than the losses caused. As said above that in the instant case, it is appropriate that the Respondent shall pay the Claimant damages 5% of the total price RMB14,000.

And because of the reasons above, each party shall bear half of the arbitration fees.

Decisions

1. Within 20 days after the release of this Award, the Respondent shall pay the Claimant damages RMB14, 000.
2. Each party bears half of the arbitration fees.

4 Observation on Draft Award 2 and Application of Art 114

Some of my colleagues suppose that there is only one correct award in a case, i.e., that qualified arbitrators should all come to identical decisions relating to same claims.

The Chartered Institute of Arbitrators once made an experiment, which they believe was unique. Five distinguished arbitrators were invited to write an award based upon the same hypothetical case.[3] The editor of the Journal comments on the result, saying "This is only to state with honesty what we all know—that often there is no definitive right' answer."[4] The editor further comments:

> In many cases, the best we can hope for is that a sensible, fair and enforce- able decision be reached. I certainly challenge any five judges—or decision- makers in any field—to reached identical decisions on matters as complex as those set out in the case. To show how unrealistic that might be, one needs only to consider for a moment one of the many House of Lords cases where there is a split decision and each of the five Law Lords has put forward his own individual reasoning.

The instant case in question is not a complex one. Questions are as follows:

Whether the Contract could be classified as a contract with a collateral condition, i.e., a conditional contract; whether the provision in Clause 6 is consistent with the provisions and principles in Art 114 of the Contract Law as a penalty clause; what the nature of the damages 30% of the total price in Clause 6, is it a liquidated damage, a penalty or stipulated penalty; what the legislative intent of the damages in Art 114 of the Contract Law; how to judge that some damages are too high and too low; when there is an explicit agreement about the liquidated damages (not the actual damages) between parties, when the claimant claims for it, should evidence of losses be submitted? I would touch on some of the questions above.

When I, being the sole arbitrator, was drafting the Award No.1, dealing with the nature of collateral conditions did consult some books by legal experts in this regard. And we know why there is some collateral condition or conditional time period to the effectiveness of a contract. That is for the need of the complex of the social life and for the purpose in facing potential risks.[5] A collateral condition in a contract must be up to five requirements: a fact of future event; the fact whether it would be accomplished or not could not be confirmed at the time of signing the contract; a fact chosen by parties at will; the contents of a collateral condition are legal; the contents of a condition shall be not contradictory with the main contents of the contract.[6] The issue lies in Clause 4 of the Contract in question. If it is regarded as a collateral condition, is it an optional clause or a statutory condition? If it is the latter, no matter it is provided in a contract or not it must be abided by. 'If it should be regarded that according to the Contract in question, delivering qualified goods by the Sellers is a statutory condition and in terms of that Clause 4 of the Contract must be regarded as a statutory condition and no matter whether or not it is provided in the Contract, the Sellers must follow it. And it is provided in the Contract that could be considered as a means of emphasis only. If that is the case, the Contract in question could not be classified as a contract with a collateral condition.'

One question more. The subject matters are 'Up-to-date products qualified with 3C Certification.' Were the Buyers very sure that the goods would be qualified as the Sellers claimed at the time? I guess the Buyers were not so sure as you might think and so that they set up the collateral condition for the purpose of reducing some risk or prevent some risk from happening.[7] In view of the above, could we judge that the collateral condition was not of statutory nature? In a sense, the transaction under the Contract in question was by sample. The samples themselves would be the confirmation of the quality of the goods by the parties and that would be consensus ad idem (meeting of the minds). After the confirmation, the two samples would have been sealed up. Then once the goods delivered fell short of the specifications, the Sellers were in breach of contract. It is said that 'A sample is the "quality clause" of a contract.'[8] The two samples were not accepted as qualified and there was no sealing of the samples and no quality clause accomplished. How could the Contract be in force and performed?

Now I would like to deal with grounds of the Award No.2. In fact the Quality Clause is not the Clause 2 only. It should be the combination of Clause 2 and Clause 4. The Sellers failed in satisfying the Quality Clause by sending two samples of sub-standard and they were defaulting.

According to Paragraphs 1 and 2 of Art 114 of the Contract Law, the Tribunal holds, as there is no concrete figure of direct losses and without evidence and the dispute was arising at the initial stage of performing the Contract and there was no substantial performance of the Contract yet. The position of the Sellers relating to the damages, i.e., that should be reduced according to Paragraph 2 of Art 114 of the Contract Law from 30% of the total price to 5%, is acceptable.

If Award No 2 is workable, I have to deal with the nature of damages in Art 114 of the Contact Law. If it is of punitive nature, it has no direct connection with actual loss. The previous agreement of the parties relating to damages should be recognized and that shows the respect to the freedom of contract. No doubt in consideration of the too high or too low of damages in terms of the actual loss, a judge or an arbitrator is in a position to make an appropriate adjustment. That shows law has another function of prohibiting the abuse of freedom of contract. Could we reduce the 30% damages of the total price to less than 20%? It might be more appropriate. In Award No.2, the Tribunal reduces the damages from 30 to 5% of the total price but without giving detailed reasons. Therefore that is not in line with the provision of liquidated damages reached by the parties contained in Clause 6 of the Contract and its punitive nature in the Contract and reflected in Art 114 of the Contract Law or the nature of the main idea of Art 114 should be construed this way.

I have to mention here. For 'penalty' or 'punitive' damages, 'there is some Chinese equivalent, you could even find a satisfactory word, expression, terms or terminology, for instance 'chengfajin' or 'fajin' and 'chengfaxin sunhai peichan,' etc. In the original Chinese version, there is no exact wording, in the provisions of Art 114 that everyone would not without any doubt that the English equivalent is 'penalty.' So some translators express Art 114 in English this way:

The parties to a contract may agree that one party shall, when violating the contract, pay breach of contract damages of a certain amount in light of the breach, or may agree upon the calculating method *of compensation for losses resulting from the breach of* contract.

If the agreed breach of contract damages are lower than the losses caused, any party may request the people's court or an arbitration institution to increase it; if it is excessively higher than the losses caused, any party may request the people's court or an arbitration institution to make an appropriate reduction.

If the parties to a contract agree upon breach of *contract damages in respect of the delay in performance,* the party in breach shall perform the debt obligations after paying the breach of contract damages.[9] (emphasis added.)

Comparing this latter English version with the former one, 'I, in this article, would not judge which is better. But I do hold that the latter one is without any legal term or terminology to express the idea of 'damage,' explicitly showing its nature. Instead, it adopts a word-for-word correspondence. Viewing it from another angle, it might be regarded as 'faithful to the original.' But it does not mean that it reflects the legislative intent.

Accordingly, there have been various views on the nature of the 'damages' and the legislative intent of the 'damages' in Art 114 and the Contract Law as well. Some jurist holds the damages in the Contract Law that is of compensative nature.[10] And there is some law professor of the view that damages in Art 114 is of double nature, compensative and punitive. But introducing various views and observations of the jurists on the nature of the 'damages' in Art 114 could not be done in this short article.[11]

5 Conclusion

Now while I am writing this article based on the data of the case, I am still in favor of Draft Award 1. I could not change my mind yet.

In terms of the small sum of the price of the Contract and the even smaller sum of claim of the Claimant, I suppose Draft Award 2 is roughly workable in that particular case if somewhat more reasons are given relating to the nature of 'damages' and the arbitrator's interpretation of it in the context of the Contract.

No matter what the nature of the damages in Art 114 is, a definite amount or an exact percentage is fixed in the Clause 6 of the Contract of the instant case or similar situation, the innocent party is in a position to claim damages and is not required to submitting supporting evidence to show its loss. But that viewpoint does not work if the innocent party claims that the defaulting action of the Respondent has caused direct economic losses exceeding the stipulated damages.

I believe if Draft Award 2 was adopted, the Sellers should pay a small sum of damages to the Buyers that would be a lesson to them. Whichever award was finalized, the parties would gain some experience by thinking the deal and case over.

Notes

1. China International Economic and Trade Arbitration Commission, Shenzhen Sub-Commission (CIETAC, Shenzhen) was renamed as CIETAC, South China, on June 18, 2004.
2. Translation is quoted from Law and Regulations of the People's Republic of China, compiled by the Legislative Affairs Office of the State Council, China Legal Publishing House, Beijing, China.
3. See Arbitrator, the Journal of the Chartered Institute of Arbitrators. Vol.66, No.2, 2000.
4. Id., p.77.
5. Id.
6. Wang Liming and Cui Jianyuan, On the Contract (Revised), Publishing House of the China University of Political Science and Law, p. 254.
7. Sui Pensheng, The Main Ideas of the Contract Law, Publishing House of the China University of Political Science and Law, June, 2003, p. 110.
8. Id. p. 491.
9. See the English version of Art 114 of the Contract Law of the People's Republic of China, China Legal System Publishing House, Beijing, China, 1999, p. 55.
10. Li Yongjun, Contract Law, Law Press, Beijing, China, January, 2004, p. 665.
11. Liu Jingyi, On the Law of Contract, the People's Court Publishing Hours, Beijing, China, August, 1999, pp. 507–508. ■

Notes on the Application of the CISG to Some International Commercial Case

1 Case One: An Australian Company vs. A Chinese Company

Main point: The disputes arising from an Agreement containing no chosen law clause between an Australian Buyer and a Chinese Seller, the case reveals the correct understanding and interpretation of and attitude toward the application of the CISG by some solicitors from Victoria state; but they were wrong not to abide by the arbitration agreement, the solicitors on behalf of their principal would have gone so far as to threaten the seller with a lawsuit by sending out an "official" statement of claim. Later, it was ridiculous that the Chinese seller would have been so unwise and would have gone so far as to file a law action of confirmation with a court of its business place, requesting that the court should confirm that the arbitration clause in the Agreement was invalided.

A. **The Parties and Some Provisions and Clauses Contained in the General Distributorship Agreement**

The plaintiff: XX PTY LTD, a company taken to be incorporated pursuant to the corporations Act 2001 (Cth) of the Victoria state of Australia and a dealer in electrical and electronic products in the Australian market, in the Agreement between the parties is Distributor and Buyer called "the Buyer."

Solicitors and Agents: XX commercial and Technology Lawyers, a law firm located in Melbourne, Victoria.

The Defendant: XXX co. Ltd, a body corporate incorporated under the laws of the p R. China, a manufacturer or supplier of domestic appliances and associated

This commentary was published in Mealey's International Arbitration Report, Vol. 25, # 5, May 2010, pp. 25–45.

The author is grateful to Madam Kui Hua Wang, senior lecturer with the School of Law, Deakin University, Australia, for providing with some materials.

Y. Huang, *Commentaries on Commercial Arbitration in Modern China*, Modern China and International Economic Law, https://doi.org/10.1007/978-981-95-0168-7_13

equipment and spare parts, in the Agreement between the parties is supplier and seller, named as "The Seller."

Products: The products covered under this Agreement shall expressly be confined to domestic appliance sold by the supplier/seller with its registered trademark XXX.

The parties entered into the Agreement in China on December xx, 2003.

The following provisions and clauses are closely relate d to the dispute:

Territory: *The territory covered under this Agreement shall be confined to the Australia only (hereinafter referred to as Territory).*

Period: *The initial validity period of the Agreement shall commerce from the date of signature by both parties and will terminate on January XX, 2008. This Agreement can be extended for another period of four (4) years subject to the terms of Art 5 (Minimum Purchase) being fulfilled. At the end of the 5th year if the quantity achieved is not less than xxxxx units in year 5, the Agreement may be further extended by another 5 years.*

(I guess that the aforesaid provisions roughly speaking could be regarded as "recital" of the Agreement.)

Art 2. Privity:*The relationship hereby established between the Supplier and the Distributor, during the effective period of the Agreement, shall be solely that of (the) Seller and (the) Buyer, and the Distributor shall under no circumstance be considered to be the agent of legal representative of the Supplier for any purpose whatsoever and shall have no right or authority to create or assume any obligation or responsibility of any kind, expressed or implied in the name of or on behalf of the Supplier.*

Art 9. Guarantee: *The Seller guarantees five year for the compressor and one year for the unit, the Seller give the Buyer 1% contract FOB value spare parts free of charge to cover any defect up to 2% by specific model, between 2% and 5% the Seller and the Buyer will share cost thereof while any product defect beyond 5%, the Seller will be fully responsible.*

Art 12. Cancellation or Termination:*(1) In case there is any breach of the provisions under this Agreement by either party during the effective period of this Agreement, the parties hereto shall first of all try to settle the matter in question as soon and amicable as possible to mutual satisfaction or if not so settled within 60 days such matters will be referred to arbitration in the Territory for resolution. (Emphasis added)*

(2)(Omitted).

Art 14. Entire Agreement:*This Agreement constitutes the entire and only agreement between the parties hereto and supersedes all previous negotiations and agreements relating to the sale of the Products, and shall not be modified or changed in any manner except by mutual consent in writing of a subsequent date signed by a duly authorized officer or representative of each of the parties hereto.*

You could find no choice of law clause in the Agreement. Nevertheless, readers would agree that there is an arbitration clause by the parties in the Agreement, namely Art 12 (1) is also playing the role of an arbitration clause.

> One of the most probable grounds for implying an agreement as the substantive applicable to the merits, is the existence of an agreement that any dispute shall be submitted to arbitration in a particular place, i.e. country, state or territory.[1]

My construction to the arbitration clause of the Agreement is that when any dispute arising from or in connection with the Agreement should be referred to arbitration in the Territory, the Australia or the victor state where the Buyer was located.

B. Quotations from the Statement of Claim by the Solicitors of the Buyer and Their Exposition on the Application of the CISG

When there were some disputes arising from the Agreement and initially the parties held some round of negotiations and consultations and reached some common understandings, the seller was optimistic that the disputes would soon be settled.

But to the surprise of the executives with the seller that they received a legal document from the Buyer's solicitors in the form of "Statement of Claim":

***In the supreme court OF vectors at Melbourne No of 2008 commercial List between*:**

XXX ***Plaintiff***

-and

XXX ***Defendant***

The address and contracting information were printed on the same page.

I would like to quote some form of the statement of claim.

9. *By reason of the fact that:*

   (a) *the Buyer and the Seller had their respective places of business in Australia and China;*
   (b) *both Australia and China are parties to the United Nations Convention on Contracts for the International Sale of Goods 1980 ("the CISG").*

The CISG applied to the sales contracts.

Particulars

Art 1(1) of the CISG. The CISG entered into force in respect of Australia on April 1, 1989, and in respect of China on January 1, 1988.

10. *There were implied terms of each sales contract by virtue of the CIGS that:*

   (a) *the Seller was obliged no deliver goods of the quantity, quality and description required by the sales contract [Art35(1)];*
   (b) *the goods had to be fit for the purposes for which goods of the same description would ordinarily be used [Art35(2)(a)]; and*
   (c) *the goods would have and retain for a reasonable period of normal use by consumers their specified qualities and characteristics.*

11. *Further and in the alternative, there were implied terms of each sales contract that the subject goods would be reasonable fit for their intended purpose, would be of merchantable quality and would comply with their description.*

Particulars

Sections 18 and 19(a) and (b) of the Goods of Act 1958 (Vic)

The Solicitors on behalf of the plaintiff accused that the Defendant was breach of the Agreement and claimed:

A. *Damages*
B. *A declaration of the Court that the obligation of the Seller to the Buyer under and pursuant to Art 9 of the Agreement shall remain in full force and effect notwithstanding of the termination of the Agreement.*
C. $
D. *Interest according to statute.*
E. *Cost.*

C. **Brief Comments on the Statement** of **Claims**

I believe that the short exposition of the application of the CISG by the solicitors engaged by the Buyer was correct and to the point.

In addition, as the solicitors on behalf of the Buyer (plaintiff) complained that the seller (Defendant) had been in breach of Art 9 of the Agreement, saying that a significant proportion of the seller's products purchased by the Buyer were subject to various faults and defects, so by reason of the matter, the Buyer has suffered loss and damage. And that was why the solicitors referred to "Section 18 and 19(a) and (b) of the Goods of Act 1958(Vic)." The solicitors did not have the full text of the sections contained in their statement of claim; I suspected the seller might have no trouble to have access to them. Now I copy out them as follows:

Sale by description

18. *Sale by description—When there is a contract for the sale of goods by description there is an implied condition that the goods shall correspond with the description; and if the sale be by sample as well as by description it is not sufficient that the bulk of the goods corresponds with the sample if the goods do not also correspond with the description.*

Goods Act 1958—SECT 19
Implied conditions as to quality or fitness.

19. 19. *Implied conditions as to quality or fitness subject to the provisions of this Part and of any Act in the behalf there is no implied warranty or condition as to the quality or fitness for any particular purpose of goods supplied under a contract of sale, except as follows:*

   (a) *where the buyer expressly or by implication makes known to the seller the particular purpose for which the goods are required so as to show that the buyer relies on the seller's skill or judgment and the goods are of description which is in the course of the seller's business to supply (whether he be the manufacturer or nor) there is an implied condition that the goods shall be reasonably fit for such purpose: Provided that in the case of a contract for the sale of a specified article under its patent or other trade name there is no implied condition as to its fitness for any particular purpose;*

(b) *where goods are bought by description from a seller who deals in goods of that description (whether he be the manufacturer or not) there is an implied condition that the goods shall be of merchantable quality: Provided that if the buyer has examined the goods there shall be no implied condition as regards defects which such examination ought to have revealed;*

(c) *an implied warranty or condition as to quality or fitness for a particular purpose may annexed by the usage of trade.*

(d) *an express warranty or condition does not negative a warranty or condition implied by this Part unless inconsistent therewith.*

I suppose that the solicitors believed that apart from the application of the CISG to the Agreement, the domestic law, particularly the law of the Victoria state of Australia should also be applied to the Agreement. The solicitors, I guess, might have firmly believed that application of the CISG did not exclude the application of their domestic law. And particularly, the referred sections aforesaid are more concrete to the situations than the corresponding Arts in the CISG.

Scholars and professionals in Australia hold that the CISG "*does not live in a vacuum. It interacts with, and operates within, the framework of domestic law, and does so at many levels.*"[2] And they are also of the viewpoint that "*Since there is little enunciation of the 'general principles' of the Convention, other than an appeal for uniform application, the national courts of common law countries may tend to fill perceived gaps in the CISG with domestic law concepts.*"[3]

According to Australian precedent in this regard, in Roder Zelt und Hallenkonstruktionen Gmbh v Rosedown Pty Ltd & Eustace,[4] a 1995 interim decision by the Federal Court, von Doussa J held that subject to leave being given, the applicant would be entitled to enforce the rights arising on avoidance under the CISG. But according to the introduction by Mr. Jacobs QC and his co-authors, there is no final determination is recorded about the case.

Mr. Jacobs and his two co-authors comment that "7.4 *The absence of a final decision by the Court deprived us of a full analysis of the pertinent provisions of the Vienna Convention,*" such as Art 8, 11, 15, 18 and 29.[5]

The three authors say that "*7.9 The case, unfortunately offers very little future guidance as to the effect of the application of the Convetion.*"[6]

The authors mention that "*7.11 However, von Dousa J also stated that: (17 ACSR at p 158) '[i]nsofar as the contract is governed by the Convention, which is now part of the municipal law of Australia, the meaning of that law, and its application to the facts, is to be determined by this court…*'".[7]

I guess that the following quotation is one of the main viewpoints of the three distinguished professionals:

> 7.13 As the Convention only governs the formation of the contract of sale and the rights and obligations of the seller and buyer arising for such a contract, the Convention is not concerned with the effect which the contract may have on the property in the goods sold (Art 4) therefore, Article 7(2) provides that:
>
> Questions concerning matters governed by this Convention which are not expressly settled in it are to be settled in conformity with the general principles on which it is based or, in the absence of such principles, in conformity with the law applicable by virtue of the rules of private international law.[8]

So the dispute arising from the Agreement between the Australian Buyer and the Chinese seller, though there is no governing law clause in the Agreement, the solicitors from the Victoria state of Australia do not hold that the parties concerned exclude the application of the CISG, no doubt the CISG is applied. Further, the application of the CISG does not exclude the application of the law of Victoria state and the federal law of that country.

On the other hand, there is explicit arbitration intention of the parties reflected in Art 12 of the Agreement with provision of referring matter in question to "*arbitration in Territory for resolution.*" I do not think that the solicitors should turn a blind eye to the arbitration agreement.

The solicitors as experienced professionals on behalf of their principal, the Buyer, would go so far as to threaten the seller with lawsuit. Namely, they sent the so-called formal "statement of claim" to the "Defendant" on mean purpose to frighten the latter. I don't believe that the solicitors' act was in accord with their code of ethics.

The above-mentioned distinguished three authors in their article briefly reveal the interaction of the CISG with statutory remedies in Australia, I am to quote more as follows:

> 8.1 As we have said, one of the factors identified as the basis for the paucity of decided cases on the Vienna Convention is Australia is the prominence and prevalence of international arbitration as the forum for the resolution of disputes.
>
> 8.2 In this regard, the Commonwealth legislated to give dominance to this form of dispute resolution, in section 7 of the International Arbitration Act 1974 (Cth) which provides:

(1) *where*

- (a) *the procedure is relation to arbitration under an arbitration agreement is governed whether by virtue of the express terms of the agreement or otherwise, by the law of a Convention country;*
- (b) *the procedure in relation arbitration under an arbitration agreement is governed whether by virtue of the express terms of the agreement or otherwise, by the law of a country not being Australia or a convention country, and a party to the agreement is Australia or a state or a person who was, at the time when the agreement was made, domiciled or ordinarily in Australia.*
- (c) *(Omitted)*

(d) *a party to an arbitration agreement is a person who was, at the time when the agreement was made, domiciled or ordinarily resident in a country that is a Convention country; this section applies to the agreement..*

(2) *Subject to this Part where:*

(a) *the proceedings instituted by a party to an arbitration agreement to which this section applies against another party to the agreement are pending in a court; and*

(b) *the proceedings involve the determination of a matter that, in pursuance of the agreement, is capable of settlement by arbitration; on the application a party to the agreement, the court shall, by order, upon such conditions (if any) as it thinks fit, stay the proceedings as involves the determination of that matter, as the case may be, and refer the parties to arbitration in respect of the matter.*

> 8.3 Thus, if the transaction involves parties to an 'arbitration agreement' and one or both of them is resident in a Convention country, the enforcement of that arbitration agreement will be respected. The Courts are not left with a discretion in this regard.[9]

I by chance got access to the documents of the transaction and case above and gave some advice to the executives of the seller, urging them to hold amicable negotiations with their counterparts and try to narrow down the issues of facts and law on which they differ with each other but holding there was no worry about the so-called litigations. The principle of compulsory reference of an international commercial dispute to arbitration in Australia explicitly reflected in the section 7 of the International Arbitration Act 1974 (Cth).

If the solicitors of the Buyer do really file the dispute with the Supreme Court of Victoria, the Seller could apply the court, and upon the application of the seller, the court shall by order stay the proceedings and refer the parties to arbitration in respect of their dispute.

D. An Unreasonable and Unexpected Event

In January 2009, I received a document titled civil Indictment (complaint) in English dated on in October 2008 from the seller. I guessed that the ones drafting the document with a computer had got the terminology from somewhere. The seller sent me the complaint for the purpose of asking me to give them (the executives) some advice about the English version of their Chinese legal document only but not on any legal issues or arbitration.

The complaint revealed that the Seller in the position as plaintiff against the Buyer as defendant might have fled a legal suit with the intermediate people's court of the place of its registration and main business,[9] first of all requesting that the court should confirm that arbitration clause in the Agreement was invalid. The Seller might officially have filed an action for conformation and intended afterward to have the disputes arising from the Agreement referred to the intermediate people's court.

The Seller states in the compliant that the disputes arising from the Agreement, both parties have tried to settle them in negotiations for quite a long time. Unfortunately, no solution has been reached due to the wide divergence between both parties. Although Clause 12 of the said Agreement contains an arbitration clause, it believes that the arbitration clause is invalid and the disputes cannot be resolved through arbitration.

The Seller in the compliant states that the Civil Procedure Law and the Arbitration Law of PRC apply. In accordance with the provisions of the Arbitration Law, if an arbitration agreement does not define or clearly specify an arbitration commission (institution), the parties may enter into an additional agreement. If the parties fail to agree, the arbitration agreement will be invalid. The arbitration clause in the Agreement does not define any arbitration commission (institution), the seller and the Buyer have not reached an additional agreement, and so the arbitration clause is invalid.[10]

After reading the document I did enquire about the matter and urge the seller to give up the ridiculous act, writing the executives of it three notes in a row to reiterate that if the disputes could not be settled through amicable negotiation, the seller or the Buyer had to refer the case to arbitration in Australia. But my advice in this regard got no response. I suspected that was a tactics of the seller, though it was no value in my mind. I was disappointed by the way the executives of the seller completely ignored my advice.

The legal doctrines and issues involved in the complaint are various; they are of basic principles, such as the proper law of the arbitration agreement (the Arbitration Law of PR. China has nothing to do with the validity of the arbitration agreement contained in the Agreement, name the Law could not be applied to the matter), the seat of the arbitration and the curia l law of arbitration and comments on the Arbitration Law of the PR. China, etc., and they are beyond the present purposes in this article, so I might not touch on them.

Up to now I could not puzzle out the reason of the action by the seller and I have got no information about the matter and have not inquired about it anymore ever since, though thereafter I by chance have met one of the in-house legal counsels of the Seller.

In my career, I have come across various commercial cases and having access to, being involved in or engaged in handling of them, I have gained knowledge and skills or enlightenment and even wisdom. In addition, I have also run across many unexpected or even absurd and ridiculous ideas and actions. Those episodes have also enriched my mind and made my life interesting or colorful more.

2 Case Two: A Chinese Company vs. A Singapore Pte. Ltd—Under the Jurisdiction of the CIETAC, South China Numbered SHEN 2008114

Main point: A choice of PRC Law clause in a contract for the international sale of goods between a Chinese corporation and a corporation from another contracting state should not be regard as exploding the application of the CISG.

A. **Briefs of the Case**

The Plaintiff: XXX Food co. Ltd, a company incorporate d located in a county, Guangxi Zhuang Autonomous Region, P R. China.

Agent: Mr. Huang, a lawyer with a law firm located in the same country with the Purchaser.

The Defendant: XXX Asia Pacific Pte. Ltd. Located in Singapore. Its parent corporation is in Indiana, America, mainly engaged in the development and manufacture of quality food (vegetables and fruits) cutting machines and according to some pamphlets attached to the file of the case that it has got subsidiaries and sales offices in principal cities worldwide.

Agent: Mr. Yu, a lawyer with a law firm located in Shanghai, PR. China.

In March 2007, the Plaintiffs the purchaser and the Defendant as the vendor entered into a sales contract consisting of standard terms in two originals in both Chinese and English prepared by the Vendor as its parent corporation has established a subsidiary named XXX China Ltd in shanghai.

The contract is brief with only nine terms and conditions and the ones which are more closely related to the disputes as follows:

1. ***Equipment***: *One (1)XX Model RA-A Dice r with stainless steel contact pars, set for 48 × 4.8 × 48 mm dices and change parts for 7.9 × 7.9 × 79 mm and 9.6 × 9.6 × 9.6 mm dices, complete with a 5 HP, 3 Ph, 50 Hz, 380 Volt motor, detail as per attached quotation.*

2. ***Total Value***: *CIF Shenzhen Port, China USDXXXXX.*

8. ***Guarantee***: *The guarantee period of equipment shall be twelve (12) months after the date of acceptance of the equipment of fifteen (15) months after the shipment date, whichever occurs first.*

9. ***Arbitration***: *All disputes arising from the execution or in connection with this contract shall be settle through friendly negotiation. In case, no settlement can be reached the disputes may then be submitted for arbitration to the China International Economic and Trade Arbitration Committee for the promotion of International Trade according to PRC laws (emphasis added). The arbitration shall be the final solution and arbitration fee shall be borne by the losing party.*

There are in the contract other provisions concerning the payment of deposit and the balance of the subject, site supervision assistance and other matters, etc.[11]

About Clause 9 of the contract, there is no equivalent wording or expression of "according to PRC laws" in the corresponding Chinese text. Further there is no specified provision such as "In the event of any discrepancy between the two aforementioned versions, the English (or Chinese) version shall prevail."

> In the request for arbitration by the purchaser claimant through its lawyer referred to the contract Law of the People's Republic of China ("Contract Law"), quoting Arts 107 and 111 (concerning the performance of obligations not in conformity with the terms of a contract and the quality of the subject matter fails to satisfy the terms of a contract) and Art 40 of the Law of PRC on protecting consumers' Rights and Interests.[1212]

B. The Application of the PR China Law and of the CISG as Well

At the oral hearing the Claimant first present its case by outlined the contents in its request for arbitration and the Chinese lawyer engaged by the Respondent in his oral defense without denying the application of the law of PRC; instead, he with ease referred to Arts 61[13] and 62[14] (where there are no provisions in a contract regarding to quality of the subject matter or the provisions are uncertain, what measures the parties to a contract should adopted or what standards shall be applied).

In view of the above-mentioned facts, the presiding arbitrator inquired of the parties whether they agreed on the application of PRC Laws. The Tribunal got official and definite replay that both party did regarded PRC law was the governing law of the contract.

Dispute was relating to the quality of the equipment; the purchaser claimed that after it received dicer, XX China Ltd located in Shanghai an associated corporation of the Vendor dispatched two erectors to the Purchaser's factory, but the erectors failed to have the dicer to produce slices of the specifications in the contract. After the erectors left, the purchaser by means of telephone and telegraph to inform the vendor (through its associated corporation in Shanghai) of the quality problem with the dice r, demanding it to send technician to handle the problem, but receiving no response. So the case was referred to arbitration.

Before the oral hearing, the author of this article mentioned the question of the application of the CISG to his co-arbitrators.

Under the sub-heading Opinion of the Tribunal in the final Award of the case, the arbitrators first of all deals with the nature of dispute and simultaneously the matter of the application of law. The piece of opinions is very brief but to the point; further it at least shows the arbitrators have known their obligation under the CISG and they have somewhat wide field of vision. I should have my English translation from the Chinese source language cited herewith. But because I would have it quoted in the Case Four in this article and actually I did have it as "precedent" contained in my Dissent relating to the Case Four, so it would be better not to have it repeated.

3 Case Three: A Hong Kong Corporation vs. A Vietnam Corporation Under the Jurisdiction of the CIETAC, South China Numbered as SHEN R2009030

Main point: In this case, in a contract of international sale of goods between a Hong Kong seller and the buyer from an assumed contracting state of the CISG, there is a chosen law clause, providing that the governing law is that of the PR. China, the buyer's Chinese lawyer held that the CISG could not be applied.

A. **The Overview of the Case**

Claimant (the Seller): XXX located in Hong Kong special Administration Region of the People's Republic of China.

Arbitration Agents: Mr. Huang, a lawyer of a law firm located in Guangzhou, Guangdong Province, P R. China. Mr. Chai, an in-house counsel with a subsidiary of the claimant. MS. Bian, an in-house counsel with the claimant.

Respondent (the Buyer): XX Plastics Co, located in Trang Bang Industrial zone, Trang Bang District, HU Chi Mingh City (Saigon), Vietnam.

Arbitration Agent Mr. Hu, a lawyer with a law firm located in Shenzhen, Guangdong Province, PR. China.

1. **Arbitration Clause and Governing Law Clause in the Disputed Contract**

The Seller and the Buyer on October xx, 2008, concluded a sale contract written in Chinese with TAI SOXL LDPE Prime Grade 3224 as the subject of Taiwan (region of China) original.

Except for the clauses for quantify, shipping information, unit price and payment, there are 34 clauses under the subtitle: General Terms and Conditions (collected as "clauses"). Two of them are as follows:

> 3. Arbitration: Any disputes arising from in connection with this contract shall be settled through amicable negotiation; if there is no settlement, any party shall refer the dispute to the China International Economic and Trade Arbitration Commission South China Sub-Commission (CIETAC, South China) for arbitration which shall be conducted in accordance with the Commissions' arbitration rules at the time of applying for arbitration, the seat is in Shenzhen, the award is final and binding upon both parties.
>
> 34. Governing Law: The governing law of this contract is the law of the People's Republic of China.

The Buyer, after paying a deposit, 20 percent of the total price, neither pay the 80 percent as agreed nor did he receive the goods under the contract. Dispute arose and on January xx, 2009, the Seller as the claimant submitted the dispute to CIETAC, South China.

B. **The Understanding and Interpretation of the Application of the CISG of the Lawyers of the Parties**

I was one member of the three-man Tribunal formulated on March xx of the same year. On May xx, 2009, the Tribunal held an oral hearing in Shenzhen. Before the oral hearing, I wanted to make sure whether Vietnam had been a contracting stare of the CISG yet, so I had to consult the lawyers on it.

I inquired of the attorneys of both parties whether Vietnam was a contracting state of CISG. The answer by the attorney of the seller was affirmative: "Yes, Vietnam is a contracting state to the convention."

Then my next question was: under such circumstances that both China and Vietnam are the contracting states to the CISG and the arbitration now is conducted in one of the contracting states, would the CISG be applicable to the present case? I got another definite answer from the attorney of the Claimant: "NO, the CISG is not applicable to the present case."

The attorney of the Respondent made no response to my question.

If we assume that Vietnam is a contracting state to the CISG, under the circumstances of the instant case, would a choice of PRC law clause in a contract between a corporation located in Hong Kong, China, and a corporation from another contracting state exclude the application of CISG?

C. The Correct Principles of Application of Civil Law in Connection with Foreign Elements in China

In the past years, I have dealt with about ten cases between that seller and its buyers mainly from Hong Kong and different regions of the Mainland of China. All the disputed contracts with standard terms prepared by the seller in advance for repeated use, namely so far as I have come across all the buyers signed the contracts formally printed by the Sellers. Some of the contracts are bilingual—in Chinese and English, some are in Chinese only. Further as time goes by I have found that the seller and its subsidiary companies in the Mainland of China are adopting the same forms of sales contracts. For the contract in Chinese only that Art34 is the applicable law clause, explicitly providing that the governing law is that of the PR China. I do not mean that the seller has not provided in its other standard contracts that they are subject to other laws.

It is expressly provided in the General principles of civil Law of PRC ("General Principles") that the application of civil law in connection with foreign elements shall be in accordance with the provisions of chapter VIII.

I would like to review chapter VIII of the General principles. It is stipulated in Art 142 that:

> The application of civil law in connection with foreign elements shall be in accordance with the provisions of this chapter.
>
> If any international treaty concluded or acceded to by the People's Republic of China contains provisions different from those in the civil laws of the People's Republic of China, the provisions of the international treaty shall prevail, unless the provisions are those which the People's Republic of China has expressed reservations.
>
> International practice may be applied on matters for which neither the law of the People's Republic of China nor any international treaty concluded or acceded to by the People's Republic of China has provided for.[15]

In 2008 Prof. Marcus S Jacobs from New South Wales, Australia, was invited to deliver some lectures at CIETAC, its sub-commissions and some law faculty in China.

He planned to come to China in September of that year. But due to some reason after he finished his article titled the United Nations Convention for the International Sale of Goods 1980 (the Vienna Convention) and International Commercial Arbitration ("Marcus' Article"),[16] colleagues at the CIETAC missed a good chance to receive him and listen to his lecture as scheduled.

If my memory serves me well, I received his draft of the article in April and March of that year. It was impressive. After reading the article, I realized that the prof Jacobs was so familiar with the matters relating to the application of the CISG to the cases under the jurisdiction of CIETAC and the interaction of the domestic law of PR China with the CISG, I felt shamed as I had not paid sufficient attention to those matters.

About review of the Art 142 of the General Principles, I have to make some quotations more from some expert and professional of the commercial arbitration circle. To tell the truth, I have not directly got access to the following quotations, instead I have re-quoted them from Marcus' Article:

> 1.72 It is submitted that a correct reading of the above Article reveals that the right position should be that CISG is superior to the PRC domestic legislation, i.e. the first hierarchy of the PRC law, as a treaty concluded or acceded to by the PRC. The PRC domestic legislation then follows as the second hierarchy in the middle. The international practice contributes as the third hierarchy. Although the CISG is above the PRC domestic legislation, it is within the broader picture of the three-tier hierarchy of the source of the PRC law.
>
> 1.73 Therefore, if the parties of international sales have chosen the law of the PRC, a Contracting State of the CISG, it is submitted that the CISF should apply as having been incorporated and become part of the PRC law (emphasis added). If the court then finds that the CISG contains provisions differing from those in the PRC domestic legislations, the provisions of the CISG shall prevail.[17]

I was wondering whether the lawyers respectively engaged by the two parties had been familiar with the provisions contained in the General principles. And I was rather doubtful whether the lawyers had reviewed their lessons or done their homework well before the oral hearing.

After conclusion of the case and in the course of sorting out data and writing this article, I have joined my co-arbitrators in handling or as a sole arbitrator dealt some cases more to that the applicant above was in an applicant capacity and the lawyer aforesaid as attorney in the arbitration proceedings. Although the claims of the applicant were generally satisfied as its defendants were in arrears, that did not mean that I would always have access to well-organized statements, sound submissions or convincing arguments from the principal and its attorney and its counterparts.

4 Case Four: An Australian Corporation vs. A Chinese Corporation Under the Jurisdiction of CIETAC, South China Numbered SHEN M2 008201

Main point: Could a Chinese party and its counterpart an Australian party by only incorporating a choice of PRC Law clause in their Agreement exclude the application of the CISG? And could the silence of the parties on the matter of the application of the CISG be interpreted to imply or should be constructed that the parties have reached an agreement that the convention do not apply to the case?

A. Briefs of the Case That Closely Related to This Commentary

Claimant (Buyer): NPL located in New South Wales, Australia.

Agents: Mr. Jones (Shareholder), Mr. Lin (Lawyer of a law firm located in Guangdong Province, China), Ms. Lin (Lawyer of the aforesaid law firm).

Respondent (Seller): MBM located in Guangdong Province of the PR. China.

Agents: Mr. Fitzpatrick (General Counsel), Ms. Li/H. (Manager), Mr. Liu/X. (Legal Counsel—in—house counsel), Mr. Wang/X.D. (Legal counsel—in-house counsel), Mr. Li/H (Legal counsel—in-house counsel), Mr. Chen/D (Lawyer of a law firm located in Guangdong Province, China), Mr. Wang/X. F. (Lawyer of the aforesaid law firm)

One day in December 2007, the Chinese Seller and the Australian Buyer entered into an Exclusive Distribution and supply Agreement ("Agreement") by which the Buyer agrees to purchase and the seller agrees to supply twelve items of medical apparatus and instruments. One of them was coded as T6.

As some disputes arising from the Agreement, the Buyer claimant according to the Dispute Resolution clause (Arbitration Clause—the author) contained in the Agreement submitted an Application for Arbitration against the Seller Respondent in December 2008. CIEETAC, South China accepted the Application.

According to the CIETAC Arbitration Rules of 2005, each party appointed an arbitrator from the panel of the CIETAC, the presiding arbitrator, who as a solicitor practices law in Hong Kong, was appointed by the chairman of the CIETAC, the author of this commentary was appointed as a co-arbitrator by the claimant, another co-arbitrator, who as a lawyer practices law in Guangdong Province, was appointed by the Respondent. The three-member Tribunal was formed in February 2009,

One day in April 2009, the Tribunal held an oral hearing in Shenzhen.

B. The Divergent Opinions on the Applicable Law Between the Majority and the Minority of the Tribunal

There had been divergence views on the applicable law between the majority arbitrators and the minority arbitrator—the author of this commentary. The divergence appeared at the commencement of and continued throughout the whole arbitral proceedings.

The majority hold that only the law of the PRC applies to the instant case.

During the proceedings or to the end of it, I had expressed my ideas on the application of the CISG in four versions successively trying to persuade my co-arbitrators; as time went by more contents were added.

Before the final award was issued and on receipt of my last but one Dissent in respect of application of the CISG. The position the majority taken with regard to the application of the CISG expressed by the presiding arbitrator in his note by email to me reads as follows:

> I have duly noted the position you are taking with regard to the application of CISG.
>
> As you will remember the parties did not make any submission, argument or even make any reference to CISG throughout the whole proceedings despite your kind reminder of the potential application of CISG at the very beginning of the hearing. So, in other words, the parties have never argued about their positions under CISG. To me, as indicated earlier to you all, the fundamental issue here is whether the tribunal should apply CIGS to the present case even if the parties did not apply, rely on, argue or even refer to CISG throughout the whole proceedings. In other words, would it be proper for the Tribunal to apply CISG in the circumstance? I should be grateful for your views/guidance on this.

C. Advice on the Application of the CISG Given b One Professional Within CIETAC, South China

There were several professionals with CIEAC, South China screened the award draft while the inner screening system operated. One of them gave his/her opinion, inter alia on the application of the CISG. I have the advice in Chinese turned into English as follows:

3. About the applicable law of the case: as both parties have chosen the law of China, and their respective places of business are in different Contracting States to the CISG, the Tribunal should first of all apply the law of China to the to the case; and then in respect of any matter that there is no provision in the law of China, the relative provision in the CISG should be applied. Don't you think so?

This piece of advice remind me of Art 6 of the Law of the People's Republic of China on Economic contracts Involving Foreign Interest or the Foreign Economic Contract Law (the "Foreign Economic Contract Law"):

> Where an international treaty which is relevant to a contract, and to which the People's Republic of China is a contracting party or a signatory has provided differently from the law of the People's Republic of China, the provisions of the international treaty shall prevail, with the exception of those clauses on which the People's Republic of China has declared reservation.[18]

The aforesaid piece of advice in respect of the application is not in line with the principle that an international treaty or convention should prevail under such circumstance. It is wrong as an American scholar once said that "[T]he CIETAC tribunal in Case 1 is applying the CISG to a dispute between parties from Contracting States, but only to the extent that the CISG's provisions 'different from the law of the People's Republic of China'."[19]

And I have once aired some views in response to the good comment of the American scholar and on the interaction of domestic law of P.R. China with the application of the CISG. It may be also be relevant.[20]

D. The Official View of the Majority Contained in the Final Award—Quotations from the Arbitral Award[21]

Jurisdiction

8. The CIETAC South China Sub-Commision[22] accepted jurisdiction over the dispute arising from the Agreement between the Parties according to the arbitration clause of the Agreement.

9. The arbitration clause, Clause 13 of the Agreement, read as follows:

The Parties agree to use their best reasonable efforts to resolve all disputes, controversies and differences which may arise out of or in connection with this Agreement in an amicable manner. In the event that direct discussions between the Parties do not result in a resolution of the dispute by voluntary mediation, with the costs and expenses of such medication being shared equally by the Parties.

In the event the Parties cannot resolve such dispute, controversies and differences by either direct discussions or mediation, the Parties agree that any such dispute, controversies and differences arising at any time with respect to the subject matter of this Agreement, including the performance or breach of the Agreement, or the interpretation of applicability of the provisions thereof, shall be finally resolved by binding arbitration under the auspices of the China international Economic and Trade Arbitration Committee ("CIETAC"). The arbitration shall be conducted in English, and the place of arbitration shall be Shenzhen, P>R China.

Governing Law.

10. Clause 12 of the Agreement provides that the applicable law shall be the laws of the People's Republic of China ("PRC")." Clause 12 of the Agreement reads as follows:

This Agreement shall be construed, and the respective rights and duties of the Parties hereto are to be determined, according to the laws of the People' principles.

11. The Agreement is a contract of sale of goods between parties whose places of business are in different countries. At the hearing, the Tribunal asked the Parties whether the United Nations Convention on Contracts for the international Sale of Goods (1980) ("CISG") should apply. The Parties did not express any view on the application of CISG at the arbitration hearing or anytime thereafter. Both Parties' have considered all the facts and legal issues in accordance with the principles of the PRC law (emphasis added).

12. The Agreement is governed by PRC law. The pleadings and arbitration hearing are also d in the instant case.

E. NPL vs. MBM: Some Dissenting Opinions on Some Issues—Such as the Application of the CISG[23]

About Material Breach of Contract

The claimant holds that:

The Respondent's intention of not performing its main obligation of supplying a key product (i.e., the T6) on the Agreement was clear, unconditional and had no legal justification and therefore ***constituted an anticipatory and material breach of the Agreement.*** Consequently the Respondent s hall not have a right to demand performance of obligations from the claimant under the Agreement, including the minimum purchase requirements." (See the claimant's Final Submission, p. 7.)

The Respondent was fully aware of the special importance of the T6 to the Claimant and ***therefore the Respondent's breach was never minor but a material breach***. (Id.)

The Respondent is of the following agreements:

Therefore the obligation to supply T6 is not certain, and declining co make T6 available in response to a general request stating no special cases or occasions and shall not constitute anticipatory breach (please refer to Art 108 of contract Law of PRC) (see the Respondent's Final statement,p.4).

... T6 is not able to materially influence the fulfillment of the purpose of the Agreement. Removal of T6 does not constitute breach of the Agreement. (Id.)

The issue of whether the failure or refuse to supply T6 constitutes a material breach of contract is still over there.

There is no similar or explicit concept of material breach in the contract Law of China. But there are some relevant provisions in the CISG.

Art 72 (1): If prior to the date for performance of the contract it is clear that one of the parties will commit a fundamental breach of contract, the other party may declare the contract avoided.

In an international arbitration, when such an issue is raised, we arbitrators would refer to any convention to which that both parties are from contracting states.

2. **About the Application of the CISG**

The initial opinion about the matter of governing law.

I in the "Initial opinion about NPL V MBM (2009-07-29)" expressed some opinion.

About the issue of governing law:

Terms 12. Application law: This Agreement s hall be construed and the respective rights and duties of the parties here to are to be determined, according to the laws of the PR China, without regard to its conflict of law.

What is the nature of the Agreement?

I believe that it is of sale of goods and the dispute arising from it should be classified as a transnational dispute.

The arbitrators should respect the party autonomy or the will of the parties. So according to Terms 12, the law of PRC is the governing law of the Agreement.

The seller is a Chinese legal entity and the Buyer is an Australian legal person. Both China and Australia are contracting states to the CISG.

Art 6 of the CISG: "***The parties may exclude the application of this Convention*** *or, subject to Art 12, derogate from or vary the effect of any of it provisions.*" We arbitrators have not found any acts done by the parties or facts happened in the course of performing the Agreement are of the nature provided in Arts 6 and 12 of the CISG.

Art 12 of the CISG: "*Any provision of Art 11, Art12 or Part 11 of this convention that allows a contract of sale or its modification or termination by agreement or any offer, acceptance or other indication of intention to be made in any form other than in writing does not apply where any party has his place of business in a Contracting State which has made a declaration under Art 96 of this Convention.* ***The parties may not derogate from or vary the effect of this article*** (emphasis added)."

3. **The Silence of the Parties on the Application of the CISG Does not Mean that They Have Reached an Agreement to Exclude the Application of the Convention**

I with the consent of the chairman of the Tribunal, on the date of the oral hearing, stated to the parties some initial opinions regarding to the application of the CISG to the instant case, suggesting that they should think it over and make response to the issue.

The CIETAC is an international arbitration institution and the Tribunal is dealing with an internationalcase.[24]

Though up to now there has no response from the parties to that issue, I suppose, according to Art I of the CISG, the convention s hall not be neglected or it shall be regarded as part of the Governing Law to the instant case.

In the course of the discussion within the Tribunal, my distinguished co-arbitrators hold or accept that as there is explicit provision in Terms 12 (of the Agreement) and the parties have not made any response to the Tribunal's inquiry as to the application of the CISG, only law of PRC is the governing law of the disputed Agreement. As the parties have considered all the facts and matters in accordance with the principles or logic contained in PRC law, Arbitrators should not impose the application of the CISG on the instant case.

I do believe that the arguments above might be sound.

But I have doubt that both parties without referring to any provisions or Articles of the CISG means that both parties' silence implies that they by means of that **have excluded** the application of the CISG.

Is that the only construction of the actor omission of the parties in this regard or in respect of the application of the CISG? could we expect that there are some interpretations more, such as that parties or their attorneys are not very sure about the application of the CISG yet, or they are, could I guess, not familiar with the CISG yet? Or they are lack of experience or practice in respect of the application of the CISG? **Or both parties had been thinking that "I should not take the lead in expressing opinion on the application of the Convention, it is better to wait and see."**

Frankly, I am superficial and have never come across any precedent that silence of the parties relating to the matter of the application of the CISG does mean that there has been or is an agreement concluded by the parties to a particular case that they **excluded** the application of the CISG. Or that silence on the matter even should be regarded as an agreement explicitly excluding the application of the convention.

I suppose there might be some factors relating to the application of the CISG to which that the parties might have considered but I am not aware or could not workout.

After pondering all the questions above, I could not find out any negative answers yet. In addition, I have got no idea why the application of the CISG would have any connection with the function of the conflict rules of China and that might be against the common will of the parties. Therefore, I still believe that the parties to the instant case **have not excluded** the application of the CISG.

As my co-arbitrators disagree with me in respect of the application of the CISG, I would accept the Award on the whole; namely, I would join my co-arbitrators in rendering the award. Nevertheless, I won't give up my viewpoint.

4. **Some Precedent or Similar Case of the Application of the CISG at CIETAC, South China**

Please refer to the award of SHEN M2008114 (Case Two aforesaid). The parties to the case are respectively from Singapore and China. Under the opinion of the Tribunal, the arbitrators in their first piece of opinions (the original is Chinese and my translation):

> The Tribunal is of the view that the claims and defense of the parties show that the instant case is relating to the conclusion and performance of a contract.
>
> Singapore and China are Contracting States to the CISG. According to Art 1 of the CISG, the convention should first of all be applied. Concerning the matter such as the validity of the contract about which there is no provision in the CISG, the relevant provisions of the law agreed by the parties should apply.
>
> Singapore and China are Contracting States to be CISG. According to Art 1 of the CISG, the Convention should first of all be applied. Concerning the matter such as the validity of the contract about which there is no provision in the CISG, the relevant provisions of the law agreed by the parties should apply.
>
> In Art 9 of the disputed contract of the instant case, there is the wording of 'according to PRC laws' in the English text, but there is no such correspondent wording in the Chinese text. At the oral hearing, both parties make quotations from PRC law, namely that the application of PRC law is the common intention of the parties. Therefore the Tribunal holds, as there is provision about the application of law in the contract and parties invoke legal provisions of PRC law, that in respect of the validity of the contract or any matter that there is no provision in the CISG, PRC law applies.

5. **Viewpoints of Specialists, Scholars and Professionals in Respect of the Application of the CISG**

I am to quote more:

> 2.2 Application of Several Laws or Standards
>
> 18-32 Frequently, rather than select and apply one national law, parties or arbitrators choose or apply different laws to govern different aspects of their relationship. This may be simply that the parties have chosen one law to govern the overall formation and interpretation of the content, but another law to govern certain aspects of performance. Further, even where parties agree one law, the parties may claim (e.g. punitive damages) and arbitrators may apply some other law which they conclude applies separate y to the chosen law. (Emphasis added)[25]
>
> 18-34 The acceptance of several laws applying in international commercial arbitration was confirmed by a resolution of the International Law Institute adopted in Athens in 1979…. In that sense, substantive Law codifications, such as Article 6 (of) CISG, anticipate different laws being applied, by allowing parties to exclude the application of the CISG or derogate from or vary the effect of any its provisions. (Emphasis added)[26]

May I make quotation more?

> I. Excluding the CISG"
>
> 2.41 Express and implied exclusion. Unlike ULIS, the CISG applies automatically when Article 1 is satisfied (Emphasis added). The parties do not opt into. It will therefore catch some contracting parties and their advisers by surprise. Nevertheless, Article 6 of the CISG,

besides allowing the parties to vary or modify particular provisions of the CISG, also allows for the exclusion of the CISG altogether. This possibility has been anticipated by the major trading associations sponsoring standard form contracts governed by English Law. They exclude all conventions, even the predecessors of the CISG, namely the 1964 Conventions Hague Conventions that produced ULIS and ULF. New law introduces uncertainty where previously there existed a tolerable measure of certainty. In addition, the CISG is tolerant of breaches of contract to a degree that might not suit the harsher environment of international commodity sales. The CISG rules on risk, moreover, could have a considerable up-setting effect on the transfer of risk in both FOB and CIF commodities contracts. Apart from such unequivocal exclusions, it is a nice question what parties will have to do to exclude to be presented where a standard from contract (as the London-based commodity association forms already do) explicitly excludes the CISG by name. The problem lies with implied exclusions. Some forum States are bound to be more exacting than others in matters of form; they might demand an explicit written exclusion. ULIS, in allowing the parties freedom to exclude the Convention in whole or in part, stated that such exclusion could be express or implied. An attempt to introduce similar language into the CISG failed, so that some doubt hangs over the subject of implied exclusion."

... ultimately, the issue turns upon whether the parties have sufficiently clearly expressed their intention to exclude the CISG under Article 6, (Emphasis added) and intention is a creature of circumstance. Taking the case of parties resident in different Contracting States, under in the absence of the clause the courts of Contracting States would have applied the CISG (Emphasis added), it has to be asked what the parties could have meant by incorporating the chosen of law as it applies to domestic contacts. It is, however, possible that they had in mind the prospect of enforcement in the courts of a non-Contracting State, in which case the choice of law clause would serve the purpose of showing that the law of that State was not to apply.[27] (Emphasis added)

I do hold that the aforesaid quotations are to the point. We should specially take account of Arts 1 and 6 of the CISG.

Please see the following quotation:

[2.6] Whether or not the application of the Convention is compulsory in a member country, once the conditions for its application are satisfied, is an issue subject to debate. On one hand, provisions of the Convention imply that the application of the Convention is compulsory, unless any restriction or deviation from whole or part of the Convention has been agreed expressly by the parties to a contract, in pursuance of art 6 of the Convention (emphasis added). On the other hand, there is nothing in the Convention stating expressly what the consequence is if a court of a member country decides that the Convention is not applicable, for whatever reasons justifies under the relevant domestic law.

In GPL Treatment Ltd V Louisiana Pacific Corp 914 Pacific Report (2d series)682;323 Oregon Reports 116: CLOUT case 137 the Canadian seller sued the US buyer for breach of the contract for the sale of cedar shakes. The sellers commenced their case under the Uniform Commercial Code (UCC) of the United States. During the trial, the sellers attempted to raise the issue of whether the Convention, rather than the UCC, should apply. The trial judge denied the motion on the ground that it was too late for the sellers to rely on the Convention to precede with their case. The sellers won their case all the way against the buyer, and thus the question of whether the Convention should apply appeared to be only a technical question. A dissenting judge of the intermediate appellate court questioned the rationale of the trial judge in denying that the Convention applied, but the Supreme Court did not address this issue at all.

Though this case was decided largely on the basis of the UCC, it may suggest that the application of the Convention may be denied by the implied agreement of the parties, which can be inferred from the acquiescence of the parties to undertake proceedings at the beginning of

> a trial without raising the issue of the Convention. This proposition, if it accurately expresses the trial judge's meaning in GPL Treatment Ltd v Louisiana-Pacific Corp, is inconsistent with art 6 of the Convention. In addition, the court of each member of the Convention must answer the question as to whether or not its country has international obligation implement the Convention within its own territory In light of these arguments, the scales will lean heavily towards the conclusion that the court of a member of the Convention probably has an obligation to apply the Convention, once the conditions for its application have been established, and its application has not been excluded in pursuance of the provisions of the Convention (Emphasis added).[28]

Being an arbitrator in China—the contracting state of the CISG, I am obliged to deal with the issue of application of the convention properly.

6. Concluding Remarks

As there is an issue of fundamental breach of contract in the case and there is no similar concept in respect of that in the PRC contract Law was that in the CISG; that could be dealt with in light of relevant provisions of the CISG; the CISG applies automatically when Art 1 is satisfied; Art 6 of the CISG allows the parties to vary or modify particular provisions of the convention and also allows for the exclusion of the CISG altogether; the parties should have sufficiently clearly expressed their intention to exclude the CISG under Art G; judges or arbitrators of each contracting stare of the CISG have an international obligation to implement the convention within its own territory. So I up to now still hold the CISG is applicable to the instant case.

7. **Additional Remarks About Some Respect of the Viewpoint Held by the Majority on the Application of Law**

I did not have this piece of remark contained in my Dissenting Opinion.

In the Para 11 of the Award quoted above, the majority of the arbitrators state that "The Parties did not express any view on the application of CISG at the arbitration hearing or anytime thereafter. Both Parties' have considered all the facts and legal issue in accordance with the principles of the PRC law." Based on that, they held that the CISG could not apply in the instant case."

I suppose that my co-arbitrators, both are veteran professionals of law, in determining whether the CISG applies to the instant case, one of the criterions or the main criterion, it seems to me, that they have adopted is a subjective judgment of the "subjective intention" of the parties. That sounds logical, but I guess they might have overlooked some objective reality and the basic principle of supremacy of international law. Further, being an arbitrator in dealing with international commercial arbitration of this category, he has to study the CISG.

5 Supplement

A. Some Qualifications for an Arbitrator

Being an arbitrator in handling a case arising from a contract of international sale of goods under the jurisdiction of CIETAC or any arbitration institutions in China, you shall at least before acceptance of the appointment or in the course of the proceedings study or review the CISG, and further study again the Chapter VII The Application of civil Law in Connection with Foreign Elements of the General Principles.

> Further, an arbitrator, in handling transnational commercial case, should consult precedent in this regard.

B. The Old Conception Contained in Art 6 of the Repealed Foreign Economic Contract Law

We should have realized that what stipulated in Art 6 of the Foreign Economic Contract Law is out of date.

Frankly, I did abide by this provision after the law came into effect on July 1, 1985, in my practice at CIETAC. What a pity I didn't realized for a period that actually it was wrong as it was in conflict with the principle that the international law prevails; namely any international treaty concluded or acceded to by the PR China is superior to the PRC domestic legislation.

Furthermore, Art 2 of the Notice on Several Issues Regarding Trial and Enforcement of civil and commercial cases Involving Foreign Interests issued by the Supreme People's Court on April 17, 2000, where it is, inter alia, stated:

> Except otherwise as stipulated in Art 126 of the Contract Law of the PRC or agree by the parties, the applicable law shall be decided properly; international conventions to which China is a Contracting State have priority except the provisions on which China has made reservation, and international usages shall be considered.

In that Notice, the Supreme Court once again reiterates the principle reflected in Art 142 of the General Principles. I have been ashamed as I, in the course of writing this article, once again perused Marcus Article. He has had the aforesaid provisions in the Notice quoted in his article. It seems to me that he is more familiar with the Notice than many Chinese arbitrators on CIETAC panel including me.

We Chinese legal professionals, especially those on the panel of the CIETAC, should have been conscious that after the General principles came into effect on January1, 1987, as there is chapter V III and Art 142, the aforesaid Art 6 of the Foreign Economic Contract Law should have been invalidated for two reasons: the new replaces the old; the Foreign Economic Contract Law was adopted at the Tenth Session of the *Standing Committee* of the sixth National People's Congress on March 21, 1985), the General principles was adopted at the ***Fourth Session*** of the Sixth National People's Congress on April 12, 1986, the new legal provision replaces the old; and in the PRC domestic legislation, the hierarchy of the General principles is higher than that of the Foreign Economic Contract Law.

But even after the Foreign Economic Contract Law and other contract laws were repealed on October 1, 1999, and the New Contract Law came into force on that day, some professionals at CIETAC could not get rid of the influence of that Art 6.

C. Arbitrators on the Panel of CIETAC Should Be Somewhat Familiar with Its Precedent

In Marcus' Article, he at length deals with some aspects of the practice and theory of the CIETAC relating the application of the CISF mainly under some parts respectively under the subheadings: **The determination of and the part played by the proper Law of the Contract in an International Commercial Arbitration involving inter alia the CISG, the application of the CISG and PRC domestic sales and the application of the CISG to sales where parties are from Hong Kong and** (the mainland of) **the PRC, Hong Kong, Macau and** (the mainland of) **the PRC, and Taiwan** (the mainland of) **the PRC**.

Prof Jacobs tells his readers or colleagues especially those from China "*[t]hat there is a very rich source of precedent in both arbitral and court decisions in other jurisdictions in regard to the interpretation of the various Articles of the CISF, CIETAC awards and Chinese Court decisions involving consideration of the CISG apparently pay no regard thereto.*"[29]

He further holds that "[t]he principle of comity would dictate that the Articles of the CISG should, insofar as possible, be given uniform international consistent meanings."[30]

In Marcus' Article, he, under the subheading **A Short Practice guide for the International Commercial Arbitration where the CISG is involved**, summarized quite a few pieces of advice to his colleagues, especially those on the panel of the CIETAC. I would like to cite one:

> 12.3 Obviously, the Arbitral Tribunal will have a thorough knowledge of the Convention and, if all possible, a working knowledge of the relevant writings on the Articles of the Convention, arbitral and court decisions concerning those Articles.[31]

I suppose those attorneys on behalf of their principals to the cases arising from international sale of goods under the jurisdiction of the Chinese arbitration in situations should be at least aware that there are similar viewpoints regarding the application of the CISG in the international commercial circle and would take account of them in their practice.

More arbitrators of common law background come to join hands with their Chinese colleagues in handling cases under the jurisdiction of the CIETAC and other arbitration institutions of China, especially those ones who are familiar with the CISG and having experience in this regard, I expect, would promote the practice to follow the principles established by precedent in China.

I quite agree with the viewpoint of prof Jacobs that "*Without the CISG, Chinese domestic legislation, by itself, was not comprehensive enough because it did not cover several important features of international sales. The CISG has corrected those vacancies and, due to global and uniform acceptance and application thereof, has had numerous positive impacts on promoting foreign trade and supporting further economic development of China*."[32]

Notes

1. Marcus S Jacobs QC, International commercial Arbitration In Australia, Law and Practice, Thomson Reuters, (loose leaves), p. 2816.
2. Marcus S Jacobs QC, Prof. Katrin Curbush-Sabine and Philip Bambagiotti, The CISG in Australian-TO-Date an Illusive Quest for Global Harmonisation: Carried in Commercial Arbitration Law Repot (Han Jian and Lin Yifei as the chief editors),CITI C Publishing House, China, Feb, 2005, p. 142.
3. Id. P149.
4. 1995057 FCR 216; (1995) ACSR 153; (1995) 13 ACLC 776, re-quoted from the article of Id. p.152.
5. Id. pp. 154–155.
6. Id., p. 157.
7. Id., p. 158.
8. Id., p. 158.
9. Id., pp. 168–170.
10. According to the provision of Art 19 of the Civil Procedure Law of the PRC, an intermediate people's court shall have jurisdiction as court of first instance over a major case involving foreign interests.
11. Art 16 of the PRC Arbitration Law stipulates that an arbitration agreement shall include, inter alia, some arbitration institute selected by the parties; Art 18 of that law provides that if an arbitration institute is not agreed upon by the parties in their arbitration agreement, the parties may reach a supplementary agreement; otherwise the arbitration agreement shall be invalid.
12. The Law of PRC On protecting consumers' Rights and Interests, Art 44 provides that: Business operators shall, if the commodities or services they supply have caused damages to the properties of consumers, bear civil liabilities by repair, remanufacture, replacement, return of goods, make-up for the short commodities return of payment for goods and services, or compensation for losses and so on as demanded by consumers. If consumers and business operators have otherwise agreed upon, such agreements shall be fulfilled.
13. Art 61 of the PRC Contract Law: Where, after the contract becomes effective, the parties did not agree on or the agreement was unclear regarding quality, price or remuneration and place of performance, etc., the parties may agree to supplement it; where no supplemental agreement is reached, it shall be determined according to the relevant provisions of the contract or trade custom—quoted from the English version by the Harmony Consultants Ltd.
14. Art 62(1)of the PRC Contract Law: If any ambiguity in relation to any matter in the contract cannot be resolved under the provision of Art 61 of the Law, the following provisions shall apply: (1) If quality requirements are unclear, the State standards or trade standards shall apply; if there is no State or trade standard, the normal standard or a specific standard that satisfies the purpose

of the contract shall apply—quoted from the English version by the Harmony Consultants Ltd.

15. It is quoted from the English version by the Harmony Consultants Led. Colleagues of mine believe that the Harmony version is more accurate or better than most of the English versions published in China, for instance the English version of the same Arts: Chapter VIII Application of Law in civil Relations with Foreigners Art 142:

    The application of law in civil relations with foreigners shall be determined by the provisions in this chapter.

    If any international treaty concluded or acceded to by the People's Republic of China contains provisions differing from those in the civil laws of the People's Republic of China, the provisions of the international treaty shall apply, unless the provisions are ones on which the People's Republic of China has announced reservations.

    International practice may be applied to matters for which neither the law of the People's Republic of China nor any international treaty concluded or acceded to by the People's Republic of China has any provisions. (http://e.iciba.com/space-4179841-do-blog-id-1035839.html).

16. Marcus S Jacobs, The United Nations Convention For The International sales of Goods 1980 (The Vienna Convention) and International commercial Arbitration by Marcus s Jacobs, carried in commercial Arbitration Review, Vol. 2, university of International Business and Economic press, China, Sep. 2009, pp.104–141.
17. See Fan Yang, the Application of CISG in the current PRC Law and CIETAC Arbitration practice, http:/lc is gw3.law.pace.edu/cisg/biblio/yang2/html. The author re-quoted from Prof Jacobs' Article, p. 115.
18. Quoted from Laws and Regulations of the people's Republic of China Governing Foreign-Related Matters compiled by the Bureau of Legislative Affairs of the State Council of the People's Republic of China and published by the China Legal System Publishing House. July 1991. (http://www.oklink.net/flfg/law/70502.htm). I have got another translation of this Art 6 from A collection of Legal Literature on Foreign Investment in China (Internal Circulation), computing center, the Ministry of Foreign Trade and Economic cooperation of PR China (that might have been composed or done in 1999):

    "When an international treaty that relates to a contract and that the People's Republic of China has concluded or joined contains provisions that differ from the law of the People's Republic of China, the provisions of the said treaty shall be applied, except for clauses in respect of which the People's Republic of China has declared reservation."

19. See Frank N. Fisanich, Note & Comment: Application of the U.N. sales convention in Chinese International commercial Arbitration: Implication for International uniformity, 10Am. Rev. Int'l Arb. 1999. Note 90 to the text. The case 1 means one of the CIETAC awards, that the scholar got access to, selected

and translated by someone in America from an official collection of CIETAC awards published by CIETAC.

20. Yanming Huang, " Grasp The key TO The case," Mealey's International Arbitration Report, vol 17, Issue8, August2002, pp. 30–62, especially "X, B Law Application, C Some Comments About The Applying the CISG By Chinese Arbitrators And Lawyers and D Could The commodity Inspection Law Apply TO The Instant Case Together with The CISG, pp. 53–60.
21. This part is quoted from the Final Award. The author has adopted some amendments to the original for the purpose of not revealing the secrets of the parties.
22. That abbreviation is somewhat different from the one I have adopted.
23. This is the final version of the Dissenting opinion by the author as a co-arbitrator of the Tribunal in handing the case and it was rendered by the author and sent to the parties with the Final Award by the secretariat of the CIETAC, South China. Some amendments have been made so that the commercial secrets of the parties should not be revealed and some corrections or adjustment have been made so that the Dissenting opinion as apart would be in line with the whole article.
24. About the status of the CIETAC in the circle of international commercial arbitration, professionals might have various opinions. For example, some colleagues comment on it by saying that "CIETAC has for several years reported an annual number of requests for arbitration well in excess of that of the ICC. Almost all of these cases involved one Chinese and one non-Chinese party. But the proposition that CIETAC administers the largest number of international arbitrations cannot be taken seriously. For one thing, until CIETAC reveals the amounts in dispute, observes will assume that most of its cases involve modest sums of money. Secondly and more importantly, CIETAC is a recognizable Chinese institution; most foreigners accept CIETAC arbitration with considerable reluctance, as a matter of negotiating pressure. Until CI ETAC can point to cases where both side are non-Chinese, and the dispute in unconnected with China, it is not even in the running with ICC" (see W. Laurence Craig, William W Park and Jan Paulsson, International Chamber of Commercial Arbitration, third edition, Oceana Publications, Ins, 2000, p. 3. The quoter respects the three colleagues' position and does not think that their comments or viewpoints quoted have no grounds. Further the quoter has to make it clear that he did not have this quotation contained in his Dissenting opinion attached to the Final Award)—the Author.
25. See Julian D M Lew QC, Loukas A Mistelis and Stefa n M Kroll, Comparative International commercial Arbitration, Kluwere Law International, 2003, p. 448. 26.
26. Id.
27. See Michael Bridge, Chapter 2: The CISG: General Issues, The International Sale of Goods Law and Practice, Oxford University Press, 1999, pp. 64–65.
28. See John Shijian MO, International commercial Law, China Legal system publishing House and LexisNexis, 2004 (third edition), pp. 79–80.
29. Id. p. 112.

30. Id.
31. Id Note 16, p. 136.
32. Id. p. 107. ■

Two Notes on the Application of the CISG to Cases Under the Jurisdiction of the CIETAC South China

1 Introduction

In the past decades, there have been a great number CIETAC arbitral awards applying the United Nations Convention On Contracts For The International Sale of Goods ("CISG") to contracts between parties located in the PR China and other Contracting States; to the contracts between parties respectively from two Contracting States of the Convention; to the contracts between parties from the Hong Kong Special Administrative Region, the Macau Special Administrative Region and the Mainland China; to the contract between parties located in Taiwan Region and in the Mainland China.[1]

But up to now I have got no access to any books based on those awards compiled by the CIETAC for its arbitrators as essential materials or supplementary reading for training its arbitrators so that they would become international minded. What a pity!

I suppose that the executives of the CIETAC should spend part of their time and energy on this piece of job.

Reading or studying CIETAC awards, you might get the impression that the awards, on the whole, are short of personality. You could hardly find out any different viewpoints among the three co-arbitrators, no matter how slight or wide the divergent opinions among them on some of the issues in a case are. Nevertheless, CIETAC awards are of many strong points but the author does not deal with them in this article.

Let's refer the Arbitration Rules of the CIETAC (effective as from May 1, 2005) Article 43 Making Award:

This commentary was published in Mealey's International Arbitration Report, Vol. 27, # 9, September 2012, pp. 19–29.

The author is grateful to Ms Qingwen Jiang with SCIA for her assistance in re-locating some materials relating to the second case in this article.

Y. Huang, *Commentaries on Commercial Arbitration in Modern China*, Modern China and International Economic Law, https://doi.org/10.1007/978-981-95-0168-7_14

> (4) Where a case is examined by an arbitral tribunal composed of three arbitrators, the award shall be rendered by all three arbitrators or a majority of the arbitrators. A written dissenting opinion shall be docketed into file and may be attached to the award but it shall not form apart of the award.
>
> (5) Where the arbitral tribunal cannot reach majority opinion, the award shall be rendered in accordance with the presiding arbitrator's opinion. The written opinion of other arbitrators shall be docketed into the file and may be attached to the award, but shall not form a party of the award.

For an award rendered by all three co-arbitrators or a majority of a tribunal, you could not locate any different viewpoints or opinions on an issue or a question. That is to say that the different opinions on issues of the co-arbitrators are not recorded or reflected in awards rendered by the tribunals handling cases under the jurisdiction of CIETAC. You could only find out the common consensus of a three-member tribunal or the majority, though now and then the pieces of opinion are actually a compromise reached after some rounds of consultations among the three co-arbitrators. You could hardly read out any individual characteristics, styles and various views of each arbitrator on some issue or question, even though actually the divergence among the three ones is common and of no substantial, so narrow and might not lead to different conclusion and decision. In a word, the different opinion would not ruin the effect or finality of an award at all.

English readers might have access to various CIETAC awards,[2] though it is limited. In this commentary, I would like to recall how I put forward my suggestions and what I stressed on the application of the CISG, hoping to show that usually how the different views would be accepted by the majority of a tribunal. A short article could only touch on this topic briefly.

Case One: A Mainland Seller V. A Hong Kong Buyer

Question: Does A Transnational Trade Contract Between A Seller From The Mainland Of China And A Buyer From The Hong Kong Special Administrative Region, With Rotterdam As The Destination Of The Subject Matter Containing An Explicit Proper Law Clause Of Applying The Chinese Con- tract Law Exclude The Application Of The CISG?

I. Overview of the Case

The China International Economic and Trade Arbitration Commission, South China Commission (CIETAC South China and since June 16, 2012, also named as Shenzhen Court of International Arbitration—SCIC, the latter name would in near future substitute the former one) on October 21, 2010, received a case arising from a contract for the transnational sale of goods.

The case was classified and numbered as SHENR2010147.

I was a member of the Tribunal of three arbitrators, handling the case, formed on December 9, 2010.

The final Award numbered as [2011] Zhongguo Maozhon Shen Cai Zi No.59 was issued on June 9, 2011. According to the decisions of the Tribunal, the losing Respondent should automatically perform the decisions within 30 days. But the

Respondent failed to abide by the decisions. The wining Claimant by the end of 2011 intended to enforce the award, asking some solicitors from Hong Kong for advice. So the case and award are known to the public domain ever after.

II. Submission of the Request for Arbitration

On July 21, 2008, the Seller Chanji Mineral Resources Trading Co. Ltd located in Changsha, Hunan Province of the Mainland of China and the Buyer XXX Metals& Minerals Co. Ltd located in the Hong Kong Special Administrative Region of the PR China (though there was the situation or in the case mentioned above, the author prefers not to reveal the Buyer's real name) entered into the Contract (numbered CJ2008-07-01, the series number within the Seller) by means of fax.

When there was dispute and could not be settled through amicable negotiation between the parties, the Seller represented by a lawyer Mr. Liu with V & T Law Firm located in Shenzhen according to the arbitration clause in the Contract referred the case to the CIETAC South China, claiming the losses suffered by it resulting from the breach of contract by the Buyer and the devaluation of the goods under the Contract, losses pertaining to the cargo storage charge, etc.

III. Clauses of the Contract Closely Relating to the Dispute

The Contract is very brief, consisting of only two pages with 17 short clauses. It begins with this sentence: The Buyer agrees to buy and the Seller agrees to sell the goods in accordance with the Contract Law of the People's Republic of China. In the following parts of this commentary, the provision is referred to as 'the provision of the application of the Contract Law of China.'

The subject matter of the Contract is 120MT Medium Carbon Ferro Manganese, the unit price is USD3640/MT CFR Rotterdam and the total amount is USD 436,800,00; Loading Port is Changsha/Shanghai/ Huangpu Port, PR China; Shipment (Delivery): On or Before August 30, 2008; Inspection: Inspection by CIQ (the abbreviation of the Entry-Exit Inspection and Quarantine of the People's Republic of China—the author) taken as final; Payment: by D/P at sight; Shipment: the carrying vessel shall be provided by the Seller, partial shipment and transshipment are all allowed; Arbitration: ...The case shall then be submitted to (the) CIETAC.

IV. Main Content of the Request for Arbitration

In the Request for Arbitration, the Seller Claimant states that on August 23, 2008, it loaded the cargo at Changsha Port and then delivered some certificates of quality and quantity and certificate of origin issued by the Entry-Exit Inspection and Quarantine Bureau of the PR China, the bill of loading, packing list issued by a shipping corporation limited, commercial invoice, shipping advice of the Seller itself to the Buyer Respondent.

On August 29, 2008, the Seller issued a collection order to China Construction Bank, Hunan Province Branch and HSBC (the Hong Kong and Shanghai Banking Corporation Limited) was appointed as the collecting bank.

On September 24, 2008, the Buyer required that as the market depreciation, so the fixed price of the goods should be reduced. In that case, the Seller reduced the unit price from USD3640/MT to USD3560/MT, and consequently reduced the total price USD436,800.00 to USD427,200.00.

On September 26, 2008, the Seller received a copy of an instruction from the Buyer to HSBC, advising the bank to pay the Seller the sum of USD427200.00, the words going "to debit the bill amount to our account no. xxxxx accrued interest and charges (if any) to our account no. xxxxxx." Actually the Buyer did not pay that sum.

On October 1, the cargo reached its destination Rotterdam. As the provision of payment by D/P at sight in the Contract was not complied with by the Buyer, the cargo could not be timely unloaded and storied properly. Therefore there was some demurrage charge.

On October 10 and 15, 2008, the Seller sent letters by courier to the Buyer, urging the latter to perform its obligations under the Contract. But there was no active result; therefore the Seller had on October 27 to store the cargo in a warehouse of a Rotterdam corporation.

On October 17, 2008, the Seller informed its collecting bank of withdrawing the set of documents (including the marine bill of loading and insurance policy, commercial invoice, packing list and certificate of origin and so on). And On October 21, 2008, it received the set of documents.

On November 19, 2009, the Seller once more urged the Buyer to comply with the provisions of the Contract by fax with some short notices together with some invoices relating to the storage charges issued by the Rotterdam corporation.

In the Request for Arbitration, the Seller states that while the cargo was stored in the warehouse in Rotterdam, its staff members respectively on December 10, 2008, and May 27, 2009, and March 22, 2010, sent brief notes by fax to the Respondent, warning that if the Buyer did not perform its obligations under the Contract, the Seller would resell the cargo to a third party and would take legal action for the breach on the part of the Buyer. Nevertheless, the Respondent took no notice of those notes.

On March 22, 2010, on adverse market, the Seller was forced in Rotterdam to resell the subject matter of the Contract to a third party; the unit price was USD2200/MT ex warehouse Rotterdam, duty unpaid. The total resale price was USD263,758.00 (the original total price was USD436,800.00).

On May 4, 2010, the Seller by courier served a letter to the Buyer, briefly recalling the course of the transaction, informing the recipient of the fact that the Seller for the purpose of reducing the loss had resold the subject matter of the Contract to a third party in Rotterdam, demanding the Buyer before May 15 to negotiate. But the Buyer turned a deaf ear to the matter.

V. The Parties' Different Views on the Issue of Proper Law

The first oral hearing was held on January 21 and the second on March 8, 2011.

About the issue of proper law, the attorney of the Seller Claimant in the course of the procedures and in the oral hearings holds and persists that both the CISG and the Contract Law of the PR China apply to the instant case.

That attorney and his assistant after the second oral hearing in their written Statement (of Attorney) dated on March16, 2011, submitted to the Tribunal explicitly state their viewpoints on all the main issues of the case, first of all saying that according to Art 93 of the CISG:

> (1) If a Contracting State has two or more territorial units in which, according to its constitution, different systems of law are applicable in relating to the matters dealt within this Convention, it may, at the time of signature, ratification, acceptance, approval or accession, declare that this Convention is to extend to all its territorial units or only to one or more of them, and may amend its declaration by submitting another declaration at any time.
>
> (4) If a Contract State makes no declaration under paragraph (1) of this article, the Convention is to extend to all territorial units of that State.

On the contrary, the attorney of the Respondent, in the course of the oral hearings when debating on some issues, insists on his viewpoint, saying that according to the explicit provision of the Contract, only the Contract Law of the (mainland) of the PR China applies to the case and the application of the CISG is excluded. He in his Statement of Attorney dated on March 15, 2011, does not touch on the issue of proper law at all.

VI. Expounding on the Issue of Proper Law in the Award of [2011] Zhongguo Maozhon Shen Cai Zi No.59

2 The First Round of Discussion Within the Tribunal

After each oral hearing, the members of the Tribunal do discuss the merits of the case and matters concerned. About the issue of proper law, I hold that the provision of the application of the Contract Law of China does not exclude the application of the CISG, and the disputed Contract is of international nature, though I have used the term of "Transnational Trade Contract" above, and the instant arbitration is within the international category. My viewpoint is based on the relevant provision in UNCITRAL MODEL Law on International Commercial Arbitration (1985).

"Article 1—Scope of Arbitration

(3) An arbitration is international if:

(b) one of the following places is situated outside the State in which the parties have their places of business:

(ii) anyplace where a substantial part of the obligations of the commercial relationship is to be performed or the place with which the subject-matter of the dispute is most closely connected."

In the award initially drafted by the presiding arbitrator under the heading of the Opinion of the Tribunal, the first sub-heading is About the Application of Law to the Instant Case:

> The parties to the case have got the agreement provided in their Contract: 'The Buyer agrees to buy and the seller agrees to sell the goods in accordance with the Contract Law of the People's Republic of China.' According to that agreement, the Tribunal confirms that the governing law of the present case is the law of the mainland of P. R. China.

I suggested that the following paragraph should be added:

> The Contract of the instant case is of transnational sale of goods, the parties to it have chosen the law of the main- land of the P. R. China as the governing law, and P. R. China is a Contracting State of the CISG. Since the parties to the Contract for international sale of goods have chosen the law of the P. R. China, China is a Contracting State of the CISG, it is an established principle that a country has adhered a convention or treaty, it is submitted that the convention or the treaty would be incorporated and become part of the domestic law of that country, therefore, the CISG should be applied to the disputed Contract alongside with the Contract Act of the P. R. China, as the CISG has been incorporated and become part of the P. R. China Law.

VII. The Second Round of Discussion

When the second draft award was available, I found there were no words on the application of the CISG; I again aired my opinion in writing to my co-arbitrators. The main points are as follows:

> The Contract is written in English, showing, inter alia, that it is a contract of transnational sale of goods.
>
> About the application of law, I do remember that the co-arbitrators did have reached consensus that the CISG applies to the instant case. In addition to my previous written opinion, we should not neglect Art 142 of the General Principles of Civil Law of the PRC.
>
> Chapter VIII Application of Law in Civil Relations with Foreigners

"Article 142

The application of law in civil relations with foreigners shall be determined by the provisions in this chapter.

If any international treaty concluded or acceded to by the People's Republic of China contains provisions differing from those in the civil laws of the People's Republic of China, the provisions of the international treaty shall apply, unless the provisions are ones on which the People's Republic of China has announced reservations. International practice may be applied to matters for which neither the law of the People's Republic of China nor any international treaty concluded or acceded to by the People's Republic of China has any provisions."[3]

(The application of civil law in connection with foreign elements shall be in accordance with the provisions of this CHAPTER..

If any international treaty concluded or acceded to by the People's Republic of China contains provisions different from those in the civil laws of the People's Republic of China, the provisions of the international treaty shall prevail, unless the provisions are those which the People's Republic of China has expressed reservations.

International practice may be applied on matters for which neither the law of the People's Republic of China nor any international treaty concluded or acceded to by the People's Republic of China has provided for—quoted from the English Version of the Harmony Consultants Limited).

"About the construction of the said Art 142, we should not be neglect that the CISG is of higher rank than that of the Contract Law in legal hierarchy (of the P. R. China domestic legislation). In the practice of the CIETAC, up to now a great number of arbitral awards applying the CISG to contracts between parties to the cases under its jurisdiction respectively from Hong Kong Special Administrative Regions, Marco Special Administrative Region, Taiwan region and the mainland of P. R. China,[4] Hong Kong and Hong Kong.[5] In the course of the proceedings, the viewpoints of the attorney of the Seller on the application of the CISG are of sound grounds."

> Only applying the Contract Law would not lead to different decisions in the instant case, but arbitrators of this Tribunal, in dealing with a case arising from a transnational trade contract, should have this eyeshot.
>
> During the hearings, the attorneys of the parties did debate on the application of the CISG. The attorney of the Seller in his statement first of all deals with the matter of the application of the CISG. Even if our Tribunal would hold that only the Contract Law of the mainland of the P. R China applies to the instant case, we are obliged to make clear the different viewpoints of the parties in this regard. Further the Tribunal has to explain why the CISG does not apply to the instant case, if we were of this opinion.

In the final award, under the heading the Opinions of the Tribunal and the Sub-Heading about the Application of law in the instant case, the wording goes:

> It is provided in the Contract that: 'The Buyer agrees to buy and the Seller agrees to sell the goods in accordance with the Contract Law of the People's Republic of China.' According to this provision, the Tribunal confirms that the governing law to the instant case is the law of (the mainland of) the People's Republic of China. The Contract of the instant case is of transnational trade; and the parties have chosen the law of (the mainland of) the People's Republic of China; China is a Contracting State to the CISG, therefore it could be deemed that the CISG also applies to the Contract, as it has been incorporated and become part of the domestic law of the Mainland of P. R. China.

When I recall what I did with the application of the CISG in dealing with the case above I couldn't help thinking of what my colleague Marcus S Jacobs QC, a pre-eminent commercial arbitral expert, says regarding to treat the CISG as a code but not just a set of decisional rules:

> Indeed, it will take a conscious effort on the part of a judge, whether from the common law tradition or other- wise, to overcome years of legal training and experience and a natural bias toward a particular and familiar legal tradition and to become internationally minded (emphasis added).[6]
>
> What I want to add is that the "on part of a judge" should be as "on the part of a judge and an arbitrator as well." In the following case, one might come to a conclusion that a lawyer from a civil law country to become internationally minded in this regard should take a conscious effort.

Case Two: A Chinese Buyer V. An American Seller

Question: Does An International Trade Contract Between A Chinese Buyer And An American Seller With The Place Of Arbitration In The PR China But Containing No Proper Law Clause Mean That The Application Of The CISG Is Excluded?

I. Briefs of the Case Relating to a Purchase Contract Between a Chinese Company and an American Company

A buyer located in Guangzhou, Guangdong Province, PR China, and a seller located in Pittsburgh, Pennsylvania, USA, on July 15, 2008 by means of fax entered into a

Purchase Contract in Chinese and English languages. It is provided in the Contract that the subject matter is a Diagnostic Ultrasound Scanner: GE Voluson 730 Expert with standard BTO5 software including 4D View PC Software ...The value of it is USD93,500.00, and the terms of payment are 100% advance T/T to the account of the Seller specified in the Contract.

The contract is based on the standard terms supplied by the buyer. That must be the contract with standard terms adopted by the buyer in most of its transactions.

When the names of the parties are mentioned below, the pseudonyms respectively for the Buyer and Seller are Guangzhou HI Ltd and MD INC.

Some clauses closely relating to the dispute are as follows:

Clause 13 Inspection and Claims: After arrival of the contracted goods, the Buyer shall apply to the China Entry-Exit Inspection and Quarantine Bureau for a preliminary inspection of the Contract goods in respect of their quality, specifications and quantity/weight. If any discrepancies are found by the Bureau regarding the specifications or quality or quantity/weight, except those for which either the insurance company of the air company (shipping company) is responsible, the Buyer shall, within 120 days after discharge or the contract goods at the port of destination, having the right either to reject the contract goods or to claim against the Seller on the strength of the inspection certification issued by the Bureau.

Clause 14 Settlement of Claim: Replace the defective contract goods with new ones, which confirm to the specifications, quality and performance as stipulated in this contract, and bear all expenses incurred to and direct losses sustained by the Buyer. The Seller shall guarantee the quality of the replacement of the Contract goods for 90 days as specified in Clause 16 hereof.

Clause 16 Guarantee of Quality: The Seller guarantees that the commodity(ies) hereof is made of the best materials with first-class workmanship, band-new, and complies in all respects with quality, performance and specification stipulated in this Contract and confirms to the technical manual of the commodity(ies) contracted. The guarantee period shall be 90 days after the acceptance.

18. Arbitration: All disputes in connection with this Contract or the execution thereof shall be amicable settle through negotiation in case no settlement can be reached between the two parties. The case under disputes shall be submitted to the Foreign Trade Arbitration Commission of the China Council for the Promotion of International Trade for arbitration...[7]

There is no applicable law clause in the Contract. When there was a dispute, the Buyer as the Claimant referred the case in accordance with the Arbitration Clause to CIETAC South China for arbitration. The case was numbered as SHEN M2010090.

II. Claims of the Claimant

In the Request for Arbitration submitted on June 10, 2010, the Buyer Claimant states that the subject matter—Diagnostic Ultrasound Scanner: GE Voluson 730 (serial number: A14206) according to the inspection certificate issued by the Entry-Exit Inspection and Quarantine of the People's Republic of China, Guangzhou, on October 27, 2008, was once imported (into China) in May 2007 for exhibitions in several cities and was displayed and used for scanning models for several times, it returned abroad in March 2008. The Scanner is thus a used one but not in conformity with the requirement provided in Clause 16 of the Contract. So the Buyer Claimant claims that the Seller Respondent:

1. Shall take back the used medical apparatus and delivers another brand-new one in line with the specifications specified in the Contract; if the Respondent doesn't re-deliver a brand-new apparatus to replace the former one, it has to refund the total price USD93,500.00, the customs duties RMB32,264.70 plus VAT RMB115,184.98;
2. All the fees and expenses incurred relating to the taking back the used apparatus and delivering a new one should be borne by the Respondent;
3. Shall pay a penalty of USD 40,105.00 (for the time being calculated to June 10, 2010) to the Claimant;
4. Shall be held responsible for the expenses of RMB40,000.00 of legal fees for engaging lawyer by the Claimant in handling this case;
5. Shall bear the notary fees of RMB5330.00 incurred to the Claimant in dealing with this case;
6. Shall bear the arbitration fees.

The Respondent fails to appear at the oral hearing other than on October 4, 2010, by email sending a cover letter to the Secretariat of the CIETAC, South China, saying that it was a broker only. Before the shipment it had informed the Buyer of the serial number of the apparatus (the Buyer in a note by email mentioned below to the secretary to the Tribunal uses the word "equipment"). The Buyer should have been able to check it with the Customs.

The oral hearing was held on September 20, 2010. And as after the oral hearing the legal representative as well as the one who on behalf of the Seller signed the Purchase Contract sent the secretary to the Tribunal the said note, and the secretary did consulting the Tribunal in October 2010 made a response. So the Tribunal did wait for a period, expecting that the Respondent might need to submit its official defense and there would be another oral hearing. So the award was issued after some delay on April 7, 2011.

III. The Viewpoints on the Application of Law and the CISG

I would like only touch on some but quite different views on the application of law and the CISG as well.

Initially, the Claimant's attorney deals with the matter of the law application, only focusing on the application of the law of PR China, holding that the Contract was finally concluded in Guangzhou, and it was mainly on the terms and conditions prepared by the Claimant; the place of delivery was Guangzhou; the place of arbitration is in China; therefore according to the doctrine of the most significant relationship, the Chinese law is applicable to this Contract.

As to the question raised by the Tribunal whether the CISG is applicable to the instant case, the attorney of the Claimant sets forth his viewpoint and reasons, saying that the parties have incorporated no governing law clause in the Contract; Art 6 of the CISG provides that "The parties may exclude the application of this Convention," since the parties explicitly express that the CISG is not applicable, that is to say that they have excluded the application of the Convention; therefore the CISG is not applicable to the present case; further as the Respondent refuses to appear at the oral hearing, that means that it gives up the right of choosing the Convention. Therefore according to the doctrine of the most significant relationship, the applicable law is Chinese law.

IV. The Brief Exposition of the Tribunal on the Proper Law of the Case

In the award, under the heading "Opinion of the Tribunal" and the sub-heading "Proper Law of the Case," the arbitrators first introduced the viewpoint of the Claimant's attorney as referred to above, and then presented the arbitrators' response to that viewpoint. The Tribunal of three arbitrators hold the above-mentioned viewpoint and reasons are of one-sided. China and America are Contracting States of the CISG. Parties to a contract are permitted to exclude the application of it, but the exclusion shall be explicit and their willingness shall be fully and clearly expressed.

Art 1(1) of the CISG provides that "This Convention applies to contracts of sale of goods between parties whose places of business are in different States:

(a) when the States are Contracting States; or
(b) when the rules of private international law lead to the application of the law of a Contracting state."

The CISG applies automatically when Art 1 is satisfied.

After inquiring into the matters, the Tribunal confirms that the parties to the instant case have not explicitly excluded the application of the CISG. According to provisions in Art 1 (1) (a), the Convention applies to contracts of sale of goods between parties whose places of business are in different States and when the States are Contracting States; the parties to the disputed Purchase Contract whose places of business are respectively in China and America, and both China and America are the Contracting States; therefore, the Tribunal holds that the CISG applies to the instant case.

The Tribunal further states that in applying the Convention, one should also take account of the characteristic of the Convention as of permissive legislation. Art 6 of it:

> The parties may exclude the application of this Convention or, subject to article 12, derogate from or vary the effect of any of its provisions.

That means that the parties to a contract may exclude the application the Convention or, subject to Art 12, derogate from or vary the effect of any of its provisions or even to have their clause re-drawn, so that to changing the meaning or the effect of the provisions of the Convention. If the parties had any variations incorporated in their contract, those varied agreements should be prevailing.

Specially mentioning the viewpoint above relating to the characteristic of the Convention as of permissive legislation was the idea of the presiding arbitrator of the Tribunal, Prof Xiao/Zhiming, a former deputy chairman of the CIETAC. Though actually neither the parties exclude the application of the Convention, nor them derogate from or vary the effect of any provisions of the Convention.

V. An Episode—A Replay by the Secretary to the Tribunal to the Respondent, Showing Communication Barriers Between Languages, Cultures and Different Jurisdictions

A. The Seller Respondent Failing to Make Any Defense and Absent from the Oral Hearing but Thereafter by Email Inquiring into the Case

The Seller Respondent did not submit any defense or materials after it had received all the arbitral notices, materials or documents by courier.

On September 20, 2010, the Tribunal held an oral hearing, the Seller Respondent failed to delegate attorney or representative to appear. Nevertheless after the oral hearing the secretary to the Tribunal informed the Respondent of that. Its legal representative Mr. L on October 8, 2010, sent a letter to the secretary by email asking for some information about the case:

> Please advise me as to the status of MA Inc. in this arbitration if I send signed copies of the information to you? I want to provide CIETAC with reference information. However, I do not want to change the status of MA Inc. in this arbitration. I do not want to enter into the arbitration process as a legal participant because the company cannot afford the costs of the process. Also, I do not think this case should have been deemed appropriate to beheld for arbitration based upon the information I am attempting to provide. I had hoped that my emailed information would allow CIETAC to check the documentation provided by Guangzhou HI Ltd and to see that the import history of the equipment was not required in the contract.

I would mention the response of the secretary to the Tribunal, for the purpose to reveal how arbitration is conducted under the jurisdiction of the CIETAC South China, wishing that that would enable colleagues of the commercial arbitration circle, businessmen and laymen to have a limited view of the practice of arbitration of the arbitral institution.

B. Prevision of the CIETAC Rules of 2005 and 2012 Pertaining Default and Making a Default Award

I would like to quote the provision relating to Default in the Arbitration Rules of the CIETAC, effective as from May 1, 2005 ("2005 Rules").

"Article 34 Default"

"1. If the Claimant fails to appear at an oral hearing without showing sufficient cause for such failure, or with- draws from an on-going oral hearing without the permission of the arbitral tribunal, the Claimant may be deemed to have withdrawn its request for Arbitration. In such a case, if the Respondent had filed a counterclaim, the arbitral tribunal shall proceed with the hearing of the counter- claim and make a default award (emphasis added)."

"2. If the Respondent fails to appear at an oral hearing without showing sufficient cause for such failure, or with- draws from an on-going oral hearing without the permission of the arbitral tribunal, the arbitral tribunal may proceed with the hearing of the counterclaim and make a default award (emphasis added). In such a case, if the Respondent has filed a counterclaim, the Respondent may be deemed to have withdrawn its counterclaim."

Now the said article is re-numbered as Article 37 Default incorporated in the CIETAC Arbitration Rules effective as of May 1, 2012, the wording remains unchanged or exactly the same as that quoted above.

What a pity, a mistake, in my humble opinion, would remain and uncorrected for some decades. I am to deal with it below. C. What the Term of Default Judgment Means in the Common Law and the Misunderstanding of and Mistranslation of It in China

Let us refer to common law dictionary and have a clear-cut understanding of the original meaning of the Default Judgment (Award).

Default judgment 1. A judgment entered againsta defendant who has failed to plead or otherwise defend against the plaintiff's claim (emphasis added). 2. A judgment entered as a penalty against a party who does not comply with an order, especially an order to comply with a discovery request (emphasis added).[88]

Default judgment, a judgment against a party for failing to appear against a party for failing to appear or to proceed with a case (emphasis added).[9]

The original meaning of "default judgment" is that a defendant fails due to the direct cause that he has failed to appear or to proceed with a case or he does not comply with an order, especially an order to comply with a discovery request.

But in China, a claimant could not win directly due to his plaintiff's failing to appear or to proceed with the case. If the plaintiff is absent, the tribunal or the arbitrator(s) dealing with or the case would continue the proceedings and make an award on the evidence before it or him (them). Namely, a plaintiff's absence from hearing is not as serious as that in a common law country, which would not be the sole factor that results to the satisfaction of all the claims of the claimant.

At CIETAC, one the one hand, a plaintiff's absence from an oral hearing or failing to submit his defense has never been the sole factor or direct cause for losing his case; on the other hand, a claimant's claims would not be all satisfied due to the absence of the plaintiff from the hearing or failing to submit his defense.

Now I would turn to the response of the secretary to the Tribunal. On November8, 2010, the secretary after consulting the presiding arbitrator by email sending her draft letter to the other two members of the Tribunal. The main text is as following:

"Please be advised that my opinion is conveyed as an arbitration secretary neutral to both parties, with the aim of providing basic arbitration information for you to consider.

(1) Jurisdiction

According to the Arbitration Clause in the contract between the Guangzhou HI Ltd and MD INC., our Commission has jurisdiction on your dispute.

(2) Authorization Certificate

You, Mr. L, could only represent the MG INC. with the company's valid authorization for you to represent the company in this arbitration proceeding. Otherwise, your communication with the Secretariat is considered only your personal opinion, not the company's.

(3) Defense and Hearing

It seems that you were trying to provide evidence for the Tribunal to consider, I would like to inform you about your status in the case.

According to Article 34 of CIETAC Arbitration Rules, "If the Respondent fails to appear at an oral hearing without showing sufficient cause for such failure, or withdraws from an on-going oral hearing without the permission of the arbitral tribunal, the arbitral tribunal may proceed with the arbitration and make a default award (emphasis added). " Since your company refused all the prior arbitral documents and did not officially respond to the secretariat, the Tribunal had held a hearing on September 20, 2010.

Submitting evidence and your written opinion or statement on the case is your company's rights, which provides you with a chance to prove your case to the arbitral tribunal. If you do not submit signed copies of your documents or statements, that is, you do not officially respond to the proceedings, which might constitute a waiver of your rights of defense in this case. Then the Tribunal holds the authority to issue the arbitral award depending on the said hearing and on the materials submitted by the Claimant (emphasis of origin).

Although your submission is late after the first hearing, the Tribunal had considered your status and agreed to allow you a chance to submit your materials in the form of signed copies. If you would like to have a look at the prior arbitration materials sent by express mail which your company refused to accept, the secretariat could send all such materials to you again upon your written request. If you would like the Tribunal to hold another hearing so that you may appear and present your case, you may so request in written to the Secretariat.

(4) Arbitration Language

According to Article 67 (1) of the CIETAC Arbitration Rules, where the parties have agreed on the arbitration language, their agreement shall prevail. Absent such agreement, the Chinese language shall be the official language to be used in the arbitration proceedings.

Since there is no such agreement on arbitration language between the Parties, the Chinese language shall be the official language to be in the arbitration proceedings. Please note that this email is in English language just for your reference (emphasis of origin). "Unless otherwise agreed by the parties, all the other arbitral correspondence will be in Chinese, and all the arbitral proceedings including the oral hearing will be conducted in Chinese only."

About the second paragraph under the hearing "3) Defense and Hearing," I pointed out to the secretary, airing my negative opinion of the Article 34 of the Arbitration Rules (effective as from May 1, 2005), saying that the translation, in my opinion, was not correct and my understanding and paraphrase containing the original meaning of the provision was that:

> If the Respondent fails to appear at an oral hearing without showing sufficient cause, or withdraws from an on-going oral hearing without the permission of the arbitral tribunal, the arbitral tribunal may proceed with the hearing (or proceed with the matter) and make an award on the evidence before it (on the basis of the facts and available evidence, on the merits of the case).[1010]

She accepted my interpretation or paraphrase, adding a paragraph containing the above-mentioned wording following the quotation of the Article 34 of the 2005 Rules. I do believe that her response containing my paraphrase was checked, accepted or approved by the administrators in charge. Any notice or document drafted, which related to any matter regarding to a case in the hands of a secretary, must go through some formalities such as checked or reviewed and then approved before it is officially issued.

3 Conclusion

I always with such intention that my commentaries would to certain extent enable readers to know that, inter alia, about what I would think and to what I would pay great attention while dealing with a case and drafting an award and how I would always be on my guard against negligence and missing some points, though minor but not less important, wishing that businessmen and their attorneys would properly deal with some matter such as that regarding to the application, and decide to choose an arbitration institution or appoint an arbitrator, not roughly say no or yes.

Notes

1. The Application of CISG in the Current PRC Law and the CIETAC Arbitration Practice, para. 1.89, http://cisgw3,law.pace.edu/cisg/biblio/yang2.html.
2. For instance, please see Editors-in-Chief Priscilla Leung Mei-fun and Wang Sheng-chang, Selected Works of China International Economic and Trade Arbitration Commission Awards (1989–1995), Authorized English Version, Hong Kong, Singapore and Malaysia Sweet & Maxwell Asia, 1998; the department under Professor Albert HKritzer arranged for the preparation of CIETAC arbitration awards on CISG proceedings. His two roadmap documents in process are found at http://cisgw3.law.pace.edu/cisg/ text/CIETAC-awards.html and http:// cisg3.law.pace. edu/cisg/text/PRC-anno.html.
3. Quoted from the English version contained in "Laws and Regulations of the People's Republic of China Governing Foreign-Related Matters" (1991.7) which is compiled by the Bureau of Legislative Affairs of the State Council of the People's Republish of China, and is published by the China Legal System Publishing House.
4. See China 20 April 1999 CIETAC Arbitration proceeding (Chemical Cleaning Product Equipment case) [Cite as: http:cisg3.law.pace.edu/cases/

990420 cl.html] referred to the paper by Fan Yang, The Application of the CISG in the Current PRC Law and CIETAC Arbitration Practice].

5. The Application of CISG in the Current PRC Law and the CIETAC Arbitration Practice, para. 1.89 http://cisgw3,law.pace.edu/cisg/biblio/yang2.html.
6. Marcus S Jacobs QC, The United Nations Convention For The International Sale of Goods 1980 (The Vienna Convention) and International Commercial Arbitration, Commercial Arbitration Review sponsored by CIETAC South China, Vol. 2, University of International Business and Economics Press, September 2009, p.110.
7. The first name of the CIETAC used since it was established in 1956 till to the beginning of 1980s.
8. See Bryan A Garner, Editor in Chief, Black's Law Dictionary, Eighth Edition, Thomson West, 2004, p. 449.
9. Random House Webster's Dictionary of the Law, 2000 by James E. Clapp, p. 254.
10. Please refer to Yanming Huang, Principles Applying in Default Proceedings and Some Misunderstanding and Mistranslation of a Default Award, Journal of International Economic Law, No.2, Volume 12 (2005), Peking University Press, May 2006, pp.332- 361. The Abstract of this article: When a party to a case neither appears at a hearing nor submits its defense, how should the tribunal proceed with the arbitration? Hoar the principles of Due Process and Natural Justice reflected? How is an award rendered? What are the original meanings of "Proceedings of Quexi Shenli (Default Proceedings)" and "Quexi Cai- jue (to render an award in the absence of one party)" in the Chinese legislation? The author shows how tribunals proceed with arbitration in one party's absence and focuses on those cases under the jurisdiction of CIETAC; reviews the practice and general principles under these circumstances in the international arbitration circle; and reveals some misreading to the principles. It also makes known that in China there have been mistakes in turning the above-mentioned legal terminologies into English.

Part VI
Some Remarks on Arbitration Clause and a Brief Book Review

Outlines

The phrase "Pre-Arbitration Proceedings" contained in the title of the last article but one may not be a proper legal term. The author has deliberated on this issue and engaged in discussions with fellow practitioners regarding the challenges faced by claimants in initiating arbitration when the arbitration clause is overly simplistic and lacks of essential elements.

In the international commercial arbitration community, it is a well-established principle that the parties' consent to arbitration must be respected. Even the simplest arbitration clause—such as "*In case of disputes, submit to arbitration*"—is generally considered valid and enforceable. However, practical issues arise when such a clause fails to specify an arbitral institution. If the parties do not operate in a jurisdiction with a tradition of ad hoc arbitration, or if they have no history of successfully resolving disputes through non-institutional arbitration, the claimant may find no clear mechanism for initiating arbitration, resulting in procedural deadlock.

It is widely accepted in the arbitration community that arbitration clauses can be concise, but they must be clear and precise. Otherwise, disputes over jurisdiction and procedure may lead to unnecessary delays and financial costs. At a minimum, an arbitration clause should include certain key elements or key words, such as:

1. A broad scope of coverage—all disputes arising from or related to the contract.
2. An explicit reference to arbitration—if disputes cannot be resolved through negotiation, either party may refer the matter to arbitration.
3. Designation of an arbitral institution—clearly identifying the arbitral body.
4. Finality and binding effect—the award shall be final and binding on both parties.

For high-value contracts, such as those involving major infrastructure projects worth billions of dollars, arbitration clauses should be drafted with even greater details and precision. In such cases, in-house counsel and legal advisors would benefit from referring to Marcel Blessing's *Drafting Arbitration Clauses*, published in (1994) 5 The American Review of International Arbitration, which is among the most comprehensive discussions on this subject, so far as the author knows.

Challenges Faced by Chinese Companies in Arbitration

The cases discussed in this article stem from the author's experiences outside arbitral institutions and tribunals. These cases reveal that some Chinese companies and their personnel are short of some necessary knowledge and experience regard to arbitration, including:

4. Choosing an appropriate arbitral institution
5. Drafting clear and enforceable arbitration clauses
6. Understanding applicable laws, treaties, conventions, and procedural rules
7. Recognizing their right to request the opposing party to provide evidence of force majeure
8. Preparing supporting evidence before making claims

In some instances, these parties fail to identify "pathological arbitration clauses" due to misapplying legal criteria. Moreover, their inability to articulate legal concepts effectively in English further complicates their position in international arbitration.

A Brief Book Review on The Voice from China

Professor An CHEN is a towering figure in the field of Chinese international economic law. His monumental work, *The Voice from China: An CHEN on International Economic Law*, is a meticulously refined masterpiece that compiles of his papers in the past years and is a landmark publication in the field, having been released in English.

The author of this book had the honor of meeting Prof. An CHEN due to his professional engagement in international commercial arbitration. Occasionally, inspired by academic discourse and encouraged by Professor An CHEN's long-standing advocacy for scholarly exchange at the International Economic Law Society, he wrote some articles that were carried in the Journal of International Economic Law, with Professor An CHEN as the chief editor.

Through Professor An CHEN's generous mentorship, the author had the rare privilege of joining a distinguished group of Chinese legal scholars and other countries as well in contributing bilingual commentaries or reviews to this remarkable work. From the perspective of an arbitration practitioner, the author in his review recalls his experience in dealing with some case, coming across some aspects similar to the case as Prof. Chen had dealt with in one of the papers collected in The Voice from China, sharing some gains and insights, simultaneously revealing some intellectual and professional enrichment in the process.

Analysis of and Comments on Two Cases of Pre-arbitration Proceedings

1 Introduction

International arbitration practitioners all pay great attention to the drafting of an arbitration clause.

Marcus S Jacobs QC, a celebrated figure in the circle of the commercial arbitration in Australia, holds that "The draftsperson of the arbitration clause must have a comprehensive knowledge of the legal principles of international commercial arbitration and, of course, where the drafting concerns arbitration with its situs in Australia, the provisions of the *International Arbitration Act 1974*(Cth) and the Schedules thereto."[1] Prof Jacobs observes this matter from the angle of a practitioner in Australia. Chinese arbitration practitioners should no doubt first of all be familiar with the provisions of the Arbitration Law People's Republic of China and the Arbitration Act or ordinance of the situs that the arbitration clause would contemplate.

A former Secretary General of the ICC International Court of Arbitration in his article based on two studies of arbitration clauses in cases submitted to the ICC's International Court of Arbitration once said that "*An arbitration clause need not be lengthy or complicated, but if it is to be effective it must be clear. Ambiguity is the worst enemy to be imagined, for it may either render an arbitration clause ineffective or, at the least, create complications that cost both time and money and thus defeat some of the very reasons that lead the parties to select arbitration.*"[2] In this article, the author gives an example of pathological arbitration clause, "*Yet another of the 1987 clause referred to 'arbitration in Seoul, Republic of Korea, before the Korean Commercial Arbitration Tribunal in accordance with the Rules of Conciliation and Arbitration of the International Chamber of Commerce.' The parties could not agree which arbitral institution was meant and after several actions before Korean courts, the arbitral tribunal appointed by ICC had to issue a partial award on the point.*

Mealey's International Arbitration Report, Vol. 27, # 4. April 2012, pp.32–41.

Y. Huang, *Commentaries on Commercial Arbitration in Modern China*, Modern China and International Economic Law, https://doi.org/10.1007/978-981-95-0168-7_15

Even a clause mentioning "the official Chamber of Commerce in Paris, France" may create uncertainty as it did in one case, the International Chamber of Commerce not being the only "Chamber of Commerce in Paris"."[3]

In the past decades, as the course of globalization deepens and expends, the international arbitration is more popular than ever. There are numerous articles about the drafting of arbitral clause. One of the most comprehensive and detailed studies in this regard is the Drafting Arbitration Clauses by Marc Blessing.[4] And with the permission of the author, I have had the article turned into Chinese.[5] Nevertheless, there are still many Chinese business men and their counsels who are lack of the ability in drafting a proper arbitral clause or short of capacity in this regard. Therefore, being an arbitration practitioner, I now and then would come across ridiculous stories relating to arbitration clauses. There is a typical one below.

2 Case One: Trouble Not Only Arising from or Relating to a Pathological Arbitral Clause

2.1 Arbitration Clause and the Provision of Governing Law

December 2009, a letter addressed to the Harmony Consultants (Shenzhen) Limited, asking my colleagues and me to give some advice.

2.1.1 Case Abstract

A Chinese corporation as the Buyer and a coal corporation located in Indonesia as the Seller at the beginning of 2008 entered into an Agreement (sale contract), there had been some trouble aroused in the course of performance. At last the Indonesian Seller in a letter to the Chinese Buyer confirmed that the former had owed the latter about USD800,000.00, among the sum USD300,000.00 was overpaid by the Buyer in their previous dealings, and USD500,000 was the freight and demurrage occurred by the cargo ship chartered by the Buyer while waiting at some port of Indonesia for loading, hoping that the sum would be set off in the future transactions.

The arbitration clause of the Agreement is as follows:

> In the event of any question or dispute arising under or out of or relating to the construction, meaning and operation or effect of this contractor breach thereof, the matter in dispute shall be referred to two arbitrators, one to be nominated by Seller and the other by Buyer and in case of the said arbitration's not agreeing then to an umpire already appointed by the arbitrators in writing before proceedings on the reference. The decision of the arbitrators, or the said umpire in the event of their not agreeing shall be final and binding on the parties to the contract. The provisions of the Inter- national Chamber of Commerce, and the rules made there- under shall apply.
>
> The arbitrator or the umpire, as the case may be, shall be entitled with the consent of the parties to **enlarge the time** (emphasis added) from time to time, for making award. The

> arbitrators/umpire shall give **a reasonable award** (emphasis added), which shall be final and conclusive on both parties. The share of cost of arbitration shall be decided by mutual discussion and such arbitration shall be per- formed in Singapore.

There are some defects or mistakes in the said clause. Some expressions are of no explicit meaning; I guess its general meaning and construct the clause as follows:

> Any issues of disputes arising from or in relation to the construction, implied meaning, the operation or effect of the contract, the matters shall be referred to two arbitrators, the Seller and the Buyer shall respectively appoint one. If the two arbitrators are in no agreement on the matters, in that case, the two arbitrators should refer the matters to an umpire already jointly appointed by them in writing before the arbitral proceedings. The decision of the three arbitrators or where the tribunal fail to reach a final consensus on the matters or there is no majority opinion, the award shall be issued in accordance with the chairperson's (or the umpire's) opinion. The ICC Rules in effect at the time shall be applied.

But the problems remain unsettled. When the parties each have appointed an arbitrator, the proceedings have not been duly commenced? Before the commencement of the arbitration proceedings, the two arbitrators have to deal with the issues or disputes referred to them? Prior to the proceedings and after the two arbitrators trying to handle the issues and disputes, they have to jointly appoint a third arbitrator as the presiding arbitrator or the empire? What rules should the two arbitrators follow prior to the proceedings?

And I had to try to work out the meaning that "to **enlarge the time**", guessing that the collocation should have been "*to extend the time limit.*"

The Applicable Law and Jurisdiction Clause in the Agreement is as follows:

> This Agreement shall be governed by and construed in accordance with the **International Arbitration Laws, in English Law to apply** (emphasis added) and each of the parties hereby submits to the non-exclusive jurisdiction of the courts of Singapore.

I do not think that provision is written in good English by qualified professionals. Excluding the clerical mistakes, one might guess the general idea of it as:

> The Agreement shall be governed by and constructed in accordance with the **International Arbitration Laws** and **the Law of England**, and the parties submit to the non-exclusive jurisdiction of the Singapore courts.

2.2 *Discussion and Analysis on Some Issues Contained or Implied in the Clauses Above*

Someone based on the materials provided by the Chinese Buyers via its lawyer put forward some questions and I had my ideas contained in some responses.

A. **Since there are some inexplicit provisions in the arbitration clause, could one holds that it is of invalidity? If the Seller based on the Agreement refers the case to a Singapore court, could the judgment be automatically recognized and enforced by an Indonesia court?**

I hold that the will of parties to settle their dispute by means of arbitration is explicit. And their will should be respected.

There is no arbitral institution definitely provided in the arbitration clause, people might think that the International Court of Arbitration of the International Chamber of Commerce (ICC International Court of Arbitration) has the jurisdiction over the dispute or the case and the tribunal-to-be would have Singapore as the situs; England law is the substantial law; and the arbitration is conduct in accordance with the ICC Rules of Arbitration; up to now there is no treaty or convention named and universally accepted as the International Arbitration Law.

Generally speaking, a valid arbitration clause has the effect and function of excluding the jurisdiction of any court. In the present case, the parties in their arbitration clause express their will to settle their dispute through arbitration and simultaneously the parties provide in their Agreement that the Singapore courts have non-exclusive jurisdiction over their case. That provision or expression would allow of more than one interpretation or lead to different constructions. If the claimant refers the case to a Singapore court and a judgment rendered is in favor of the Chinese Buyer, neither the Indonesia administrative nor the courts of it have any obligation to enforce a foreign judgment; the means of judicial aid between two countries would cost you much time and energy. Even if there is an judicial agreement between the governments of the People's Republic of China and Indonesia, the competent departments of China are obliged to server their nations (persons and firms and corporations). But the correspondent ministries such as Ministry of Justice and Ministry of Foreign Affairs of a third state are not obliged to serve a Chinese corporation in this regard.

If you don't elaborate your reasons, but just simply deny or affirm the validity of the arbitration clause, you would bump into difficulties, and encounter resistances or obstacles. People with various standpoints would interpret it from different angles and are sure to find out reasons contained or implied in the arbitration clause in favor of them.

As the Seller acknowledges the basic facts, that it still owes the Buyer a sum of USD800,000.00, the Buy could actively contact the Seller and try to negotiate with the Seller, seeking any possible means to resolve the current problems between the parties, including how to continue their transactions. The Buyer could put forward some solutions or proposals in its letters or notes containing some clear-cut arbitration clause, by exchanging letters that the new arbitration clause might replace the old one in the Agreement. That depends on some skills and tactics.

B. **It is provided in the Arbitration Clause that "*The Arbitrators/ umpire shall give a reasonable award, which shall be final and conclusive on both parties.*" Does the provision mean that unless the award is reasonable and to the satisfaction of both parties, otherwise it would not be final and conclusive on both parties? Does it mean that the award is subject to a judgment by a court regarding whether it is reasonable or not?**

Further as in the Applicable Law and Jurisdiction Clause that "*each of the parties hereby submits to the non-exclusive jurisdiction of the courts of*

***Singapore*,” does that provision of non-exclusive jurisdiction not exclude the jurisdiction of the courts of the P. R. China and the courts of Indonesia or the courts of other states? Does the application of the Rules of Arbitration of the ICC require that arbitrators should be appointed from its panel?**

I make response to the above questions, saying that about an arbitral clause, professionals in the circle would judge its validity as a whole. People know that there might be defectiveness in an arbitral clause or the clause is a pathological one. If the will of the parties is explicit and could be implemented, some defects could be overlooked or neglected. For instance the wording in the present case that the “*award shall be reasonable.*”

Whether an award is reasonable could not be judged or appraised by a party with its own criteria only. The tribunal is not bound by that provision. Otherwise the arbitration could not be conducted. On the whole only few awards are to the satisfaction of all the parties concerned, that is to say, you could hardly come across a party that the award is against would be satisfied.

The ICC has its panel. But in the present case, applying ICC Rules doesn't mean that parties have to appoint arbitrators from its panel.

C. **Opinions from a Singapore lawyer**

In my practice, in connection with any aspects of international commercial arbitration, I am willing to consult colleagues of other countries or regions, even if we would see eye to eye. Colleagues of different countries of jurisdictions have different careers with various experiences. Those colleagues of various backgrounds would view and examine the same issue with various angles and therefore their opinions and mine would be of mutual complementary.

I on December 17, 2009, copied down the aforesaid clauses and by email sent to a lawyer, who is also an arbitration practitioner, from Singapore, inquiring:

> How could it be constructed and would it work in Singapore? Could any party refer the dispute arising from the contract to the Singapore International Arbitration Centre?
>
> It reminds me of another arbitration clause, ‘Arbitration in Seoul, Republic of Korea, before the Korean Commercial Arbitration Tribunal in accordance with the Rules of Conciliation and Arbitration of the International Chamber of Commerce.[6] It did work but caused the parties concerned great trouble. At last, the arbitral tribunal appointed by ICC.
>
> Would you be so kind as to spare some minutes on it and give me some valuable pieces of advice?

The response from Mr. Yan Ing Loong[7] is as follows:

> 2. Recently, in 2009, Singapore's highest court (the Court of Appeal) considered the effect of a clause which required all disputes to be ‘resolved by arbitration before the Singapore International Arbitration in accordance with the Rules of Arbitration of the International Chamber of Commerce.’ The Court of Appeal upheld the clause as a valid arbitration clause.
>
> 3. One difficulty with the clause set out in the e-mail (and this same difficulty applies to the Korean arbitration clause referred to in the article by Stephen Bond) is that it is unclear which arbitral institution is intended to administer the arbitration (assuming that parties intended an institutional arbitration). For example, possible arbitral institutions in Singapore include

the SIAC (Singapore International Arbitration Centre), and the ICC itself (the ICC's Asia Office is situated in Singapore)." Therefore, it may be arguable that the clause has several possible interpretations:

(a) The arbitration is to be administered by the ICC Office in Singapore in accordance with the ICC Rules;
(b) The arbitration is to be administered by the SIAC in Singapore in accordance with the ICC Rules; or
(c) The parties intended to have an ad hoc arbitration, without any arbitral institution administering the arbitration, and the ad hoc arbitration tribunal are to apply the ICC Rules.

4. It is not immediately clear which interpretation is likely to be the correct one. One possible course of action to consider is to make discrete enquiries as to whether SIAC / ICC would be prepared to administer the arbitration, to 'test the waters'.

5. I should also point out that there may be a number of other issues which arise from the arbitration clause (among others):

(a) The reference to 'the provisions of the International Chamber of Commerce, and the rules made thereunder shall apply' is not as clear as it should be. The relevant arbitration rules in question are actually the 'Rules of Arbitration of the International Chamber of Commerce.' The point is that the International Chamber of Commerce does make other rules which do not concern arbitration (e.g., ICC Incoterms and ICC's Uniform Customs and Practice for Documentary Credits).
(b) The phrase 'the matter in dispute shall be referred to two arbitrators, one to be nominated by Seller and the other by Buyer and in case of the said arbitration's not agreeing then to an umpire already appointed by the arbitrators in writing before proceeding on the reference' is a bit confusing. Presumably, the two arbitrators have to proceed on the reference first before it can be seen whether or not the two arbitrators are in agreement. Yet the clause says that the umpire has to be appointed (which would be the case if the two arbitrators disagree after proceeding on the reference) before proceeding on the reference. It is not how this phrase is to be interpreted (if it is a valid arbitration clause to begin with).
(c) The arbitration clause states that the costs of the arbitration 'shall be decided by mutual discussion' What if parties cannot agree on the costs of the arbitration (particularly if the losing party refuses to pay any costs of the arbitration to the winning party)? Do the arbitrators still have power to award costs of the arbitration to the winning party?"

According to the understanding of me, about the costs of the arbitration, the Singapore lawyer is not sure whether the general principle—the losing party bearing the costs—applies to the case. But the author of this article nevertheless believes that if the parties can't agree on the costs of the arbitration, the three-member tribunal still have power to award costs of it to winning party. But before the arbitrators come to their conclusion, there would be an argument between the parties.

More than two years is gone since December 12, 2009, when my colleagues and I were consulted. In the course of drafting this article (in March 2012), I sent a note by email to the Chinese Buyer's former in-house counsel, inquiring about the dispute. She told me there had been no transactions between the Chinese Buyer and the Indonesia Seller and the Buyer had never claimed the sum of USD 800,000.00 and the interests incurred ever since.

The sum of USD800,000.00 plus interest of more than three-year is a big, medium or small one? It just depends on who you are and how it flows or is used.

The sum in that case was just like a small stone thrown into the Pacific Ocean, without sound or sending up no spray. The case and story arising from the Agreement would be also soon forgotten by those who have access to the case materials.

3 Case Two: Troubles and Questions Mainly Pertaining to the Provision and Event of Force Majeure

3.1 Conclusion of a Contract and a Dispute Arising

March 2011, I received a letter titled the Cause of a Hong Kong Arbitration ("the Cause") with some appendixes from a law firm located in Guangzhou on behalf of a trading company to ask for advice, for the purpose of analyzing the prospect of referring the case to the Hong Kong International Arbitration Centre.

The Cause reveals that on July 16, 2010, a Buyer, a trade company in Guangzhou, and a Seller, a company in Hong Kong entered into a Sale and Purchase Contact for Steam Coal of Indonesia origin and a Supplementary Agreement of three clauses.

It is provided in the Contract that the Seller shall before August 8, 2010, deliver the Buyer 35,000MT (± 10%) of coal at a loading port in South Kalimantan, Indonesia; the price shall be USD78 per MTCIF Discharge Port (a port in China as may be designated by the Buyer and confirmed by the parties by exchange of emails for each shipment).

After the conclusion of the Contract, on July 22, 2010, the Buyer had a letter of Credit ("LC") of a sum of USD2,730,000.00 issued in favor of the Seller, stipulating, *inter alia*, that the latest date of shipment was August 8, 2010, and the discharge Port (destination) is Shantou, Guangdong Province, PR China.

July 27, 2010, the Seller wrote to the Buyer, requesting that the latest date of shipment amended to August 14, 2010. The Buyer in response held that the amendment could not be accepted.

The Seller could not deliver the coal on the date stipulated in the LC, so that the Buyer was unable to deliver the coal to its end user and therefore resulting in breach of contract between the Buyer and its end user, and as a consequence of it the Buyer suffered losses. But the Buyer neither provided me with contract between it and its end user nor other documents relating to their deal.

The Seller on August 13, 2010, wrote to the Buyer, saying that it failed to deliver the goods due to *force majeure* concretely there were heavy rain and floods in Indonesia, according to Clause 14.1 (quoted below), both parties shall not be liable to each other.

On August 26, 2010, the Seller in a letter to the Buyer (one of my colleagues in his circle letter to his colleagues with the Harmony initially discusses the case also mentions this letter, see below) requested to re-arrange shipment. The Buyer did not accept the suggestion; instead, the Buyer insisted that unless the Contract was performed; otherwise there could be no new transaction. Subsequently, the Buyer wrote to the Seller, asking the latter to compensate the former in accordance with the stipulation in the Contract (including the Supplementary Agreement). Deadlock arose and could not be resolved. So the Buyer through its lawyers to wrote to the Harmony.

3.2 *Comments on Various Aspects of the Transaction or the Case to the Law Firm of the Buyer*

In a letter containing comments on various aspects to the lawyers of the Buyer, I quoted those terms and conditions and some contents of appendixes to the Cause from the Buyer about the transaction.

A. **The terms and conditions closely related to the dispute**

Payment (9)

Within 5 working days of the signing of this Contract, Buyer shall open an irrevocable, transferable Letter of Credit to Seller. The Letter of Credit shall be issued through Buyer's bank acceptable to Seller, and shall be payable against Seller's drafts drawn at sight on the opening bank and against the documents specified in Clause 9.2 and 9.3 of this Contract. (9.1)

Force Majeure (14)

Seller shall not be liable to Buyer nor shall Buyer be liable to Seller for any delay or failure in the performance of obligations under this Contract **if such delays or failure is due to or results or is consequential upon force majeure** (emphasis added). The term "force majeure" shall include natural calamities, acts of public enemies, insurrections, strikes, fires, war, explosions, **floods and severe weather** (emphasis added). (14.1)

The party whose performance of any obligation is affected by reason of any of the causes referred to in Clause 14.1 shall promptly give notice thereof by facsimile to the other party followed, as soon as practicable, by a notice in writing setting forth the particulars of the relevant event and, if **possible, supporting evidence** (Emphasis added). The date of such notice shall be the first day under which the provisions of Clause 14.1 may apply. The party issuing such notice shall take reasonable steps to resume with the least possible delay compliance with its obligations under this agreement, but shall not be required to settle any strike, lockout or other labor difficulty on terms not acceptable to it. (14.2)

The party shall also notify promptly of the cessation of any event referred in Clause 14.1 by facsimile to the other party. The date of such notice shall be the last day under which the provisions of Clause 14.1 may apply. (14.3)

Mutual Collaboration (15)

Seller and Buyer recognize that circumstances may arise which could not have been foreseen at the time this Contract was entered into and agree that they will use their best efforts to solve any problems due to such unforeseeable circumstances in a spirit of mutual understanding and collaboration.

Arbitration (16)

All disputes arising from the execution of this Contract shall be settled through amicable consultation by Buyer and Seller. In case no settlement can be reached within 60(sixty) days after commencement of such consultation, the disputes shall be finally settled by arbitration in Hong Kong International Arbitration Centre. (16.1)

Seller and Buyer shall continue to perform all their obligations under this Contract pending publication of the Arbitrators' award and such performance shall be without prejudice to any final adjustment in accordance with the award. (16.2)

Governing Law (17)

The validity, construction and performance of this Contract shall be interpreted, governed and determined in accordance with the laws of Hong Kong.

The three clauses in the Supplementary Agreement are translated by me as follows:

Apart from force majeure, if the Seller fails to deliver the goods due to some reasons on the part of it, the parties shall settle the problem through negotiation. If no settlement could be reached, the Seller shall pay the Buyer two percent of the total price of the Contract as compensation; (1)

When the Buyer claims, relevant documentary proofs should be produced; (2)

When it is established that two the percent should be paid, the Seller shall remit the sum in ten working days by T/T to the account of the Buyer. (3)

B. Intention and claim of the Buyer

The Buyer intends to act as claimant to refer the dispute to arbitration in Hong Kong, requesting the Seller to abide by the provisions in the Clause 1 of the Supplementary Agreement paying two percent of the total amount of the LC USD2,730,000.00, namely USD54,600.00. Actually there is no explicit sum provided in the Contract, so the Buyer refers to the sum of the LC.

C. Opinions on various questions raised or reflected by the Buyer and its lawyers

The validity of the Arbitration Clause

Clause14 is explicit. I, in my in writing to the Buyer, say that if the Buyer wants to spend fewer fees, it could try to require that the case referred to a sole arbitrator and having the case examined on the basis of documents only, wishing that the Seller would have no objection. But there is no such explicit and concrete provisions in the Arbitration Clause (the provisions of an arbitration clause could be broad enough to cover many aspects or matters, such as the arbitration language, the nationality and the number of arbitrator, the applying rules other than governing law, etc.); if the Seller as respondent doesn't agree, there would be some trouble.

Estimated arbitration and legal fees

In Hong Kong, the hourly rate of a veteran arbitrator or a solicitor may be HKD5000-6000.00. If there is a sole arbitrator and an oral hearing lasts for a day (say seven hours), being a claimant and if it engages a solicitor, the Buyer has to pay in advance at least HKD70,000.00. Administration fees collected by the Hong Kong International Arbitration Centre and other costs are not included. If an award in favor of the Buyer is rendered, and if the Seller respondent does not automatically perform the decisions of the tribunal, the winning claimant has to engage some solicitor to apply to a court in Hong Kong for enforcing the award. A sum more should be spent.

About the possibility of referring the dispute to the Small Claims Tribunal of Hong Kong (hears minor monetary claims involving amounts not exceeding $50,000. The hearing is informal and no legal representation is allowed).

If the Buyer wants to have a try, referring the case to the Small Claims Tribunal, the Seller respondent could simply in its defense point out that there is an arbitration clause in the Contract; the case would be set aside.

Notice about the *force majeure*

The letter in English dated August 13, 2010, as Appendix 5 by the Seller to the Buyer:

> Pls be informed that the execution of the Contract has been affected by severe bad weather in South Kalimantan, Indonesia. Heavy rain has caused major flooding in the coal mines and on the coal transportation roads. As a result, the Contract cannot be implemented as intended.

The fourth and fifth paragraphs of the letter are as follows:

> In accordance with Clause 14.1 of the Contract, we hereby declared force majeure due to 'floods and severe weather'.
>
> In accordance with Clause 14.1 of the Contract, your company and our company are not liable to each other for any delay of failure in the performance of obligations under the Contract as such delay or failure is due to or consequential upon force majeure.

In the response to Buyer's law firm, I say:

> My I draw your attention to the words and expressions in Clause 14.2 '**if possible, supporting evidence**.' There is no explicit and mandatory requirement that supporting evidence concerning any force majeure should be provided. Generally speaking, parties concerned should provide such evidence issued by a local chamber of commerce. The existing pieces of evidence don't reveal that your client has challenged the fact that there had been force majeure, and asked the Seller to produce evidence proving that there was event of force majeure.

Some words on the Appendix 6, the Sellers' new suggestion and the Appendix 7, a letter by the Buyer to the Seller

In Appendix 6, the Seller raised the question of new arrangement, saying to delay the shipment to October 10, 2010, and suggested that the Buyer has a new LC rendered.

Appendix 7 is a letter in Chinese dated on August 27, 2010, by the Buyer to the Seller. In the letter, the Buyer first recalled the course of the transaction and then the Buyer accused of the Seller of being unable to deliver the goods, complaining that caused the Buyer in breach of the contract with its end user, revealing that resulting in the great losses of the Buyer. In this letter, the Buyer says that:

> According to the Contract and the Supplementary Agreement, your company shall pay my company two percent of the total price of the Contract. On August 12, 2010, an invoice was sent to your company. Please pay the sum by T/T to the appointed account in the invoice.
>
> We have taken notice that in your letter dated August 26, 2010, you offer that you could deliver goods on October 10, 2010. My company also wishes that more transactions and closer cooperation done with your company. Nevertheless, your company has to act in accordance with the Contract; otherwise there would be chance for a new contract.

The Seller informed the Buyer of the force majeure, saying, *inter alia*, that because of that, the transaction under the LC could not be done as provided, namely the coal could not be shipped in accordance with the date stipulated in the LC. The Seller required the Buyer to have a new LC issued. The request itself is not improper. The Buyer should have corresponding provisions contained in the contract with its end user.

Description of the case in the Cause

Base on the materials provided by your law firm, namely on the documents or appendixes to the Cause, there is no evidence showing that the Seller intended to break the Contract. The Seller did fail to deliver the goods according to the stipulations of the LC. According to the last paragraph of the Cause, it is hard to confirm there was no event of *force majeure*. And there is no circumstance that entitles the Buyer to exercise the right provided in the Clause 1 of the Supplementary Agreement, that is to say that the Buyer is in a position to claim the two percent of the total price of the LC.

If you want to proof that the condition provided in the Clause 1 of the Supplementary Agreement fulfils, and the Seller has to pay the Buyer damages, for the time being there is no evident evidence yet.

The key reason for that is that there is no explicit and mandatory stipulation in Clause 14.1 of the Contract requiring that when there is *force majeure*, the Seller has to provide supporting evidence—certificate rendered by a local chamber of commerce. Instead, the wording is "*if possible, supporting evidence.*"

In the course of exchanging letters between the parties, the Buyer had never required the Seller to provide such supporting evidence, though the Buyer was entitled to require the Seller to do so.

3.3 Alleged Breach of Contract Between the Seller and the Buyer

A veteran solicitor, one of my colleagues with the Harmony Mr. T.C Foo[8] had his initial opinion expressed in a circular letter to his colleagues referring to the dispute is as follows:

> The case is not so simple as it appears. Further detailed information and instructions are required for assessment of liability on the part of the Seller.

He quoted the Clause 14.1 and 14.2 and then says:

> There is a letter dated 26th August 2010from the Seller to the Buyer saying that due to rainstorm delivery of the goods (coal) could not be made in the middle of August 2010 and the loading of the goods would be made on 10th October 2010.
>
> Anything done by the Buyer after this letter? Did the Buyer receive a formal notice in writing with sup- porting evidence from the Seller after this letter? **Did the Buyer write to the Seller requesting for evidence of force majeure, namely flooding or severe weather? And if not why not?** (Emphasis added) Did the Buyer accept the shipment on or after 10th October 2010 as suggested by the Seller? Did the Buyer response to the letter of 26th August 2010? Any correspondence exchanged between the Buyer and the Seller in relation to the delayed shipment? What happened after 10th October 2010? Did the Buyer accept the wrongful repudiation on the part of the Seller? Any negotiations or consultation for settlement between the parties? If not why not? We need such further instructions and information, in particular the official weather charts of South Kalimantan, Indonesia at all material times to show or not to show the rain storm and sever weather, before we are in a position to examine the liability of the Seller in respect of the alleged breach of the contract. The official weather charts are important evidence to rebut the allegation of force majeure. Can we get the charts from Indonesia?
>
> If there is a prima facie case of breach on the part of the Seller not due to force majeure, then the dispute shall be settled by arbitration in Hong Kong.
>
> There is also legal argument to be involved. **In common law, penalty is not allowed against a party for breach of the contract** (Emphasis added). The injured party can claim against the defaulting party pre-estimated damages or actual damages sustained by the innocent party. Under the contract, the governing law is the law of Hong Kong. Thus the common law applies. In the eyes of Hong Kong law, the Supplemental Agreement is badly worded. **To make it valid and effective, we have to prove by expert evidence that according to the trade practice in the coal industries,2%ofthe purchase price is NOT penalty, but pre-estimated damages** (Emphasis added). There is decision in conveyancing cases that 10% of the purchase price is not penalty, but pre-estimated damages for breach the agreement for sale and purchase. Can we find such authority in cases concerning sale and purchase of coal?

Professionals could see that my colleague examines the case from a different angle. I suppose that the Buyer and his lawyers or even most of the lawyers in the Mainland China (other than those who are trained in common law countries and regions) could hardly understand why penalty is not allowed against a party for breach of a contract and why the provision of the Clause 1 of the Supplementary Agreement pertaining to the two percent of the total price of the Contract paid to the Buyer as compensation could not work alone in Hong Kong when Hong Kong law is the governing law as it does in the mainland China when the substantive law is the Law of the PR China.

Another colleague of the Harmony as a solicitor from Hong Kong also briefly touches on the problem of "*relevant documentary proofs*" mentioned in Clause 2 of the Supplementary Agreement. He is puzzled over it, inquiring what it means. Further he tells me that according to his inference based on the business address of the Seller located in Hong Kong, he doubts the competence of the Seller. He holds that the Seller has not proved what the exact reason of the weather. But on the other hand, the question should be raised to the Buyer: Why it did not require the Seller to produce evidence or certificate to prove that there had been *force majeure*, and what the exact *force majeure* was?

People could find out, from the independent opinions of my two colleagues as solicitors from Hong Kong and by me, that there are some questions concerning the event and evidence of *force majeure* overlapped each other.

I could not understand why in the era of internet, there was difficulty that would prevent the Buyer from collecting some information such as weather charts of South Kalimantan, Indonesia.

The Buyer and its law firm did receive the comments or opinions above. And then there was no information from Guangzhou.

4 Conclusion

Based on my notes in dealing with the cases I have this article written, hoping that they would not slip from my mind soon. These two cases are neither very typical nor complicated. I have not only revealed my opinions but also introduced some valuable pieces of advice from lawyers or solicitors of common law, arbitration practitioners of different backgrounds and with different experiences and from various angles or standpoints, sharing their knowledge and viewpoints, wishing that businessmen and their lawyers include house counsels especially those located in the mainland China might get some enlightenment.

The two cases are not involving huge sums or claims; however they do contain some interesting points and businessmen might draw some lessons from them.

Notes

1. Marcus S Jacobs QC, *International Commercial Arbitration in Australia Law and Practice, Thomson Reuters, 2009, p. 1851.*
2. See Stephen R. *Bond, How to Draft an ICC Arbitration Clause (Revised), ICSID REVIEW Foreign Investments Law Journal, Vol. 7. No. 1, Spring 1992*, pp. 153–167 and the Chinese version by Yanming Huang carried in *Arbitration and Law* (Sponsored by the CIETAC and some other institutes), Issue 1, Feb 1996, pp 24–33.

3. Original note: *Société Asland v. Société European Energy Corporation, L.G.I Paris, 1990 Revue del'arbitrage, at 521, noted by Pluyetteat 353. The French Court held that the parties had manifestly chosen the ICC which is the recognized arbitration center in Paris for resolving international disputes.*
4. Marc Blessing, *Drafting Arbitration Clauses*, published in (1994) 5 *The American Review of International Arbitration.*
5. Please refer to *Arbitration and Law* (sponsored by CIETAC and other two institutes), Law Press, China, June 2007, Issue 106, pp. 66–100.
6. *Id. at* *2. p. 156.
7. Partner with Sidley Austin LLP International Lawyers.
8. Solicitor and notary with Liu, Choi & Chan, Solicitors & Notaries of Hong Kong.

Precise and Thorough Analyses—Illustrating a Guru's Profound Knowledge—A Brief Commentary on the Voice from China: An CHEN on International Economic Law

Opening this great monograph titled the Voice from China: An CHEN *on International Economic Law (The Voice from China), I am very delighted* with and impressed by Prof CHEN's scholastic achievements on the subject and his skills in mastering English.[1]

Prof. CHEN is an eminent jurist and the forerunner of China's international economic law discipline. He was the Chairman of the Chinese Society of International Economic Law in which I was once a member of the Society and a mere subordinate under his supervision. I wish to touch and simultaneously share my views on some aspects of the cases and the Legal Opinions in the Voice from China (Chapters 20, 21, 22 and 23) from the perspective of a craftsman—an arbitrator. In order to save space, abbreviated case names and subjects related would be applied.[2]

Case 1, A UK Co X v. a UK Insurance Co Y. In December 1996, an entity from Cayman Islands and Chinese Co.B entered into a contractual joint venture agreement ("**the Agreement**") and a contractual joint venture ("**the CJV**") was established in China. Later Co X replaced the Cayman entity. Under the insurance policy issued by Co Y with Co X as the assured, the risks undertaken cover losses arising out of acts of expropriation occurring during the policy period of February 20, 2001, to February 19, 2004. Due to the issuance of **Circular No. 31 (1998)** by the PRC's State Council and **Circular No. 43 (2002)** by the General Office of the State Council ("**the Two Circulars**"), Co X claims that the Two Circulars constitute an **Act of Expropriation**, and therefore requesting compensation for losses from Co Y-by reference to the insurance policy that stipulated about (possible) compulsory take over by the Chinese government. Co Y denies and Co X refers the case to arbitration in British.

The key issues before Prof. CHEN are whether the Two Circulars are of the nature or give such effects of an Act of Expropriation of the assets of the CJV; if the answer

This article was carried in Journal of International Economic Law, China, Vol. 21, # 4, 2014, pp. 635–716

Y. Huang, *Commentaries on Commercial Arbitration in Modern China*, Modern China and International Economic Law, https://doi.org/10.1007/978-981-95-0168-7_16

is affirmative, Co X could base on the alleged Act of Expropriation to claim the coverage under the insurance policy; thereafter Co Y would gain the subrogation (of insurer) from Co X. In another word, the said issues could be expressed in a manner to cover situations where an agreement is in line with the provisions of the Act of PRC on Chinese-Foreign Contractual Joint Venture ("CJV Act") and has received approval by some competent governmental authorities of China. Under such circumstances, have those internationally accepted basic legal principles, *such as "**autonomy of the parties' will**" and "no-retroactivity of law,"* been fully accepted by or already taken root in China as a country ruled by law?[3]

***Case 2**, Xiamen Zhonghe Industry Co., Ltd (Zhonghe) v. Bunge Singapore Pte. Ltd* (Bunge). Zhonghe as buyer and Bunge as seller on February 25, 2004, entered into the Contract S04-071 ("**the Contract**") with Brazilian soybeans of 55,000 metric tons as the subject matter. It is provided in the Contract that Zhonghe shall through a first-class Chinese bank acceptable by Bunge open a letter of credit in favor of the seller[4]

> After the conclusion of the Contract, several shipments of Brazilian soybeans exported to China were found containing germicide carboxin-processed soybeans (or **Brazilian soybeans highly toxic carcinogenic pesticide** or adulteration of red-coated Brazilian soybeans) including a shipment under the Contract between Zhonghe and Bunge; therefore the General Administration of Quality Supervision, Inspection and Quarantine of China (**"AGSIG"**) issued a Warning Notice and then some **Public Announcements** in a succession prohibiting the importation of Brazilian soybeans. Public Announcement 71 even declared that Bunge was temporarily revoked **of the capacity of exporting Brazilian soybeans to China.**
>
> **The core issues that Prof. CHEN faces are whether the prohibitions** (or **administrative ordinances, administrative prohibitive orders or mandatory regulations or rules) issued** by AGSIG have comprehensive and powerful legal binding force over Chinese importers, Chinese banks and their respective branches overseas; whether China is the place of performance of the obligation to open the letter of credit under the Contract; **when English laws are applicable,** whether the mandatory rules or orders in Chinese legal system are of mandatory effects over Chinese legal entities and therefore the Contract was frustrated due to the said prohibitions and their binding force.
>
> Bunge holds that the prohibitions by AQSIQ on soybeans adulterated with germicide carboxin cannot be fully supported by Chinese laws. According to the provisions of the Act of PRC on Food Sanitation adulteration of the impurities or fake products therein had to be conducted with an intention; therefore the legislative authority for the decisions made by AQSIQ upon the soybeans is not sufficient. Further, Bunge is of the view that the Public Announcement 71 was temporary suspension and actually in existence for 9 days only and so it has not reached the point that it would frustrate the Contract as a whole. Zhonghe should have applied some Chinese bank or its branch overseas to open the letter of credit during the period of 23~25 of June 2004. Failing this, Zhonghe shall be responsible for the liabilities. "According to the Contract, English laws (shall) apply when a dispute is referred to arbitration (emphasis added). English laws only *recognize(s)that a breach at the place of performance of the contractual obligations can possibly lead to the frustration of contract." Further, Bunge* holds that pursuant to the Contract, China is not the place of performance of the obligation to open the letter of credit, and opening of the credit letter which is in violation of Chinese laws cannot be taken as the ground for frustration under English laws. The Chinese lawyer engaged by Bunge holds the view that whether one corporate could apply for a letter of credit mainly depends on the applicant's status and financial standing,

but no concrete negative evidence against Zhonghe is produced. The Chinese lawyer argues that the Public Announcement 71 had no material influence on the establishment of the letter of credit under the Contract.[5]

In his Legal Opinions, when dealing with issues pertaining to Case 1, Prof CHEN has not overlooked or missed out any provisions concerned from the Constitution to all the laws, acts, regulations, rules, and administrative orders and even the promises by China when entering into WTO. For instance, he lists some facts that as a member of WTO, China has not only *promised to "ensure the full conformity of its laws, regulations, and rules with the provision of the WTO Agreement," but also taken measures in* this regard."[6] When treating the problems relating to Case 2, he respectively identifies the Contract and the clause that "English laws shall be applied," and that the Contract was signed by Bunge's subsidiary Bunge International Trading (Shanghai) Co., Ltd ("**Bunge Shanghai**") residing in Shanghai with Zhonghe.[7]

Revealing his deep knowledge of the Convention on the Law Applicable to Contractual Obligations ("**Rome Convention**"), the effective Contacts (Applicable Law) Act 1990 (of British), the precedents established by English courts in their long established judicial practice and conflict of laws rules which have been refined and summarized by authoritative English scholars and widely accepted by the international community, analyzing their mutual relations and different forces, step by step, Prof. CHEN discusses the issues and expounds his viewpoints by accurately referring to the relevant provisions of various acts or laws and legal theories.

Prof. CHEN reaches his conclusion that in Case 1 the Two Circulars and their provisions are of no **Expropriation** effects, and confirms that the *two major principles of law, i.e., "**autonomy of the parties' will**" and*"**non-retroactivity**" have actually taken root in China and are applicable to the case. And in Case 2, he firmly believes that the **administrative prohibitive orders or mandatory orders** contained in the Publication Announcements, such as the Announcements 71 by AQSIQ, are of binding effects over Chinese legal entities concerned, that China is the place of performance of the obligation to have the letter of credit opened and the Contract was frustrated due to the mandatory orders.

Perusing the chapters, the author cannot help recall the days when China was at the initial period of reform and began to rejoin the international community. It was also the initial period of the rule by law in China. In 1985–1986, I assisted a senior superior in preparing a legal opinion for a Hong Kong banking group. The opinion concerned a loan agreement in which the banking group acted as lender, a Chinese company as borrower, and two Chinese corporations as guarantors. The agreement was governed by the laws of New York State. The lawyers engaged by the banking group had to engage some lawyer in the mainland China to carry out inquiries to identify and confirm the status, the business scope, the financial standing and other conditions of the borrowers and the guarantors; that the matters relating to the loan and guaranty were normal and in conformity with the laws, acts, regulations or policies of China; that the borrower and his guarantors had got consents from competent departments of China; and the decisions relating to the loan made by the boards of directors of the borrower and the guarantors and representatives who would sign the loan agreement and other documents concerned. The main business of one of the two guarantors had been in Hong Kong for over 100 years; nevertheless its registration place of the business was in Beijing. Though it was of good credit in Hong Kong, it was required according to the regulations by the State Administrative Bureau of Exchange Control to apply for approval for the guaranty and to obtain the approval certificate. At that time, there were few statutes enacted or promulgated by National People's Congress or its standing committee; instead, there were quite a lot internal documents or official documents of red colored titles ("hong tou wen jian" in Chinese). But it was obviously, while the applicable laws of the loan agreement were the laws of the New York State, the banking group and their lawyers relied expressly upon the provisions of the laws, acts, regulations or even the then popular internal documents of China containing some polices in this regard. All the legal issues or matters identified and confirmed in the legal opinions issued by the lawyer from mainland China were the preconditions for the finally conclusion of the loan agreement. The signing of the loan agreement was done upon the receipt of the legal opinions by the banking group and its lawyers.

In Case 1, Co Y acts in reasonable manner, timely asking a Chinese legal expert for advice which forms as his basis for defense. If Co X, when in doubt of the retroactivity of the Two Circulars and whether it is of the nature of expropriation, should have acted as Co Y in asking a Chinese legal expert for advice, Prof. CHEN's legal opinions would have been issued for him and such legal opinions would have even better effect. After all, Co X had referred the case to arbitration, as his sum of investment was USD12,000,000.00, the coverage of the policy would not have been less than that sum or probably plus 10 percent and the sum claimed would have not been less than the sum either. In this case, Co X had paid fees for his lawyers, for the arbitration administrative charges closely relating to the time spent by the registrar and his deputies and the fees for the arbitrator(s). If Co X had asked for advice before referring the case to arbitration, the sum paid for a Chinese legal expert and his legal opinions would be a very small proportion comparing with the fees and changes that he would have paid for arbitral process.

> Concerning Case 2, I have mentioned above that I was once an assistant to a senior superior in rendering legal opinions to a banking group from other jurisdiction. When the governing laws were those of the New York State, the banking group's lawyers had never overlooked the lex personal is of the borrower and guarantors of other jurisdiction. In contrast, in Case 2, the Chinese lawyer engaged by Bunge has given me an impression that he did not take proper notice or even probably turned a blind eye to the laws or mandatory orders of China.
>
> The lex personal is of Zhonghe should not have been neglected, such as those pertaining to the capacity for private rights or duties, any Chinese legal entities should be abided by them or the Chinese legal entities must be subject to those laws, acts, regulations or administrative orders. If there are any prohibitions on the importing or exporting to China food or material for food processing with **pesticide,** knowledge about these prohibitions or the absence of such knowledge would have different serious consequences. Prof. CHEN has proved that he is well professed of all aspects of the matters concerned I would like to stress that the Contract is of an important feature in international trade. For example, parties are from the contracting states to the CISG, then the provisions of the CISG will be regarded as being integrated into their respective national law of PR China and Singapore. If the parties do not expressly exclude the application of the CISG or derogate from or vary the effect of its

> provisions, save the reservations, doesn't the CISG apply to the case? When the governing law is of English law, does it mean that the CISG could be absolutely excluded?[8]
>
> I am fully accept that Prof. CHEN is correct in quoting Art 3(3) of *the Rome Convention "[T]he fact that the parties have chosen a foreign law, whether or not accompanied by the choice of a foreign tribunal, shall* not, where all the other elements relevant to the situation at the time of the choice are connected with one country only, prejudice the application of rules of the law of that country which cannot be derogated from by contract, herein after called 'mandatory rules'."

It seems to me that the application of the CISG to the case could not be excluded. If the parties don't exclude the application of the CISG in the Contract, it will be necessary to look at Art 7(2) of the CISG:

> Questions concerning matters governed by this Convention which are not expressly settled in it are to be settled in conformity with the general principles on which it is based or, in the absence of such principles, in conformity with the law applicable by virtue of the rules of private international law.[9]

If in the instant case the CISG could not be excluded, should we rely on the lex personal is of Zhonghe as Prof. CHEN does and we may further refer to Art 127 of the Contact Act of PRC:

> The Administration of Industry and Commerce and other relevant administrative authorities shall, within the scope of their respective the functions, supervise and deal with any unlawful conduct by way of contract prejudicial and detrimental to national or public interest. If such conduct amounts to a crime, criminal responsibility shall be pursued according to laws.

The provision contained in Art 127 above, once more from another angle reminds anyone of the binding effects of Chinese mandatory orders or rules and serious consequence of being against them.[10]

In addition, I guess it might be better to tell Bunge and his Chinese lawyer, if they insist on the view that the mandatory rules or orders in the Chinese legal system could be ignored and the award should be made in favor of Bunge that under the Contract Brazilian soybeans containing highly toxic carcinogenic pesticide could be exported to China, the award should be set aside or its enforcement be refused. Some lines on a case revealing that misconduct of arbitrator "[W]hich justified setting aside an award *Telkon SALtd v Anthong Boswood QC" are as follows*[11]*:*

> The South African High Court found that the arbitrator had committed **errors of law** (emphasis added) which amounted to gross irregularities in the conduct of the arbitration and set the award aside.[12]

We should be aware that nowadays any awards tainted with extremely serious or egregious errors amount to a breach of public policy. To allow such fundamentally flawed awards to stand uncorrected would undermine confidence in the integrity of the arbitral process. That concept or principle is expressly reflected in the Arts 34 and 36 of the UNCITRAL Model *Law on International Commercial Arbitration.*[13]

From the Legal Opinions by Prof. CHEN, we arbitrators could get some enlightenment. In our awards under the subtitle "the Opinions of the Tribunal," the tribunal should ensure that no issue and claim is missed out, all matters, key issues, facts and the merits of the case should be thoroughly explored. If arbitrators are short of that ability, failing to explain why a claim or counterclaim is sustained or refused, their awards rendered would be far from convincing in giving reasons.

It is in the twenty-first century that Prof. CHEN issued his Legal Opinions. Sets of laws, acts, regulations or rules that are orientated toward the needs of a market economy have been basically enacted or promulgated. All the provisions he quotes are transparent in the sun. The effects of those "internal documents" are fading. Nevertheless, the problem lies in whether one is an old hand. Not familiar with all the aspects of the matters concerned, without profound knowledge and deep understanding of all the issues concerned, without skills in mastering in one's mother-tongue and English plus its legal terminology, one could hardly deal with those hard-nuts properly.

The era of reform and opening to the international community has provided Prof. CHEN with a golden opportunity and in return for the era and on behalf of the discipline of the international economic law of China he advocates with admirable clarity and strength; his voice is echoing along the long road to the heights.

> I guess Prof. CHEN must be familiar with the saying of Karl Marx, "A *foreign language is a weapon in the struggle of life." No pains no gains.* Without decades of hard working, reading, writing and studying, no one is able to write in idiomatic English.

His professional papers are carried in authoritative journals and then collected in this monograph. Acting as a distinguish representative of discipline of the China's international economic law and the circle of China international arbitration, he has made his marks on the international stage and added academic literature thereon.

It is revealed in the Voice from China, that Prof. CHEN as a junior teacher in 1953 shifted from law to Marxism and Leninism. When over 50-year old, in his prime years, he at last got the chance to return to the law *field as he says that "Just stated to race at the age of spurt." On the other* hand, it could be regarded as lucky. In the spring of reform and opening to the outside, he has lost no chance to "rouse to catch up, overcome shortage by diligence." His doctoral candidates remember that he usually would not turn off his desk-lamp until midnight or early morning. In the past decades, he has never idled away. His brilliant works are reflecting the long road he has traveled.

In his poem of self-encouragement in 2005 even when he was aged 76, he revealed his determination that he would never stop in his academic researching and creating course[14]

> Regretfully it is so late in a daytime Half of a lifetime had been spent in vain, Thanks to the setting sun so brightly shines, the old ox insists in carrying a broken cart to the end Never stop in speeding up its hoof-pace in time, As long as its surplus energy still remains.

That reminds me of the similar poem by an American poet Robert Frost:

> Devotion
> The heart can think of no devotion, greater than being shore to the ocean, holding the curve of one position,
> Counting an endless repetition

Notes

1. The author is grateful to Brian C. W. Wong, Barister of Hong Kong and Prof. Thomas Chiu of HKCT Institute of Social Science for their valuable pieces of advice, such as on idiomatical ways of saying things.
2. See An CHEN, The Truth Among the Fogbound "Expropriation" Claim: Comments on British X Investment Co. Versus British Y Insurance Co. Case; The Approach of "Winning from Both Sides" Used in the "Expropriation" Claim: Re-comments on British X Investment Co. Versus British Y Insurance Co. Case; On the Serious Violation of Chinese Jus Cogens: Comments on the Case of Importing Toxic Brazilian Soybeans into China (Expert's Legal Opinion on Zhonghe Versus Bunge Case); Isn't the Strict Prohibition on Importing Toxic Brazilian Soybeans into China "Illegal"?-A Rebuttal to Lawyer Song's Allegation, in An CHEN, The Voice from China: An CHEN *on International Economic Law, Springer, 2014, pp. 635–716.*
3. See An CHEN, On the Serious Violation of Chinese Jus Cogens: Comments on the Case of Importing Toxic Brazilian Soybeans into China (Expert's Legal Opinion on Zhonghe Versus Bunge Case), in An CHEN, The Voice from China: An CHEN on International Economic Law, Springer 2013, p. 679. About this view point, Barrister Brian C. W. Wang from Hong Kong, who majoring in law for many years in British, is of the opinion: This may not be an accurate position of English law.
4. Ibid.
5. See An CHEN, The Truth Among the Fogbound "Expropriation" Claim: Comments on British X Investment Co. Versus British Y Insurance Co. Case, in An CHEN, The Voice from China: An CHEN on International Economic Law, Springer, 2013, p.643.
6. Ibid., pp. 643–646.
7. See An CHEN, On the Serious Violation of Chinese Jus Cogens: Comments on the Case of Importing Toxic Brazilian Soybeans into China (Expert's Legal Opinion on Zhonghe Versus Bunge Case), in An CHEN, The Voice from China: An CHEN on International Economic Law, Springer 2013,pp. 687–688.
8. See Art 6 of the CISG.
9. See An CHEN, On the Serious Violation of Chinese Jus Cogens: Comments on the Case of Importing Toxic Brazilian Soybeans into China (Expert's Legal Opinion on Zhonghe Versus Bunge Case), in An CHEN, The Voice from China: An CHEN on International Economic Law, Springer 2013, pp. 687–689.

10. Quoted from the English Edition of the Contact Act of PRC by Harmony Consultants Ltd.
11. See Michael Hwang and Amy Lai, Do Egregious Errors Amount to a Breach of Public Policy?Arbiration, Vol. 71, No. 1, 2005, p. 24. And the Note 21 on the same page: The errors considered material were that the arbitrator: (1) failed to apply his mind properly to certain questions he had to decide; ... (4) failed to decide another material question, which effectively resulted in a ruling favoring one party, paras.10.8–10.84.
12. Ibid., pp.1–24.
13. Ibid., p. 24.
14. *An CHEN, The Voice from China: An CHEN on International Economic Law, Springer*, 2014, pp. li–lii.

The manufacturer's authorised representative in the EU is Springer Nature Customer Service Centre GmbH, Europaplatz 3, 69115 Heidelberg, Germany. If you have any concerns regarding our products, please contact ProductSafety@springernature.com

Printed and bound by CPI Group (UK) Ltd, Croydon, CR0 4YY
26/10/2026
02239437-0005